MW01041639

*Improving Training Effectiveness
in Work Organizations*

SERIES IN APPLIED PSYCHOLOGY

Edwin A. Fleishman, George Mason University
Series Editor

Improving Training Effectiveness in Work Organizations

Volume Editor:

J. Kevin Ford
Michigan State University

Associate Editors:

Steve W. J. Kozlowski
Michigan State University

Kurt Kraiger
University of Colorado at Denver

Eduardo Salas
*Naval Air Warfare Center Training
Systems Division*

Mark S. Teachout
USAA

LEA LAWRENCE ERLBAUM ASSOCIATES, PUBLISHERS
1997   Mahwah, New Jersey

Lawrence Erlbaum Associates, Inc., Publishers
10 Industrial Avenue
Mahwah, New Jersey 07430

Cover design by Mairav Salomon-Dekel

Library of Congress Cataloging-in-Publication Data

Improving training effectiveness in work organizatons /
volume editor J. Kevin Ford ; associate editors, Steve W. J.
Kozlowski ... [et al.].
      p. cm. — (Series in applied psychology)
    Includes indexes.
    ISBN 0-8058-1387-X (acid-free paper)
    1. Employees—Training of. 2. Training needs. 3.
Cognitive learning. I. Ford, J. Kevin (John Kevin) II.
Kozlowski, Steve W. J. III. Series.
HF5549.5.T7I3764 1996
658.3'12404—dc20   96-18085
                                 CIP

Printed in the United States of America
10 9 8 7 6 5 4 3 2 1

Contents

Foreword

There is a compelling need for innovative approaches to the solution of many pressing problems involving human relationships in today's society. Such approaches are more likely to be successful when they are based on sound research and applications. This *Series in Applied Psychology* offers publications that emphasize state-of-the-art research and its application to important issues of human behavior in a variety of societal settings. The objective is to bridge both academic and applied interests.

A longstanding application of psychology has been in the area of workplace training and development. Applied psychologists have developed needs assessment methodologies, training design approaches, training delivery mechanisms, and training evaluation procedures. Research has examined basic issues of knowledge and skill acquisition, retention, and transfer as well as the factors that impact these training outcomes.

Important advances and new perspectives regarding learning and development are emerging from a variety of applied disciplines, such as industrial and organizational psychology, instructional psychology, human factors, and applied cognitive psychology. The training field has just begun to develop, integrate, and synthesize new perspectives and to generate new applications for improving training practice.

This book brings together a set of original chapters by prominent scholars in the area of training and development. The contributors include applied psychologists and human resource specialists who successfully bridge in their own careers the academic and applied interests that this book series strives to serve. The chapters provide a state-of-the-art assessment as well as a framework to guide future research and practice.

As more organizations recognize their human resources as the key to competitive advantage, training and development have become even more vital for organizational effectiveness. *Improving Training Effectiveness in Work Organizations* provides insight into the ways that applied psychologists can inform theory and, at the same time, help organizations to more effectively develop their human resources.

—Edwin A. Fleishman, Editor

Preface

The purpose of this edited volume is to present a number of innovative chapters involving cutting-edge research issues in training and training effectiveness in work organizations. Each chapter provides an integrative summary of a research area with the goal of developing a specific research agenda. Such a focus is meant not only to stimulate thinking in the training field, but also to direct future research. The book focuses on four major topic areas: (a) integrating the advances in the cognitive sciences with training needs assessment, design, and evaluation approaches; (b) viewing learning as a continuous process relevant to training, socialization, and employee development; (c) expanding our perspective on factors impacting training effectiveness; and (d) improving the linkage between training research and practice.

This edited volume concentrates on moving the training field forward by incorporating new ideas, theories, and measures into training. Each chapter provides a research agenda for the area covered. The book goes beyond existing training books. First, the book concentrates on new ideas and critical methodological and measurement issues, rather than summarizing existing literature. Second, the volume clearly articulates a research agenda for the future, rather than providing general prescriptions. Third, the volume provides chapters on emerging issues in training that have important implications for improving training design and effectiveness. Finally, the volume focuses on various levels of analysis (intraindividual, interindividual, team, and organizational issues) and the factors that are relevant to better understanding training effectiveness from these different perspectives. This provides a theoretically driven scientist/practitioner orientation to the book.

The book's genesis is from a conference on training effectiveness held at Michigan State University. The purpose of the conference was to bring together active researchers in the area of training effectiveness so that they could share their recent empirical and conceptual work, interact with others holding similar interests, and work together to establish a substantive agenda for future research efforts. The conference was unique in at least two ways. First, the presentations concentrated on work in progress and directions for future research, rather than on completed work. Second, the traditional individual discussant role was replaced by small-group discussions involving all participants.

The major objective of the structured group interactions was to move toward a training research agenda. Based on the success of the conference, enthusiasm was generated to take some of the ideas from the conference and develop a book that focused on cutting-edge issues. This book represents these efforts. Such an edited book would not be possible without help from a number of individuals. The editors of this book are grateful for the work of Marcy Schafer, the administrative assistant for the book. She read, edited, reread, and reedited each chapter in this volume. Her professional approach helped make this book a reality. We also want to thank Ray O'Connell and his staff at Lawrence Erlbaum Associates for their assistance and cooperation. Our special thanks go to a terrific group of authors who enthusiastically took up the challenge to address cutting-edge issues in training research. The efforts of these authors made our job as editors a pleasure. This volume displays the talents of a core of researchers interested in moving the field of training forward.

—J. Kevin Ford

1

Advances in Training Research and Practice: An Historical Perspective

J. Kevin Ford
Michigan State University

Formal literature on applied psychology and workplace training extends back to the turn of the century, with studies and initiatives devoted to safety training in industries such as mining and railroads. Early developments in management theory also featured training components. For example, Taylor's (1911) development of the scientific principles of management was premised on core assumptions about the ease of training workers to perform effectively by segmenting jobs into simple tasks.

An independent literature on training emerged during the 1920s. Applied psychology textbooks of the period began to cover training as a topic distinct from the more traditional topics of selection, motivation, accident prevention, and fatigue (e.g., see Burtt, 1929; Viteles, 1932). However, this acceptance of training as an independent topic was not universal. Jenkins (1935) dismissed the relevance of industrial training to applied psychology and relegated it to the educational psychology arena. In a footnote in his applied psychology textbook, he stated the following: "Little evidence is available concerning training in industry. For dependable information on training, in general, the reader may turn to any of the better documented textbooks of educational psychology" (p. 129).

An examination of current applied psychological literature on workplace training issues would provide significantly larger amounts of material for Jenkins to consider. In fact, learning and the application of learning to the job has emerged as a key aspect of applied psychological approaches to work. Textbooks in the field devote one or more chapters to training-related issues. The *Annual Review of Psychology* routinely reviews the issues relevant to workplace training.

1

The key journals in the field, such as the *Journal of Applied Psychology* and *Personnel Psychology*, have shown an increase in the number of articles devoted to training issues such as needs assessment, design, methods, and evaluation. In addition, the *Training Research Journal* was recently introduced with the expressed purpose to encourage multidisciplinary efforts regarding workplace training.

This emerging research interest parallels large increases in the amount and diversity of workplace training initiatives in organizational settings. One estimate suggests that over $210 billion is spent every year in the United States alone on workplace training (Carnevale, Gainer, & Villet, 1990). The pressure for more training has expanded due to the increasingly popular view that people, rather than technology, represent the primary source of enduring competitive advantage. In addition, the increasing scope and complexity of the changes occurring in the workplace, such as team-based work systems, the focus on quality, and reengineering, require a highly trained and knowledgeable workforce.

The purpose of this chapter is to provide a historical lineage of the training field from an applied psychological perspective. Although there are many ways in which such an analysis could be completed, the focus here is on three key reviews of the training literature. These reviews provide a window through which the changes in applied psychological research relevant to training can be viewed. The first comprehensive review was completed by McGehee in 1949. In his review of training in industry, training literature of the pre-World War II era (1934–1938) is compared with the advances made a decade later (1944–1948). The second review was completed by Campbell in 1971. Notably, this review of personnel training and development was the first training chapter to be completed for the *Annual Review of Psychology*. Campbell's work reviewed changes and developments in the field during the 1950s and 1960s, and thus serves as a bridge between McGehee's work and the most current literature review. The third review is the most recent review of training literature in the *Annual Review of Psychology*, and was completed by Tannenbaum and Yukl in 1992. It provides an examination of more current perspectives in the training field. Together, the three reviews span over 50 years of research on learning and other training-related issues—from its inception to its more mature status as a distinct field of inquiry today. This 50-year time frame allows for the examination of the shifts in training research.

Each of the reviews is divided into two sections. The first section describes the scope and direction of applied research on training and development at the time of the review. The second section identifies concerns and cutting-edge issues raised by the reviewers regarding how applied psychology could become more responsive to increasing our understanding of training effectiveness. In this way, an analysis can be made of how well the cutting-edge issues of an earlier review were addressed by subsequent research. Based on this historical analysis, current research "gaps" that are in need of further study are identified. This chapter concludes with a discussion of the theoretical and operational frameworks required to push the frontiers of the training field into the 21st century.

STARTUP EFFORTS: IN SEARCH OF APPLIED PSYCHOLOGICAL RESEARCH

Prior to the seminal textbook on training (McGehee & Thayer, 1961), in 1949 McGehee provided what could be the first systematic review and analysis of the emerging field of industrial training. For the review, McGehee examined hundreds of articles and chapters on training, and classified their content as well as their focus on research or practice. He provided a wonderful picture of early attempts to integrate applied psychology with organizational training issues.

Scope and Direction of Applied Research on Training

In terms of scope and direction, McGehee (1949) noted that the dictionary definition of *training* was relatively narrow—applicable only to those processes involved in gaining proficiency in a specific skill or competence. McGehee saw industrial training as much broader in scope with programs also designed to induct the new worker, improve the performance of experienced workers and managers, and to "inform the worker concerning basic economics and to counteract collectivistic ideology" (p. 84).

In regard to trends, McGehee (1949) cited survey results from the 1946 National Industrial Conference Board that the amount of training had increased about threefold since 1938 for supervisors, production workers, and top executives, and had increased 200% for apprentice training. In addition, 29% of the companies who responded to the survey reported that they had a separate training function. Most of the training was conducted by experienced foremen and experienced workers without the assistance of specialized training departments. McGehee's concern about the quality of training when training responsibility was not specifically delegated is evident in his statement that "too often what is everybody's business is nobody's business" (p. 87).

McGehee compared the trends from the 1934 to 1938 sample of articles with those of 1944 to 1948. He found that, from 1934 to 1938, 39 research articles, descriptive (practitioner) papers, or book chapters were written that dealt specifically with training, whereas there were 82 such publications from 1944 to 1948. He also noted that there were over 300 articles on training, most of which were mostly anecdotal and nonpsychological in nature. The increase in applied psychological research was mainly seen in articles on supervisory and management personnel. Although there was an increased interest in training, McGehee noted that there was not an appreciable increase in research studies.

McGehee also categorized the topics covered in the training literature. He showed that the majority of research–based papers focused on learning principles from laboratory studies or from the educational process in public schools. The major innovations during the 1944 to 1948 period were the emphasis on determining the appropriate training content and the importance of and methods to use for training evaluation. McGehee also cited the large amount of military research on training that could be of value to industrial training, such as (a) applying psychological principles of learning to training, (b) evaluating training, (c) standardizing training through job analysis and the development of lesson plans, and (d) designing equipment for the operator.

Cutting-Edge Issues

McGehee (1949) concluded his review with a discussion of persistent problems in training that required the development of new techniques and methods. These problems reflected these basic issues: (a) who to train, (b) what the content of training should be, (c) what methods are to be used in training, (d) who is to do the training, and (e) how the outcomes of training activities are to be evaluated.

McGehee asserted that there was a need for more systematic approaches to assessing the training needs of individual workers, such as "auditing" individuals in the workforce as to needed skills and the projection of potential labor needs in the future. To better determine training content, McGehee stressed the need for more research on the reliability and validity of various job-analysis approaches to training needs assessment, and the need to move to an individualized instruction approach to training tied to the results of the job analysis. He also stressed the need for more research on the proper sequencing of training content, the appropriate use of massed versus spaced practice, and the best approaches for maximizing trainee motivation for transfer. One promising technique he discussed was role playing. He cited the need for greater understanding of the situations or conditions under which this technique was most effective.

The research issue of who was qualified to be a trainer was discussed in terms of selecting individuals in the plant who have the greatest aptitude for instructing others. He cautioned that centralized training should not take over actual training, but rather supervisors and others should be trained to be the trainers—this would allow for these individuals to become partners in the planning of training for the department. In this way, McGehee was an early proponent of the now popular train-the-trainer systems.

The final issue to be considered was the evaluation of training. McGehee (1949) cited that the main reasons for the lack of training evaluation were the lack of statistical skills and research techniques by training personnel and the lack of support by top management for controlled studies that interfered with daily work routines. He noted that industry cannot expect decisive aid from applied psychology in improving training effectiveness unless there was movement away from the immediate solutions for immediate problems mentality to a broader perspective that addressed the more fundamental issues of effectiveness, in which the immediate issues were rooted.

GROWTH AND EXPANSION: IN SEARCH OF ORDER AND DIRECTION

In contrast to the McGehee (1949) review, in 1971 Campbell noted that the field of personnel training and development had become so diverse it was difficult to know where to draw the boundaries. The interest in issues of learning and organizational effectiveness had led to extremes ranging from basic research on learning simple tasks (nonsense words) to complex, large-scale organizational development activities. His overall goal for the review was to focus on the middle ground between the two extremes, and to describe the state of the art in training especially as it was relevant to applied psychological issues.

Scope and Direction of Applied Research on Training

Many of the cutting-edge issues identified by McGehee (1949) were becoming a reality in the training field. For example, McGehee and Thayer (1961) provided the training field with a systematic approach to training needs assessment and methodologies for determining who and what to train. The instructional psychology and military literatures were developing and using the instructional systems design model for linking training needs assessment to training objectives, design, and evaluation.

Campbell (1971) also noted that, during the 1950s the field of psychology was fertile ground for continued studies aimed at more micro, individual-level learning processes—largely conducted in laboratory settings. For example, early studies examined the factors influencing the learning of psychomotor tasks and transfer of learning to different tasks. This research by experimental psychologists surfaced principles of learning that could be applied to improve training design. One principle stated the importance of an identical match between elements of training and expected practices in the transfer setting. However, the generalizability of these studies was limited because they focused on simple tasks in isolated settings.

Campbell stressed that a critical advance in the field was due to the work of Gagne (1962). Gagne applied a number of learning principles developed from

laboratory research to ongoing military operations. He found that these principles were a necessary, but not sufficient, condition for learning. Instead,
research highlighted the need to conduct a thorough needs analysis and to
properly sequence the learning events to guide the learner toward greater skill
acquisition and retention. This work is consistent with the call by McGehee
(1949) to attend to issues of sequencing and design.

In terms of training methods and techniques, the emphasis in the literature
at that time was heavily weighted toward managerial development. For example, the 1950s and 1960s saw the development and expansion of the National
Training Laboratory in Bethel, Maine, and the advancement of the concept of
an unstructured group laboratory approach to learning interpersonal attitudes
and skills. Campbell (1971) also described other training methods, such as
computer-based instruction, the managerial grid, cross-cultural training, and
training for the hard-core unemployed. In fact, the number of different training
methods and techniques greatly expanded from those levels cited by McGehee
(1949). Although this proliferation of programs and techniques provided trainers with many choices, Campbell noted that firms were, on the whole, not
pleased with the quality of the training offered.

Cutting-Edge Issues

Upon reviewing the training literature, Campbell (1971) concluded that, "by
and large, the training and development literature is voluminous, nonempirical,
nontheoretical, poorly written, and dull" (p. 565). He also decried the lack of
maturity and faddish nature of the training enterprise. Fads are based on moving
from one training method to another without much thought as to answering
the more important question of what is to be learned.

To counteract these problems with the training field, Campbell discussed a
number of important cutting-edge directions for future research. First, he
stressed the need for applied psychology to move away from a focus on hardware
and training techniques and return to the key process issue of "what is to be
learned." As an example, he noted the need to take a more programmed
instruction approach to all training efforts (i.e., specifying terminal behaviors,
decomposing learning tasks into its structural components, and seeking an
optimal sequencing of these components in a rational way). He also cited the
historic theoretical foundation of training around learning principles, but,
similar to McGehee (1949), pointed to the need to give more serious attention
to needs assessment, the identification of training content (what to learn), and
the sequencing of that content.

Second, he cited the lack of theoretical models. He noted that although
education, training, and development may be key's to success for many of our
national problems, few efforts were being made to systematically address these
issues from a more scientific perspective. He stressed the need to develop

theoretical models to predict when and why certain types of training activities would lead to greater skill acquisition, retention, and transfer.

Third, Campbell (1971) concluded that the training field needed empirical studies that took a systems approach to the interaction of training and other organizational systems. For example, there was a need to move away from an either–or approach to training evaluation and instead focus on the differential effects of training strategies within complex organizational environments. More specifically, he challenged the field to begin the long and difficult process of developing a broad database on the factors that could impact training effectiveness.

Fourth, he focused on the need to devote attention to the methods and concepts of behavioral modification for its promise in linking theory and practice. He also suggested the need for more information on key training areas of the future, including training via television, team training, and simulation training. Campbell hoped that attention to these cutting edge issues would lead to a more promising field of training within the next 20 years.

GAINING LEGITIMACY: THE ROAD TO MATURITY

In 1992, Tannenbaum and Yukl concentrated their review on topics of training needs assessment, design, selected training methods, trainee characteristics, pretraining and posttraining environments, and evaluation. They also considered recent advances in cognitive learning theories, high-technology training methods, team training, and on-the-job managerial development. Tannenbaum and Yukl noted that the practice of training has continued to grow at a rapid rate, with estimates that employers are expending $30 billion on formal training and another $180 billion on informal on-the-job training each year.

Scope and Direction of Applied Research on Training

The Tannenbaum and Yukl (1992) review demonstrated that many of the challenges offered by Campbell (1971) for needed research direction had received attention. New techniques and methods of needs assessment were developed, resulting in new approaches for sequencing training content and learning events. More important, theoretical frameworks were developed to better understand the process of skill acquisition, retention, and transfer. A new research base highlighted the multiple factors that can impact training effectiveness, including trainee characteristics, training design principles, and work context. In addition, much work was done on behavioral modeling techniques, and there was an expanding literature on team training and computer-based instruction. The scope and direction of training research were also expanded to include research on training as a system within a larger organizational context. For example, one research trend is the investigation of the linkage of training practice and strategic planning processes of the firm (Noe & Ford, 1992).

A major shift in emphasis from the 1960s to the early 1990s was the move toward a cognitive perspective on learning. Applied psychologists began to suggest ways to apply cognitive and instructional psychology principles and concepts such as mental models and metacognitive activities. This movement holds promise for improving our understanding of how to structure learning environments, what it means to learn during training, and how learning in training transfers to the job (Kraiger, 1995). The focus of the cognitive orientation on how learning occurs complements the more behaviorist orientation that concentrates on what is to be learned. This shows there is much to be gained from an integration of the two perspectives and approaches.

Finally, the review by Tannenbaum and Yukl (1992) highlighted the expanding scope of training research to explicitly include issues in the pretraining and posttraining environments. From this perspective, training can not be perceived as an isolated event, but instead as a part of the ongoing dynamic and changeable processes in work organizations. Therefore, to more fully understand training effectiveness, research has begun to develop more sophisticated models, and has generated many different types of interventions to motivate and facilitate skill acquisition and transfer. For example, researchers have examined the impact of trainee participation and choice in attending training programs, as well as the impact of posttraining activities such as relapse-prevention programs and training effectiveness.

Cutting-Edge Issues

Tannenbaum and Yukl (1992) provided a number of general directions for future research. First, they stressed the need for continued movement toward incorporating cognitive concepts into the field of training. Although they see the prospects of applying cognitive concepts to training as exciting, they cautioned not to let this line of research become a mere fad.

Second, they contended that there is a need to pay more attention to training as a system embedded within an organizational context. This includes examining factors in the pretraining and posttraining environments that can impact training success.

Third, they stressed the need to focus more attention to the issues of why, when, and for whom a particular type of training program is effective. The researchers noted the blurring distinction between formal training and less formal learning activities for employee development, and the need to examine how individuals learn within an organizational setting. They contended that research can help inform us on how to integrate developmental experiences and formal training activities. Finally, they suggested that research is needed on how different features of high-technology methods, such as computer-aided instruction and interactive videodisc instruction, can facilitate learning and retention.

BUILDING ON SUCCESSES: A NEW AGENDA FOR RESEARCH AND PRACTICE

The three reviews highlight the tremendous changes that have occurred in the training field over the last 50 years. From its rudimentary beginnings, workplace training has emerged as a distinct field of inquiry. From its initial focus on training methods and techniques, the field has expanded to consider the relationships between various work context factors and their impact training effectiveness. From its atheoretical roots, applied psychological approaches to important training issues have led to the development of theoretical models and conceptual frameworks for learning and transfer. These three reviews illustrate these advances, as well as aid our appreciation of where the field has been and how it has arrived to where it is today. The reviews also demonstrate that research addressing the cutting-edge issues of yesterday creates new needs and directions for today.

The conference that served as the catalyst for the present volume on applied psychological issues and training was focused on future challenges to the field. Round-table discussions were conducted regarding areas in need of research that have the potential to have a major impact on training effectiveness. Critical issues were identified, and a consensus among the participants developed around four research themes. These later became the framework for this book.

In particular, the chapters in this book are organized into the following four research areas: (a) integrating advances in cognitive sciences with traditional approaches to training needs assessment, design, and evaluation approaches; (b) viewing learning as a continuous process relevant to training, socialization, and employee development; (c) developing frameworks of training within an organizational context; and (d) applying psychology to improve the linkage between training research and practice. Each of these research areas are described next along with a short summary of how each chapter addresses a particular research issue.

Integrating Advances in Cognitive Sciences With Workplace Training: Implications for Training Needs Assessment, Design, and Evaluation Models

One research issue concerns the need to more fully integrate recent advances in cognitive research into the training field. The promise of cognitive constructs to improve our understanding of training can only be realized with increased efforts to translate the basic cognitive concepts into fruitful lines of inquiry relevant to organizational training. In addition, improvements in training practice can only come about when methods and techniques are developed based on cognitive research that improves the way in which training needs assessment, training design, or training evaluation is conducted.

Traditional training research in applied psychology has tended to focus on studying the development of relatively simple skills for relatively short retention periods. The need to train for higher order cognitive skills, such as problem solving and troubleshooting, is largely the result of changes in the workplace (e.g., technological innovation, self-directed work teams, and the multiskilling of jobs). The movement toward higher order skills requires an orientation toward building individual expertise.

In general, cognitive theorists have defined *expertise* as the achievement of consistent, superior performance through the development of specialized mental processes acquired through experience and training. Although different terminology may be used, there is an emerging consensus within the learning theory literature on the concepts that distinguish novice and expert performance; they include the development of procedural knowledge and automaticity skills, mental models, and metacognitive and self-regulatory skills (Glaser, 1990).

Recent efforts have been made to summarize these emerging perspectives in the cognitive sciences, and to suggest implications of this work for training research (e.g., see Cannon-Bowers, Tannenbaum, Salas, & Converse, 1991; Howell & Cooke, 1989; Lord & Maher, 1991). These reviews provide solid background for cognitive issues such as the organization of memory, the storage and retrieval of information, and other cognitive operations. Yet there is a need to show how the study and practice of training could be appreciably different by taking a more cognitive perspective. Ford and Kraiger (1995) took some initial steps by identifying specific constructs from cognitive and instructional theory that have relevance for improving our understanding of training effectiveness. They suggesteed that there is a need for advances in training research that synthesize our understanding of learning and human behavior.

Part I of this volume presents three chapters that directly address the applicability of key cognitive constructs and the development of methods to improve training assessment, design, and evaluation. Rogers, Maurer, Salas, and Fisk (chap. 2, this volume) apply the issues of automatic and controlled processing to training needs assessment. They present a new methodology for task analysis (Controlled and Automatic Processing Task Analytic Methodology [CAPTAM]), and link the information obtained from this approach to improving training design.

Coovert and Craiger (chap. 3, this volume) present the concept of the "Petri Net" as a way to detail the interactions required among individuals for effective skilled performance. Identifying the components of a Petri Net provides a new approach to understanding the requirements for teamwork, and allows for the incorporation of creative strategies for training design.

Goldsmith and Kraiger (chap. 3, this volume) detail the importance of knowledge organization and the use of structural assessment as a method for identifying how individuals organize training information. Implications of one such structural assessment methodology (Pathfinder) for improving training evaluation are emphasized.

Viewing Learning as a Continuous Process: Implications for Training, Socialization, and Employee Development

The globalization of world markets, new ways of organizing work, changes in workforce demographics, new technology, and literacy problems are forces that are making new demands on organizations for improving competitiveness. The jobs of today often require complex cognitive skills to deal with more highly technical and sophisticated manufacturing and customer service systems as well as the interpersonal skills necessary to function effectively in work teams (Goldstein & Gilliam, 1990). Consequently, continuous learning has been touted as increasingly important for organizational effectiveness.

With a continuous learning orientation, learning is considered an everyday activity for all employees, with training as one of various key mechanisms for improving knowledge and skills. Unfortunately, most of the existing research in the training field has examined the effectiveness of individual training programs. Such research implicitly makes at least two assumptions: (a) training programs within an organization are independent from one another in terms of their impact on employees, and (b) most learning in organizations occurs during formal training programs.

These two assumptions are less tenable in the world of work today and in the future. Therefore, the training field is in need of new conceptual models and approaches to consider training programs as interdependent, and to focus on integrating other learning activities with more formal training approaches. In this way, the concept of "learning" takes on a more integrated, long-term orientation, rather than the event-oriented, short-term perspective that much of the existing research investigates.

Part II of this book provides three chapters that address the issues related to viewing learning from this broader perspective. In particular, Baldwin and Magjuka (chap. 5, this volume) contend that training cannot be considered as an isolated event or singular activity. Instead, they reconceptualize training as an episode that occurs among many other organizational episodes experienced by employees. The authors build a conceptual framework that highlights the events and cognition that occur prior to the delivery of a training intervention that can impact trainees' motivation to learn and develop.

Chao (chap. 6, this volume) highlights the important role of socialization as an ongoing learning experience for individuals. Contrasted with the more formal structured experiences of training, socialization is a long-term, informal process. During this process, individuals learn what their role within the organization is, and how they must adjust to the demands of the job and the nature of the organizational culture. The process takes place at the conscious level through explicit learning experiences, as well as at the unconscious level through implicit learning. Chao highlights how socialization can be a complement, a substitute for, and a barrier to formal training.

Noe, Wilk, Mullen, and Wanek (chap. 7, this volume) focus on the importance of continuous learning and employee development in today's competitive environment. The authors define *employee development*, and identify what activities are considered developmental. They build and describe a conceptual framework of the individual and organizational characteristics that influence the frequency and type of development activity in which employees may participate.

Developing Frameworks of Training Within an Organizational Context: Implications for Training Evaluation and Transfer

Kraiger, Ford, and Salas (1993) noted that there is an important difference between the concepts of training evaluation and training effectiveness. *Training evaluation* focuses on whether training leads to the desired level of proficiency indicated by the training objectives. A key question to be addressed prior to training evaluation is "what is to be learned?" (Campbell, 1988). It is concerned with issues of measurement and design, the accomplishment of learning objectives, and the attainment of requisite knowledge and skills.

Training effectiveness deals with the broader issues involved in understanding why training did or did not lead to the desired level of proficiency. This requires the development of conceptual models that identify the factors prior to, during, and/or following a training intervention that could impact learning, retention, and the transfer of training. Such models begin with a focus on viewing training in context, rather than in isolation of individuals and workplace constraints. These models are critical for uncovering whether a training program was ineffective due to the characteristics of the program or to factors outside the control of the training system.

More effort has traditionally been devoted to issues of training evaluation than to the more complex issues of examining training in context. Noe (1986) provided one of the first training models that concentrated on linking individual characteristics to trainee motivation and training success. Recent research has identified individual factors such as self-efficacy and situational factors such as supervisor and coworker support as having an impact on learning and training transfer. More efforts in this area are clearly needed.

Part III of this book includes three chapters that provide new directions for research focusing on training within the realities of the workplace. Mathieu and Martineau (chap. 8, this volume) expand our understanding of training by focusing on the role of training motivation. The authors develop a conceptual framework that depicts the relationship between training motivation and training evaluation criteria. They also identify key individual differences and situational factors that can impact trainee motivation prior to and following training.

Alliger and Katzman (chap. 9, this volume) go beyond the traditional evaluation focus on the assessment of mean group differences. The authors describe the need to consider when one would expect changes in group variability scores due to a training intervention. Previous research and theory on the effects of variability such as practice effects are presented, and research on the measurement of change is summarized. A conceptual model of the conditions necessary to permit prediction of variability change due to training is then presented and analyzed.

Kozlowski and Salas (chap. 10, this volume) contend that training activities must be considered as embedded within an organizational context. They develop a conceptual framework that integrates concepts drawn from organizational systems theory with more traditional training constructs. In particular, the authors emphasize the ways in which the organizational context can either support or contradict the knowledge and skills gained during training. Research propositions are generated that concentrate on how to develop a congruent organizational system that supports the expression of trained skills.

Applied Psychology and Training: Methods for Improving the Linkage Between Training Research and Practice

Early work in applied psychology and training was almost exclusively practice-driven. McGehee's (1949) cutting-edge issues focused on critical practice issues of who to train, what to train, what methods are best to use, and how to evaluate effectiveness. Campbell (1971) bemoaned the continued focus on direct practice and the lack of theory and empirical research on training.

Since the 1970s, there has been an explosion of research on training-related issues. This research has been more firmly driven by conceptual models of skill acquisition and transfer. Continuation of these empirical and conceptual advances are needed in the field, and underlie the rationale for developing this book. Nevertheless, it is also critical that advances in the field are directly linked to improving training practice. For example, the performance appraisal field embraced the cognitive revolution and examined issues of encoding, storage, and retrieval patterns of raters. Although conceptually rich, implications for improving practice were indirect and as a result, research has since decreased in importance.

Researchers and practitioners have warned that there is only limited influence between training research to practice and from practice to research. In fact, one of the main reasons for the development of the new journal *Human Resource Development Quarterly* was to allow more synergy between research and practice. Theory development in training is not often used to inform and improve practice while the experiences of training practice are seldom used to more fully articulate needed research directions. There is clearly a need for a more synthetic approach to move the field forward, rather than the current mode where research and training practice are separate and compartmentalized.

One reason that theory and practice may not be as strongly linked is the lack of effort devoted to developing methods or approaches that help make this linkage easier to accomplish. This volume presents two chapters on how to link research and practice more closely together.

In Part IV, Salas, Cannon-Bowers, and Blickensderfer (chap. 11, this volume) provide a framework for increasing what they term *reciprocity*, or mutual exchange between research and practice. They suggest the development of principles, guidelines, and specifications as a way to translate theory into ways to improve training practice. The mechanisms for translating research results into practical suggestions for improvement are demonstrated through the application of research on team decision making under stress and cockpit air crew coordination training.

Klein and Ralls (chap 12, this volume) take as a starting point the detailed analysis of what occurs in practice. Across different organizations, they take a qualitative approach to the study of training transfer and the intended and unintended consequences of technology training on workplace processes and characteristics. They use this detailed analysis of practice to drive the development of research propositions around issues of employee sensemaking; distribution of power and expertise; and job design, structure, and culture.

In the final section, Part V, Salas, Cannon-Bowers, and Kozlowski (chap. 13, this volume) provide some final observations relevant to training research and practice. These observations include a review of the key themes that have emerged from the preceding chapters. In addition, the authors highlight new ways for linking training research with the changing needs of the training field.

CLOSING REMARKS

The analysis of the three reviews reveal that the scope and direction of training research has been greatly expanded and refined. Training research is no longer searching for an identity. With maturity has come legitimacy. The increasing importance of training and development activities in organizations provides a unique opportunity for developing and addressing issues that can lead to new ways of understanding learning and training effectiveness.

The cutting-edge issues in training research revolve around the areas that form the framework for this book. The authors have taken on the challenging task of advancing the field through the conceptual development of new and innovative ideas in training. They have also provided illustrations of how theoretical developments could be applied to make improvements in training practice.

The overarching goal of this book, then, is to stimulate thinking that advances theory and guides practice to improve training effectiveness. The success in this endeavor must be examined in the context of the changing role of training and development as we move into the 21st century. Thus, an indicator of success might be the extent to which future reviews of training research build on the themes addressed in this book, as well as whether new cutting-edge issues arise from the research that is sparked by the ideas presented in this volume.

REFERENCES

Burtt, H. E. (1929). *Psychology and industrial efficiency*. New York: Appleton.

Campbell, J. P. (1971). Personnel training and development. *Annual Review of Psychology, 22*, 565–602.

Campbell, J. P. (1988). Training design for performance improvement. In J. P. Campbell, R. J. Campbell, & Associates (Eds.), *Productivity in organizations* (pp. 177–216). San Francisco: Jossey-Bass.

Cannon-Bowers, J. A., Tannenbaum, S. I., Salas, E., & Converse, S. A. (1991). Toward an integration of training theory and technique. *Human Factors, 33*, 281–292.

Carnevale, A. P., Gainer, L. J., & Villet, J. (1990). *Training in America: The organization and strategic role of training*. San Francisco: Jossey–Bass.

Ford, J. K., & Kraiger, K. (1995). The application of cognitive constructs and principles to the instructional systems model of training: Implications for needs assessment, design, and transfer. In C. L. Cooper & I. T. Robertson (Eds.), *International review of industrial and organizational psychology* (Vol. 10, pp. 1–48). London: Wiley.

Gagne, R. M. (1962). Military training and principles of learning. *American Psychologist, 17*, 83–91.

Glaser, R. (1990). The reemergence of learning theory within instructional research. *American Psychologist, 45*, 29–39.

Goldstein, I. L., & Gilliam, P. (1990). Training system issues in the year 2000. *American Psychologist, 45*, 134–145.

Howell, W. C., & Cooke, N. J. (1989). Training the human information processor: A review of cognitive models. In I. L. Goldstein & Associates (Eds.), *Training and development in organizations* (pp. 121–182). San Francisco: Jossey-Bass.

Jenkins, J. G. (1935). *Psychology in business and industry*. New York: Wiley.

Kraiger, K. (1995, August). *Paradigms lost: Applications and misapplications of cognitive science to the study of training*. Invited address presented at the 103rd annual convention of the American Psychological Association, New York.

Kraiger, K., Ford, J. K., & Salas, E. (1993). Application of cognitive, skill-based, and affective theories of learning outcomes to new methods of training evaluation. *Journal of Applied Psychology, 78,* 311–328.

Lord, R. G., & Maher, K. J. (1991). Cognitive theory in industrial/organizational psychology. In M. D. Dunnette & L. M. Hough (Eds.), *Handbook of industrial and organizational psychology* (2nd ed., Vol. 2, pp. 1–62). Palo Alto, CA: Consulting Psychologists Press.

McGehee, W. (1949). Training in industry. In W. Dennis (Ed.), *Current trends in industrial psychology* (pp. 84–114). Pittsburgh: University of Pittsburgh Press.

McGehee, W., & Thayer, P. W. (1961). *Training in business and industry.* New York: Wiley.

Noe, R. A. (1986). Training attributes and attitudes: Neglected influences of training effectiveness. *Academy of Management Review, 11,* 736–749.

Noe, R. A., & Ford, J. K. (1992). Emerging issues and new directions for training research. *Research in Personnel and Human Resources Management, 10,* 345–384.

Tannenbaum, S., & Yukl, G. (1992). Training and development in work organizations. In M. R. Rosenzweig & L. W. Porter (Eds.), *Annual review of psychology* (Vol. 43, pp. 399–441). Palo Alto, CA: Annual Reviews.

Taylor, F. W. (1911). *The principles of scientific management.* New York: Harper & Row.

Viteles, M. S. (1932). *Industrial psychology.* New York: Norton.

I

Integrating Advances in Cognitive Science With Training Assessment, Design, and Evaluation Constructs

2

Training Design, Cognitive Theory, and Automaticity: Principles and a Methodology

Wendy A. Rogers
University of Georgia

Todd J. Maurer
Georgia Institute of Technology

Eduardo Salas
Navel Air Warfare Center Training Systems Division

Arthur D. Fisk
Georgia Institute of Technology

For more than a century, psychologists have realized the importance of making aspects of a task habitual or automatized, thereby reducing the amount of thought or attention required for performance of the overall task (Bryan & Harter, 1899; James, 1890; Solomons & Stein, 1896). Since these early studies, much experimental work has been conducted to understand the characteristics of such automatization (for a review, see Shiffrin, 1988). Training programs should be structured to capitalize on the benefits of automatization to optimize both training and ultimate human performance (Howell & Cooke, 1989). To capitalize on automatism, a task-analytic strategy must be used that aids in the identification of tasks and task components that can and cannot be automatized. The goal of this chapter is to present the details of a task-analytic framework designed to capitalize on cognitive theory of automatization to maximize training effectiveness.

Recent task-analytic approaches have emphasized the importance of cognitive psychology for the successful understanding of the training needs within a task domain (Goldstein, 1993; Redding, 1989; Regian & Schneider, 1990;

Terranova, Snyder, Seamster, & Treitler, 1989). Relative to more traditional instructional system development approaches, a task analysis based on principles of cognitive psychology has an empirically and theoretically driven focus. The cognitive approach provides a link between determining the tasks and components that need to be trained and the best methods for training them.

Our approach builds on the research on automaticity. The lessons learned can be used in training settings by practitioners who possess a minimum of experience with the relevant psychological principles. We present the theoretical basis as well as the practical application of the Controlled and Automatic Processing Task Analytic Methodology (CAPTAM). The elegance of CAPTAM lies in its empirical grounding. The framework presented herein provides specific, theoretically based information about what to look for in task decomposition. The utility of the approach is that it can assist in developing an empirically based plan of action for training the necessary skills for a particular job. Such a plan can minimize costs and maximize training effectiveness.

It should be noted that CAPTAM is not suitable for all situations. The diversity of training situations in organizations today necessitates having a variety of task-analytic approaches. We believe that our approach has a wide range of applicability, however, and one of the goals of the present chapter is to illustrate some of the potential applications and provide the basics necessary for additional applications. This chapter also explicates the situations for which CAPTAM may not be the best approach and delineates some of the areas in which more research is required for the successful application of cognitively oriented task-analytic approaches.

CONTROLLED AND AUTOMATIC PROCESSING THEORY AND TRAINING

The importance of an approach to training that capitalizes on automatization or overlearning has been reported in recent reviews of the training literature (Goldstein, 1986, 1993; Howell & Cooke, 1989). Goldstein (1986) discussed the criticality of overlearning (which may be analogous to automatization) for situations in which the task will not receive a lot of practice in the work setting, to maintain performance levels under stress and over time, and to ensure asymptotic performance on all criteria. More recently, Goldstein (1993) described automaticity as a "crucial point in instructional theory" (p. 110). Howell and Cooke (1989) discussed the importance of automaticity to free up attentional resources for the more demanding aspects of complex tasks. These authors all emphasize the importance of automaticity for training. However, they do not provide the means by which to implement the theory of automatic processing to training.

Skilled performance of most complex tasks requires the coordination and integration of many task components. To illustrate with a common example, consider the task of driving a manual shift automobile. One must coordinate the components of shifting gears; manipulating the gas, brake, and clutch pedals; steering; monitoring the activities of other drivers and pedestrians; and route planning. The complexity of the task is tremendous for novice drivers. For skilled drivers, many of the task components no longer require attention (they have become automatized); the task can be performed with ease, and often concurrently with other tasks such as listening to the radio or carrying on a conversation. The important issue, here, is how an individual makes the transition from a novice to a skilled performer.

Logan (1985) referred to *automatization* as the hands and feet of skill. There are certain characteristics that define whether something is a controlled or an automatic process (Schneider, Dumais, & Shiffrin, 1984; Shiffrin & Dumais, 1981). Controlled, strategic processes are required for the performance of novel tasks, as well as for tasks that are varied in nature and require the devotion of attention. For example, in the task of driving, monitoring the behavior of other vehicles on the road requires attentional resources. Some controlled processes consume attentional resources such that it becomes difficult to perform other tasks concurrently. Consider the concentration involved when merging onto a busy highway; generally, conversation stops, the driver tunes out the sounds of the radio, and attention is focused on the task of merging successfully. Controlled processes are serial in nature, meaning that they are carried out in a step-by-step fashion. Anderson (1982) likened novice performance on some tasks to following a recipe. The steps required to save a document on a word processor, for example, may be fairly detailed for novice users, whereas for the more experienced user, the task has been consolidated into a single-step procedure. The requirement to perform controlled processes serially results in their being performed slower and often under the explicit control of the individual.

The characteristics of automatic processes are nearly opposite those of controlled processes. After extensive and consistent practice (described later), some tasks or task components may become automatized. As a result, because they no longer require a step-by-step application, they are performed faster, are more efficient, and are generally more accurate. Automatized task components no longer require the devotion of attentional resources and, hence, may be performed in parallel with other tasks. Many components of driving become automatized and enable experienced drivers to multitask. The entire process of shifting gears (i.e., remove pressure from gas pedal, depress clutch, change gears, and begin to release clutch while pressing gas pedal) becomes automatized, such that experienced drivers do not even pause in their conversation.

Another characteristic of automatic processes is that, once they are initiated, they run to completion unless a conscious effort is made to inhibit them. A simplistic example is that, when handwriting the word *bitter*, you will automatically dot the *i* and cross the *t*s, and it is actually very difficult to inhibit this process while maintaining your normal writing speed. Automatic processes can occur without intention in the presence of an eliciting stimulus. For instance, one might pick up the telephone and immediately begin to dial an often called number, even when that was not the intention. Another example involves the automatic attention response that accompanies hearing one's own name.

There are many benefits of automatic processing: (a) attentional requirements are minimized, enabling one to perform more than one task simultaneously; (b) performance becomes fast, efficient, and accurate; and (c) performance also becomes immune to potentially deleterious effects of stress (Hancock 1984, 1986), alcohol (Fisk & Schneider, 1982), fatigue, and vigilance situations (Fisk & Schneider, 1981). Recent research also suggests that automatized task components are better retained over a 1-year retention interval than the more controlled, strategic task components (Fisk & Hodge, 1992).

For the purposes of illustration, automatic process development has been described in the context of the relatively simple task of driving an automobile. Many training system designers will be interested in tasks that are much more complex. For example, consider training fighter pilots, supervisors in nuclear power plants, and air traffic controllers. Although such tasks are extremely complex, the basic principles of automatic process development are applicable. The majority of tasks performed are actually a combination of controlled and automatically processed components. Consequently, training of the automatic components can have significant benefits for overall performance. Performance will be enhanced and more cognitive resources will be available for the strategic aspects of the job. In complex task domains, the ultimate training goal is the same as in learning to drive an automobile (i.e., to automatize those components that can be trained to automaticity).

IMPLICATIONS OF THEORY
TO TRAINING INTERVENTIONS

The concepts of automatic and controlled processing can be used to maximize the utility of training interventions by: (a) maximizing performance resulting from training, (b) minimizing training time and associated costs, and (c) incorporating critical cognitive components into training design. A fourth prospect surrounding validity of selection systems used to predict training performance is also explored here.

Utility in the simplest sense can be optimized by maximizing performance improvements and minimizing associated costs of achieving those improvements. The appropriate use of automaticity principles in training design may maximize ultimate performance attained by trainees at the conclusion of training (Myers & Fisk, 1987; Regian & Schneider, 1990). It can maximize both retention and transfer of that performance, which is particularly critical for training to have any real long-term payoff on the job (Fisk & Hodge, 1992; Whaley & Fisk, 1993). The development of automaticity is especially crucial for situations in which skills may go unused for long intervals (e.g., CPR training; Fisk, Hertzog, Lee, Rogers, & Anderson, 1994; Fisk & Hodge, 1992). Moreover, Fisk, Lee, and Rogers (1991) demonstrated that the transfer of automatized task components is quite successful if the component is applied in a similar fashion across tasks (Czerwinski, Lightfoot, & Shiffrin, 1992; Rogers, 1992; Schneider & Fisk, 1984).

The identification and training of consistent components can speed training, reduce failure rates, and make salient consistencies that might not normally be evident until years have been spent on the job (Schneider, 1985). For example, Wightman and Lintern (1985) reviewed various types of part-task training for aviation skills. They concluded that simplification (wherein difficult tasks are made easier) is most successful for tasks that are initially very difficult to learn, such as: (a) compensatory tracking in which the error source is unclear (Gordon, 1959; Poulton, 1974), (b) pitch-and-roll tracking in a flight simulator (Briggs & Waters, 1958), and (c) aircraft carrier landing skills (Wightman & Sistrunk, 1987). This approach is often cheaper and less frustrating for trainees trying to master a seemingly impossible task (Fisk & Rogers, 1988a). Another part-task training technique, segmentation, involves providing more training for the difficult components of the task. This approach has been successful in domains such as simulator training of aircraft carrier landing skills (Wightman & Sistrunk, 1987).

Once consistencies have been identified, the training program can make the consistent relationships salient to the trainee. Eberts and Schneider (1985) demonstrated that feedback during training that made salient the consistent relationships between control input and system output produced superior performance relative to other types of feedback conditions. It may also be possible to physically highlight significant items during training (Hodge et al., 1993) and sequence the training program, such that component skills that are important for higher order skills are trained first. For example, in their training program directed toward reading, Frederiksen, Warren, and Rosebery (1985a, 1985b) first trained perceptual encoding, then decoding, then context utilization. Similar principles of sequencing would be beneficial for many complex tasks that build on component skills, such as learning transmission codes prior to working directly with a radio transmitter or learning the Morse code alphabet prior to being able to decode messages (Bryan & Harter, 1899).

Trainers can also make use of compressed time procedures (speeding up the process) to make salient consistent relationships that occur infrequently in the work environment but are nevertheless important. Vidulich, Yeh, and Schneider (1983) utilized a compressed time procedure to provide subjects with a higher number of trials on an inflight refueling task. For a task that requires 5 minutes to occur in real time, they simulated the procedure in 20 seconds. Relative to a control group, the subjects receiving more trials in the compressed procedure were more accurate. Similar benefits of massing practice on particular task components was demonstrated for procedural items such as cockpit check, cockpit familiarization, and starting procedures (Flexman, Roscoe, Williams, & Williges, 1972).

Appropriate use of consistency principles may also reduce overall training time (Schneider, 1985). This can mean real gains because training time may be one major source of cost (facility/equipment time, trainer time, trainee time away from the job assignment, etc.). Optimal training design may also help to reduce washout, accidents, washback, and withdrawals. For example, part-task training techniques may be utilized to make complex tasks initially tractable such that novice performers are not overwhelmed (McGrath & Harris, 1971; Wightman & Lintern, 1985). Once some of the components have been automatized, trainees can be gradually transitioned to the complete task. The degree to which automaticity has been acquired can be evaluated through secondary performance techniques, with interference problems, or through embedded measurement techniques (Kraiger, Ford, & Salas, 1993).

It is important to keep in mind that both part- and whole-task training will likely be necessary for optimal performance (Schneider & Detweiler, 1987). In addition, tasks that require integration or temporal coordination of the components may benefit most from whole-task training (Folds, Gerth, & Engelman, 1987; Klapp, Martin, McMillan, & Brook, 1987). Beginning a training program with part-task training and then proceeding to whole-task training may be most efficient (Fisk & Rogers, 1988a). Procedural and psychomotor tasks often benefit from part-task training, and simply allowing subjects to become familiar with task dynamics also results in improved performance.

The applied psychology literature has acknowledged that different abilities may be relevant at different stages of skill acquisition. It has also been suggested that the information-processing requirements of the tasks performed may make a difference in the extent to which general cognitive ability, perceptual and psychomotor abilities (Ackerman, 1987; Murphy, 1989), or even task-specific abilities (Fleishman & Mumford, 1989a, 1989b) are relevant to performance. This suggests that when using ability tests to select personnel into training programs, one may need to carefully consider which stages of skill acquisition one wishes to predict with the greatest accuracy (Barrett & Maurer, 1993; Schneider, 1985). Some consideration has been given to changing ability requirements and issues related to utility estimates for selection programs (Bobko, Colella, & Russell, 1990). However, most existing task/job analyses have not focused much on analyzing tasks according to the degree of consistency they involve (for an exception, see Fisk & Rogers, 1992).

There are a multitude of task- and job-analytic techniques in existence (Fleishman & Mumford, 1989b; Gael, 1988; Harvey, 1991), but little work has examined qualitative difference's in tasks related to automaticity principles. For all of the reasons outlined previously, such a task-analytic framework would be useful.

THE TRADITIONAL TRAINING PROCESS

Goldstein (1986, 1993) described an instructional systems perspective for the systematic development of training programs. His model of an instructional system consists of the following phases: (a) needs assessment, (b) training and development, (c) evaluation, and (d) training goals. This type of approach represents the traditional training process in industrial/organizational psychology.

An understanding of controlled and automatic processes may be relevant to each phase of the training development process. In terms of needs assessment, the goal is to gain an understanding of which tasks and task components can be automatized and which remain controlled. This information may then be used in the training and development phase to develop the most appropriate instructional program. Within the evaluation phase, trainers can rely on empirically verified methods for determining automatic process development (i.e., the ability to perform a secondary task without decrement; Schneider et al., 1984). Finally, the training goals may be structured around the development of automatized component processes.

The discussion in the present chapter is most relevant to the needs assessment and training phases of Goldstein's (1993) model. The chapter focuses on how to determine which tasks and task components can become automatized, and describes specific applications of this approach for the development of training systems.

WHAT TASKS OR TASK COMPONENTS
CAN BE AUTOMATIZED?

Shiffrin and Schneider (1977) and Schneider and Shiffrin (1977) made extensive use of a procedure by which one can measure and study automatic and controlled processes in the laboratory. They used what is referred to as a *visual-memory search paradigm*. In this task, the subject is presented with one or more items to hold in memory and then several items appear as the display set. The subject's task is to decide as quickly and accurately as possible if one of the items from the memory set is one of the items in the display. The matching item is referred to as the *target* and the other items in the display are referred to as *distractors*. This is a useful laboratory task for illustrating automaticity principles: Although it is simple, it requires information-processing components of real-world tasks, such as visual search, keeping things in memory, coordinating information, and so on.

Automatic process development is assessed in the search paradigm by manipulating the type of practice provided. It is important to distinguish between two types of practice. The first is consistent mapping (CM) practice. In CM practice, the targets and distractors are drawn from different sets and are completely nonoverlapping. Stimuli are always responded to in the same way over trials. For example, suppose the memory set items were the letters A and B. Every time one of these letters appeared in the display, the subjects would always make the same prespecified response. After much consistent practice, the subjects would develop an automatic response. They would immediately respond when they saw either one of those letters, and their reaction time (RT) would be independent of the number of items in the display.

The other type of practice is called varied mapping (VM) practice. In VM, the target and distractor items are drawn from the same set. Thus, on some trials, a particular letter might be a target and be attended to, but on other trials that same letter might serve as a distractor and have to be ignored. Because VM practice does not allow the same response to a given stimulus across all trials, subjects can never develop an automatic response. The key to the development of automatic processes is consistency. Tasks or task components that are consistent may be automatized.

Although much of the early work investigating the characteristics of automatic and controlled processing was conducted using relatively simple stimuli, such as letters and numbers, more recent research has extended the basic findings to more complex stimuli and more complex task situations (Cannon-Bowers, Salas, & Grossman, 1991; Fisk & Rogers, 1992). To illustrate, two domains are briefly discussed: map reading skills (Fisk & Eboch, 1989) and reading skills (Frederiksen et al., 1985a, 1985b). In their map reading experiment, Fisk and Eboch (1989) required subjects to make judgments about the population size of counties presented on a map. Population density was designated by a color code (e.g., red > green > blue > grey > purple > yellow > brown). In the CM condition, the color code legend did not vary, whereas in the VM condition, the legend changed across trials. A comparison of the CM and VM training conditions revealed dramatic performance differences. For the CM, relative to the VM condition, there was a significantly greater reduction in RT across practice, more of a reduction in response variability, and reaction time became less susceptible to increases in comparison load. The data from a complex map reading task revealed that extensive CM practice results in performance that is characteristic of automatic processing. Frederiksen et al. (1985a, 1985b) demonstrated that consistent component training could effectively improve reading skills. For example, poor readers often encode words based on single letters. Consistent training to automatically encode multiletter units (TION) resulted in improved reading performance.

The range of research demonstrating the reliability of the distinction between automatic and controlled processing lends credence to the idea that such
distinctions are important for a wide range of practical applications. In addition,
the extant data provide illustrations of the characteristics of processing under
conditions of stress (Hancock, 1984, 1986), long-term retention intervals (Fisk
& Hodge, 1992), less-than-perfect consistency (Fisk & Jones, 1992; Schneider
& Fisk, 1982a), and context-dependent consistency (Fisk & Rogers, 1988b;
Rogers, Lee, & Fisk, 1995).

PRINCIPLES OF AUTOMATIC PROCESS
DEVELOPMENT

The principles that govern the development of automatic processes are comparable across many levels of task complexity, degree, and kind of consistency.
Although consistency may be operationalized somewhat differently across
tasks, it generally indicates the learning and application of invariant rules,
invariant components of processing, or invariant sequences of information-
processing components that are essential to successful task performance (Fisk
& Lloyd, 1988; Fisk, Oransky, & Skedsvold, 1988). The characteristics of
performance on tasks that have been trained in a consistent fashion are
comparable. Performance after training is generally faster, more reliable, less
effortful, less consuming of cognitive resources, resistant to decline over
retention intervals, and less sensitive to situations of high stress, high
workload, and fatigue (Schneider et al., 1984). The fact that even complex
rule-based knowledge can benefit from consistent training bodes well for
practitioners faced with the task of training individuals to perform complex
tasks in complex environments (Fisk et al., 1988).

Based on the multitude of research that has been conducted to understand
the boundaries and intricacies of skill development in general and automatic
process development in particular, a series of processing principles have been
developed. These principles represent agreed upon facts about phenomena
necessary for understanding behavior and reflect human performance guidelines that may be important for understanding, designing, and developing
training programs for complex tasks (Fisk & Rogers, 1992). These principles
are summarized next.

Principle 1

Performance improvements will occur in situations where stimuli are responded
to in a consistent manner across exposures. There is a plethora of research
demonstrating the benefits of consistency for a range of stimuli, including letters
and numbers (Schneider & Shiffrin, 1977), words and categories (Fisk &

Schneider, 1983; Schneider & Fisk, 1984), spatial stimuli (Ackerman, 1986; Eberts & Schneider, 1986), and auditory stimuli (Poltrock, Lansman, & Hunt, 1982).

Principle 2

Consistent relationships at abstract or higher order levels (i.e., consistencies among stimuli), and consistent rules should be identified. Fisk and Schneider (1983; Schneider & Fisk, 1984) assessed performance for category search in which the memory set was a category label (fruit) and the items in the display set were category exemplars (apple). They found that the CM–VM differences were robust with these stimuli, and that learning could occur at the level of the higher order category, as opposed to the word level (Fisk & Jones, 1992). That is, individuals trained with the exemplars apple, orange, pear, and melon could transfer what they had learned to new members of the trained category (lemon, strawberry). In many real-world tasks, the stimulus-to-response consistency may be at a higher level that is not immediately obvious. Patterns of information or rules may be consistent, but individual stimulus items may vary across situations. To illustrate, in football what distinguishes a player as the appropriate receiver is a function of the dynamics of the situation (Walker & Fisk, 1995). The decision is made on a combination of cues (defensive players and offensive receivers; Hodge et al., 1993). These issues have been addressed in several studies examining practice effects in situations demanding that the subject attend to consistencies at a more abstract level. For example, CM–VM differences have been demonstrated for a pattern of letters rather than an individual letter (Myers & Fisk, 1987), for the consistency of rules rather than individual items (Fisk et al., 1988), chesslike tasks (Fisk & Lloyd, 1988), map reading (Fisk & Eboch, 1989), learning arithmetic base five (Fisk & Gallini, 1989), reading skills (Frederiksen et al., 1985a; 1985b), and perceptual decision-making tasks (Kramer, Strayer, & Buckley, 1990).

Principle 3

The degree of performance improvement is directly related to the degree of consistency. In many real-world settings, the situation or task demands may not be completely consistent. There may be noise in the system where a stimulus might be paired inappropriately, or the task may be sufficiently difficult that errors are made on the part of the subject. Schneider and Fisk (1982a) demonstrated that conditions that were at least 67% consistent yielded significant performance improvements, and that performance was more indicative of automatic processing than of controlled processing (Lee & Fisk, 1993).

Principle 4

Contextual cues should be used to mimic the effects of consistency and may activate automatic sequences of behavior. Less than perfect consistency may also yield practice benefits and efficient performance in situations where the context provides cues about consistency. Fisk and Rogers (1988b; Rogers, Lee, & Fisk, 1995) demonstrated that subjects could benefit from contextually defined consistency, such that performance was superior to VM performance. For example, the functions associated with particular keys across word-processing systems are context-dependent. The F1 key may save the document on one system, whereas it may close the document in another system. The menus, screen layout, and even the keyboard may serve as contextual cues about the functions for a particular system.

Principle 5

Long-term retention differs across task components (automatically processed components vs. controlled components). Fisk and Hodge (1992) assessed retention at intervals up to 1 year after practice, and found that the performance characteristics of automatic processes were well maintained even after long periods of disuse. Across experiments, they found more decline in search conditions that required information coordination (switching between memory scanning and visual search), suggesting that, although the automatic processes may not have decayed, the strategic, controlled processing aspects of the task did (Fisk et al., 1994).

Principle 6

Consistent task components must be identified and trained to levels of auto-maticity to minimize mental workload. As described earlier, automatic processes are less consumptive of attentional resources. Thus, the more task components that can be automatized, the less mental workload there will be (at least in terms of attentional requirements; Schneider & Fisk, 1982b).

Principle 7

Training to levels of automaticity will also make performance reliable under environmental stressors such as alcohol, fatigue, heat, noise, and so on. Research suggests that consistent task training can make performance resistant to the effects of heat stress, alcohol intoxication, and fatigue (Fisk & Schneider, 1981, 1982; Hancock, 1984, 1986).

Principle 8

Pretraining of task components to automaticity may be beneficial for complex tasks. Pretraining and part-task training techniques are beneficial for automatizing task components that can then be recombined for the whole task (Eggemeier, Fisk, Robbins, & Lawless, 1988; Fisk & Eboch, 1989).

Principle 9

Part-task training may also be beneficial for complex tasks. Part-task training may be particularly useful for tasks that are initially too difficult for novices too perform (Wightman & Lintern, 1985).

A PROPOSED TASK-ANALYTIC METHODOLOGY

The principles described in the previous section form the basis for CAPTAM. It is well known that complex, multicomponent tasks lead to improved performance if: (a) the dominant task components are consistent and have received extended practice, or (b) the lower level task components are automatized such that they do not interfere with the higher level attention-demanding aspects of the task. The major purpose of instruction for skill acquisition is to ensure that the consistent elements of the situation are clear to the learner, and that the learner receives many correct executions of the consistent task components. The relatively broad-based applicability of the principles of automatic processing serves as the foundation for CAPTAM. The major thrust of our approach is to determine where the consistencies lie in a given task domain; that is, whether they are simple stimulus–response consistencies, higher order rule-based consistencies or even less than perfectly consistent. Armed with this information, we can draw on the experimental literature to determine how best to train individuals to benefit from the consistencies of the task.

The following section discusses the details of CAPTAM.

CONTROLLED AND AUTOMATIC PROCESSING TASK ANALYTIC METHODOLOGY

In any job or task analysis, it is important to specify several fundamental issues. First is the source (or sources) from whom the job data will be obtained. Many discussions of this issue center on whether it is most appropriate to query job incumbents or supervisors or to use trained observers, and so on (Cornelius,

1988). It is argued here that it is important to gather job-related data from people at different levels of job experience. The different descriptions provided by novices versus experts can provide insight into those task components that change as a function of skill acquisition. Similarities among the descriptions highlight those tasks or task components that remain constant irrespective of skill level.

The second issue involves the methods of obtaining data (Goldstein, 1986). Common methods include observation, questionnaires, and interviews. CAPTAM makes extensive use of observation, along with group interviews. Other methods might also be applied within this framework.

The third issue concerns the type of job descriptor. One needs to determine whether the focus is on the tasks and activities performed, the physical demands, working conditions, abilities and skills, and so on. In CAPTAM, the foci are the education and training required to perform the tasks, the degree to which task components may be automatized, and the differences in task performance under various conditions of stress and overload. To that end, descriptions of the specific tasks and activities, working conditions, and abilities and skills required are all of direct relevance.

The final issue to be specified is the purpose of the analysis: What is the outcome of the analysis and intended use of the outcome data? In the present case, the goal is to develop a training program that maximizes training effectiveness through identifying tasks with consistent components that can then be trained. The following section provides a more in-depth discussion of what the task/job analysts should be looking for. The general goal is to look for task consistencies that can be trained. Task consistency may not be immediately obvious. Task analysts should be cognizant of this fact and look for higher order or rule-based consistencies.

The goal of this section is to provide a set of guidelines or prescriptive statements about how to conduct the task analysis. By necessity (and also by design), the guidelines are at the level of psychological processes and are applicable to a wide range of job settings. Several examples of applications are also provided to illustrate CAPTAM.

Novice and Expert Comparisons

Determine where novices have difficulties that are not evident for experts. Such task components or decision points would likely be amenable to consistent training for automaticity.

Determine where the performance of novices, but not experts, breaks down under conditions of stress, time pressure, fatigue, and so on. Evidence suggests that well-learned automatic task components are immune to deleterious effects of such conditions.

Determine the task components or decision points for which experts report high workload. These task components may be amenable to part-task training procedures, such that attentional demands are initially reduced during training so that novices will not be cognitively overloaded during training (Wightman & Lintern 1985). Task components that remain difficult even for experts may be virtually impossible for novices and might require special training procedures.

Declarative Versus Procedural Knowledge

Different types of knowledge acquisition require different types of training. Anderson (1982) made a distinction between declarative knowledge, which is fact knowledge (knowing what), and procedural knowledge, which is knowledge of procedures (knowing how). Both declarative and procedural task components can benefit from consistent training, although the training procedures will differ for the two types of knowledge acquisition.

Determine what information is necessary to perform this task. Focus on the kind of background knowledge the worker must have for the task (or task component). Determine aspects of the task that are easy for the expert to write down or verbalize. Tasks that primarily require declarative knowledge require training that encourages memorization. Consistent task components can be trained, such that eliciting stimuli will automatically evoke associated declarative information.

Determine the steps involved in performing the task. Consistent training of the more procedural components can result in the compilation and proceduralization of the process, such that component steps are combined and one stage leads directly to the next (Anderson, 1982). An example of proceduralization is the fact that one initially follows a "recipe" for performing tasks with several steps (adding a series of numbers), but consistent practice minimizes the steps and makes the process more efficient. In some cases, consistent practice can lead to direct memory access, such that the execution of the recipe or algorithm is no longer even necessary (Logan, 1988). A comparison of expert and novice descriptions of the steps involved in a task is especially important because experts may not be able to describe each of the component steps of the process due to automatization or proceduralization.

Identification of Consistencies

Identify local level consistencies, such as basic stimulus–response associations. These types of consistencies may be the easiest to identify. If a particular response is made every time a stimulus is presented, that is a local level consistency. For example, if an alarm is associated with turning off a machine in all contexts, under all goal conditions, no matter what, then that stimulus–response association would be classified as *completely consistent*.

Identify where consistent categories of information exist. For example, an insurance salesperson is trained to sell the "optimal" package to all individuals. However, optimality is determined by a combination of factors that are consistent together. Similar issues would arise with a loan officer at a bank. Good credit will not always be associated with a loan, but the combination of good credit, collateral, and a good job might be consistently associated with a successful loan application.

Identify where consistent rules exist. A consistent rule for an air traffic controller is to maintain a certain distance between aircraft. However, responses will vary to specific aircraft at different points in time.

Identify context-specific consistencies. Compare responses to stimuli under different contexts. The range of important contexts varies across job domains. For example, for trainees who are required to use many software systems on the same computer, emphasis on the consistencies within a system is most important. Training contextually relevant responses is particularly important for police officers and military personnel. These individuals must learn to differentiate friend or foe before shooting, and these decisions are contextually determined.

Identify where and how task goals consistently change performance. As with contexts, the best approach is to observe the response's made to stimuli under different goal conditions. To illustrate, the response made to pilots when an air intercept controller is given the goal of "identifying aircraft" will be very different from those given with the goal of "defend friendly air space from hostile intruders." Consider also the differences between the strategy of a reader with the task of editing a manuscript for content versus a reader with the goal of proofreading the grammar of the manuscript. Although the stimulus is the same (the manuscript), the different goal changes the level of reading.

Interviewing Techniques

The first major step in CAPTAM involves the collection of data pertaining to the task domain to be trained. The task analyst may apply the consistency principles within a variety of job-analysis techniques. The choice may depend on the nature of the task being analyzed. One approach that has been successfully applied involves semistructured interviews of individuals within the job context (Eggemeier et al., 1988). Several critical components of the interviews are described in detail. The personnel requirements and form of the interview play a key role in the acquisition of the data necessary for the development of the training program based on the principles of controlled and automatic processing.

The interview team ideally consists of one or two individuals who are familiar with the basic principles of controlled and automatic processing theory. Working knowledge of these principles may be obtained from Schneider et al. (1984), Shiffrin (1988), and Shiffrin and Dumais (1981). Given this basic knowledge, the interviewers are better able to ask the appropriate questions and interpret the answers within the context of controlled/automatic processing theory. Another member of the interview team should be a subject matter expert (SME). By definition, an SME is an expert in the task domain of interest. He or she is invaluable in guiding the questions during the interviews to ensure that all facets of the task domain are considered. It is important to note that the SME serves as an interviewer, not an interviewee.

The choice of whom to interview is another factor that determines the success of the interviews. It is important to include individuals with a range of experience within the task domain of interest. Both novices and highly skilled individuals should be included. An ideal group would consist of one or two individuals from each skill level. (It is important not to include supervisors and employees in the same group; the task analyst also must be cognizant of the social dynamics of a particular group and how they may influence the data.) A particular interview session might include an interviewer(s), an SME, and two to four interviewees ranging in experience levels. The group interview format allows direct comparison of the answers provided by individuals of different skill levels, and the interchange among the interviewees may also provide important information. It may also be useful to conduct one-on-one interviews to alleviate potential "shyness" of some individuals to express their opinions in a group setting.

It is critical to include individuals of varying skill levels because the differences and similarities in their reports provide information relevant to identifying consistent task components as well as other training decisions. For example, a novice communications operator might claim that remembering transmission codes is a major component of the job. However, an expert might state that remembering the codes is trivial. This is an obvious case of something that the experts have learned that the novices are still struggling with. This task component is a candidate for consistent component training. If the codes are consistent at some level, training of transmission codes could reduce the influence of that component on overall performance even for novice communication personnel. Training to the level of automatization would free up attentional resources to be devoted to performing the other components of the task.

There will also be task components that both novices and experts cite as critical for successful task performance. For an air traffic controller, maintaining an updated representation of the relative positions of aircraft will always be critical and require attention. These task components are characteristic of controlled processes that remain attention demanding even for very skilled performers. That is not to say that the task components do not benefit from practice. However, once asymptotic performance levels are reached, performance may still be slow, serial in nature, and resource-consumptive.

On-Site Observation

Following the interviews, the task analysts should conduct some on-site observations of the task domain. Direct observation may validate the differences between experts and novices. The observers should particularly note where the sequences and categories of activities differed from those reported in the interviews (for both novices and experts). In addition, the observers should focus on the speed with which critical tasks are performed, how tasks may differ depending on the goal of the performer, and how task performance is affected by stress, fatigue, and time pressure.

The task analysis is an iterative process. Following the on-site observations, another interview session might be helpful to clarify points of confusion and to allow the interview team to further probe any issues that arise during their observations.

The CAPTAM approach is different from traditional job analyses in a number of ways. First, the approach specifies analyzing individuals with a range of expertise, rather than focusing on the best performers. The interest is in the differences in responses to the same question due to variation in expertise (rather than using frequency or task importance ratings). In addition, the approach takes a more dynamic, process-oriented perspective, in that changes in skill acquisition from novice to expert are of critical importance. It is not sufficient to simply list the knowledge, skills, and abilities required for each task. Instead, the analysts must determine (a) which tasks can become automatized with practice and which ones remain controlled and strategic; (b) whether and how context, fatigue, stress, time pressure, and so on influence performance; and, finally, (c) whether it is possible to remove performance limitations through training or if strategic components should be emphasized in training.

APPLICATIONS OF CAPTAM

Approaches that are conceptually similar to CAPTAM have shown some success in real-world training scenarios. Schneider, Vidulich, and Yeh (1982) reported a training program aimed at developing the component, spatial skills required to perform air traffic control for in flight refueling. Theirs was an early attempt to develop a training program founded on basic research showing the need to develop automatic component skills. Their results support the suggestion that substantial performance improvements could be obtained by careful analysis of complex tasks and the identification of a method for representing and training the consistent elements of an overall complex task. More recently, Regian and Schneider (1990) developed a procedure based on automaticity theory for the selection and training of Naval Air Intercept Control trainees.

Fisk and Eggemeier (1988; Eggemeier et al., 1988) reported a direct application of consistent component training to rich, real-world tasks performed as part of the military tactical command and control mission. Their approach was basically a precursor to CAPTAM. They first identified the consistent trainable components in the operational environment through extensive interviews and observations. The interview and observation data indicated that there were several clearly identifiable high-level components in an aerial refueling mission (e.g., locating the tanker and receiver aircraft, directing the aircraft into the proper refueling position). Analyses of these high-level components permitted identification of several categories of controller skills required for the mission. Each of those skills was then analyzed to identify consistent elements, which resulted in the identification of a variety of consistent task components involving perceptual and motor functions. To illustrate, detecting the direction of the aircraft turn requires that the controller utilize a consistent relationship between movement of the return on the display and the aircraft direction of motion. The results of the Eggemeier et al. application indicate that the task analytic methodology could be successfully applied—first to identify consistent components, and then to develop a part-task training approach based on those consistent components.

One occupation in which the identification of consistencies has been attempted with the ultimate goal of improving training is that of a firefighter. Firefighting represents a task domain in which decisions must frequently be made under extreme time pressure. Klein and associates (Klein, 1989; Klein & Calderwood, 1988; Klein, Calderwood, & Clinton-Cirocco, 1986) gathered useful information from semistructured interviews in their critical decision method of retrospective verbal protocols. Their method involves having experts provide answers to questions concerning critical incidents that had taken place within the previous year. The decision points (when nontrivial alternative courses of action are available) are then probed with interview questions. The results reported by Klein et al. (1986) support the proposal that perceptual information and recognitional processes are critical to performance:

> The most striking finding was how rarely we found any evidence that the FGCs [Fire Ground Commanders] attempted to compare or evaluate alternatives at all. … Most commonly, the FGCs claimed that they simply recognized the situation as an example of something they had encountered many times before and acted without conscious awareness of making choices at all. (p. 577)

In fact, of the 156 decision points measured, 127 represented situations in which events triggered an immediate recognition of what to do.

Klein and Calderwood (1988) suggested that training programs should emphasize sensitivity to critical factors that distinguish prototypical situations, with the overall goal being to instruct individuals on how to conceptualize situations quickly and effectively. The CAPTAM approach capitalizes on the consistencies apparent in the prototypical situations, and structures the training program around those consistencies. In all likelihood, the consistencies would be at higher levels (the type of fire), rather than at the specific stimulus level. However, many components of the firefighter's job would be consistent at the specific stimulus level, and these task components would also benefit from consistent training. Examples of such consistent task components include operating equipment, maneuvering ladders, locating hidden fires, shoring up weak structural components, and searching for evidence of arson (Bownas, 1988).

It is useful to consider additional domains in which the CAPTAM approach might be applied. There are numerous categories of jobs that would be amenable to our approach. In Volume 2 of the *Job Analysis Handbook for Business, Industry, and Government* (Gael, 1988), a variety of applications of job-analysis techniques are reported. The occupations include nurse, human service worker, clerical worker, computer programmer, life insurance agent, supermarket cashier, bus operator, police officer, firefighter, telecommunications craft worker, steel worker, heavy equipment operator, automobile mechanic, computer logic chip production operator, and plant nursery operator. The design of training programs for all of these domains could benefit from CAPTAM. The remainder of this chapter discusses several of these applications to demonstrate the range of applicability of CAPTAM. These examples are based on task analyses conducted by other researchers. A full implementation of the CAPTAM approach would include the actual interviews, observations, and task analysis. However, these examples are intended to demonstrate the applicability of the approach to a variety of domains and to the training and development phase of an instructional system.

Clerical Worker

Gandy (1988) reported the results of a job analysis of clerical jobs. A review of Gandy's results reveals that many of the task categories might benefit from training according to the principles of controlled and automatic processing. Filing and sorting activities, bookkeeping and financial activities, computing and coding, operating machines, typing and data entry, and taking dictation are all activities that have consistent components that could be trained to levels of automaticity. According to Gandy, these activities account for 50% of the time spent by clerical workers. Consequently, if training time were spent making these activities as efficient and resource-independent as possible (automatic), the overall job performance of the clerical worker would be improved and job output increased.

Computer Programmer

At the level of programming, there are clearly consistencies within programming language (syntax, error messages, subroutines). There may also be some consistencies across computer languages. In addition to these lower level consistencies in the job of a computer programmer, there are also higher order consistencies that may be trainable. For example, although the details will differ across applications, the general structure of databases may be quite consistent. If database designers are taught to look at the higher order consistencies, they may be better able to transport their skills across a range of domains.

A recent theory of software comprehension (Boehm-Davis, Harris, & Littman, 1993) suggests that experienced programmers develop "clichés" that are standardized units or chunks of code. Clichés may be used to segment a problem into manageable units and enhance software comprehension. These clichés may represent higher order consistencies in programming that could be directly trained.

Supermarket Cashier

Nearly all of the important and frequent tasks performed by supermarket cashiers would be amenable to training according to the principles of consistency. Task analysis has revealed the following tasks for supermarket cashiers: memorize prices; associate price with item; make change; count money; subtract, divide, and multiply during customer transactions; bag groceries; operate register; and grab items from basket and place on check stand counter (Fogli, 1988). Some of these tasks are inconsistent, (e.g., the prices of items change on a weekly basis). For items in the produce department, the cashier need not remember the price, but simply remember the code number for the scale. Hence, this task is consistent at a higher level (cf. Fisk et al., 1988). The majority of the tasks are completely consistent and could be readily trained under CM conditions. We should emphasize again that these suggestions for task components that could be consistently trained were based on someone else's task analysis. Using CAPTAM, we would have more confidence in our recommendations. We would have interviewed novice and expert cashiers and compared their difficulties to illuminate training needs. Both groups would probably comment on the difficulty of trying to remember changing prices from week to week (a varied task component). However, it is likely that only the novices would report difficulty remembering produce codes because the codes are consistent and expert cashiers would already have learned them. Similarly, making change may be difficult for novices, but not for experts. This example illustrates how CAPTAM would provide more information relative to a traditional task analysis.

CONTRIBUTIONS, RESTRICTIONS, AND FUTURE RESEARCH

The CAPTAM approach can be helpful for any kind of job, at least in terms of understanding the training needs of the particular job. The empirical and theoretical bases of CAPTAM are directly relevant to the training of those components that can become automatized. It is an indisputable fact that if your attention must be devoted to lower level (perceptual) components of tasks, those resources are not available for the higher level components of the task. To date, the approach has been particularly helpful for task domains that have heavy perceptual components. Additional research in more complex cognitive domains will test the generality of the approach (Orasanu, 1990).

It is important to keep in mind that, as trainers begin to encompass more complex behaviors, they must be concerned about the issue of "scaling up" the processing principles acquired from simpler tasks. Recent research on Decision Making Evaluation Facility for Tactical Teams (DEFTT) begins to tackle some of the issues involved in applying consistent principles to complex training environments (Hodge et al., 1993).

An open question remains as to whether more strategic components of tasks can be trained in a similar manner. That is, the approach may not work well in terms of training the strategic aspects of jobs. Clearly, the task analysis will provide information about which parts of jobs will continue to require cognitive effort. New research should focus on the degree to which part-task training, identification of consistencies, and so on will also be helpful for tasks that remain attention-demanding even after extensive training.

Within the training environment, CAPTAM could be used for the development of scenarios and the design of simulators. An understanding of the principles of consistency would enable designers to develop the most appropriate situations, which provide practice leading to the development of automaticity for the relevant task components.

Within the organizational environment, trainers must consider social problems and organizational factors that may influence the design of training programs. Task analysts can also contribute more knowledge about the utility of different methods of implementing the consistency principles and translating them into familiar job-analytic techniques. It will be particularly useful to compare approaches that rely on verbal questionnaires, open-ended versus closed interviews, verbal protocols, ratings, and so on. The question, of course, is which approach is the most useful for delineating the consistencies in a particular domain. More than likely, we will discover that a convergence of analytic techniques is most beneficial, and, that the most appropriate approach will probably differ across task domains. However, guidelines could be provided based on the aforementioned comparison of various techniques.

CONCLUSION

This chapter presented a brief overview of automatic and controlled processing theory to illustrate the foundations of CAPTAM. It presented the details of CAPTAM and some application examples. The goal here was to provide practitioners with a task-analytic framework with which to develop training programs that capitalize on consistent components of tasks. There is a wealth of information in the cognitive and training literature that may be applied to practical problems. CAPTAM relies on the principles of consistency and automaticity to enable the development of maximally effective training programs.

To review, the distinctions between controlled and automatic processing have revealed that the characteristics differ greatly according to the dominant mode of processing for a particular task or task component. Tasks that are primarily performed automatically or that consist of some automatized components are performed faster, more accurately, with less demand on attentional resources, with less susceptibility to stressors such as heat and fatigue, and are better retained across time. The benefits of automatic processing are manifold—the greater the degree to which training programs can capitalize on automatized components, the more effective such programs will be.

CAPTAM represents a framework for identifying the consistent components of tasks through interviews and observations. This chapter provided guidelines for identifying consistent components based on empirical laboratory data. In addition, it reported several real-world scenarios in which approaches similar to CAPTAM have been successfully applied (Eggemeier et al., 1988; Schneider et al., 1982). Finally, it presented some illustrative examples of domains in which the CAPTAM framework could potentially be applied.

The purpose of this chapter was to provide an overview of a tool for practitioners who must develop maximally effective training programs. CAPTAM is empirically and theoretically grounded. The application of this framework yields a set of trainable tasks and task components. A training program can then be developed that will capitalize on the principles of automaticity and maximize the benefits of training. Ideally, CAPTAM will be refined through its application to a range of domains. The development of a successful training ideology is an iterative process that cycles through theory and application. Future applications-oriented research will likely yield additional guidelines for extracting the consistent components from real-world domains. These updated principles and guidelines will then inform subsequent task analyses.

ACKNOWLEDGMENTS

Portions of this methodology were adapted from Eggemeier et al. (1988), Fisk and Eggemeier (1988), Fisk and Rogers (1992), and Fisk, Scerbo, and Schneider (1983). Initial development of the task-analytic technique was funded by a contract (No. F33615-85-C-0010) between the Air Force Human Resources Laboratory—Logistics and Human Factors Division, and Systems Exploration, Inc. The views expressed herein are those of the authors and do not necessarily reflect the official position of the organizations with which they are affiliated.

REFERENCES

Ackerman, P. L. (1986). Individual differences in information processing: An investigation of intellectual abilities and task performance during practice. *Intelligence, 10*, 101–139.

Ackerman, P. L. (1987). Individual differences in skill learning: An integration of psychometric and information processing perspectives. *Psychological Bulletin, 102*, 3–27.

Anderson, J. R. (1982). Acquisition of cognitive skill. *Psychological Review, 89*, 369–406.

Barrett, G. V., & Maurer, T. J. (1993). *The task/job analysis–predictor development process: Beyond g and general construct categories in tailored employment ability testing.* Unpublished manuscript, University of Akron, Ohio.

Bobko, P., Colella, A., & Russell, C. J. (1990). *Estimation of selection utility with multiple predictors in the presence of multiple performance criteria, differential validity through time, and strategic goals* (Tech. Rep.). San Diego, CA: Navy Personnel Research and Development Center.

Boehm-Davis, D. A., Harris, J. E., & Littman, D. C. (1993, February). *Toward a goal-based theory of software comprehension.* Proceedings of the First Mid-Atlantic Human Factors Conference, Virginia Beach, VA.

Bownas, D. A. (1988). Firefighter. In S. Gael (Ed.), *The job analysis handbook for business, industry, and government* (Vol. 2, pp. 1255–1264). New York: Wiley.

Briggs, G. E., & Waters, L. K. (1958). Training and transfer as a function of component interaction. *Journal of Experimental Psychology, 56*, 492–500.

Bryan, W. L., & Harter, N. (1899). Studies on the telegraphic language: The acquisition of a hierarchy of habits. *Psychological Review, 6*, 345–375.

Cannon-Bowers, J. A., Salas, E., & Grossman, J. D. (1991). *Improving tactical decision making under stress: Research directions and applied implications.* Presented at the 27th International Applied Military Psychology Symposium: A focus on Decision Making Research, Stockholm, Sweden.

Cornelius, E. T. (1988). Practical findings from job analysis research. In S. Gael (Ed.), *The job analysis handbook for business, industry, and government* (Vol. 1, pp. 48–68). New York: Wiley.

Czerwinski, M. P., Lightfoot, N., & Shiffrin, R. M. (1992). Automatization and training in visual search. *American Journal of Psychology, 105*, 271–316.

Eberts, R., & Schneider, W. (1985). Internalizing the system dynamics for a second–order system. *Human Factors, 27*, 371–395.

Eberts, R., & Schneider, W. (1986). Effects of perceptual training of sequenced line movements. *Perception and Psychophysics, 39*, 236–247.

Eggemeier, F. T., Fisk, A. D., Robbins, R. J., & Lawless, M. T. (1988). *Application of automatic/controlled processing theory to training tactical command and control skills: II. Evaluations of task-analytic methodology.* Proceedings of the annual meeting of the Human Factors Society, Santa Monica, CA.

Fisk, A. D., & Eboch, M. (1989). Application of automatic/controlled processing theory to training component map reading skills. *Applied Ergonomics, 20*, 2–8.

Fisk, A. D., & Eggemeier, F. T. (1988). Application of automatic/controlled processing theory to training tactical command and control skills: I. Background and task-analytic methodology. *Proceedings of the Annual Meeting of the Human Factors Society*, Santa Monica, CA.

Fisk, A. D., & Gallini, J. K. (1989). Training consistent components of tasks: Developing an instructional system based on automatic/controlled processing principles. *Human Factors, 31*, 453–463.

Fisk, A. D., Hertzog, C., Lee, M. D., Rogers, W. A., & Anderson, M. (1994). Long-term retention of skilled visual search: Do young adults retain more than old adults? *Psychology and Aging, 9*, 206–215.

Fisk, A. D., & Hodge, K. A. (1992). Retention of trained performance in consistent mapping search after extended delay. *Human Factors, 34*, 147–164.

Fisk, A. D., & Jones, C. D. (1992). Global versus local consistency: Effects of degree of within-category consistency on learning and performance. *Human Factors, 34*, 693–705.

Fisk, A. D., Lee, M. D., & Rogers, W. A. (1991). Recombination of automatic processing components: The effects of transfer, reversal, and conflict situations. *Human Factors, 33*, 267–280.

Fisk, A. D., & Lloyd, S. J. (1988). The role of stimulus-to-rule consistency in learning rapid application of spatial rules. *Human Factors, 30*, 35–49.

Fisk, A. D., Oransky, N. A., & Skedsvold, P. R. (1988). Examination of the role of "higher-order" consistency in skill development. *Human Factors, 30*, 567–582.

Fisk, A. D., & Rogers, W. A. (1988a). *A review and critical analysis of automaticity, part/whole training, and team training as a basis for high performance skills training development* (ADF-IBM-8801). Atlanta: Georgia Institute of Technology.

Fisk, A. D., & Rogers, W. A. (1988b). The role of situational context in the development of high-performance skills. *Human Factors, 30*, 703–712.

Fisk, A. D., & Rogers, W. A. (1992). The application of consistency principles for the assessment of skill development. In W. Regian & V. Shute (Eds.), *Cognitive approaches to automated instruction* (pp. 171–194). Hillsdale, NJ: Lawrence Erlbaum Associates.

Fisk, A. D., Scerbo, M. W., & Schneider, W. (1983). Issues in training for skilled performance. In A. T. Pope & L. D. Haugh (Eds.), *Proceedings of the Human Factors Society, 12*, 392–396.

Fisk, A. D., & Schneider, W. (1981). Control and automatic processing during tasks requiring sustained attention: A new approach to vigilance. *Human Factors, 23*, 737–750.

Fisk, A. D., & Schneider, W. (1982). Type of task practice and time-sharing activities predict deficits due to alcohol ingestion. *Proceedings of the 26th Annual Meeting of the Human Factors Society*, Santa Monica, CA.

Fisk, A. D., & Schneider, W. (1983). Category and word search: Generalizing search principles to complex processing. *Journal of Experimental Psychology: Learning, Memory, and Cognition, 9*, 177–195.

Fleishman, E. A., & Mumford, M. D. (1989a). Individual attributes and training performance. In I. L. Goldstein (Ed.), *Training and development in organizations* (pp. 183–255). San Francisco: Jossey-Bass.

Fleishman, E. A., & Mumford, M. D. (1989b). Abilities as causes of individual differences in skill acquisition. *Human Performance, 2*, 201–223.

Flexman, R. E., Roscoe, S. N., Williams, A. C., Jr., & Williges, B. H. (1972). Studies in pilot training: The anatomy of transfer. *Aviation Research Monographs, 2*, 1–87.

Fogli, L. (1988). Supermarket cashier. In S. Gael (Ed.), *The job analysis handbook for business, industry, and government* (Vol. 2, pp. 1215–1228). New York: Wiley.

Folds, D. J., Gerth, J. M., & Engelman, W. R. (1987). *Enhancement of human performance in manual target acquisition* (Tech. Rep. No. USAFSAM-TR-86-18). Atlanta: Georgia Institute of Technology, Systems Engineering Laboratory.

Frederiksen, J. R., Warren, B. M., & Rosebery, A. S. (1985a). A componential approach to training reading skills: Part 1. Perceptual units training. *Cognition and Instruction, 2*, 91–130.

Frederiksen, J. R., Warren, B. M., & Rosebery, A. S. (1985b). A componential approach to training reading skills: Part 1. Decoding and use of context. *Cognition and Instruction, 2,* 271–338.

Gael, S. (1988). *The job analysis handbook for business, industry, and government.* New York: Wiley.

Gandy, J. A. (1988). Clerical jobs. In S. Gael (Ed.), *The job analysis handbook for business, industry, and government* (Vol. 2, pp. 1181–1191). New York: Wiley.

Goldstein, I. L. (1986). *Training in organizations: Needs assessment, development, and evaluation* (2nd ed.). Monterey, CA: Brooks/Cole.

Goldstein, I. L. (1993). *Training in organizations: Needs assessment, development, and evaluation* (3rd ed.). Pacific Grove, CA: Brooks/Cole.

Gordon, N. B. (1959). Learning a motor task under varied display conditions. *Journal of Experimental Psychology, 57,* 65–73.

Hancock, P. A. (1984). Environmental stressors. In J. S. Warm (Ed.), *Sustained attention in human performance* (pp. 134–177). New York: Wiley.

Hancock, P. A. (1986). Sustained attention under thermal stress. *Psychological Bulletin, 99,* 263–281.

Harvey, R. J. (1991). Job analysis. In M. D. Dunnette & L. M. Hough (Eds.), *Handbook of industrial and organizational psychology* (Vol. 2, pp. 71–174). Palo Alto, CA: Consulting Psychologists Press.

Hodge, K. A., Rothrock, L., Krosnick, W., Nagel, K. L., Kirlik, A. C., Walker, N., & Fisk, A. D. (1993). *Training for decision making under stress: An empirical investigation of part-task training for perceptual and rule-based decision making* (HAPL–9301, Contract N61339-91-C-0115). Orlando, FL: Navy Training Systems Center.

Howell, W. C., & Cooke, N. J. (1989). Training the human information processor: A review of cognitive models. In I. L. Goldstein (Ed.), *Training and development in organizations* (pp. 121–182). San Francisco: Jossey-Bass.

James, W. (1890). *The principles of psychology* (Vol. 1). New York: Holt, Rhinehart & Winston.

Klapp, S. T., Martin, Z. E., McMillan, G. G., & Brook, D. T. (1987). Whole-task and part-task training in dual motor tasks. In L. S. Mark, J. S. Warm, & R. L. Huston (Eds.), *Ergonomics and human factors: Recent research* (pp. 125–130). New York: Springer-Verlag.

Klein, G. A. (1989). Do decision biases explain too much? *Human Factors Bulletin, 32,* 1–3.

Klein, G. A., & Calderwood, R. (1988). *How do people use analogues to make decisions?* Proceedings of the Case-Based Reasoning Workshop, San Mateo, CA: Morgan Kaufman Publishers.

Klein, G. A., Calderwood, R., & Clinton-Cirocco, A. (1986). Rapid decision making on the fire ground. *Proceedings of the annual meeting of the Human Factors Society,* Santa Monica, CA.

Kraiger, K., Ford, J. K., & Salas, E. (1993). Application of cognitive, skill-based, and affective theories of learning outcomes to new methods of training evaluation [Monograph]. *Journal of Applied Psychology, 78,* 311–328.

Kramer, A. F., Strayer, D. L., & Buckley, J. (1990). Development and transfer of automatic processing. *Journal of Experimental Psychology: Human Perception and Performance, 16,* 505–522.

Lee, M. D., & Fisk, A. D. (1993). Disruption and maintenance of skilled visual search as a function of degree of consistency. *Human Factors, 35,* 205–220.

Logan, G. D. (1985). Skill and automaticity: Relations, implications, and future directions. *Canadian Journal of Psychology, 39,* 367–3286.

Logan, G. D. (1988). Toward an instance theory of automatization. *Psychological Review, 95,* 492–527.

McGrath, J. J., & Harris, D. H. (1971). *Adaptive training. Aviation research Monographs* (Vol. 1). Champaign, IL: Aviation Research Laboratory.

Murphy, K. (1989). Is the relationship between cognitive ability and job performance stable over time? *Human Performance, 2,* 183–200.

Myers, G. L., & Fisk, A. D. (1987). Training consistent task components: Application of automatic and controlled processing theory to industrial task training. *Human Factors, 29,* 255–268.

Orasanu, J. M. (1990). Diagnostic approaches to learning: Measuring what, how and how much. In N. Frederiksen, R. Glaser, A. Lesgold, & M. Shafto (Eds.), *Diagnostic monitoring of skill and knowledge acquisition* (pp. 393–405). Hillsdale, NJ: Lawrence Erlbaum Associates.

Poltrock, S. E., Lansman, M., & Hunt, E. (1982). Automatic and controlled attention processes in auditory target detection. *Journal of Experimental Psychology: Human Perception and Performance, 8*, 37–45.

Poulton, E. C. (1974). *Tracking skill and manual control.* New York: Academic Press.

Redding, R. E. (1989). Perspectives on cognitive task analysis: The state of the state of the art. *Proceedings of the 33rd annual meeting of the Human Factors Society*, Santa Monica, CA.

Regian, J. W., & Schneider, W. (1990). Assessment procedures for predicting and optimizing skill acquisition after extensive practice. In N. Frederiksen, R. Glaser, A. Lesgold, & M. Shafto (Eds.), *Diagnostic monitoring of skill and knowledge acquisition* (pp. 297–323). Hillsdale, NJ: Lawrence Erlbaum Associates.

Rogers, W. A. (1992). Age differences in visual search: Target and distracter learning. *Psychology and Aging, 7*, 526–535.

Rogers, W. A., Lee, M. D., & Fisk, A. D. (1995). Contextual effects on general learning, feature learning, and attention strengthening in visual search. *Human Factors, 37*, 158–172.

Schneider, W. (1985). Training high performance skills: Fallacies and guidelines. *Human Factors, 27*, 285–300.

Schneider, W., & Detweiler, M. (1987). The role of practice in dual–task performance: Toward workload modeling in a connectionist/control architecture. *Human Factors, 30*, 539–566.

Schneider, W., Dumais, S. T., & Shiffrin, R. M. (1984). Automatic processes and attention. In R. Parasuraman & D. R. Davies (Eds.), *Varieties of attention* (pp. 1–27). Orlando, FL: Academic Press.

Schneider, W., & Fisk, A. D. (1982a). Degree of consistent training: Improvements in search performance and automatic process development. *Perception and Psychophysics, 31*, 160–168.

Schneider, W., & Fisk, A. D. (1982b). Concurrent automatic and controlled visual search: Can processing occur without resource cost? *Journal of Experimental Psychology: Learning, Memory, and Cognition, 8*, 261–278.

Schneider, W., & Fisk, A. D. (1984). Automatic category search and its transfer. *Journal of Experimental Psychology: Learning, Memory, and Cognition, 10*, 1–15.

Schneider, W., & Shiffrin, R. M. (1977). Controlled and automatic human information processing: I. Detection, search and attention. *Psychological Review, 84*, 1–66.

Schneider, W., Vidulich, M. A., & Yeh, Y. Y. (1982). Training spatial skills for air-traffic control. *Proceedings of the 26th Annual Meeting of the Human Factors Society*, Santa Monica, CA.

Shiffrin, R. M. (1988). Attention. In R. C. Atkinson, R. J. Herrnstein, & R. D. Luce (Eds.), *Stevens' handbook of experimental psychology* (pp. 739–811). New York: Wiley.

Shiffrin, R. M., & Dumais, S. (1981). The development of automatism. In J. A. Anderson (Ed.), *Cognitive skills and their acquisition* (pp. 111–140). Hillsdale, NJ: Lawrence Erlbaum Associates.

Shiffrin, R. M., & Schneider, W. (1977). Controlled and automatic human information processing: II. Perceptual learning, automatic attending, and a general theory. *Psychological Review, 84*, 127–190.

Solomons, L., & Stein, G. (1896). Normal motor automatism. *Psychological Review, 3*, 492–512.

Terranova, M., Snyder, C. E., Seamster, T. L., & Treitler, I. E. (1989). Cognitive task analysis: Techniques applied to airborne weapons training. *Proceedings of the 33rd annual meeting of the Human Factors Society*, Santa Monica, CA.

Vidulich, M. A., Yeh, Y. Y., & Schneider W. (1983). Time compressed components for air-intercept skills. *Proceedings of the 27th annual meeting of the Human Factors Society*, Santa Monica, CA.

Walker, N., & Fisk, A. D. (1995, July). Human Factors goes to the gridiron. *Ergonomics in Design*, 8–13.

Whaley, C. J., & Fisk, A. D. (1993). Effects of part-task training on memory-set unitization and retention of memory-dependent skilled search. *Human Factors, 35*, 639–652.

Wightman, D. C., & Lintern, G. (1985). Part-task training for tracking and manual control. *Human Factors, 27,* 267–283.

Wightman, D. C., & Sistrunk, F. (1987). Part-task training strategies in simulated carrier landing final approach training. *Human Factors, 29,* 245–254.

3

Modeling Performance and Establishing Performance Criteria in Training Systems

Michael D. Coovert
University of South Florida
J. Philip Craiger
University of Nebraska at Omaha

The subdiscipline of training within industrial/organizational psychology is rich with issues for research and application. One need only examine recent review articles to obtain a feel for just how broad the topic area is (cf. Baldwin & Ford, 1988; Cannon-Bowers, Tannenbaum, Salas, & Converse, 1991; Kraiger, Ford, & Salas, 1993; Tannenbaum & Yukl, 1992). This chapter focuses on a small piece of the domain, and encourage's readers to think of human performance in training from new perspectives.

A conceptual and methodological approach is introduced that allows the researcher and practitioner alike to approach the modeling of human behavior while training and the measurement of performance within those systems from a new perspective. A modeling tool primarily used outside of training is described, but the authors' belief is it would be beneficial for the training community. This chapter represents the training task and establishes measures of performance within a training system. Goldstein (1991) stated that the evaluation process of training systems within organizations revolves around two procedures: establishing measures of success during training (see Ostroff, 1991), and using research designs to determine what changes occurred during the training process. The approach described here is well suited for meeting both of those needs. This chapter focuses primarily on establishing measures of success in terms of effectiveness and efficiency, whereas a complementary paper

(Coovert, Cannon-Bowers, Campbell, & Salas, 1994) described the analysis of Petri Net data from a traditional research design perspective.

It is the authors' belief that, through the application of computer- and simulation-based approaches, such as those describe here (Coovert, Craiger, & Cannon-Bowers, 1995; Sanders, 1991), one can answer a variety of questions related to performance in training systems. Some of those questions include the following: Are there certain tasks during training where effective individuals (teams) perform faster (slower) than those individuals (teams) who are not as effective? Is there strategies that emerge from the behavior of effective individuals and teams? And, is it more likely that effective individuals (teams) follow one path in a network of possible behaviors more often than individuals (teams) that are not as effective?

Petri Nets are presented as a modeling tool for use in training. The nets are useful in developing training programs such as intelligent tutoring systems. They also provide a theoretical perspective for viewing individuals in training for cognitively demanding jobs. Specifically, the role of mental models in problem solving and decision making is addressed, followed by: (a) knowledge representation for different types of tasks, (b) differences in expert–novice problem-solving strategies, (c) decision-making errors, and (d) mental models in team tasks. Each of these areas is important in its own right, and Petri Net modeling strategies can facilitate an understanding of each topic. The chapter concludes with a discussion of computational psychology and future challenges for intelligent tutoring systems in training.

MENTAL MODELS IN PROBLEM SOLVING AND DECISION MAKING

Craik, in *The Nature of Explanation* (1943), was one of the first to propose that an important underlying mechanism of problem solving and decision making involves thought experiments. Humans, either explicitly or implicitly, generate internal mental representations or models of the world in which they live to evaluate and predict possible future states. Although a single accepted definition of a *mental model* has proved elusive to the field, for the purposes of this chapter, a rigorous definition proposed by Johnson-Laird (1990) is used:

> ...a mental model can be defined as a representation of a body of knowledge—either long-term or short-term that meets the following conditions:
> • Its structures correspond to the structure of the situation that it represents.
> • It can consist of elements corresponding only to perceptible entities, in which case it may be realized as an image, perceptual or imaginary. Alternatively it can contain elements corresponding to abstract notions; their significance depends crucially on the procedures for manipulating models.

- Unlike other proposed forms of representation, it does not contain variables. (p. 488)

A mental model is composed of symbols that serve as abstract representations of real-world entities, and processes that represent the relationships between the symbols, as well as how they interact and affect each other. As such, mental models are executable working representations of the world. Several theoretical cognitive structures have been proposed to explain how people represent knowledge and reason, including: schemata (Bartlett, 1932), scripts (Schank & Abelson, 1977), frames (Minsky, 1975), and semantic networks (Quillian, 1968). The defining attribute of mental models is that they are dynamic. Individuals manipulate symbols that represent real-world entities to understand and predict possible states of the world (Rouse & Morris, 1986). The mental model construct has proved to possess an interdisciplinary applicability—being proposed as an explanatory mechanism for human decision making and problem solving in a number of scientific domains, including: psycholinguistics, cognitive science, artificial intelligence, and most subdisciplines of psychology.

Skill- Versus Rule- Versus Knowledge-Based Cognitive Control

Advanced skills training often has at its center the learning of effective skills for decision making and problem solving. As such, it is important to understand the various types of cognitive control involved with these processes. The set of cognitive processes that affect decision making and problem solving is a hierarchy of subprocesses, each of which affects performance. Rasmussen (1980, 1987; Olsen & Rasmussen, 1989) developed a taxonomy of cognitive control that purports to explain how cognitive processes translate into behavior. Three levels of control are defined. *Skill-based* control is characterized by routine and automated processes, such as those associated with perceptual-motor skills. *Rule-based* control is characterized by feed-forward goal-oriented behavior based on rules developed empirically through experience or training. The rule-based level is concerned with the immediate state of the problem—identifying task and environmental cues that are relevant to the immediate situation, and matching these cues with stored rules to select the most appropriate rule for application. The highest conceptual representation is the *knowledge-based level*, which serves a metalevel control function—a global plan of action concerned with goal setting, selecting appropriate behaviors, and monitoring goal-directed progress.

During decision making, control of reasoning is transferred among the levels, with the direction of transfer being context-dependent (i.e., the immediate problem state determines the level instantiated). For example, once an individual identifies an appropriate rule, the automated skill-based control is activated, resulting in a change in the decision/task environment, with control returning to the knowledge-base level to monitor goal progress. Control then transfers back to the rule-based level, and so on.

The relative effect of each level of control on the overall process of decision making and problem solving is difficult to determine a priori; it probably depends on the tasks and problem domain. For tasks requiring problem solving and decision making, the rule- and knowledge-based levels undoubtedly have a large impact on performance. Depending on the behaviors being trained, various aspects of skill-, rule-, and knowledge-based cognitive control are employed.

Expert and Novice Differences

Research suggests fundamental differences in the ways in which experts and novices solve problems. Specific differences exist between the two in how knowledge is represented and information is processed. Apparently, experts represent problems at "a higher level of abstraction" than do novices. Experience with diverse problem types allows them to develop heuristics that they employ as a means of reducing the search space of the problem (Newell & Simon, 1972). In contrast, novices, appear to focus on the surface features of a problem; when faced with a difficult task, their strategy involves incrementally decomposing the task and solving the subproblems. This is important information for trainers to have because it allows the monitoring of trainee progression from novice to more advanced states.

A possible explanation of differences between novices and experts is provided by research on case-based reasoning, which suggests reasoning by analogy appears to be a widely used general problem-solving strategy (Kolodner, 1991). Case-based reasoning is premised on the fact that humans draw on experiences with past problems when confronted with new problems. Kolodner contended that humans store experiential and problem-relevant knowledge in long-term memory in the form of cases that are indexed by similarity. Enormous quantities of experiential knowledge allow experts to employ analogical reasoning efficiently by providing them access to similar strategies that were successfully used in solving past problems. Novices use the same strategy. However, they have little problem-solving experience, and the complexity of problems they do experience often prohibits them from developing efficient indexing procedures (i.e., they are unable to determine the contextual factors that are relevant to problem solving).

Interestingly, when presented with a novel situation, expert behavior appears to be that of a novice. Like the novice, the expert exhausts the collection of rules and the knowledge required to solve the problem in an expert manner, leading them to focus on the surface features of the problem. Reason (1987) proposed that the primary differences between experts and novices style of problem solving (framed within cognitive control), is that experts have a much larger set of rules, and that they are formulated at a higher level of abstraction (emphasizing general problem structure rather than surface features). Therefore, differences between experts and novices regarding elements of cognitive control are at the skill- and rule-based levels; there is apparently little else that is different between the two.

Decision-Making Errors

Understanding and evaluating performance in terms of information processing is facilitated through an analysis of both correct and incorrect performance (Simon, 1979). From an information-processing perspective, errors can be partitioned into two general classes: slips and mistakes. A *slip* is a failure to execute a planned action (Norman, 1981), whereas a *mistake* is characterized as a failure to achieve a desired outcome although a plan of action was carried out correctly (Newell & Simon, 1972). Obviously it is important, in training, to be able to differentiate between the two. (As described later, the construction of lattice networks of anticipated behaviors during training is one way to achieve this differentiation.)

Reason (1987) defined three types of errors: skill-based slips, rule-based mistakes, and knowledge-based mistakes. Skill-based slips are considered monitoring failures, whereas rule- and knowledge-based mistakes are considered failures in problem-solving strategies. *Skill-based slips* occur due to omitted or mistimed attentional checks (problems with the perception of cues). *Rule-based mistakes* are thought to occur due to incorrect or inappropriate matching of environmental/task cues to available rules (improper interpretation of cues, or selection of inappropriate rules). *Knowledge-based mistakes* are caused by either an incomplete or incorrect mental model, or bounded rationality (Simon, 1986). Reason outlined a number of limitations and biases that lead to errors in performance, including: rigidity of rule-bound thinking (the misapplication of familiar rules to new situations), the availability of heuristic's (employing rules or heuristics based on the ease with which they come to mind; Tversky & Kahneman, 1982), selective processing of information (not taking into account all relevant cues), and incorrect or incomplete knowledge (inadequate training). Obviously, there is a big advantage in being able to identify the type of error made during training because that will suggest the most promising remedial course of action. Cognitive errors are most apparent when anticipated responses are made explicit with a structure, such as that provided by Petri Nets.

Mental Models and Teams

Because teams are composed of individuals, individual decision making is an important underlying component of team decision making (TDM). However,

TDM cannot be characterized as simply the aggregate of decision making by the individual members. This fact is apparent when the distinction between *teams* and *groups* is noted. Although the terms are sometimes used interchangeably, teams are conceptually distinct from groups and coacting aggregates (Penner & Craiger, 1992). Forsyth (1983) defined a *group* as loosely structured aggregates of individuals who influence one another through interaction. Teams are inherently more complex—structurally and behaviorally—than are groups. Teams are characterized in terms of well-defined divisions of labor, interdependence, compensatory behavior, and (often) hierarchical structure (Dyer, 1984).

These characteristics suggest that there is more to TDM than simply the sum of decision making by the individuals, and empirical evidence supports this. McIntyre, Morgan, Salas, and Glickman (1988) found a relationship between the effectiveness of a team and the ability of its members to predict such team aspects as: (a) the needs and behavior of other team members, (b) the task requirements, and (c) the behavior of other team members. These results suggest that team members must not only have developed a mental model of their own task, but they must also develop mental models of tasks executed by other team members, as well as the team decision-making structure as a whole. As is seen shortly, construction of a Petri Net representation of the team task can be an effective aid to use in training individuals, not only in their own role in the team task, but also in establishing a mental model of the team's task.

Summary

When establishing performance standards for training, it is useful to consider several things. First, an information-processing perspective of the trainee provides a theoretical background appropriate for how the individual will (or should) construct a mental model of the task. Second, the type of information being learned by the trainee will determine the relative importance of skill-, rule-, or knowledge-based cognitive control. Third, understanding mental models and cognitive control strategies can lead to a concrete way of establishing effective behavioral strategies for use in training novices. Another way of saying this is that if experts (because of their mental representation and cognitive control strategies) tend to follow a specific path in a network of behaviors, deviations from that path on the part of novices can serve as a metric to measure trainee performance against. Also, for time-critical behavior, efficiency in traversing the behavioral network can also be assessed. Finally, for situations in which teams are trained, it would be especially useful model team performance utilizing the same methodology employed for individual performance.

A modeling methodology that can be used to represent individuals and teams in training systems is represented next. The approach is general, in that it can be used to represent both active and passive elements in the training system while allowing the construction of lattice networks of behavior. Attributes of behavior within the system, such as effectiveness and efficiency, can also be quantified for evaluation; thus, allowing for the establishment of performance criteria and standards.

MODELING BEHAVIOR WITH PETRI NETS

An Overview of Petri Nets

Conventional tools such as flow diagrams, narrative descriptions, and time-line analysis are useful for a variety of modeling problems. However, they impose constraints on the representation, and are not powerful enough for certain types of tasks. Specifically, those tools make it difficult or impossible to expose critical time-dependencies, task concurrencies, and event driven behavior.

Petri Nets are a useful and powerful modeling tool and overcome the aforementioned shortcomings. The methodology was proposed by C. A. Petri (1962) as a general purpose modeling tool for asynchronous systems. Systems that have been successfully modeled by Petri Nets have such diverse characteristics as being: distributed, asynchronous, concurrent, and stochastic. The approach is especially useful because individuals at work often perform tasks in an asynchronous manner with stochastic properties. The ability to construct models with these properties make's Petri Nets an attractive tool for modeling an individual's behavior. Furthermore, because this methodology affords the capability of modeling parallel activities (and conflict), aggregates of individuals (subteams and teams) can also be modeled.

Petri Nets have both graphical and mathematical dimension's. The graphical aspect makes them a useful tool for representing a system in a visual manner. This facilitates the development of the mental model (Rouse & Morris, 1986) of the training task on the part of the trainee. The graphical component also makes it an excellent communication medium for the trainer to employ. As a mathematical tool, algebraic equations, state equations, or other mathematical models are established, which control the behavior of the system. The mathematical underpinnings of the nets allow for rigorous analyses of various types. The mathematics of Petri Nets are not discused here (see Reutenauer, 1990). Since Petri's early work, the nets have been the focus of much research to embellish and extend their capabilities. A good overview of recent developments and extensions can be found in Jensen and Rozenberg (1991).

Although there are special types of Petri Nets, they were not differentiated in this chapter. Rather, the purpose here is to provide the reader with a low-level introduction to the process of constructing a representation of systems using a few basic constructs and rules. Readers interested in special issues are encouraged to explore the literature (cf. Jensen & Rozenberg, 1991; Peterson, 1981; Reisig, 1992) on the topic of interest, and to employ various software packages for the analysis of their models (cf. Alphatech, 1992; Chiiola, 1990; Metasoftware, 1992; Perceptronics, 1993).

Basic Components. The basic components of the nets are quite few, yet these limited building blocks can be used to construct and represent complex and powerful models. There are three basic elements in a Petri Net. The first is a representation of an active component of the system being modeled. *Active* components are represented as rectangles or squares (□   □), and are used to represent agents or events; they are generally referred to as transitions. *Passive* components are the second system type, and they are represented as circles (O). Passive components also represent channels, preconditions, or postconditions, and are generally referred to as places. *Connections* between the active and passive system components are made through arrows (→ ←), with the arrow head indicating the direction of the relationship (the flow of information). For example, an active component connected to a passive component and the passive connected to a subsequent active one is represented as: □→O→□

As a graphical tool, a Petri Net is similar to a flow chart or block diagram; it is this visual component that makes it an excellent tool for communication. But these nets go beyond flow charts and block diagrams, in that they incorporate tokens, which are used to simulate dynamic and concurrent activities of a system. Tokens reside in places and move throughout the net as the transitions "fire." The firing of a transition is controlled by rules associated with the transition. In the simplest case, a transition is enabled and fires as soon as a token resides in the place that precedes it. Tokens are used to represent abstract or nonabstract entities within a model, and are depicted as a solid circle (●).

Formally, the structure of a Petri Net is a bipartite directed graph (a more expansive definition is provided in the appendix), $G = [P, T, A]$ where $P = \{p_1, p_2, ..., p_n\}$ is a set of finite places, $T = \{t_1, t_2, ... , t_m\}$ is a set of finite transitions, and $A = \{P \times T\} \cup \{T \times P\}$ is a set of directed arcs. The set of input places of a transition (t) is given by $I(t) = \{p \mid (p,t) \ \varepsilon \ A\}$, and the set of output places of transition (t) is given by $O(t) = \{p \mid (t,p) \ \varepsilon \ A\}$.

Hence, only three elements are used to construct a Petri Net model: Transitions reflect active model components, places represent passive components, and directed arcs add structure in terms of possible linkages between places to transitions and transitions to places. Tokens represent the current state of the system (wherever a token resides, that activity is being performed or that place is being occupied). The mathematics of the system underlie the structure and controls the behavior of the system, and is graphically depicted as the flow of tokens throughout the net. In the net described later, stochastic time-based models and probability structures are set in place to model the system.

The construction of a Petri Net model is illustrated using a laboratory task. The task is straightforward and, thereby, provides a clear example of the application of the technique. Yet it is complex enough to provide the reader with a feel for what the construction of a Petri Net model would entail for an organizational training system. (Coovert had the following model built in Percnet/hsi software [Perceptronics, 1993] that executes on a Sun workstation; and Dorsey [1994] had a model of a three-individual decision-making team working in the combat information center aboard a Navy warship.)

Replenishment at Sea.   The replenishment at sea (RAS; Hogan, Sampson, Raza, Millar, & Salas, 1987) exercise is useful to study many aspects of team training. The exercise simulates the frequent Navy job of transferring supplies from a supply ship to a receiving ship while at sea. The task, as implemented in the laboratory, consists of the supply ship that resides on one table and is separated by approximately 30 centimeters of "ocean" from the receiving ship that is on a second table.

Two methods exist for transferring cargo between the ships. The first is a battery-operated, remote-controlled crane on the receiving ship. The second method employs two towers (one on each ship) equipped with a pulley and rope.

The receiving ship is manned by two individuals: a pulley operator and a crane operator. The pulley operator, in addition to moving the pulley with the supply ship operator, also helps the crane operator unload and store cargo that arrives on the receiving ship. The crane operator works the crane and assists the pulley operator in the unloading and storing of supplies.

The supply ship, manned by the supply ship operator, provides three containers for holding cargo: two platforms and one net. Each container has separate weight capacities and can be attached to either the crane or the pulley. Holds on the supply ship are loaded with various blocks, cylinders, and metal bars representing fuel, ammunition, food, supplies, and spare parts. The supply ship operator has three duties: (a) attaching the platforms to the pulley and crane, (b) loading cargo onto the platforms, and (c) helping the pulley operator move the pulley back and forth between the two ships. Table 3.1 summarizes the duties for each individual in the RAS task.

A Hierarchical Petri Net Representation of RAS

The RAS team exercise using the graphical aspect of modified Petri Nets is described now. At the highest level, RAS can be represented as in the top panel of Fig. 3.1. This figure depicts the beginning and end of the exercise; the team is represented as double circle—the double circle indicates there is a subnet "below" that place. The net below is an elaboration of that higher level representation. Here, the three individuals are an elaboration of the team (see the middle panel of Fig. 3.1).

TABLE 3.1

Individual Operators and Their Duties for the Replenishment at Sea Exercise

Operator	Duties
On the supply ship	
1. Supply ship operator (S)	S1. Loads cargo onto the platforms. T13–T23; P10–P16
	S2. Attaches and unattaches platforms to the crane and pulley. T24–T32; P17–P22
	S3. Operates the pulley in conjunction with the pulley operator. T33–T41; P23–P28
On the receiving ship	
1. Crane operator (C)	C1. Operates the crane.
	C2. Assists the pulley operator with unloading and storing supplies.
2. Pulley operator (P)	P1. Operates the pulley in conjunction with the supply ship operator.
	P2. Assists the crane operator with unloading and storing supplies.

Note. For the supply ship operator, the transitions associated with each duty are listed Fig. 3.2.

A key notion in this modeling approach is the ability to elaborate a portion of the model. In traditional job-analysis terms (Harvey, 1991; Levine, 1983), this is the decomposition of the job into duties, tasks, activities, and elements. In this approach, such nonovert behaviors as decision making (Coovert & McNelis, 1992; Lord & Maher, 1991) and situational awareness are also made explicit. This provides an additional level of detail and clarity to the problem being modeled, and it allows for the establishment of performance standards. Sometimes this additional information cannot be gathered according to traditional job analytic techniques, but is easily gathered via protocol analysis, such as verbal protocol analysis (Ericsson & Simon, 1984; Newell & Simon, 1972).

Just as the team was elaborated into individuals, individuals can be elaborated for a detailed representation of their actions. The lower panel of Figure 3.1 presents an elaboration of the supply ship operator's position at the job duty level. Moving from left to right in the figure, the first transition indicates the duty level has been activated. The operator must now decide which duty (loading, attaching/unattaching, operating the pulley) is appropriate to perform. When the decision is made, the appropriate transition fires and control moves to yet another double circle, which means there is another subnet. In this situation, each of the three duties can be further elaborated into tasks.

The second level elaborations for the loading, attaching/unattaching, and operating pulley duties into tasks are presented in Fig. 3.2. Looking at the loading elaboration in the top panel, this is a specific representation of what the supply ship operator does to accomplish that function of the job. The far left of the figure depicts is the start for the subnet and the transition that enables it.

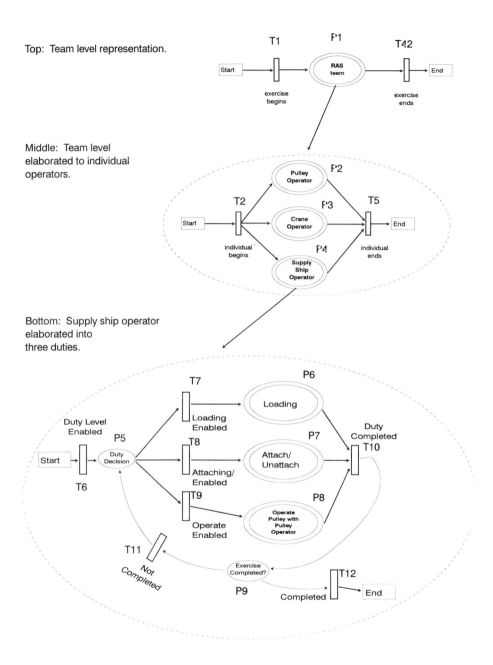

FIG. 3.1. Highest meaningful representation of the Replenishment at Sea (RAS) exercise (top panel) and two elaborations: the first from the team level to the individual level (middle panel), and the second elaborating the supply ship operator job into three duties (bottom panel).

Top: Elaboration of the loading duty.

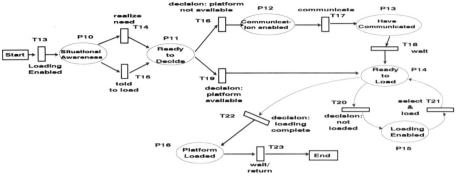

Middle: Elaboration of the attach/unattach duty.

Bottom: Elaboration of the operate pulley duty.

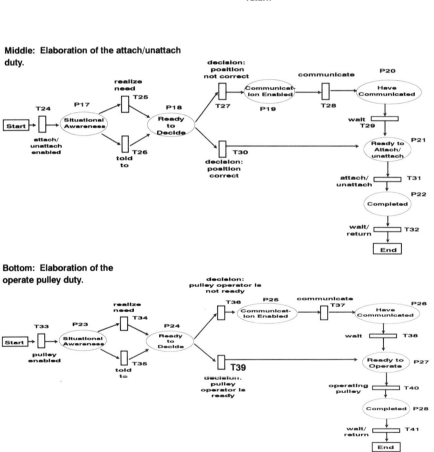

FIG. 3.2. Elaboration of the supply ship operator's duties into task activities.

58

The individual maintains "situational awareness" regarding the loading process, and then either realizes the need to load supplies or is told to load supplies by one of the other team members. Next, the operator is ready to decide if the correct platform is available. If it is available, the ,"decision: platform available" transition fires and the lower arc is followed to the "ready to load" place. If the platform is not available, the "not available" transition fires and the individual communicates with the receiving ship, waits for the correct platform to become available, and is ready to load. This circular process (i.e., ready to load → decision: not loaded → loading enabled → select & load → ready to load), continues until the platform is loaded. Once completed, the "loading completed" transition fires and control moves back up to the duty level elaboration (lower panel of Fig. 3.1) where the "duty completed" transition fires and the token subsequently resides in the "exercise completed?" place. The crane and the pulley operators' job'sre decomposed and modeled in a similar manner.

Development of Performance Criteria

A major advantage of this type of representation is that it can be used to provide or establish performance standards or performance criteria for individuals or teams in training. That is, at any of the levels of representation, performance criteria can be established and associated with that level. Two types of measurement—time and probability—are most appropriate for this task. (Other types of tasks or training systems might employ different measures of performance; there is nothing in the technique that forces the developer of a model to employ the measures described here.)

Time refers to the latency associated with a transition (or a person's performance), whereas probability refers to the odds of taking one path in a network versus another. This allows one to think of an individual's performance on two performance dimensions: (a) effectiveness (optimal vs. nonoptimal) and (b) efficiency. Analysis of the model in terms of these two variables allows one to respond to some of the questions posed at the beginning of the chapter.

To illustrate this point, we ran 20 three-individual teams on the RAS exercise and videotaped their performance. Working from the videotapes, we measured performance in terms of time spent and probabilities across the 12 minutes of the task. Some of this information for the supply ship operator is provided in Fig. 3.3. The figure provides the amount of time spent at each transition, as well as the probability that one path versus another was taken when the graph splits. The first thing to notice is that supply ship operators from effective teams entered the "operate pulley subnet" more frequently than did the operators from ineffective teams (34% vs. 25%, respectively). Effective team supply ship operators also realized the need to operate the pulley more often than did the ineffective team operators (87% vs. 82%, respectively): The former had to

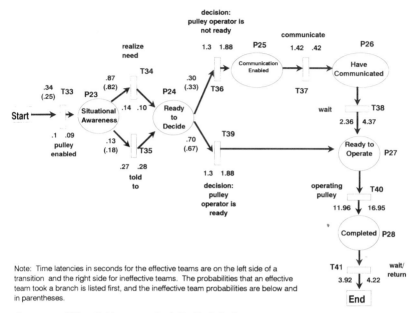

Note: Time latencies in seconds for the effective teams are on the left side of a transition and the right side for ineffective teams. The probabilities that an effective team took a branch is listed first, and the ineffective team probabilities are below and in parentheses.

A sequence of firings that is an example of *effective behaviors*:

T33, P23, T34, P24, T39, P27, T40, P28, T41; with a total execution time of 17.42 sec.

Three sequences of firings represent *ineffective behaviors*:

1) (must be told to act, communicate and wait) T33, P23, T35, P24, T36, P25, T37, P26, T38, P27, T40, P28, T41; total execution time of 28.21 sec.

2) (realize the need to act, but must communicate and wait) T33, P23, T34, T36, P25, T37, P26, T38, P27, T40, P28, T41; total execution time of 28.03 sec.

3) (must be told to act) T33, P23, T35, P24, T39, P27, T40, P28, T41; total execution time of 23.42 sec.

FIG. 3.3. Specification of the operate pulley duty for the supply ship operator, along with times and probabilities for effective and ineffective performance. This information is used for defining *effectiveness* and *efficiency of performance*.

communicate with the pulley operator with less frequency than did the latter (30% vs. 33%, respectively).

This is one way to develop the probabilistic structure of the model, which would then be used in training or in further computer-simulation work. Another approach would be to have trainers (subject matter experts) define the appropriate behavioral paths (as is done in intelligent tutoring systems employing discourse management networks). It is common for novices to follow one set of paths; as they gain expertise, they modify their behavior in the network so that after time, it resembles the paths taken by experts. A graphical lattice structure can easily be constructed that represents the behavioral paths taken by an individual throughout the exercise. As experience is gained, the primary lattice structure is modified: Certain branches of the tree would be "pruned" as the individual develops an optimal strategy and no longer takes inefficient paths. Note that this is one way of representing and evaluating the different behaviors that typify expert versus novice behavior. It's assumed that the expert has the correct mental model of the task, and this leads to the appropriate effective streams of behavior. Figure 3.3 provides the structure for effective behavior and three structures for ineffective behaviors. Analysis of the ineffective behavior sequences can lead to inferences about the incorrect mental model or cognitive control structures employed by the novices.

Similar comparisons can be made on the average amount of time spent at each transition. On average, the supply ship operators from effective teams spent less time deciding if the pulley operator was free (1.30 vs. 1.88 sec.), but spent more time communicating with the pulley operator when they needed to (1.42 vs. .42 sec.). In a similar comparison, after the communication, the effective teams spent less time waiting for the pulley operator to be free (2.36 vs. 4.37 sec.), and they were more efficient operating the pulley (on average, taking only 11.96 vs. 16.95 sec. for the ineffective teams). Finally, the operators from effective teams spent less time before beginning a new task than did the ineffective teams (3.92 vs. 4.22 sec., respectively).

This analysis is how the stochastic nature of the model can be determined if it is to be used for computer studies or as the control structure for an intelligent tutoring system. For each task element, a value (mean) and a distribution (normal, exponential) are identified, and these are associated with the transitions in the model. With these two types of information (latency, probability), one can construct working models of individual and team performance. We know the odds of taking one path versus another are known. One behavior will be performed and another will not. For each critical element of behavior (transition), it is known how long it will take (within stochastic boundaries).

Hence, a Petri Net model has two components: A graphical one (presented in the figures) and a mathematical one. Certain time parameters have been associated with events in this model (Fig. 3.3), but the mathematical structure underlying the graphical one has not been made explicit. The reader can obtain a feel for the execution of the mathematical representation if you mentally simulate the execution of the representation. Begin with the middle panel in Fig. 3.1 and choose the supply ship operator; move to the lower panel for an elaboration at the duty level; and then move to the appropriate task elements specified in Fig. 3.2. Decide which team you will be (effective or ineffective), and then follow the branches and spend the appropriate amount of time at each transition. Upon completion, move back to the duty level, where you may choose to perform another duty or move back to the top level, where you could examine another operator. The computer-simulation model executes all of the figures for each individual concurrently, just as the individuals perform their actions concurrently during the exercise.

Further examples of effective and efficient behaviors are provided in Figs. 3.4 and 3.5. These lattice networks could easily be employed in training to demonstrate optimal ways of performing the task.

SUMMARY

This portion of the chapter introduced the modeling capability of Petri Nets. Graphically, they are an attractive tool for modeling various aspects of training systems. The example herein demonstrated the process of making performance in a training exercise explicit. This explicitness can be used as a communication technique to convey the process of performance to trainees, facilitating the development of a mental model.

The process of developing criterion standards was described. This process can be used during training as well as afterward (e.g., criterion standards in a job sample test). Our measures focused on the amount of time required to perform certain task elements that can be combined or aggregated (see Coovert, Salas, Cannon-Bowers, Craiger, & Takalkar, 1990), as well as alternative strategies (behaviors in a lattice network expressed as probabilities) that effective individuals (experts) employed, as compared with less effective (novices) individuals. Time and probability serve as performance standards during training, thus meeting the need as stated by Goldstein (1991). Our demonstration relied on data from real teams, but criterion standards could have easily been generated by basing latency estimates on models of human performance (Howell & Cooke, 1989; Wickens, 1992), and by using Petri Net simulation software to generate performance envelopes for each individual operator and for the team as a whole.

As a final point, these models can be further embellished through the incorporation of workload information (Perceptronics, 1993; Wickens, 1992). By constructing a conflict matrix, an assessment of the amount of workload throughout the training can be made. For example, a task that has a large visual componet is being performed, and the operator needs to perform a second task concurrently. If the second task has a large visual component the conflict would be high, whereas if the second task had no visual component the conflict would be low or nonexistent. For certain types of jobs, especially those with a large information-processing load, being able to represent workload and model its fluctuation during training is an invaluable capability. For a complete example of this, see Coovert and Dorsey (1994).

Team Level: T1, P1

⇓

Individual Level: T2, P4

⇓

Duty Level - attach platform to crane   T6, P5, T8, P7

⇓

Task Activity Level (attach)   T24, P17, T25, P18, T30, P21, T31, P22, T32

⇓

Duty Level - loading crane   T10, P9, T11, P5, T7, P6

⇓

Task Activity Level (loading x 3)   T13, P10, T14, P11, T19, P14, T20, P15,
T21, P14, T20, P15, T21, P14, T20, P15,
T21, P14, T22, P16, T23

⇓

Duty Level - attach platform to pulley T10, P9, T11, P5, T8, P7

⇓

Task Activity Level (attach)   T24, P17, T25, P18, T30, P21, T31, P22, T32

⇓

Duty Level - loading pulley   T10, P9, T11, P5, T7, P6

⇓

Task Activity Level (loading x 2)   T13, P10, T14, P11, T19, P14, T20, P15, T21,
P14, T20, P15, T21, P14, T22, P16, T23

⇓

Duty Level - operate pulley   T10, P9, T11, P5, T9, P8

⇓

Task Activity Level (operate pulley) T33, P23, T34, P24, T39, P27, T40, P28, T41

⇓

Return to Duty, Individual, and Team Levels   T10, P9, T12, T5, T42

FIG. 3.4. Sequence of behaviors for the supply ship operator. Beginning at the team level, elaboration moves to the individual level, to the supply ship operator, followed by several duties: attaching a platform to the crane, loading the platform attached to the crane, attaching a platform to the pulley, loading the platform attached to the pulley, and operating the pulley in conjunction with the pulley operator. Finally, the return to the duty,

63

A sample sequence of effective and ineffective behavioral streams to use in training for the replenishment at sea task. The letters refer to operators (S = supply ship, C = crane, P = pulley) and ships (ss = supply ship, rs = receiving ship), and numbers refer to the duties performed by that operator (see again Table 1 for a listing by operator). Letters side-by-side indicate sequential performance, while stacked letters indicate concurrent performance.

Sequence of effective behaviors to train:

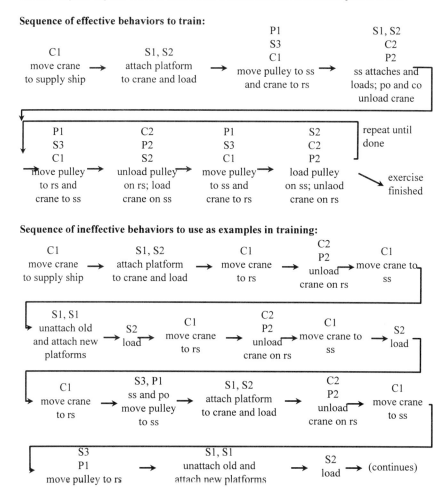

FIG. 3.5. Example sequences of effective and ineffective behavioral streams.

DISCUSSION

The purpose of this chapter was to describe how, through the use of Petri Nets, models of performance during training can be constructed, and how measures of performance in terms of effectiveness and efficiency can be established. The approach has been to take a top–down decomposition of the target of the training. In our example, we began with a team task and elaborated it to the individual level, with further elaborations to the duty and task levels. At critical elements within the activities of the tasks, measures such as time and probability were taken. Our example relied on three types of measures: the number of times an event occurred, the time associated with the event, and the probability one arc in a network was taken relative to another. The count and time data were especially useful in establishing measures of efficiency during training; the probability data were also useful for describing effectiveness of performance in a network of possible behaviors.

Given the task to be trained, a model could also be constructed from the bottom up by beginning with the smallest meaningful elements of interest (e.g., keystrokes, eye fixations) and chaining these together until a behavioral stream is complete. Then one could move up in a representational hierarchy, constructing the next layer out of these more elemental blocks, and continue the process until it would no longer be useful to represent behavior during training at a higher level. The methodology is not restricted to modeling only observable tasks. In our examples, we included the unobservable activity of decision making. However, the researcher or practitioner must be able to identify the appropriate levels at which to model behavior and to establish criterion measures of performance.

The graphical representation of behavior with the nets can also be a big help when communicating with trainers as well as trainees. The trainers can view the network and ensure it represents their mental model of how the trainee should behave. Furthermore, because the lattice structures are straightforward and precise, they facilitate the communication of differences between expected behavior and the behavior of a trainee having difficulty. The model can help communicate information in a manner that will facilitate the construction of an appropriate mental model on the part of the trainee. In those instances where difficulty arises, the trainer can point to the specific place in the net where the trainee is experiencing difficulty and provide precise feedback. The same strategy can be employed when efficiency is of concern. The sequence of behaviors that are not being performed quickly enough can be highlighted, and the trainee can receive the feedback that, although he or she forms an optimal path through the network, delays are occurring at specific points. In a similar manner, the network of behaviors followed by the trainee can be compared to the paths taken by experts, and deviations can be communicated to the trainee.

Modeling With Effective Procedures

Computational psychology is a hybrid scientific discipline devoted to the study of the human mind from the perspective of computation. In the abstract, the mind and computers function as symbol processors, and human cognition and information processing can be understood by representing these in computer models. The roots of computational psychology can be traced to the notion of "effective calcuability". *Effective calcuability* is an idea concerning what it means to compute: any procedure or process that can be carried out stepwise with well-defined rules (i.e., through effective procedures; Cohen, 1986; Dewdney, 1989). Computational psychologists have extended the idea of the effective procedure to the study of human behavior. They viewed the human mind "as a representational system, psychology being the study of the various computational processes whereby mental representations are constructed, organized, interpreted and transformed" (Boden, 1988, p. 36).

The idea that psychological processes can be represented and studied through their explicit representation and manipulation by computer modeling and simulation was presented early to the psychological community by Newell, Shaw, and Simon (1958). The information-processing/computer-modeling formalism developed slowly, gaining momentum when other respected scientists advocated the idea (Feigenbaum & Feldman, 1963; Miller, Galanter, & Pribram, 1960). Especially intriguing is the latter work by psychologist G. A. Miller and associates. Miller et al. (1960) believed that stimulus–response explanations of behavior (the trend at the time) ignore the mechanisms that translate environmental stimuli into behavioral responses. They argued that behavior should be explained in terms of hierarchical plans and goal-directed behavior, and that the study of behavior was best achieved through computer modeling. Computer models were thought to be appropriate for the study of many aspects of human behavior, including memory, language, personality, and motor control.

Proponents of computational psychology espouse that employing effective procedures as explanatory mechanisms forces a rigorous representation of theory, and that explicitly coding behaviors and the possible consequences forces one to be more critical of the necessary aspects of the theory. When expressed in natural language, omitting a single essential ingredient in a theory may not be missed, but when coded as a program small deviations quickly become apparent (Coovert et al., 1995; Winston, 1984). In addition to being an effective means for modeling and understanding behavior, computational models are attractive because they force theorists and researchers to be explicit in terms of all the building blocks of behavior within the confines of the theory. Computer modeling of individuals is especially attractive for training because interventions are designed to impact certain specific components of behavior. Thus, the model can provide ahead of time the effectiveness of the intervention, as well as its impact on the whole of behavior.

Critical Issues in ITS Development

Research on the role of computers as intelligent tutoring systems (ITSs) has made significant advances in the last few decades (Boder & Cavallo, 1991).

ITSs are gaining acceptance in the mainstream educational institutions as a means of providing instruction for subjects as diverse as language, arithmetic, algebra, geometry, logic, and computer programming. Moreover, ITS research has resulted in new ideas and theories regarding how knowledge should be structured and presented to an individual to maximize learning, as well as assisting in an understanding of the cognitive processes involved in problem solving and decision making. Notwithstanding the widespread potential for the application of ITS in education and training, the process of developing and successfully implementing an ITS is a fairly complicated task. Experience has shown that there are numerous factors that should be considered to determine whether the development of an ITS is feasible, practical, or desirable.

It is essential that the characteristics of the problem domain are taken into consideration in the design phase. Most ITSs that have been developed and successfully implemented have focused on fairly specific problem domains. Experience has shown that it is difficult to develop an ITS, or any intelligent computer system, that contains knowledge from disparate problem domains *and* performs well in terms of its ability to emulate expert behavior. If a problem domain is fairly broad, an ITS may not be feasible.

There are two possible limitations of the use of ITS for training cognitive skills. First, it may be impossible to a priori define all the possible scenarios that team members may encounter in an operating environment. Second, and related to the first, an ITS is low in physical fidelity for tasks requiring perceptual-motor skills, unless these skills are computer related. However, the efficiency notion of time in the Petri Net models can serve as an indicator when perceptual-motor skills might require further training. A possible solution is a "piece meal" approach to training—using ITS for training cognitive skills, and using traditional hands-on training for developing perceptual-motor skills.

The Changing Nature of Work

The last half of the 20th century has seen fundamental changes in the nature of work. A primary cause of this change is a move from an industrial-based to an information-based economy. The advent and diffusion of information technology has led to the changes in the traditional structure of existing jobs and the creation of new jobs that are fundamentally different from those of yesteryear. The character and structure of new information-based jobs require different skills than those of the industrial-based age, particularly in terms of information processing and increased demands on decision making, problem solving, and training (Coovert, 1995; Forester, 1986; Howard, 1995). The development and diffusion of new training methods that adequately address these skills lags behind technology, resulting in the application of training methodologies that are often deficient for addressing higher lever cognitive skills (Bainbridge, 1989). Traditional training methods have concentrated on developing perceptual-motor and familiar cognitive skills, and making these skills such that they are performed automatically. A difficulty arises in operating environments that evolve dynamically over time—where relationships among environmental cues can be characterized as *complex*, a consequence of which is a much larger problem space (a larger set of possible situations that an individual may encounter). In these environments, an individual is likely to find him or herself in a novel situation. For these types of jobs, defining various states of the problem space an individual may encounter may not be possible a priori. Consequently, it may be impossible to develop and include training modules directed at acquiring skills for these novel situations. For these jobs, the requirement is developing self-directed problem-solving skills and instilling individuals with the requisite skills that allow them to "think on their own" when encountering a novel situation (Bainbridge, 1989).

It is interesting that the technology that changed the fundamental nature of many jobs has also led to the creation of new tools that can be employed to train and measure worker's performance in complex tasks. In particular, computer-based training methodologies are slowly making their way into the mainstream (Bainbridge, 1989). However, the task of developing an ITS is not a simple one. Developing an ITS is a money- and labor-intensive task, requiring (at least) a knowledge source (either subject matter experts or knowledge engineers) and a programmer.

In conclusion, those who must establish performance criteria for individuals in training often face a formidable task. The approach presented here is meant to assist individuals in the development of training criteria. Petri Net modeling can be used to establish criteria at a variety of levels (task, individual, team), and it can facilitate the diagnosis of exactly where in the task the individual is having difficulty. If the trainee problems are based on performance efficiency, all that may be required is further hands-on practice. However, if the issue is effectiveness, there may be an uncertainty with the trainee's mental model of the task. Fortunately, the methodology facilitates not only the identification of such problems, but their remediation as well.

A further strength of the methodology is that it can be used as a computational tool to establish measures of performance, either through simulation studies or by employing the net as a control structure in an ITS.

APPENDIX: A MORE COMPLETE
DEFINITION OF A PETRI NET

A more complete definition presents a *Petri Net* as the 5-tuple, $PN = (P, T, F, W, M_o)$ where:

$P = (p_1, p_2, \ldots , p_m)$ is a finite set of places

$T = (t_1, t_2, \ldots, t_n)$ is a finite set of transitions
$F \subseteq (P \times T) \cup (T \times P)$ is a set of arcs representing flow relations
$W{:}F \rightarrow \{1, 2, 3, \ldots\}$ specifies a weight function
$M_0{:}P \rightarrow \{1, 2, 3, \ldots\}$ specifies the initial marking (e.g., places with tokens and how many tokens)

A net structure $N = (P, T, F, W)$ without a specific initial marking is denoted by N. The initial marking of a Petri Net is denoted by (N, M_0).

REFERENCES

Alphatech, Inc. (1992). *Modeler*. Burlington, MA: Author.

Bainbridge, L. (1989). Cognitive processes and training methods: A summary. In L. Bainbridge & S. A. R. Quintanilla (Eds.), *Developing skills with information technology* (pp. 177–192). New York: Kaufmann.

Baldwin, T. T., & Ford, J. K. (1988). Transfer of training: A review and directions for future research. *Personnel Psychology, 41,* 63–105.

Bartlett, F. C. (1932). *Remembering*. London: Cambridge University Press.

Boden, M. A. (1988). *Computer models of mind*. New York: Cambridge University Press.

Boder, A., & Cavallo, D. (1991). An epistemological approach to intelligent tutoring systems. In M. Yazdani & R. W. Lawler (Eds.), *Artificial intelligence in education* (Vol. 2, pp.111–134). Norwood, NJ: Ablex.

Cannon-Bowers, J. A., Tannenbaum, S. I., Salas, E., & Converse, S. A. (1991). Toward an integration of training theory and technique. *Human Factors, 33,* 281–292.

Chiiola, G. (1990). *GreatSPN*. Torino, Italy: University di Torino Press.

Cohen, D. I. A. (1986). *Introduction to computer theory*. New York: Wiley.

Coovert, M. D. (1995). Technological changes in office jobs: What we know and what we can expect. In A. Howard (Ed.), *The changing nature of work* (pp. 175–208). San Francisco: Jossey-Bass.

Coovert, M. D., Cannon-Bowers, J. A., Campbell, G., & Salas, E. (1994). *A methodology for measuring team performance using Petri Nets*. Manuscript submitted for publication.

Coovert, M. D., Craiger, J. P., & Cannon-Bowers, J. A. (1995). Innovations in modeling and simulating team performance: Implications for decision making. In R. Guzzo & E. Salas (Eds.), *Team effectiveness and decision making in organizations* (pp. 149–203). San Francisco: Jossey-Bass.

Coovert, M. D., & Dorsey, D. (1994). Performance differences between experts and novices as modeled with Petri nets. *Proceedings of the Fourth International Dynamic Modeling in Organizations conference*. Berlin: Springer-Verlag.

Coovert, M. D., & McNelis, K. (1992). Team decision making and performance: A review and proposed modeling approach employing Petri nets. In R. W. Swezey & E. Salas (Eds.), *Teams: Their training and performance* (pp. 247–280). Norwood, NJ: Ablex.

Coovert, M. D., Salas, E., Cannon-Bowers, J. A., Craiger, J. P., & Takalkar, P. (1990). Understanding team performance measures: Application of Petri Nets. *In Proceedings of the 1990 IEEE International Conference on Systems, Man, and Cybernetics* (pp. 387–393). Washington, DC: IEEE Computer Society Press.

Craik, K. (1943). *The nature of explanation*. New York: Cambridge University Press.

Dewdney, A. K. (1989). *The turing omnibus*. New York: Computer Science Press.

Dorsey, D. (1994). *Performance modeling with Petri Nets*. Unpublished master's thesis, University of South Florida: Tampa.

Dyer, J. L. (1984). Team research and team training: A state of the art review. In F. A. Muckler (Ed.), *Human factors review: 1984* (pp. 285–323). Santa Monica, CA: Human Factors Society.

Ericsson, K. A., & Simon, H. A. (1984). *Protocol analysis: Verbal reports as data*. Cambridge, MA: MIT Press.

Feigenbaum, E. A., & Feldman, J. (1963). *Computers and thought*. New York: McGraw-Hill.

Forester, T. (1986). *The information technology revolution*. Cambridge, MA: MIT Press.

Forsyth, D. R. (1983). *An introduction to group dynamics*. Monterey, CA: Brooks/Cole.

Goldstein, I. L. (1991). Training in work organizations. In M. D. Dunnette & L. M. Hough (Eds.), *Handbook of industrial and organizational psychology* (2nd ed., Vol. 2, pp. 71–164). Palo Alto, CA: Consulting Psychologists Press.

Harvey, R. J. (1991). Job analysis. In M. D. Dunnette & L. M. Hough (Eds.), *Handbook of industrial and organizational psychology* (2nd ed., Vol. 2, pp. 71–164). Palo Alto, CA: Consulting Psychologists Press.

Hogan, R., Sampson, D., Raza, S., Millar, C., & Salas, E. (1987). *Research with small groups: Two realistic tasks* (Tech. Rep.). Orlando, FL: Naval Training Systems Center.

Howard, A. (Ed.) (1995). *The changing nature of work*. San Francisco: Jossey-Bass.

Howell, W. C., & Cooke, N. J. (1989). Training the human information processor: A review of cognitive models. In I. L. Goldstein (Ed.), *Training and development in work organizations: Frontiers of industrial and organizational psychology* (pp. 121–182). San Francisco: Jossey-Bass.

Jensen, K., & Rozenberg, G. (Eds.). (1991). *High-level Petri nets: Theory and application*. Berlin: Springer-Verlag.

Johnson-Laird, P. N. (1990). Mental models. In M. J. Posner (Ed.), *Foundations of cognitive science* (pp. 469–500). Cambridge, MA: MIT Press.

Kolodner, J. L. (1991). Improving human decision making through case-based decision aiding. *AI Magazine, 12*, 52–68.

Kraiger, K., Ford, J. K., & Salas, E. (1993). New methods of training evaluation [Monograph]. *Journal of Applied Psychology, 78*, 311–328.

Levine, E. L. (1983). *Everything you always wanted to know about job analysis*. Tampa, FL: Mariner.

Lord, R. G., & Maher, K. J. (1991). Cognitive theory in industrial/organizational psychology. In M. D. Dunnette & L. M. Hough (Eds.), *Handbook of industrial and organizational psychology* (2nd ed., Vol. 2, pp. 1–62). Palo Alto, CA: Consulting Psychologists Press.

McIntyre, R. M., Morgan, B. B., Jr., Salas, E., & Glickman, A. S. (1988). *Team research in the eighties: Lessons learned*. Unpublished manuscript, Naval Training Systems Center: Orlando, FL.

Metasoftware. (1992). *Design CPN*. Boston MA: Author.

Miller, G. A., Galanter, E., & Pribram, K. H. (1960). *Plans and the structure of behavior*. New York: Holt, Rinehart & Winston.

Minsky, M. (1975). A framework for the representation of knowledge. In P. H. Winston (Ed.), *The psychology of computer vision* (pp. 211–277). New York: McGraw-Hill.

Newell, A., & Simon, H. H. (1972). *Human problem solving*. Englewood Cliffs, NJ: Prentice-Hall.

Newell, A., Shaw, J. C., & Simon, H. A. (1958). Elements of a theory of human problem solving. *Psychological Review, 55*, 151–166.

Norman, D. A. (1981). Categorization of action slips. *Psychological Review, 88*, 1–15.

Olsen, S. E., & Rasmussen, J. (1989). The reflective expert and the prenovice: Notes on skill-, rule- and knowledge-based performance in the setting of instruction and training. In L. Bainbridge & S. A. R. Quintanilla (Eds.), *Developing skills with information technology* (pp. 3–8). New York: Wiley.

Ostroff, C. (1991). Training effectiveness measures and scoring schemes: A comparison. *Personnel Psychology, 44*, 353–374.

Penner, L. A., & Craiger, J. P. (1992). Individual performance in a team context: The weakest link. In R. W. Swezey & E. Salas (Eds.), *Teams: Their training and performance* (pp. 57–73). Norwood, NJ: Ablex.

Perceptronics. (1993). *Percnet/hsi*. Woodland Hills, CA: Author.

Peterson, J. L. (1981). *Petri Nets and the modeling of systems*. Englewood Cliffs, NJ: Prentice-Hall.

Petri, C. A. (1962). Kommunikation mit automaten. Schriften des IIM Nr. 2, Institute furInstrumentelle Mathematik, Bonn. [Tech. Rep. RADC-TR-65-377] New York: Griffiss Air Force Base.

Quillian, M. R. (1968). Semantic memory. In M. Minsky (Ed.), *Semantic information processing* (pp. 227–270). Cambridge, MA: MIT Press.

Rasmussen, J. (1980). What can be learned from human error reports? In K. Duncan, R. Gruneberg, & D. Wallis (Eds.), *Changes in working life* (pp.64–77).New York: Wiley.

Rasmussen, J. (1987). Cognitive control and human error mechanisms. In J. Rasmussen, K. Duncan, & J. Leplat (Eds.), *New technology and human error* (pp.23–30). Chichester, England: Wiley.

Reason, J. (1987). Generic error-modeling systems (GEMS): A cognitive framework for locating human error forms. In J. Rasmussen, K. Duncan, & J. Leplat (Eds.), *New technology and human error* (pp.63–83). Chichester, England: Wiley.

Reisig, W. (1992). *A primer in Petri net design*. Berlin: Springer-Verlag.

Reutenauer, C. (1990). *The mathematics of Petri Nets*. Hartford, England: Prentice-Hall.

Rouse, W. B., & Morris, N. M. (1986). On looking into the black box: Prospects and limits in the search for mental models. *Psychological Bulletin, 100*, 359–363.

Sanders, A. F. (1991). Simulation as a tool in the measurement of human performance. *Ergonomics, 34*, 995–1025.

Schank, R. C., & Abelson, R. P. (1977). Scripts, plans, goals, and understanding. Hillsdale, NJ: Lawrence Erlbaum Associates.

Simon, H. A. (1979). What the knower knows: Alternative strategies for problem solving tasks. In F. Klix (Ed.), *Human and artificial intelligence* (pp.89–101). Amsterdam: North Holland.

Simon, H. A. (1986). Alternative visions of rationality. In H. R. Arkes & K. R. Hammond (Eds.), *Judgment and decision making: An interdisciplinary reader* (pp. 97–113). New York: Cambridge University Press.

Tannenbaum, S. I., & Yukl, G. (1992). Training and development in work organizations. *Annual Review of Psychology, 43*, 399–441.

Tversky, A., & Kahneman, D. (1982). Availability: A heuristic for judging frequency and probability. In D. Kahneman, P. Slovic, & A. Tversky (Eds.), *Judgment under uncertainty: Heuristics and biases* (pp. 163–178). New York: Cambridge University Press.

Wickens, C. D. (1992). *Engineering psychology and human performance* (2nd ed.). New York: Harper-Collins.

Winston, P. H. (1984). *Artificial intelligence*. Reading, MA: Addison-Wesley.

4

Applications of Structural Knowledge Assessment to Training Evaluation

Timothy E. Goldsmith
University of New Mexico
Kurt Kraiger
University of Colorado at Denver

An organization conducts a needs assessment to design a series of computer training courses for its clerical employees. The needs assessment reveals that most clerical workers lack key knowledge and skills in primary applications (e.g., knowing how to copy files, change printer options, etc.). The analysis also reveals that most workers lack an understanding of the conceptual relationships among the operating system, applications, work-related tasks, and menu commands. For example, they may not know how DOS and Windows are alike and different, how to pull material from one application to another, or how the same task can be accomplished in several different applications. Evaluating learning for training courses designed to teach basic knowledge and skills may consist of recognition tasks ("Which of the following is the command for saving a file?") or work samples ("Execute the key strokes to save a file under a new name"). But how can one evaluate training designed to provide trainees with conceptual knowledge about the relationships among operating systems, applications, and tasks?

In recent years, a number of authors have discussed ways in which advances in cognitive and instructional psychology may be relevant to the design, conduct, and evaluation of training (see Cannon-Bowers, Tannenbaum, Salas, & Converse, 1991; Ford & Kraiger, 1995; Howell & Cooke, 1989; Kraiger, Ford, & Salas, 1993). This chapter focuses on a method for assessing an individual's knowledge and competence in a particular subject matter. It moves from more general discussions, such as those by Howell and Cooke(1989) and Kraiger et al. (1993), to a specific, conceptually based, validated method for evaluating learning during training. This method, which is called *structural assessment*, also has implications for the processes of needs assessment and training design. However, this chapter focuses mainly on evaluation applications.

Structural assessment is rooted in theoretical developments in cognitive psychology and cognitive science. It is largely based on the assumption that an individual's competence in an area is reflected by how he or she represents knowledge of the domain. This chapter's objectives are to describe the theoretical basis of structural assessment, detail the steps required to actually perform an assessment, and illustrate the method with results from several validation studies. This chapter also shows that a cognitively based approach to assessment offers several advantages over traditional methods of evaluating training effectiveness. The chapter concludes by describing several lines of research that address both methodological and practical issues associated with structural assessment, including extensions of the approach to designing training programs. To provide a context for appreciating the advantages of structural assessment, traditional methods of knowledge assessment from the training field are first briefly reviewed.

APPROACHES TO ASSESSING KNOWLEDGE

Traditional Approaches to Assessing Knowledge

We reviewed knowledge assessment (learning evaluation) methods from 57 training studies from the industrial/organizational (I/O) literature published between 1960 and 1992. Potential studies were identified from two prior reviews (Alliger & Janak, 1989; Baldwin & Ford, 1988), or studies known by either author. The two most popular methods for assessing learning were paper-and-pencil tests (used in 29% of all studies) and role plays or simulations (used in 22% of all studies). Less frequent methods were performance tests or work samples and ratings of learning by the trainees or their peers or supervisors.

In the typical study, paper-and-pencil tests are constructed to resemble traditional multiple-choice tests commonly administered in school classrooms. Test content is drawn from the training content, and multiple items are constructed and administered to trainees upon the completion of the program (Bretz & Thompsett, 1993; Bunker & Cohen, 1977). In some instances, the tests resemble certification or standardized achievement tests, representing knowledge expected of all incumbents in title (Froehlich, 1962; Gordon & Kleiman, 1976). Undoubtedly, such tests are popular because they are easy to develop and administer, and because they produce variance in trainees' scores. However, there is not always a theoretical basis for their use, and there is no clear link between the evaluation measure and either the learning objectives or instructional strategies (Kraiger & Jung, in press). For example, Harrison (1993) used an eight-item multiple-choice test to compare the efficacy of knowledge-based and experiential approaches to cross-cultural training. The objective of the knowledge-based approach was to provide trainees with factual information about a country, whereas the objective of the experiential approach was to train specific applied behaviors (McCaffery, 1986). Although Harrison used the paper-and-pencil test to evaluate both programs, it is clear that a recognition-based test was more appropriate for the knowledge-based course than for the experiential course.

Not only can such criteria be criticized as inappropriate in many contexts, but other inadequacies of such traditional methods have been widely discussed elsewhere (Frederiksen, 1984). Among the most important shortcomings of this approach is the inability of the method to assess higher order learning or understanding (Kraiger et al., 1993), and the possibility of criterion contamination due to differences among trainees in test-taking ability and test anxiety (Gagne & Beard, 1978).

Role plays or simulations have been used most commonly to assess learning of managerial or human relations skills. Typically, trainees are given a carefully contrived scenario and asked to apply the concepts covered in training (Decker, 1982; Moses & Ritchie, 1976). For less complex jobs, work samples have been used in the same manner (Gordon & Cohen, 1973). To the extent that the conditions in the role plays or work samples resemble actual job conditions, such criteria may be reasonable predictors of later performance on the job, and may also be assumed to be content-valid. However, such criteria may be time-consuming and expensive to administer. More important, the construct validity of these measures as indicators of knowledge acquisition can be questioned. Proper behaviors can be imitated without much learning taking place. Also, the absence of a correct behavior provides little guidance in diagnosing what knowledge is missing. For example, suppose that, during a pilot simulator exercise, one member of an air crew fails to inform another that a gauge is not operating properly. From this test alone, it may not be clear whether the omission of the desired behavior (i.e., communicating potential problems) was because the first member did not notice the gauge, did not see the importance of informing the other, forgot to inform the other, or did not understand the relationship between situational awareness and communication.

In summary, traditional approaches by I/O psychologists to knowledge assessment have employed measures that rely on verbal recognition or behavioral reproduction as indices of learning. Besides practical, psychometric, and administrative problems, these measures can be criticized for being relevant for only a narrow range of cognitive learning outcomes (Kraiger et al., 1993), for ignoring research advances in other psychological domains, and for being atheoretical (Campbell, 1971; Wexley, 1984).

In contrast to training research in the field of I/O psychology, research in cognitive and instructional psychology has provided insights into both the nature of learning and methods of assessing learning. A primary goal of this chapter is to describe one particular type of cognitive assessment—the structural assessment of knowledge. This discussion emphasizes the methods for implementing a structural assessment and previous efforts to validate the approach. To build a stronger link between training evaluation measures and theories of learning, the chapter reviews research from cognitive psychology on knowledge representation and skill acquisition that has implications for knowledge assessment. Following this, it discusses the theoretical basis of structural assessment.

Cognitive Assessment of Knowledge and Skill

The central idea behind a cognitive assessment is the link between domain competence and domain representation. Presumably an important characteristic of knowledge in any field of study is its structure or organization. The concepts, ideas, terms, and rules that make up a knowledge domain are interrelated in ways that give rise to their meaning and to the meaningfulness of the domain. This chapter refers to this type of representation as the knowledge structure of a domain. A domain's *knowledge structure* is defined in one sense by the textbooks, research articles, training manuals, or whatever other written documents exist in the domain. In another sense, the knowledge structure of a domain can be seen to exist in the minds of domain experts. An important distinction exists between the knowledge of a domain and an individual's representation of that knowledge (Palmer, 1978). When the knowledge representation of an individual is referred to, the term *cognitive structure* is used. From this perspective, education and training can be viewed as the process of acquiring a cognitive structure that matches the domain's knowledge structure (Shavelson, 1972).

Over the past 25 years, the field of cognitive psychology has shifted from the study of general cognitive processes to the investigation of domain-specific knowledge—knowledge that helps one perform tasks (Chi, Glaser, & Rees, 1981). At a theoretical level, this leads to questions such as: What does it mean to be knowledgeable in a domain? What differentiates experts from novices? How can knowledge be measured or assessed? Investigations of the latter question have led to the development of methods for eliciting, representing, and assessing domain-specific knowledge—methods that can be applied to training evaluation.

Two lines of research have influenced the development of the structural assessment approach. First, studies of expert–novice group differences have clearly demonstrated the value of well-organized task-relevant information and subsequent task performance. For example, McKeithen, Reitman, Reuter, and Hirtle (1981) showed that expert computer programmers organized their knowledge of programming languages along semantic dimensions, whereas novice programmers organized the language along syntactic lines. Similarly,

Lesgold et al. (1989) found that organization of radiology knowledge predicted residents' skills in diagnosing x-rays. Generally, although this research has reinforced the value of structural knowledge for representing group differences, these studies have not directly addressed the issue of assessment methods at the individual level.

A second relevant line of research has been conducted by educational psychologists. This work has attempted to link an individual's cognitive structure to other measures of learning or competence in traditional academic subjects. Research in this area has shown that a student's cognitive structure becomes more similar to an expert's with instruction (Acton, 1991), and that the similarity between a student's structure and an expert's structure is a good predictor of course achievement or competence (Champagne, Klopfer, & Anderson, 1980; Diekhoff, 1983; Goldsmith & Johnson, 1990; Shavelson & Stanton, 1975). These studies indicate that structural assessment has value as a measure of academic learning, and offer promise of value in the training arena.

For structural assessment to be applied to mainstream training evaluation, a number of practical and theoretical questions must be addressed. Practically, there are issues in developing measures, including: How does one define the knowledge structure of an instructional domain? How does one elicit and represent a learner's cognitive structure of that domain? There are also questions of evaluation: What methods are best suited for comparing learners' structures with an idealized representation? How does one determine what is the "best" representation? Finally, as any new evaluation method must be validated, the following questions must be considered: What is the relationship between structural assessments and other indices of competency? What are the limits of structural assessment? Are there conditions where it does not predict domain performance? These and related questions have been the focus of recent research in the area.

Before addressing specific methodological issues, the theoretical foundations of structural assessment are discussed. First, what is the relationship between ideas of knowledge representation from cognitive psychology and the structural assessment of knowledge? What theoretical view of knowledge representation is assumed by structural assessment? What assumptions underlie the empirical elicitation of knowledge? To be construct-valid, an evaluation method must have a solid theoretical foundation. The following section, summarizes the theoretical basis for the structural assessment of cognitive knowledge.

Theoretical Basis of Structural Knowledge Assessment

Structural assessment is founded on the assumption that knowledge is relational. As one becomes more knowledgeable in a domain, one moves beyond accumulating declarative and procedural knowledge (knowledge of facts and acts) and begins to organize knowledge by building meaningful relations among known concepts (Jonassen, Beissner, & Yacci, 1993). The term *knowledge structure* simply refers to an organization of concepts, rather than simply a collection of facts or a set of rules. Knowledge structures exist at a higher level of abstraction than facts or rules. Facts and rules are only meaningful or accessible in a domain because of their underlying knowledge structure. Although not all of knowledge may be represented by relationships, it is assumed that much of domain expertise is reflected in the structural relations among central concepts. Recent evidence suggests that these conceptual relations can be empirically elicited.

Two theoretical issues should be clarified before discussing the structural assessment technique: (a) the relationship between assessment and representation of knowledge, and (b) the role of similarity in the elicitation and representation of conceptual relationships. First, cognitive psychologists have long focused on the representation of knowledge. They have found that the manner in which individuals organize and represent knowledge influences their performance on numerous tasks, including perception, problem solving, and decision making. Thus, one can infer that an individual's representation of that knowledge is closely related to his or her level of domain competence. Accordingly, the objective of structural assessment is to evaluate individuals' domain competence by assessing how they represent structure in that domain. The outcome of a structural assessment is a description of *what* an individual knows.

In contrast, the outcome of traditional assessment is often an index of *how much* someone knows. Although summary indices such as percent correct and percentile ranking are useful for rating performance, these measures offer little descriptive information beyond classification or ranking. As is seen here, structural assessment provides more explicit feedback about the "correctness" of learning.

Second, how can perceived similarity or relatedness be used to elicit a representation of knowledge? To answer this question, one needs to be explicit about what it means to be *related*. Two concepts may be related because they are causally linked, they covary in space or time, they belong to the same category, and so forth. Ultimately, it is the shared meaning of concepts that underlies their judged relatedness. The important role of similarity in thinking and knowing (Noble, 1956), and more specifically in generalization, discrimination, pattern recognition, and memory retrieval, has been well documented (Collins & Loftus, 1975; Shepard, 1958; Tversky, 1977).

Psychological similarity and cognitive structure are related. *Structure* generally refers to the organization of a set of elements viewed from the perspective of the whole set. However, *structure* is defined by similarity relations. Both local relations and global patterns of relations give rise to structure. Once a semantic structure is defined, it serves as a basis for judging concept relatedness. Hence, similarity and structure are complementary concepts, each drawing on the other for its existence and both tied closely to meaning itself.

Cognitive structures are acquired through successive integration and differentiation across a set of concepts. During early learning, people accumulate knowledge of facts and procedures. These facts and procedures can be represented as concepts. As people learn, they begin to make associations among elements previously perceived as unrelated, and then form discriminations where previously unseen. For example, in a sales training course, a trainee may learn that a follow-up call is related to closing a sale or to repeat business. Subsequent learning results in discrimination of elements previously seen as related. The trainee may learn that follow-up calls are more appropriate in one context than another. Eventually, the trainee takes a pattern of relationships and organizes them in a meaningful way.

For purposes of assessment, it is not necessary to assume that similarity holds any causal role in carrying out intelligent activities. Rather, the importance of the construct of similarity lies in its potential to reflect domain competence. Within structural assessment, direct judgments of concept relatedness are assumed to reflect an individual's level of competence in a domain. Specifically, concept relations produced by a competent individual will have particular structural characteristics, such that valid inferences about the person's level of competence can be made on the basis of these relations.

STEPS OF STRUCTURAL ASSESSMENT

This section describes the basic steps required to implement a structural assessment: (a) defining a referent structure of a discipline, (b) eliciting an individual's judgments of relatedness among the important concepts of the domain, (c) deriving from these judgments a cognitive structure of the individual, and (d) evaluating this derived cognitive structure. Within each step, there are multiple options. There is currently an ongoing program of research investigating the methods themselves with the goal of developing and organizing a set of procedures that will provide a valid, reliable, and efficient evaluation of domain knowledge.

Defining a Referent Structure

The first step in structural assessment is to define the domain according to subject matter experts. The result of this step is called the *referent structure*. The referent structure plays the important role of serving as a standard against which cognitive structures, say from students of the domain, are evaluated. The referent structure is obtained by identifying a set of central concepts in the area and obtaining experts' judgments of relatedness between pairs of these concepts. The referent structure is then derived by applying scaling methods to these expert judgments.

A set of core concepts is usually obtained by examining training manuals or textbooks, and by focused interviews with subject matter experts. This step is similar in many respects to a traditional needs assessments. In fact, Ford and Kraiger (1995) proposed specific methods by which structural assessment can be adapted to the needs assessment process.

An important question is, how many concepts should be selected to adequately represent a domain? There is some evidence that the quality of the resulting cognitive structures is a function of the number of defined concepts (Goldsmith, Johnson, & Acton, 1991). In past research, we have typically selected between 20 and 30 concepts from a larger set of concepts that subject matter experts have identified as important to the domain and have been covered as part of the course material. Recently, P. J. Johnson, Goldsmith, and Teague (1995) described a method by which only a subset of all possible pairs of concepts can be used to obtain conceptual structures. The resulting structures derived from subsets of pairs were shown to have the same degree of predictive validity as structures derived from all possible pairs. The primary advantage of using only a subset of pairs to derive a knowledge representation is that the total number of concepts can be increased, allowing for a more comprehensive coverage of the domain. For example, the Johnson et al. study used 60 concepts to define the domain of college algebra. In the training domain, Jung and Kraiger (1994) collected ratings on a subset of pairs to assess a problem-based instructional program for undergraduate civil engineers.

Elicitation

The next step is to elicit a learner's judgments of conceptual relationships among the concepts. The elicitation procedure must be capable of capturing structural knowledge (the relationships among important concepts in the domain). A variety of methods have been used to obtain concept relationships, including word associations (P. E. Johnson, 1964), ordered recall (Cooke, Durso, & Schvaneveldt, 1986), card sorting (Shavelson & Stanton, 1975), and direct numerical rating of pairwise relatedness (Fenker, 1975; Goldsmith et al., 1991). This latter approach has several advantages, including: (a) the validity of direct ratings has been demonstrated (Cooke et al., 1986), (b) the method is easy to explain to learners, (c) the judgment task is simple, and (d) the resulting data can be directly represented using methods described next.

Direct pairwise ratings require trainees to rate pairs of concepts on a relatedness scale (a 7-point scale might be anchored by 7 = *highly related*, 1 = *not at all related*). These ratings are analyzed using methods described next. A small subset of the pairs (20–30) can be rated twice to assess the internal consistency of a learner's ratings. Knowledgeable trainees can usually rate up to 200 concept pairs in 20 minutes. If ratings on all possible pairs are collected, this translates into 20 concepts $[n \ (n-1) \ / \ 2]$. If a subset of pairs is rated as described earlier, the number of concepts assessed in the same time could increase to 60 or more.

Representation

Representation means a physical portrayal of the structure or organization of concepts. Relatedness ratings are virtually uninterpretable in their raw form, due largely to the number of ratings and presence of noise or error in the judgments. However, a matrix of relatedness ratings can be transformed by one of several scaling algorithms to derive a more meaningful, interpretable representation. Scaling approaches assume that the inherent structure is derivable from the perceived similarities of a set of items. Several scaling methods have been used to derive representations (Cooke & McDonald, 1987).

Multidimensional scaling (MDS) is a frequently used method (Kruskal, 1964) that represents a set of concepts as points in an n-dimensional Euclidean space. Other scaling algorithms, such as cluster analysis (S. C. Johnson, 1967) and additive trees (Sattath & Tversky, 1977), result in dendogram (branching) representations. Examples of applications using these procedures include Fenker (1975), who used MDS to represent the learning of structural relationships in a statistics and design course, and Schoenfeld and Herrman (1982), who used hierarchical clustering to represent structural changes in students' understanding of mathematical concepts.

A scaling procedure called Pathfinder has proved to be a useful method for representing domain knowledge (Schvaneveldt, Durso, & Dearholt, 1989). The Pathfinder scaling algorithm transforms a matrix of relatedness or similarity ratings into a representation in the form of a network structure. In this network structure, each of the rated concepts is depicted as a node in the network, and the relatedness between concepts is depicted by how closely they are linked. An advantage of Pathfinder over alternative methods is that it does not impose a hierarchical solution, thereby presumably allowing for greater freedom in reflecting an individual's inherent cognitive structure. Figure 4.1 shows an example of a Pathfinder representation of a knowledge domain for automotive mechanics. This network was obtained after averaging relatedness ratings from two proficient mechanics. The concepts represent general systems within engines (cooling system), specific engine components (radiator), and several common engine malfunctions (overheating). Because this is an expert representation, the concepts have been organized (by skilled mechanics) into meaningful clusters of concepts. The network has been used to guide the development of a training program.

Evaluation

The final step in structural assessment is to evaluate an individual's cognitive structure. In a training context, evaluation may be used to assess

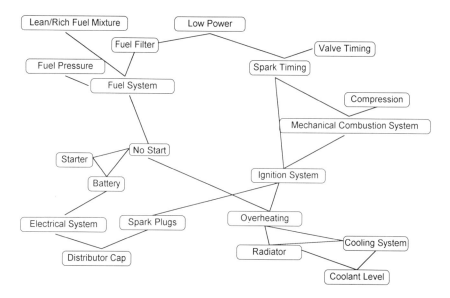

FIG. 4.1. A structural assessment representation of the knowledge of automotive mechanics.

pretest–posttest change, or to assess mastery of training content. Thus, what is the level of competence indicated by a particular cognitive structure? This evaluation may be conducted through either a qualitative assessment of the derived structure (Hamrick, Harty, & Ault, 1987; P. E. Johnson, Cox, & Curran, 1970) or a quantitative assessment (Preece, 1976; Shavelson, 1972). The latter strategy is often preferred because it permits criterion-referenced evaluation and provides specific feedback to trainees.

In recent years, researchers have derived several methods for quantitatively evaluating cognitive structures. One evaluation is called closeness, and it involves comparing two network representations (Goldsmith & Davenport, 1990). Closeness is a measure of the configural similarity between two network structures containing identical concepts. Closeness can be used as a referent-based measure of the quality of a cognitive structure. Competence in an individual's cognitive structure is assumed if it is similar to the referent or target structure.

For any two networks, closeness varies from zero to one. If the networks are complementary (the presence of a link in one network implies the absence of the link in the other, and vice versa), closeness equals zero. If the networks are identical, closeness equals one. Two networks would be identical if, for each concept, all concepts linked to that concept were identical.

To calculate closeness, corresponding nodes between the two network structures are compared. The basis for making these comparisons is the idea of a neighborhood. Each node (concept) in the network is defined by a set of neighbors that consists of those other nodes that are directly linked to it. For example, in Fig. 4.1, if "coolant level" is only related to "cooling system," "radiator," and "overheating," then the latter three concepts define the neighborhood of coolant level. Two nodes are then compared by comparing their respective neighborhoods. A ratio is formed of the number of common neighbors divided by the total number of neighbors in both structures. (Technically, the actual comparison is made by examining the intersection and union of the two neighborhood sets. For each node, the ratio of the cardinality of the intersection to the cardinality of the union is computed.) The final index of closeness is simply the average of these ratios over the set of nodes.

Closeness is a referent-based measure because the quality of an individual's cognitive structure is evaluated in reference to an agreed on standard. The referent structure of a domain may be identified by collecting relatedness ratings from a set of domain experts, such as the mechanics used in Fig. 4.1. Often the referent structure comes from the course instructor or is derived from averaging concept ratings across several high performers or subject matter experts. Acton, Johnson, and Goldsmith (1994) examined the predictiveness of different types of referent structures, and concluded that a referent structure based on averaged expert ratings is as good, and often better, than the actual course instructor. This finding is important because it indicates that the quality of learner representations is not dependent on idiosyncratic characteristics of the instructor—characteristics that could manifest both in the instructor's own conceptual structure and in his or her composing and grading traditional exams.

A second method of evaluating a cognitive structure is a measure of the coherence of an individual's conceptual relations. Coherence measures the internal consistency of a set of similarity relations, thus it is a referent-free measure of quality. The coherence measure is a correlation between the direct relatedness ratings and a set of derived indirect ratings. The basic assumption behind coherence is that the degree of similarity between two objects has implications for how these objects are related to other objects. The exact nature of this implication comes from the triangle inequality law. If Concepts A and B are perceived as similar, and B and C are seen as similar, then A and C should also be perceived as similar. This same logic holds for more than three objects. Thus, coherence, is a property that results from obedience to a type of generalized triangle inequality law.

A coherence index is obtained by comparing a learner's direct relatedness rating for a pair of concepts and an indirect rating derived from examining the similarity between those two concepts and all other concepts in the rated set. This comparison is again based on the idea of a neighborhood. A set of neighbors is defined for each concept, consisting of those other concepts that are "highly related" (where *highly related* is defined as some particular cutoff value along the rating scale). An indirect rating of similarity is computed for each pair of concepts by comparing the concepts' neighborhoods. The more similar the direct and indirect ratings, the higher the coherence of the data.

Generally, both closeness and coherence may be calculated to evaluate cognitive structures. They will usually, but not always, be correlated. There may be instances in which one metric is more relevant to learning outcomes than another. For example, for basic training courses, an instructional objective might be that trainees simply begin to organize information in a meaningful (consistent) way. Coherence would be the more appropriate evaluation measure. In other settings, training may be used to prepare trainers to perform in a specific domain, such as sales. In this instance, it may be desirable that, by the completion of training, trainees develop cognitive structures that resemble those of high performers (Kraiger et al., 1993). The closeness scale may be more appropriate under such conditions.

ADVANTAGES OF STRUCTURAL ASSESSMENTS

Given this overview of the process of structural assessment, it is instructive to elaborate on several of its advantages over traditional forms of testing. These are reviewed not to suggest that traditional testing is inappropriate, but to call attention to the conditions where structural assessment may be a viable alternative or complementary approach to assessing learning.

First, to traditional testing methods, which merely provide descriptions or summaries in contrast of how much someone knows, structural assessment results in a representation of a learner's knowledge. There is an explicit description (a physical representation) of what someone knows. This representation offers a potentially richer source of information for directing additional training or remediation. For example, a trainer and trainee may review the trainee's representation of knowledge before or after training and determine gaps in knowledge, flaws in logic, or incorrect relations that must be unlearned before correct structures can be built (diSessa, 1982).

Second, in contrast to traditional methods, such as multiple-choice tests, which rely heavily on memory retrieval, structural assessments are less susceptible to retrieval deficits because of the nature of the elicitation method. Learners cannot complain that they knew the information, but could not retrieve it. Similarly, structural assessments are more likely to be sensitive to tacit knowledge. *Tacit knowledge* refers to knowledge that is not explicitly taught, but is nonetheless critical to successful performance. It reflects competence in certain areas that is not readily demonstrated through a set of explicit procedures (Wagner, 1987). By definition, tacit knowledge cannot be measured by traditional tests of explicit knowledge. However, tacit knowledge may be revealed through the way in which a learner represents relations among critical concepts.

For example, in a study of insight, subjects were told a puzzle story and asked to deduce the reason for the behavior of the focal character (Dayton, Durso, & Shepard, 1990). Pathfinder representations of key elements in the story were collected from subjects immediately after they heard the story. Some subjects immediately deduced the reason, but most did not. The remaining subjects were coached (provided clues) to assist in the deductive process. Some of these subjects did deduce the reason with assistance, but others still could not. The Pathfinder representations of the former group of subjects were more similar to those of the subjects who deduced without help than they were to the subjects who could not deduce even with help, suggesting that the structural assessment revealed some tacit understanding of the key story elements.

Structural assessment may minimize "teaching to the test." A potential problem with conventional testing is that, once instructors become knowledgeable of the criteria (the specific questions or types of questions that are asked), they begin to direct their training to facilitate test performance, rather than on-the-job competence. Recall that cognitive structure is viewed as an emergent property and a description of knowledge, although not knowledge per se. Although potentially one could teach to a structural assessment test, the nature of the instruction would be neither interesting nor reinforcing to most trainees (Jonassen ct al., 1993). Simply informing trainees that the ignition system and spark timing are highly related is unlikely to result in any real understanding of the concepts. Meaningful instruction focuses on defining what concepts mean and showing how concepts are related to one another (Tennyson & Cocchiarella, 1986; Tessmer, Wilson, & Driscoll, 1990).

Finally, structural assessment offers a clear description of what it means to be knowledgeable of a particular discipline. By describing the knowledge structure of a discipline, the ideal or referent structure is made explicit. The goal of training is then made objective; trainees should acquire a cognitive structure that resembles the referent structure (Howell & Cooke, 1989; Kraiger, 1988; Merrill & Tennyson, 1977).

CONSTRUCT VALIDATION
OF STRUCTURAL ASSESSMENTS

This section summarizes research that has begun to provide construct-oriented evidence of the validity of structural assessments. Demonstrations of construct validity require cumulative evidence that an operational measure is theoretically and empirically related to the latent construct it was designed to assess. Investigations of the construct validity of training evaluation measures provide both challenges and opportunities (Kraiger & Salas, 1993). The challenge is that one must link the measure to the construct (a cognitive structure), as well as show that the measure is sensitive to changes in the construct as a function of the training intervention. The opportunity is that training programs provide both dynamic environments and quasi experimental designs for testing hypotheses about the measure. One may provide construct-oriented evidence of the validity of a behavioral measure by showing that it varies for participants in a behavior modeling course, but not for those in an attitudinally based course.

Investigations of the construct validity of any measure begin by clearly specifying the latent construct, then demonstrating that scores on the measure behave in predictable ways, given the definition of the construct. Throughout this chapter, the following definition of *structural assessment* is used: Structural assessment provides a measure of an individual's cognitive structure of a set of elements that represent a knowledge domain. This organization is defined by the relations among elements. The outcomes of structural assessments should reflect known differences in knowledge, skill, or aptitude; change as a function of training; and predict performance in the domain for which the knowledge elements were defined, elicited, and represented. Several recent studies that support the construct validity of structural assessments are summarized next.

Group Differences

If structural assessments are valid measures of knowledge organization, then these assessments should vary across individuals who differ in aptitude, skills, or experience in various content domains. This is, in fact, the case.

In perhaps the earliest study using the general methods of structural assessment as defined earlier (including Pathfinder networks), Schvaneveldt et al. (1985) examined differences in cognitive structures of three groups of fighter pilots. Seventeen student pilots, 10 instructor pilots, and 9 air national guard pilots served as subjects. The groups varied considerably in experience as measured by flying time. Thirty concepts were selected from the domain of air combat maneuvering with the aid of subject matter experts and training materials. Pilots then rated the relatedness of the concept pairs on a 10-point scale. MDS and Pathfinder were used to derive representations of the individual sets of ratings. Discriminant function analysis was used to classify pilots using either their raw relatedness ratings, euclidean distances from MDS solutions to the ratings, or path distances from the Pathfinder solutions. The results show that individuals could indeed be classified into their original groups on the basis of their ratings of concept relationships. Further, classification was more accurate using distances from the derived structures than from the raw ratings, showing that the transformation of the raw ratings by the scaling procedures enhanced group differences. Scaled representations of knowledge were useful for distinguishing levels of expertise.

In a more recent validation study, P. J. Johnson et al. (1995) attempted to predict ACT math scores from college students' relatedness judgments of math concepts. The subjects were 101 introductory psychology students, all of whom had taken the ACT test. Subjects rated the relatedness of all pairs of 24 terms from college algebra on a 7-point relatedness scale. A referent structure for the domain was derived from averaging the ratings of four additional students from the same subject pool who had scored 30 or above on the math ACT test.

First, students' ratings were correlated with the averaged referent ratings to obtain an "index of goodness" for each student. These goodness scores were then correlated with the students' math ACT scores, resulting in a correlation of $r = .57$, $p < .001$. Hence, raw concept ratings are a good discriminator of prior experience level. Next, Pathfinder networks were derived for each student and also for the referent. The closeness measure was used to compare each student's network with the referent network, and these values were correlated with math ACT scores. The correlation this time was $r = .58$, $p < .001$. When the covariance of raw ratings was partialed out of the closeness measures, closeness still accounted for a significant amount of variance in the ACT scores ($r = .32$, $p < .01$). This result suggests that the scaling method is uncovering important structural information not directly accessible in the raw ratings.

Changes Over Time

If structural assessments are valid measures of knowledge organization, they should also improve in quality as a function of instruction—specifically, that both closeness (structural similarity) and coherence are greater as a result of student learning. Several recent studies support this prediction.

Acton (1991) studied undergraduate and graduate students in two subject areas: statistics/design and computer science. Both areas contained a set of sequential courses where the earlier courses generally served as prerequisites for later courses (a Pascal programming course followed by a course on data structures). Sets of 24 concepts were identified for each domain. Referent structures were obtained from course instructors. Students rated the relatedness of each pair of concepts at the end of each semester-long course. The results show that both the similarity of a student's structure to the expert referent structure and the coherence of a student's structure increased with experience in the domain.

Similar results have also been found in training applications. Kraiger and Salas (1993) reported change in closeness and coherence scores from pre- to posttraining administrations for a group of Navy pilots receiving air crew coordination training. Kraiger, Salas, and Cannon-Bowers (1995) reported higher closeness scores on posttest for graduate students receiving computer training. Jung and Kraiger (1994) had civil engineering majors directly map structural dynamics concepts (tension, pressure) onto a blank representation (a cognitive map drawn by the professor with most concepts removed for testing purposes). The quality of student representations was significantly greater after a 2½-week field training experience, and significantly predicted student performance in a subsequent structural dynamics course.

Predictive Validity

If structural assessments are valid training evaluation measures, they should be empirically related to performance in domains that are logically related to the training content. This prediction has been investigated in several studies in both educational and training domains.

Over the past two decades, researchers have investigated the relationship between cognitive structures and traditional measures of learning. The results are generally encouraging, showing that the similarity between students' and experts' derived cognitive structures is a good predictor of classroom exam performance. These findings leave little doubt about the validity of the general structural assessment approach.

In the authors' own work, the structural assessment of classroom knowledge in multiple studies over numerous academic domains, was examined including college algebra, biology, civil engineering, cognitive psychology, computer programming, statistics, and research methods. Students are asked to rate the relatedness of pairs of course-relevant concepts. The ratings are collected either with a paper-and-pencil test administered in class or by personal computer at a campus computer pod at the students' convenience. Typically, a 5- or 7-point relatedness scale is used. The predictive validity of these assessments has been investigated by examining the correlations between course performance (final exam grades) and either the raw relatedness ratings or different transformations (different scaling methods), or different methods of comparing student ratings with referent ratings (see P. J. Johnson et al., 1995, for details). Regardless of the method, the predictive validity coefficients typically fall into the range of .50 to .75 (Goldsmith et al., 1991; P. J. Johnson et al., 1995). Transformed ratings generally predict better than raw ratings, indicating the advantage of the structural information uncovered by scaling procedures.

In the training domain, Kraiger (1993) collected relatedness judgments among 13 concepts covered in a sales training course in the telecommunications industry. The concepts were drawn from an interview with the course facilitator, who also supplied the expert solution (via relatedness judgments). Pairwise judgments were collected both before and after training, as were responses to a 20-item true–false test written to reflect the 13 concepts. The results show that closeness scores were more highly correlated with sales performance (number of units sold, gross revenue) collected 1 and 2 months after training than were scores on a true–false test.

In a similar investigation, Kraiger et al. (1993) performed a structural assessment on 11 graduate students immediately after they completed a 3-hour training program on SPSSx programming. Pairwise judgments of similarity were collected for 18 concepts drawn from the training material. Transfer of training was assessed by students' performance on two programming assignments approximately 12 weeks posttraining. Posttraining coherence scores correlated between .32 and .39 with performance on the two assignments.

Kraiger et al. (1993) also used structural assessment to evaluate a training program to prepare students for a PC-based simulation of a Naval decision-making task. The task required subjects to identify incoming unmarked contacts, interpret ambiguous or conflicting information, and decide whether to shoot or clear the contact. Subjects rated 21 concepts drawn from the training content domain before and after watching a 30-minute training video. Training content was manipulated by providing half the subjects (students) with the goals and objectives of the decision-making task (an advance organizer) before training, and providing half the subjects with the same information after training. As hypothesized, closeness scores were significantly more related to performance on the simulation task for subjects receiving the advance organizer before training ($r = .63$) than for subjects receiving the same information after training ($r = -.11$). Thus, the relationship between assessment scores and subsequent domain performance may be moderated by instructional quality.

Summary

Although there is a need for additional research, the evidence to date supports the construct validity of structural assessments, at least those conducted with Pathfinder. Pathfinder representations (a) reflect meaningful differences in subjects' knowledge or expertise, (b) change as a function of training and learning, and (c) predict both final exam performance and performance in posttraining domains. In future studies, it is important to show that these results generalize to other knowledge domains. It is also important to rule out alternative explanations for the findings. For example, general intelligence might be an unmeasured variable causing spuriously high relationships in previous studies. More intelligent people might generally create higher quality representations. Such persons might also score higher on ACT tests or perform well on the job (Schmidt & Hunter 1981). Research to date supports the contention that structural assessments are specific to domain learning.

OTHER ISSUES

Other Applications of Structural Assessment

This chapter focused on applying structural assessments to issues of training evaluation. Structural assessments can also be used in other ways to support training effectiveness. For example, mental models and knowledge structures of subject matter experts may be an area of interest to researchers and course designers during the needs assessment process (Ford & Kraiger, 1995; Hong & O'Neill, 1992; Howell & Cooke, 1989). The focus of the assessment process may go beyond individual tasks and knowledge elements to the interrelationships among those tasks and elements as perceived by incumbents. Not only does structural assessment provide tools for eliciting and representing expert knowledge structures, but, because the structures are not directly measured, structural assessment circumvents the problem that experts are often unable to articulate their knowledge (Kraiger, 1988).

Structural assessment may be used in a number of ways during the needs assessment process. The initial step of defining the content domain (described earlier) provides an alternative to traditional approaches of specifying tasks or requisite knowledge, skills, and abilities. Additionally, key concepts can be elicited and represented both for domain experts and novices. This information may serve several purposes. Expert solutions can be compared to determine whether there is one or many paradigms for understanding and solving problems on the job. If expert solutions vary widely, perhaps learners should be encouraged to build their own idiosyncratic knowledge structures (through discovery learning), rather than trying to provide a single "best" model through instruction (Jonassen et al., 1993). Expert solutions can also be compared to novice solutions to determine appropriate training content. For example, if expert models contained interrelated concepts related to problem diagnosis, but novice models did not, then training could emphasize diagnostic cues during problem solving. The quality of individual knowledge representations (assessed by either closeness or coherence) could then be used during person analysis to identify who should be trained.

The results of a structural assessment can also support the design and development of training. Training effectiveness may increase if quality knowledge structures are important to domain performance, and training is designed to foster development of those knowledge structures. There has been little research on how to best teach knowledge structures in training contexts. The study by Kraiger et al. (1995) described previously suggests that the use of advance organizers may be one helpful instructional method. By definition, *advance organizers* provide a framework or structure that enables trainees to organize the presented information (Mayer, 1979). Ideally, comparative organizers, which explicitly delineate similarities and differences between two sets of ideas, may be shared (Ausubel, 1968). One attractive feature of advance organizers is that they merely provide a departure point, but learners are still free to develop unique knowledge structures through training or experience. Glaser and Bassok (1989) have recommended that advance organizers include a graphical representation of the performance process, and structural assessment may certainly be used for this purpose.

A second instructional design for promoting the developing of trainee knowledge structures is situated learning embedded in realistic contexts (Glaser & Bassok, 1989). Situated learning involves the instruction of knowledge and skills in contexts reflecting the way they will be used in real life (Collins, 1991). Because learning tasks becomes situationally specific, the learner is better able to organize domain-specific knowledge and incorporate problem-based goal structures into a meaningful cognitive structure. Structural assessment may be used to support an intervention such as this. Through interviews with subject matter experts, the performance domain can be identified, as well as the knowledge domain. Through elicitation and representation, cognitive structures can be mapped that explicitly show the link between job knowledge and the conditions in which that knowledge may be applied. Training can then be constructed to expose trainees to common problems, and their performance can be reviewed with respect to the referent structure (are they asking the right questions or applying the right knowledge given the problem?).

diSessa (1982) proposed a method called *schema stretching* for teaching knowledge. The teacher asks questions to ascertain the learners' current cognitive structure, then proposes problems or questions so that responding requires learners to "stretch" or expand their current knowledge structure to solve the problem. For example, when teaching someone to drive, one could ask at what distance one should break to stop a car, and what factors would affect this decision. If speed was the only mediating factor given, then the instructor could ask the learner what would happen if the breaks were applied at that speed and that distance, but on a snow-packed road. A structural assessment could guide this process by providing an initial depiction of both the instructor's and learner's knowledge structure, as well as by mapping progress and resistance during the instructional process.

Research Needs

Despite the promising results of applying structural assessment to issues of training effectiveness, much work remains to be done. Recent research on structural assessment has focused principally on two issues: (a) establishing a replicable methodology for eliciting, representing, and evaluating knowledge structures; and (b) demonstrating the validity of such assessments through their relations to relevant criteria. Several lines of research are needed for structural assessment to find its way into the mainstream of training evaluation.

One research line should continue to focus on methodological issues for improving the reliability and predictive validity of the technique. Although there is a set of procedures for effectively implementing a structural assessment, there is clearly room for improvement. Further research in any of the four major steps of structural assessment is warranted. A second line would focus on theoretical issues. There is a need to more closely link structural assessment measures to learning constructs. On the one hand, structural assessments have been advocated as measures of mental models (Jih & Reeves, 1992; Kraiger et al., 1993), which are dynamic entities composed of multiple knowledge forms (declarative, procedural, etc.). On the other hand, the "building blocks" of a structural assessment are concepts—elements of declarative knowledge. Jonassen et al. (1993) suggested that structural knowledge is a link between declarative knowledge and procedural knowledge. Therefore, it is important to determine whether the structural assessment method is limited to assessing declarative knowledge only, or whether it is also sensitive to procedural knowledge. One straightforward way to address these issues would be to administer content-relevant structural assessment measures after training courses that focused on one form of knowledge or the other, and determine whether posttest assessments were qualitatively and quantitatively different from pretests (Kraiger & Jung, 1995). The same strategy could be employed to determine whether other learning outcomes may be captured by the structural assessment approach. Structural assessments may be useful for determining whether participants in an organizational diversity course truly perceive diversity activities as relevant to good business practices.

Given that the predictive validity of cognitive structures has been demonstrated, do such structures have any causal implications? How literally can these representations be taken? Because experts all agree that certain concepts are tightly clustered, what does this imply for training a novice? Logically, the demonstration of a correlation between closeness scores and performance does not necessarily imply that having certain conceptual relations underlies certain competencies. Rather, all that safely can be said is that individuals who are expert are characterized by certain cognitive structures. However, it is quite possible that these relationships do have causal implications for domain performance. If they do, it would be possible to use the derived representations to individualize training. In other words, specific deficits could be identified on the basis of specific departures from the idealized structure, and this information could be used to design an individualized training program. One could envision an interactive program (an intelligent tutoring system) that would continually update a cognitive structure of a user, and, on the basis of comparisons with an idealized end state, redirect training routines.

It may also be useful to explore the causal mechanisms underlying the link between training interventions and the formation of qualitatively superior cognitive structures. Rouse, Cannon-Bowers, and Salas (1992) hypothesized that teams perform better when team members share similar cognitive structures for the task domain. They suggested that training members toward the criterion of shared or matched expectations for task outcomes would be an effective strategy for directly imparting shared cognitive structures. Studies of specific training events, such as the Kraiger et al. (1995) investigation of advance organizers, may be useful for furthering an understanding of how knowledge structures are formed, and how training may be best constructed. Other studies of this nature are necessary to further explicate and test causal mechanisms linking instruction to the formation of useful knowledge structures.

An issue of both practical and theoretical importance concerns the choice of the referent structure (for scoring closeness). Most applications to date have been conducted in classroom settings, where it is appropriate to define the referent structure as the instructors' cognitive structure. However, in training applications, a referent structure may be elicited from not only the trainer, but also high performers on the job. It might be expected that job performers and trainers would hold qualitatively different cognitive structures, but it is also possible that experts may differ among themselves, particularly if they are experienced and have had the opportunity to individualize their work. The implications of differences among experts on the evaluation of trainees' cognitive structures are unclear.

CONCLUSION

This chapter described a structural assessment of an individual learner's knowledge and skill in a specific domain. The method is based on sound theoretical foundations from cognitive science, psychometric theory, and scaling theory. The basic steps in a structural assessment are to define the structure of the domain, and then elicit, represent, and assess an individual's cognitive structure of the domain. A set of procedures currently exist that provides a valid, reliable, and efficient method for performing structural assessments. Once a set of terms is identified for a task domain and a referent structure obtained, the rest of the procedures are quickly and efficiently carried out by computer. The ease of administering and scoring the assessment makes immediate feedback possible on a student's performance as soon as he or she is finished giving concept relationships. Although structural assessments are not intended to replace traditional assessments, they do offer an important dimension to assessment that is lacking in traditional methods.

REFERENCES

Acton, W. H. (1991). *Comparison of criterion referenced and criterion free measures of cognitive structure.* Unpublished doctoral dissertation, University of New Mexico, Alburquerque.
Acton, W. H., Johnson, P. J., & Goldsmith, T. E. (1994). Structural knowledge assessment: Comparison of referent structures. *Journal of Educational Psychology, 86,* 303–311.
Alliger, G. M., & Janak, E. A. (1989). Kirkpatrick's levels of training criteria: Thirty years later. *Personnel Psychology, 42,* 331–342.

Ausubel, D. P. (1968). *Educational psychology: A cognitive view*. New York: Holt, Rinehart & Winston.

Baldwin, T. T., & Ford, J. K. (1988). Transfer of training: A review and future directions for research. *Personnel Psychology, 41,* 63–105.

Bretz, R. D., Jr., & Thompsett, R. E. (1993). Comparing traditional and integrative learning methods in organizational training programs. *Journal of Applied Psychology, 77,* 941–951.

Bunker, K., & Cohen, S. L. (1977). The rigors of training evaluation: A discussion and field demonstration. *Personnel Psychology, 30,* 525–541.

Campbell, J. P. (1971). Personnel training and development. *Annual Review of Psychology, 22,* 565–602.

Cannon-Bowers, J. A., Tannenbaum, S. I., Salas, E., & Converse, S. A. (1991). Toward an integration of training theory and technique. *Human Factors, 33,* 281–292.

Champagne, A. B., Klopfer, L. E., & Anderson, J. H. (1980). Factors influencing the learning of classical mechanics. *American Journal of Physics, 48,* 1074–1079.

Chi, M. T. H., Glaser, R., & Rees, E. (1981). *Expertise in problem-solving* (Tech. Rep. No. 5). Pittsburgh, PA: University of Pittsburgh, Learning Research and Development Center.

Collins, A. M. (1991). Cognitive apprenticeship and instructional technology. In L. Idol & B. F. Jones (Eds.), *Educational values and cognitive instruction: Implications for reform* (pp. 121–138). Hillsdale, NJ: Lawrence Erlbaum Associates.

Collins, A. M., & Loftus, E. F. (1975). A spreading activation theory of semantic processing. *Psychological Review, 82*(6), 407–428.

Cooke, N. M., Durso, F. T., & Schvaneveldt, R. W. (1986). Recall and measures of memory organization. *Journal of Experimental Psychology: Learning, Memory and Cognition, 12,* 538–549.

Cooke, N. M., & McDonald, J. E. (1987). The application of psychological scaling techniques to knowledge-elicitation for knowledge-based systems. *International Journal of Man-Machine Systems, 28,* 533–550.

Dayton, T., Durso, F. T., & Shepard, J. D. (1990). A measure of the knowledge reorganization underlying insight. In R. W. Schvaneveldt (Ed.), *Pathfinder associative networks: Studies in knowledge organization* (pp. 267–277). Norwood, NJ: Ablex.

Decker, P. J. (1982). The enhancement of behavior modeling training of supervisory skills by the inclusion of retention processes. *Personnel Psychology, 35,* 323–332.

Diekhoff, G. M (1983). Testing through relationship judgments. *Journal of Educational Psychology, 75,* 227–233.

diSessa, A. A. (1982). Unlearning Aristotelian physics: A study of knowledge-based learning. *Cognitive Science, 6,* 37–75.

Fenker, R. M. (1975). The organization of conceptual materials: A methodology for measuring ideal and actual cognitive structures. *Instructional Science, 4,* 33–57.

Ford, J. K., & Kraiger, K. (1995). The application of cognitive constructs and principles to the instructional systems model of training: Implications for needs assessment, design, and transfer. In I. Robertson & D. Cooper (Eds.), *The international review of industrial and organizational psychology* (Vol. 10, pp. 1–48). London: Wiley.

Frederiksen, N. (1984). The real test bias: Influences of testing on teaching and learning. *American Psychologist, 39,* 193–202.

Froehlich, H. P. (1962). Training conditions, ability, and academic outcomes. *Journal of Applied Psychology, 46,* 67–71.

Gagne, R. M., & Beard, J. G. (1978). Assessment of learning outcomes. In R. Glaser (Ed.), *Advances in instructional psychology* (Vol. 1, pp. 261–294). Hillsdale, NJ: Lawrence Erlbaum Associates.

Glaser, R., & Bassok, M. (1989). Learning theory and the study of instruction. *Annual Review of Psychology, 40,* 631–666.

Goldsmith, T. E., & Davenport, D. M. (1990). Assessing structural similarity of graphs. In R. W. Schvaneveldt (Ed.), *Pathfinder associative networks: Studies in knowledge organization* (pp. 75–87). Norwood, NJ: Ablex.

Goldsmith, T. E., & Johnson, P. J. (1990). A structural assessment of classroom learning. In R. W. Schvaneveldt (Ed.), *Pathfinder associative networks: Studies in knowledge organization* (pp. 241–254). Norwood, NJ: Ablex.

Goldsmith, T. E., Johnson, P. J., & Acton, W. H. (1991). Assessing structural knowledge. *Journal of Educational Psychology, 83,* 88–96.

Gordon, M. E., & Cohen, S. L. (1973). Training behavior as a predictor of trainability. *Personnel Psychology, 26,* 261–272.

Gordon, M. E., & Kleiman, L. S. (1976). The prediction of trainability using a work sample test and an aptitude test: A direct comparison. *Personnel Psychology, 29,* 243–253.

Hamrick, L., Harty, H., & Ault, C. (1987). Concept structure interrelatedness competence (ConSic): A tool for examining and promoting cognitive structure. *School Science and Mathematics, 87,* 655–664.

Harrison, J. K. (1993). Individual and combined effects of behavior modeling and the cultural assimilator in cross-cultural management training. *Journal of Applied Psychology, 77,* 952–962.

Hong, E., & O'Neill, H. F., Jr. (1992). Instructional strategies to help learners build relevant mental models in inferential statistics. *Journal of Educational Psychology, 84,* 150–159.

Howell, W. C., & Cooke, N. J. (1989). Training the human information processor. In I. L. Goldstein (Ed.), *Training and development in organizations* (pp. 121–182). San Francisco: Jossey-Bass.

Jih, H. J., & Reeves, T. C. (1992). Mental models: A research focus on interactive learning systems. *Educational Technology, Research, and Development, 40,* 39–54.

Johnson, P. E. (1964). Associative meaning of concepts in physics. *Journal of Educational Psychology, 55,* 84–88.

Johnson, P. E., Cox, D. L., & Curran, T. E. (1970). Psychological reality of physical concepts. *Psychonomic Science, 19,* 245–247.

Johnson, P. J., Goldsmith, T. E., & Teague, K. (1995). Similarity, structure, and knowledge: A representational approach to assessment. In P. D. Nichols, S. F. Chipman, R. L. Brennan, (Eds.), *Cognitively diagnostic assessment* (pp. 221–249). Hillsdale, NJ: Lawrence Erlbaum Associates.

Johnson, S. C. (1967). Hierarchical clustering schemes. *Psychometrika, 32,* 241–254.

Jonassen, D. H., Beissner, K., & Yacci, M. (1993). *Structural knowledge: Techniques for representing, conveying, and acquiring structural knowledge.* Hillsdale, NJ: Lawrence Erlbaum Associates.

Jung, K. M., & Kraiger, K. (1994, April). *A multi-faceted evaluation of problem-based instruction.* Paper submitted for presentation at the annual meeting of the Society for Industrial/Organizational Psychology, Nashville, TN.

Kraiger, K. (1988, April). *Implications of expert/novice differences for training assessment and design.* Paper presented at the annual meeting of the Society for Industrial/Organizational Psychology, Dallas, TX.

Kraiger, K. (1993). *Further support for structural assessment as a method of training evaluation.* Paper presented at the annual meeting of the American Psychological Association, Toronto, Canada.

Kraiger, K., Ford, J. K., & Salas, E. (1993). Integration of cognitive, behavioral, and affective theories of learning into new methods of training evaluation [Monograph]. *Journal of Applied Psychology, 78,* 311–328.

Kraiger, K., & Jung, K. M. (in press). Linking training objectives to evaluation criteria. In M. A. Quiñones & A. Dutta (Eds.), *Training for the 21st century technology: Applications of psychological research.* Washington, DC: American Psychological Association.

Kraiger, K., & Salas, E. (1993, May). *An empirical test of two cognitively-based measures of learning during training.* Paper presented at the annual meeting of the Society for Industrial/Organizational Psychology, San Francisco.

Kraiger, K., Salas, E., & Cannon-Bowers, J.A. (1995). Measuring knowledge organization as a method for assessing learning during training. *Human Factors, 37,* 804–816.

Kruskal, J. B. (1964). Multidimensional scaling by optimizing goodness- of-fit to a nonmetric hypothesis. *Psychometrika, 29,* 115–129.

Lesgold, A., Rubinson, H., Feltovich, P., Glaser, R., Klopfer, D., & Wang, Y. (1989). Expertise in a complex skill: Diagnosing x-ray pictures. In M. T. Chi, R. Glaser, & M. J. Farr (Eds.), *The nature of expertise* (pp. 311–342). Hillsdale, NJ: Lawrence Erlbaum Associates.

Mayer, R. E. (1979). Can advance organizers influence meaningful learning? *Review of Educational Research, 49,* 371–383.

McCaffery, J. A. (1986). Independent effectiveness: A reconsideration of cross-cultural orientation and training. *International Journal of Intercultural Relations, 10,* 159–178.

McKeithen, K. B., Reitman, J. S., Reuter, H. H., & Hirtle, S. C. (1981). Knowledge organization and skill differences in computer programmers. *Cognitive Psychology, 13,* 307–325.

Merrill, M., & Tennyson, R. D. (1977). *Teaching concepts: An instructional design guide.* Englewood Cliffs, NJ: Educational Technology Publications.

Moses, J. L., & Ritchie, R. J. (1976). Supervisory relationships training: A behavioral evaluation of a behavior modeling program. *Personnel Psychology, 29,* 337–343.

Noble, C. E. (1956). Psychology and the logic of similarity. *The Journal of General Psychology, 57,* 23–43.

Palmer, S. E. (1978). Fundamental aspects of cognitive representation. In E. Rosch & B. B. Lloyd (Eds.), *Cognition and categorization* (pp. 259–303). Hillsdale, NJ: Lawrence Erlbaum Associates.

Preece, P. F. W. (1976). The concepts of electromagnetism: A study of the internal representation of external structures. *Journal of Research in Science Teaching, 13,* 517–524.

Rouse, W. B., Cannon-Bowers, J. A., & Salas, E. (1992). The role of mental models in team performance in complex systems. *IEEE Transactions on Systems, Man, and Cybernetics, 22,* 1296–1308.

Sattath, S., & Tversky, A. (1977). Additive similarity trees. *Psychometrika, 42,* 319–345.

Schmidt, F. L., & Hunter, J. E. (1981). Employment testing: Old theories and new research findings. *American Psychologist, 36,* 1128–1137.

Schoenfeld, A. H., & Herrman, D. J. (1982). Problem perception and knowledge structure in expert and novice mathematical problem solvers. *Journal of Experimental Psychology: Learning, Memory, and Cognition, 8,* 484–494.

Schvaneveldt, R. W., Durso, F. T., & Dearholt, D. W. (1989). Network structures in proximity data. In G. H. Bower (Ed.), *The psychology of learning and motivation* (Vol. 24, pp. 249–284). New York: Academic Press.

Schvaneveldt, R. W., Durso, F. T., Goldsmith, T. E., Breen, T. J., Cooke, N. M., Tucker, R. G., & De Maio, J. C. (1985). Measuring the structure of expertise. *International Journal of Man-Machine Studies, 23,* 699–728.

Shavelson, R. J. (1972). Some aspects of the correspondence between content structure and cognitive structure in physics instruction. *Journal of Educational Psychology, 63,* 225–234.

Shavelson, R. J., & Stanton, G. C. (1975). Concept validation: Methodology and application to three measures of cognitive structure. *Journal of Educational Measurement, 12,* 67–85.

Shepard, R. N. (1958). Stimulus and response generalization: Tests of a model relating generalization to distance in psychological space. *Journal of Experimental Psychology, 55,* 509–523.

Tennyson, R. D., & Cocchiarella, M. J. (1986). An empirically based instructional design theory for teaching concepts. *Review of Educational Research, 56,* 40–71.

Tessmer, M., Wilson, B., & Driscoll, M. (1990). A new model of concept teaching and learning. *Educational Technology Research and Development, 38,* 45–53.

Tversky, A. (1977). Features of similarity. *Psychological Review, 84,* 327–352.

Wagner, R. K. (1987). Tacit knowledge in everyday intelligent behavior. *Journal of Personality and Social Psychology, 52,* 1236–1247.

Wexley, K. N. (1984). Personnel training. *Annual Review of Psychology, 35,* 519–551.

II

Viewing Learning as a Continuous Process: Implications for Training, Socialization, and Employee Development

5

Training as an Organizational Episode: Pretraining Influences on Trainee Motivation

Timothy T. Baldwin
Richard J. Magjuka
Indiana University School of Business

We need reminding that trainees do not just fall out of some great trainee bin in the sky; they probably have rather long and varied organizational histories, which have created certain attitudes, values and behaviors relative to specific training experiences.
— Campbell (1989, p. 479)

A considerable amount of writing in the organizational literature has suggested that the context or environment in which interventions take place will have profound effects on the outcomes of those interventions. In a recent review of the research literature on applications of organizational work teams, Sundstrom, DeMeuse, and Futrell (1990) concluded that work team effectiveness depends as much on organizational contextual factors as on skilled internal group functioning. Although there is ample anecdotal evidence to suggest that contextual factors are similarly influential to training effectiveness, most prior empirical research on industrial training applications has been limited to issues of skill assessment, instructional design, and trainee aptitudes. Systematic consideration of the context of training interventions has only recently begun.

An assumption common to most training guidebooks is that the learning context can be managed or designed in a way that will affect trainee cognitions and, ultimately, training effectiveness. However, this assumption tends to oversimplify the complexity of managing contextual factors in organizations. We contend that the complexity stems in large part from the difficulty of predicting how employees will attach meaning to management acts, and the

99

reality that, for organization employees, training is not an isolated event or singular activity, but an episode that occurs among many other organizational episodes experienced by those employees.

The purpose of this chapter is to develop the notion of training as an organizational episode. Viewing training as an episode draws particular attention to events and cognitions that occur prior to the delivery of a training intervention. This chapter focuses on identifying and developing a framework of those pretraining contextual factors that may influence trainee motivation.

Our hope is that viewing training as an episode will induce greater research attention paid to the pretraining context, and will yield a richer understanding of the predictors of training success and failure. Without consideration of key contextual factors prior to training, one cannot draw correct conclusions about training effects. From a practical perspective, the specific interest here is in those contextual factors that can be managed to improve the probability of successful training episodes.

The chapter is divided into two sections. First, a conceptualization of training as an organizational episode is presented and the research implications of such a perspective are illustrated. An episodic perspective requires an understanding of the cumulative effects of contextual factors on trainee perceptions and necessitates expansion of current training research strategies. This section incorporates Bandura's (1986) social cognitive theory as a foundation for understanding the role of pretraining contextual influences as predictors of successful (or unsuccessful) training episodes.

Second, the pretraining contextual factors that are most likely to influence trainee perceptions are highlighted. Also presented are a framework and a set of propositions designed to focus research investigation of such factors. The identification of contextual factors is based on inferences drawn from the human resource management literature (Latham & Crandall, 1991; Tannenbaum & Yukl, 1992), as well as the authors' own recent research and involvement in a number of organizational training initiatives. The variables are categorized under the labels of (a) *training introduction*, (b) *training cohort*, and (c) *transfer climate*. Consistent with Bandura's theory, the central proposition here is that pretraining contextual factors are salient influences on trainee cognitions and motivation, and will affect the degree of training success independent of what occurs in the instructional program. The chapter concludes with a summary and discussion of important research directions.

TRAINING AS AN ORGANIZATIONAL EPISODE

Every training experience can be viewed as an episode—a series of cumulative stimuli experienced by the trainee and the cognitions associated with those experiences (Lighthall, 1989). The standard for evaluating the beginning and end of an episode is normative: Training episodes are socially constructed and trainees determine the beginning and end of an episode by synthesizing their experiences from multiple sources. Although this definition suggests that defining an episode is a subjective activity, there is an interplay between subjective interpretation and objective contextual factors that combine to influence someone's determination of an episode's boundaries.

The beginning of most training episodes is well before any instruction begins or any trainer is involved. In most organizational training contexts, trainees and trainers consider a training episode to include stimuli associated with the introduction of a training initiative, determination of a training cohort, the delivery of training content, and the return of the trainee to the work situation. Moreover, a trainee's perspective of all parts of an episode will be filtered through past training experience, experiences of colleagues, and other concurrent organizational activity.

The current definition of *training* as a socially constructed episode necessitates expanding traditional training research in two important ways. First, the significance of any training design practice lies in the meaning attached to the activity by the trainees, not the trainers, managers, or other outside parties. From this perspective, implementing a training intervention in an organization represents a series of acts (introduction, cohort selection) that signify meaning to trainees, regardless of whether a particular message is intentionally being communicated by the initiator of the message (usually a manager or trainer). Although the existing training research has generally treated training design elements as objective stimuli with a common meaning, an important research agenda is to examine how trainees attach meaning to different design elements, and assess the motivational effect—positive and negative—of those design elements.

From this perspective, an important point is that any training episode represents a natural slice of organizational life and occurs within a particular organizational culture. Organizational training takes place amid individuals doing their jobs, functioning on teams, and being exposed to a host of other organizational activities unrelated to the training in question. Participants have learned organizational rules that guide their behavior in that culture, and their reaction to different training episode stimuli will reflect their interpretation of the appropriate rules to apply.

Consider the apparently straightforward activity of setting training performance goals. The focus of most goal setting research has been on the objective characteristics of effective goals. There has been relatively little interest in examining the interpretation of goals by the trainee. Goal setting studies have rarely considered the influence of the situation, the location within a training process, or the cumulative experiences of training participants.

From an episodic perspective, when an organization and its managers formulate performance goals, the act potentially communicates more to respondents than numerical targets and behavioral strategies. The communicated signal attached to goals may be positive or negative. When goals are formulated, one signal to employees may be that management has a clear idea concerning the outcome of a process and is willing to assume some responsibility for the accomplishment of the established goal. However, it could also be the case that employees interpret the provision of goals in a negative fashion. For example, experience in a particular firm could suggest that goals are merely "wishes," with no accountability and no consequences for not attaining goals.

The general point is that the motivating influence of any training design element is partially contingent on the trainees' accumulated experience with that design element in other organizational settings. Activities such as goal setting do not represent practices that are idiosyncratic to training. Businesses set profit goals, people have sales goals, and managers evaluate subordinates in terms of attaining personal goals. The meaning that employees attach to such goal setting activities will affect the interpretation of goal setting in training.

A second issue suggested by this definition is that if a researcher wishes to understand the determinants of effectiveness for an episode, it is necessary to assess more than one cross-sectional snapshot of a single training design element. An episodic view requires researchers to study the cumulativity of training design elements. Only when the sequence of salient pretraining messages is examined will it be possible to adequately assess the effect of the design practice on trainee motivation and learning.

In a recent study of trainee participation in the pretraining process, Baldwin, Magjuka, and Loher (1991) found that participation was related to self-reported trainee motivation, but only when the participative input was reflected in the ultimate training received. As the authors noted, the concept of participation in the training process has been treated favorably by adult learning theorists and training researchers. However, the presumed positive effect of participation in training has been empirically observed only when investigators have looked at incomplete participation episodes—whereby trainees were asked for input but were not subsequently told whether their input was reflected in the training to be received. When a complete participation episode was considered, results showed that a participative choice that was not ultimately received actually detracted from the motivation to learn and subsequent learning. The implication of this research is that accurate attributions of trainee motivation and learning are increased to the extent that more complete episodes are assessed.

Different combinations of training design elements can exert a cumulative effect very different than a design element examined in isolation. Trainees may weigh more heavily a design element signal at one stage in an episode as opposed to another stage. It could be that those stimuli encountered most proximate to training delivery exert the greatest influence on trainee motivation. In any case, the potential impact of cumulative effects throughout a training episode suggests the importance of broadening the training research lens.

In summary, by treating the training process as an episode, research must undergo a significant shift that underscores the importance of the organizational context. Employees determine the beginning and end of an episode by synthesizing their experiences gained from all sources to establish boundaries. Emerging from this perspective are a host of important research questions that remain relatively unexplored. For example, which design elements are significant and get the attention of trainees? Do various constituencies interpret similarly the meaning of design elements? Within any single constituency, are there systematic differences in how subgroups (managers vs. professionals vs. clerical staff) react to the identical design element? Do different training cohorts affect trainee expectations and motivation? What organizational climate factors contribute to high degrees of trainee motivation? To address such questions, those conducting training research must better understand the work setting and social identities of potential trainees.

Social Cognitive Theory

The current definition of *training* as an episode suggests the important interaction of pretraining events and trainee cognitions related to those events. As noted by several recent authors (Latham, 1988; Martocchio, 1992; Mathieu, Martineau, & Tannenbaum, 1993), Bandura's (1986) social cognitive theory provides a useful theoretical model for predicting, understanding, and increasing the motivational determinants of successful training episodes.

Social cognitive theory posits reciprocal determinism among the person's cognitions, the environment, and overt behavior. Put simply, behavior influences and is influenced by both cognitive and environmental contingencies. Bandura (1986) contended that individuals regulate their behavior based on their beliefs about their ability to accomplish a task (self-efficacy), and their beliefs about the environmental consequences of their behavior (outcome expectancies).

Self-efficacy is defined as people's judgments of their capabilities to organize and execute courses of action required to attain designated types of performances. It is concerned not with the skills people have, but with judgments of what they can do with whatever skills they possess (Bandura, 1986). When individuals believe they are capable of high performance, they are more likely to attempt the appropriate behavior to achieve their goals. Self-efficacy has been found to influence sales performance, productivity in a manufacturing setting, and job attendance (Barling & Beattie, 1983; Frayne & Latham, 1987; Latham & Frayne, 1989). In training environments, it has been linked to positive outcomes of computer software training (Gist, Schwoerer, & Rosen, 1989), interpersonal skills training (Gist, Stevens, & Bavetta, 1990), and military training programs (Eden & Ravid, 1982; Tannenbaum, Mathieu, Salas, & Cannon-Bowers, 1991). Low self-efficacy has been found to be so detrimental to training success that behavior will not change even when outcome expec-tancies are high (Frayne & Latham, 1987).

Outcome expectancies have also been linked to training outcomes. Al-though expectancies can take many forms, both personal and organizational, training success is maximized when trainees perceive that desirable outcomes (or avoidance of undesirable outcomes) are attained as a result of completing a program satisfactorily.

In summary, based on Bandura's (1986) model, the influence of contextual variables on training outcomes of learning and transfer is posited to occur via trainee cognitions of self-efficacy and/or outcome expectancies. More specifi-cally, trainee motivation will be maximized to the degree that trainees: (a) have maximum confidence that they can learn and transfer; and (b) believe that there is some value, personal or organizational, from learning and applying training content. The authors' recent work has convinced them that factors in the pretraining context are central to the formation of those trainee percep-tions. Of particular interest are those contextual factors related to (a) how a training initiative is introduced and labeled, (b) the nature of the training cohort, and (c) the perceived climate for transfer of skills to the job.

Figure 5.1 presents a framework of pretraining contextual variables imposed on an abbreviated model of social cognitive theory. The proposed framework represents a pretraining episode; it is a preliminary attempt to highlight the potential influence of contextual factors on individual cognitions that have been linked to positive training outcomes. The framework is incomplete at present because empirical work is needed to specify the nature of the relation-ships and important contingencies. Of course, performance in training is determined by factors other than trainee motivation (ability, training content relevance), and any meaningful training episode certainly continues through

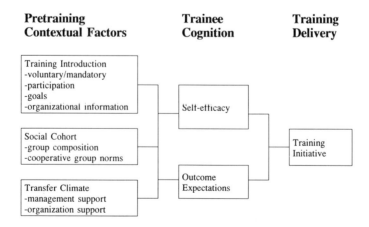

FIG. 5.1. A pretraining episode.

the posttraining transfer environment. However, this chapter's focus is limited to consideration of linkages between pretraining contextual factors and trainee motivation.

The value of the framework is to aid those interested in studying the pretraining context by highlighting variables to be considered and where future work is needed. With development, it has the potential to provide managers and trainers with a prescriptive tool for creating "training friendly" contexts and enhancing the favorability of their firm's learning culture. The next section discusses each of the contextual variables identified in the framework, and generates research propositions regarding the relationship of pretraining context to self-efficacy and outcome expectations.

TRAINING INTRODUCTION

The conception of training as an episode acknowledges that all management actions send signals that convey meaning to organizational employees (Pfeffer, 1981). The signals may be explicit or implicit, and the meanings attached are either consistent or inconsistent with management intentions. With respect to training initiatives, a small, but growing body of research has begun to explore the signals attached to the way training is introduced in an organization. The term *introduced* is used in the broadest sense to include who may attend, the nature of trainee input in the process, and the formal goals and labels assigned to a training initiative. It has been the authors' experience that the introduction of training varies widely across firms and certainly within different initiatives within the same firm. This section focuses on three aspects of training introduction that warrant focused research attention.

Voluntary/Mandatory

Among the most basic of trainee questions related to organizational training is, Do I have to attend? That is, is participation in a training initiative subject to employee discretion (voluntary) or considered a condition of employment (mandatory)?

Traditional wisdom is that motivation to learn is enhanced if trainees attend of their own volition (Dewar, 1984; Lawler, 1986). These authors generally contended that voluntary programs establish an attractive context for involvement and are an efficient means of gaining the attendance of those best suited to program objectives. The assumption is that a functional form of self-selection is fostered by a voluntary program, and that such programs help avoid accommodating employees not interested in nor well suited to program objectives (Mohrman & Ledford, 1985). Some research has found voluntary participation to be related to higher motivation to learn and more positive trainee reactions (Cohen, 1990; Hicks & Klimoski, 1987; Mathieu, Tannenbaum, & Salas, 1990).

However, recent evidence from organizational settings suggests that volunteer participation may not always yield the most desirable membership. Some administrators of voluntary programs have complained that those who volunteer are often those most interested in getting out of work (Kanter, 1986). In addition, Baldwin and Magjuka (1991) found that engineers who perceived training to be mandatory reported greater intentions to apply what they learned back on the job than did engineers who viewed their attendance as voluntary. The authors attributed the result to trainee perceptions that mandatory status was one of the most salient signals of organizational importance. That is, the motivation to learn was, in part, induced by the outcome expectancy that the program was important to organizational decision makers or otherwise it would not be mandated. Those who viewed the program as voluntary were interpreting that as a signal of the relative lack of importance of training relative to a host of other mandated organizational activities.

Tannenbaum and Yukl (1992) contended that one important moderator of the effect of voluntary–mandatory status may be the different attitudes toward training in a particular firm. In the Baldwin and Magjuka (1991) study, the vast majority of engineers reported that their prior training experiences had been favorable. However, in the study by Hicks and Klimoski (1987), few employees who could have volunteered did so, suggesting that employees in that organization perceived training to be of low value. It seems plausible that when prior training experience has not been favorable, any mandated attendance for training may be dysfunctional.

An episodic perspective complicates the study of voluntary–mandatory, in that the formal designation of a program is not presumed to be an objective reality. Rather, it is the trainee's subjective perception of program status, aside from the formal designation, that most significantly affects outcome expectancies. The formal designation may coincide with trainee perceptions, but few would argue that some interventions labeled *voluntary* are often perceived by trainees as implicitly mandatory. Similarly, programs formally tagged as *required* are often dismissed as, *not really required for me*.

From a pragmatic standpoint, this appears to be a dilemma for training managers left with the task of conveying importance without risking the detrimental effects of mandating or "forcing" people to attend. Some organizations have opted to mandate a certain amount of training time, but allow trainee discretion in choosing the type of training attended. In any case, it is important that future researchers acknowledge the importance of perceived status on trainee perceptions and not use the formal designation as a sufficient indicator of that perceived status. One also needs to know much more about the implications of training designations and the conditions where mandated instruction can be most successful. Mandating training allows for a more representative cohort and alleviates the recurring training problem of attracting those who need the training least (Baldwin, Magjuka, & Fulford, 1990).

Nonetheless, fears of trying to train those "forced" to attend linger as well. Future research on the antecedents and consequences of perceived program status across a variety of training environments is needed to inform future research and practice.

Trainee Participation

Closely related to the issue of voluntary–mandatory program status is the issue of trainee participation in the pretraining period. Few issues in behavioral science are more loaded with ideological and moral connotations than that of participation in decision making. Participatory learning processes are viewed by some as a moral imperative (Sashkin, 1984). We concur with Locke and others (Locke & Schweiger, 1979) that, at least in organizational contexts, such systematic ideology in favor of participation is inappropriate in the absence of practical evidence that participation influences important trainee expectations and outcomes.

A recurring prescription for enhancing the effectiveness of training interventions is to involve employees in decisions about the training process (Newstrom & Lilyquist, 1979; Wlodkowski, 1985). Participation might include soliciting trainee input on courses to be delivered, content of those courses, and/or how the courses are to be scheduled and conducted (Baldwin et al., 1991). Adult learning theorists posit that, because adults will learn only what they feel a desire to learn, involvement in training decisions should be a potent pretraining motivator (Knowles, 1984).

Although it may seem intuitive that the involved trainee will be more motivated and ultimately more successful, there is scant empirical evidence to support those propositions (Noe, 1986). Indeed, some recent authors have questioned the premise that participation is motivational at all (Latham, Winters, & Locke, 1992). Baldwin et al. (1991) found no significant overall positive relationship between participation and learning, nor between self-reported motivation and learning. Similarly, neither Hicks and Klimoski (1987) nor Mathieu et al. (1993) found a significant relationship between pretraining choice and learning.

The recent evidence challenging the value of pretraining participation is consistent with prior research on participation in instructional settings. Anderson (1959) summarized a number of studies comparing authoritarian and democratic approaches to teaching. He found no trend with respect to a learning criterion, but democratic approaches were generally superior with respect to a morale criterion. Outside of learning contexts, other reviews of research on participation have generally concluded that participation has greater effects on morale or satisfaction than it does on motivation to perform and performance (Wagner & Gooding, 1987). Perhaps, as Latham et al. (1992) suggested, the potential benefits of participation may be more informational than motivational, and, if so, such benefits may be more easily obtained in training contexts via direct informational strategies and/or goal setting.

It is premature to conclude from the existing evidence that a trainee's involvement in the pretraining period does not have some value. In some contexts, employees' participation may be interpreted as signifying the value of egalitarianism and highlighting the importance of every employee's input. Research has shown that participation can be a powerful signal of inclusion and may serve to validate organizational culture and values (Meyer & Rowan, 1977; Pfeffer, 1981). Pretraining involvement might presumably lead to better attendance, peer support, and less likelihood of disruptive behaviors.

The equivocal findings serve to further highlight the importance of an episodic perspective. Participation represents a design issue that can signify a variety of meanings to individuals throughout an organization and within different organizations. Trainees interpret their participation as a sequence of activities that incorporates the provision of options, selection of an alternative, and knowledge of the results of selection decisions.

Goals

A third dimension of the way in which training is introduced concerns the nature of the goals and labels assigned to a training initiative. Setting specific difficult goals has been shown to lead to higher performance in a wide variety of settings, and is among the most robust findings in the organizational literature (Locke & Latham, 1990). Although forms of goal setting, such as learning objectives and advance organizers, have long been a part of the language of instructional design (Goldstein, 1992), only recently have training researchers begun to explore the effects of assigned goals as a mechanism for enhancing training outcomes (Cohen, 1990).

Cohen (1990) found that trainees with goals prior to training entered training with higher levels of motivation to learn. In a comparison of the effects of participation and goal setting, Baldwin, Magjuka, and Loher (1992) found that the most direct path to increased learning was an assigned goal, which prompted notetaking, regardless of the degree of input the trainees had in the selection of their training content. The presence of an assigned goal overwhelmed the negative or frustration effects associated with a group of trainees who had an opportunity to voice a preference for a training topic, but were not given their preferred choice.

Despite these preliminary findings, the consequences of goals in training contexts are not self-evident. The training content is often more complex than traditionally studied goal setting tasks, and it has been shown that the goal setting effect is more pronounced for simple versus complex tasks (Locke & Latham, 1990).

Moreover, an important stream of recent work suggests that it is important to distinguish between two different types of goals: (a) learning goals, in which individuals seek to increase their ability or master new tasks; and (b) performance goals, in which individuals seek to maintain positive judgments about their ability (Elliott & Dweck, 1988). Latham and Crandall (1991) characterized this same distinction as between process (behavioral) and outcome (results achieved) goals. Recent findings indicate that outcome goals can actually be detrimental to the learning process if they are set in the early stages of skill acquisition. Kanfer and Ackerman (1989) found that the higher the attentional demands of the learning stage, the less effective the setting of an outcome goal is on behavior.

From an episodic perspective, the source of goal information can be a crucial factor in the motivating influence of goals in organizations. For example, a strategic objective established for a training initiative by the chief executive officer (CEO) or other top-level manager has been credited with having a powerful effect on trainee motivation (Dixon, 1993).

Research is needed that links emerging conceptual work to the practice of setting goals in a variety of instructional contexts. Administrators impressed with the demonstrated potential of goals rightly ask questions such as: (a) Are there differences in trainee expectations associated with different goal sources? (b) Is trainee motivation likely to be influenced more by program- or task-specific goals? (c) Are there environmental conditions where specific, difficult goals might constrain motivation and learning? (d) How should appropriate difficulty levels be established? and (e) Who should set and monitor goals?

In short, research must be aimed at understanding how to best harness this powerful mechanism to maximize training outcomes. The simple maxim to set specific, difficult goals is insufficiently prescriptive for varied training content and contexts. One needs to know far more about the effects of different types and timing of training goals, different sources of goal information, and the practical construction of appropriate goals in industrial training contexts.

Organizational Information

Evidence suggests that there is often considerable uncertainty among employees concerning the organizational purpose of proposed training and how training content and objectives contribute to strategic organizational objectives (Hall, 1984). Firms often do not directly communicate to employees answers to their questions concerning the significance of training involvement. It seems reasonable that the more information regarding a training experience that can be provided in advance to trainees, the better. Recent evidence suggests that those trainees who received information about the training prior to their attendance reported more favorable reactions and greater intentions to transfer learning than did those receiving little information (Baldwin & Magjuka, 1991). However, time and resources in an organization are scarce, and little is known about the type and depth of information that is best suited to enhancing training outcomes.

In a study of computer skills training, Martocchio (1992) found that labeling the training context as an *opportunity* resulted in lower computer anxiety and higher learning than in a neutral context. Those in the opportunity training context also reported higher computer efficacy beliefs. Training classes were labeled as *opportunities* via wording in the introduction to trainees, which focused on aspects of their personal gain, positive experience for others, and control over their work environment. Neutral introductions were neutral with respect to threat and opportunity.

Findings from the Martocchio (1992) study are consistent with the power of labeling documented by Dov Eden and others in their work on the Pygmalion effect (Eden, 1984; Eden & Ravid, 1982; Eden & Shani, 1982). Results show that information conveying high expectations to both trainer and trainee can lead to the development of stronger efficacy and outcome expectations and to higher training achievement.

Considerable research has examined realistic job previews and expectations, and has concluded that met expectations are associated with higher satisfaction and lower withdrawal behaviors (Premack & Wanous, 1985). The whole domain of expectations about training has to be explored more fully. Some organizations sell their training programs as a major inducement to join the firm, creating high expectations of those programs. Unmet expectations may have strong negative consequences on performance in training and even tenure in the organization.

Emerging evidence suggests that the labels attached to both training content and to trainees themselves can have a powerful impact on training effectiveness. Information and labels have the power to detract from as well as enhance training outcomes (Langer, 1979). Given the relative ease and cost-effectiveness of labeling strategies, training researchers and professionals must learn more about the ways in which training information can be effectively labeled and managed to facilitate trainee motivation and learning.

Research Implications

The manner in which training is introduced in an organization has the potential to influence trainee motivation and ultimately the effectiveness of the initiative. Pretraining introduction contains many cues about training; some are conveyed by managers, but others are conveyed by peers or reflected in organizational policies or practices. Although it seems clear that the introduction of training can be either a facilitator or inhibitor of subsequent training effectiveness, much more research is needed to flesh out the nature of relationships and important contingencies.

One general notion that guides several of our propositions is that there are significant differences among employee groups in interpreting elements of training episodes. Employees who encounter similar socialization experiences will develop a shared view—a group norm on how episodes are defined and evaluated. Job function, work experience, and organizational level exert a strong socializing force on employees. As one example, employees on the shop floor might find it difficult to ever accept the proposition that any important organizational activity is voluntary. At the same time, senior executives may find it equally difficult to accept that any training activity is ever really mandatory and could not be superseded by other more crucial organizational responsibilities.

The influence of organizational level and job function extends beyond membership in a particular firm. It is predicted that group norms reflect a mixture of beliefs that are unique and tied to a particular firm, and beliefs that are universal and shared by members of a job function or organizational level across many different firms. From a research standpoint, training investigators need to more fully sample contexts as well as subjects. Research needs to expand to sample different types of trainees, different training groups, and different types of training climates to get a better understanding of how training introduction interacts with organizational roles and culture to influence individual attitudes and learning.

In an effort to stimulate a more focused future research agenda, a set of research propositions related to the way in which training is introduced in the organization is presented. The propositions reflect the notion that the objective features of a particular introduction are subordinate in importance to trainee perceptions of those factors. The propositions also highlight the differences among different levels and functions in the firm.

Proposition 1: Program status, pretraining participation, and goals will be interpreted differently by employees with different job functions and at different organizational levels.

Proposition 2: Outcome expectations associated with mandatory training will be affected by employees' overall view of effectiveness of the previous training in the firm.

Proposition 3: For most organizational training, training perceived as mandatory will be associated with as high or higher levels of trainee motivation than will voluntary status because:

Proposition 3a: Employees will expect that required membership status leads to a higher probability of success in attaining the objectives of any intervention.

Proposition 3b: Required membership status communicates a message to employees that the firm is committed to the future success of the training initiative.

Proposition 3c: The alternative, voluntary attendance does not signify importance in most organizations. That is, employees will reason: "Everything that is important and valued in our firm is required and everything that is unimportant or peripheral tends to be voluntary."

Proposition 4:   Trainee participation in the pretraining period will not, per se, yield higher trainee motivation. The motivational influence of participation will be contingent on the outcomes of that participation and the informational gain from participation.

Proposition 5:   The effects of goals on trainee efficacy and outcome expectations will be affected by the source of the goal.

Proposition 5a: Training goals set by management will be more influential than those set by training designers or instructors.

Proposition 6:   The effects of goals on trainee efficacy and outcome expectations will be affected by the type of goal.

Proposition 6a: Learning goals will produce different expectations than performance goals.

Proposition 7:   Trainee efficacy and outcome expectations will be affected by the type of information and labels associated with a training initiative.

Proposition 7a: Training perceived as opportunity will induce higher efficacy and expectations.

TRAINING COHORT

Although individual on-the-job instruction was once the norm, much organizational training now takes place in formal training contexts and in a social setting of peers and others. Given that people are often trained in groups, the impact of the group's composition and norms on trainee perceptions and learning may be considerable. Although the literature on group dynamics, peer effects, and social influences on performance is rich, application of this literature to training has been sparse. Trainees take careful note of who else attends their training, and the nature of the working relationship with the training cohort (Are we expected and/or rewarded for working together? Is it really a competitive exercise?, etc.); their perception of these factors will influence motivation and learning.

Group Composition

Although few training observers would disagree that the composition of the training cohort can influence trainee perceptions, little research has been conducted on the effects of the composition of training groups. Feldman (1989) suggested that key group composition factors that can positively influence individual attitudes and learning include homogeneity of skill levels at entry, small size, and a high degree of interaction among trainees.

The limited empirical evidence supports the notion that trainees should be comparable in aptitude and skill prior to entering a program (Langer, 1979). One problem associated with training individuals of dissimilar aptitudes is that the training ends up being provided at the lowest common denominator—training from which everyone, regardless of aptitude, job level, or specific assignment, can learn (Feldman, 1989). Such generic training often provides neither enough useful information nor enough feedback and sense of accomplishment to make the training effective (St. John, 1980). Moreover, Langer (1979) found that the mere presence of a highly placed or skilled person can potentially undermine the effective use of routine skills among those lower in the organization or less skilled.

However, in today's business reality, a strong argument can be made in favor of seeking a heterogeneous training cohort. Pairing employees with their counterparts from different organizational units as well as customers, subordinates, vendors, and representatives from other organizational levels can provide an opportunity for idea exchange and facilitate cross-level understanding (Latham & Crandall, 1991).

From an organizational perspective, the question of appropriate group composition is highly contingent on program objectives. For some programs (fast-track management development), the organization would probably hope to attract a homogeneous group of the most motivated and capable employees—the best and the brightest. In other instances, the most desirable group might be a cross-section of employees who vary in their background and knowledge of a particular subject matter. Fostering creative and innovative behavior may be one training objective where diverse training cohorts make sense. In some cases, it may even be that organizations would want a homogeneous group of the least skilled employees to participate on the premise that they have the most to gain from the program in question.

A central premise of this analysis is that employees may not interpret the objectives of composition decisions in a manner consistent with management. For example, Van Maanen (1978) suggested that differences in the extent to which newcomers are separated from veterans and high-potential candidates are trained separately from others will impact the attitudes, beliefs, and performance of employees.

With respect to the size of a training cohort, Penner and Craiger (1992) pointed out that, under most circumstances, as group size increases, individual learning performance declines. This decline is generally due to a decline in motivation attributed to evaluation effects (Harkins & Szymanski, 1989). Harkins and Szymanski proposed that the potential for evaluation of a person's performance influences how motivated he or she is to perform well. Group size is one crucial factor that will influence subjective estimates of the likelihood of such an evaluation occurring. As group size increases, individual members believe that the probability that their individual performance can be identified and evaluated decreases.

Clearly, the selection of "whom and how many to train together" is an important pretraining decision that will have potentially profound effects on trainee attitudes and learning. Although the existing evidence suggests that small, homogeneous groups are preferred, rigorous scientific investigation of group composition in training is in its infancy. We need to learn much more about the conditions under which homogeneity, heterogeneity, and size lead to positive trainee attitudes and outcomes. Composition may also be a crucial influence on the formation of cooperative group norms.

Cooperative Group Norms

Most instructors argue for the value of learning from each other and helping one another learn. Recent evidence, although not from industrial contexts, generally supports the value of cooperative learning for enhancing training performance (Latham & Crandall, 1991). In a meta-analytic review, Johnson, Maruyama, Johnson, Nelson, and Skon (1981) concluded that cooperation is better for productivity than is competition or individualization for all but rote-decoding tasks. In a comprehensive review of 46 studies conducted in school settings, Slavin (1983) reported that 63% showed cooperative learning methods to have significantly positive effects on student achievement, 33% showed no differences, and 4% found higher achievement for individual methods. Lookatch (1989) similarly concluded that cooperative learning is viewed positively by trainees and promotes greater rapport, discussion, and enjoyment of the learning process.

The favorable results should not be interpreted to mean that just bringing trainees together will yield fruitful cooperative learning. As Slavin (1983) noted, learning is a completely individual outcome that may or may not be improved by cooperation. Promoting productive cooperative learning requires attention to the composition of the group (discussed earlier) and the creation of a strong group norm of shared responsibility and individual accountability.

The key element in cooperative learning regards the development of group norms. Trainees may be in a position to cooperate and believe that they are capable of cooperating, but may choose not to do so because they believe it will have little or no effect on their personal outcomes. Mullen and Baumeister (1987) used the term *diving* to describe a situation in which, because of group norms, an individual is motivated to perform at less than his or her best. One form of diving proposed by Mullen and Baumeister can result from a group norm that discourages excellence in performance by any group member. This is essentially the rate-busting effect discussed by Roethlisberger & Dickson (1939). The other kind of diving occurs when the group determines that excellence in performance is inappropriate for a particular individual. For example, high-status members of a team may communicate the message to other members that excellence in performance from a low-status member is not appropriate. As a result, the low-status member does not attempt to do his or her best.

An important element in creating cooperative norms is the nature of rewards. Slavin (1983) suggested that the mere presence of rewards will not enhance learning. Rather, the rewards must be consistent with the learning structure. To maximize the effects on learning, individual learning structures should be accompanied by individual or competitive rewards, and cooperative learning structures should be accompanied by group rewards. As Slavin noted, the provision of rewards based on group performance creates group member norms supporting performance. If group success depends on the learning performance of all group members, group members can be expected to try to make the group successful by encouraging each other to excel.

The basis for group rewards could take a number of forms, including the selection of the lowest member score (weakest link) or an average of all group member scores. Although rewards given to groups are likely to be less finely tuned to individual performance than rewards given to individuals, group members are hypothesized to create a sensitive and effective reward system for each other when the efforts of all group members are required for group success. In traditional learning groups, members are seldom held responsible for each other's learning. If cooperative learning is to lead to better training outcomes, it is clear that the reward structure must encourage cooperation.

One of the most compelling arguments in favor of cooperative learning is the potential for high performers to raise the level of learning of low performers (Johnson & Johnson, 1984). Findings suggest that a trainee who has the substantive support of other trainees will have higher self-efficacy and superior coping mechanisms than would be the case without such support (Johnson & Johnson, 1984). In organizational settings, where interdependence is high, the success of the group can often be a function of the "weakest link"; in such cases, it is obviously crucial to facilitate the learning of all members.

Even within a group reward context there still must be a level of individual accountability. For example, although the existence of a social facilitation effect has been well documented for many years (Cottrell, 1972), there is also evidence that, under some conditions, social interaction can be detrimental to motivation and performance. In a study of training designed to help people interpret a financial report, Saxe (1988) found that it was moderate levels of interaction that led to significantly higher performance on a written achievement test, as opposed to either low interaction or high interaction. This suggests that an excess of interaction may produce a form of "social loafing" or "free rider" effect, whereby a person believes that because he or she is one of several people working on a task, he or she can do relatively little but still reap the benefits of the group's performance (Kerr & Bruun, 1981; Latane, Williams, & Harkins, 1979). In the Saxe study, it may have been that the high-level interaction subjects focused on pooling answers, rather than concentrating on ensuring that all team members understood the material (Latham & Crandall, 1991).

For cooperative learning to be successful, it must involve individual accountability. It may well be that working in a group under certain circumstances does increase the learning of all individuals in that group more than would working in other arrangements. But a measure of group productivity provides no evidence of that one way or the other. Only individual learning assessments can indicate which learning method is superior. For example, if a group produces an excellent project report, but only a few members really contributed to it, it is unlikely that the individuals in that group learned more than they might have if they had to produce their own individual outcome. Therefore, although it seems entirely appropriate to link training initiatives with business outcomes and team projects, it is important to keep in mind that all learning is ultimately an individual phenomenon, and accountability at the individual level is still key.

Research Implications

Like training practice, traditional training research has had a decidedly individual focus. Training professionals have implicitly viewed the instructor–student and student–materials interactions as the two most important foci of training investigations (Johnson & Johnson, 1984). By contrast, the peer interaction and group dynamics that take place have often been viewed as either irrelevant or, at best, a convenient opportunity for networking or coincidental byproduct of a training initiative.

Recent authors have contended that the focus on individualistic learning environments is unfortunate given the potential of cooperative learning to enhance training enjoyment and outcomes. Although the evidence is not unequivocal, studies over the years have consistently shown that cooperative learning can produce more favorable trainee reactions, increased learning, creative insight, and quality of decision making (Johnson & Johnson, 1984). However, the best results for cooperative learning have emerged from relatively small and homogeneous learning cohorts, with group rewards that support shared responsibility—conditions that have not characterized much training activity in the past. Given potential differences in the propensity to work successfully in group situations, it may also be that those who choose to work cooperatively will achieve the most positive outcomes.

Although the potential research avenues in this area are exciting, little empirical work has been done on the impact of group dynamics in industrial training applications. Most of what was discussed previously is derived from educational and social psychology experiments. Much more work in industrial training contexts is needed to build an understanding of group composition and cooperative learning effects. The industrial training literature would benefit significantly from empirical evidence related to the conditions under which particular group structures, norms and rewards influence trainee motivation and learning. Several research propositions designed to focus future research efforts are presented below.

Proposition 1:   Trainee self-efficacy and outcome expectations will be influenced by the size and homogeneity of the group cohort.

Proposition 1a: Homogeneity in group composition will lead to higher degrees of trainee satisfaction with the training process. Trainee motivation and learning will be contingent on program objectives.

Proposition 2:   Trainees in cooperative learning contexts will report more positive reaction to the learning process and higher motivation to learn than those in individual learning conditions.

Proposition 3:   Trainees in cooperative learning contexts will have higher learning performance than those in individual learning contexts only when group rewards and individual accountability are present.

Proposition 4:   Cooperative learning contexts with group rewards will enhance the learning of the lowest performing group members.

Proposition 5:   The positive effects of cooperative learning settings will be maximized when trainees are given the choice to work cooperatively.

TRANSFER CLIMATE

Although much of the preceding discussion focused on trainee cognitions and learning outcomes, it is the transfer of training that is of paramount concern for training researchers and practitioners (Baldwin & Ford, 1988). Perhaps generally thought of as a posttraining issue, it is suggested here that the outcome expectancies associated with transfer of training are significantly influenced by pretraining contextual cues (Broad & Newstrom, 1992). It is trainees' perceptions of the transfer climate that are important (Does my manager see the value in this training? Will I be able to use it?), and pretraining conditions have obvious potential to influence such perceptions. It is suspected that much of the transfer climate is communicated to trainees prior to any instruction. This section discusses the two broad dimensions of transfer climate: (a) management support, and (b) organizational support.

Management Support

Ubiquitous in discussions of successful organizational interventions is the notion of *management support* (Van Maanen & Schein, 1979). Few would argue that, for training to be maximally effective, supervisors need to express their commitment to training as well as commit their time and resources. In a study across five organizations, Cohen (1990) found that trainees with more supportive supervisors entered training with stronger beliefs that training would be useful. Baldwin and Magjuka (1991) found that trainees who entered training expecting some type of supervisory follow-up reported stronger intentions to transfer what was learned to the job. Although it is clear that the supervisor plays a critical role in facilitating the transfer of training, less clear are the specific processes by which supervisors can promote motivation and learning, particularly in the pretraining context.

In a survey of 98 full-time working master of business administration (MBA) students, Baldwin and Magjuka (1991) found that organizational employees may make a distinction between management "permission" and more meaningful management support. Management often spends money and takes people's time, but that does not really constitute support. If managers devoted their own time to kick off the program, attended sessions (perhaps even agreed to lead some sessions), and committed to follow-up with participants, then the survey respondents felt the training was being truly supported.

A well-established tenet of organizational behavior is that performance is a function of ability, motivation, and the opportunity to perform (Dunnette, 1972). One element of management support that has received recent attention involves providing the opportunity for skill application (Ford, Quiñones, Sego, & Sorra, 1992). In a study of Air Force technical training, Ford et al. (1992) found support for the proposition that a trainee's supervisor provides more or fewer opportunities to perform trained tasks based on his or her perceptions or attitudes toward the trainee. Here again, the power of expectations is much like that found in work on the Pygmalion effect noted earlier (Eden, 1984). The Ford et al. (1992) study also demonstrated the reciprocal effect posited in our framework—that self-efficacy both affected and was affected by opportunity. Individuals high in self-efficacy were more likely to actively seek the opportunity to perform the tasks they were trained for, and to perform the more complex and difficult tasks.

A form of management support closely related to providing opportunity is the removal of situational constraints. Building on the work of Peters, O'Connor, and Eulberg (1985), Latham and Crandall (1991) noted that there are at least eight constraints that can hinder the transfer of training to the job setting: (a) the lack of job-related information, (b) tools and equipment, (c) materials and supplies, (d) required services and help from others, (e) time availability, (f) physical aspects of the work environment, (g) job-relevant authority, and (h) budgetary support.

Situational constraints can obviously have a negative impact on the transfer of trained skills. To the extent that a manager can minimize constraints, trainee outcome expectations should be positively affected. Continuation of the work on opportunity and situational constraints would be fruitful in helping clarify and prioritize specific manifestations of what has been an ambiguous construct labeled *management support*.

Organizational Support

Organizational support factors are those variables that may affect trainee outcome expectations, but are primarily determined by persons or events external to the immediate supervisor or job role (Latham & Crandall, 1991). Among the most critical organizational support factors are promotion/reward systems and peer influence.

Several writers recently emphasized the importance of training activity that is aligned with the strategy of the firm (Jackson, Schuler, & Rivero, 1989; Latham, 1988). Others have argued that major disincentives to trainee motivation (negative outcome expectations) are a lack of supportive organizational reward systems, such as pay for performance, promotion from within, skill-based pay, and rewards for managers who encourage employee development (Hall, 1984; Salinger, 1973).

Although the importance of congruent and supportive organizational systems seems self-evident, there is substantial evidence that it is not being applied in the training context (Latham & Crandall, 1991; Robinson & Robinson, 1989). Furthermore, empirical research linking management and organizational support is still in its infancy, and would benefit from concerted descriptive and construct definition work.

After 20 years of perennial lamenting in the training literature, it is still the case that little posttraining evaluation occurs. Saari, Johnson, McLaughlin, and Zimmerle (1988) summarized results from a large-scale survey of management development in 611 organizations, and concluded that few conduct any evaluation at all. The lack of accountability and rigorous evaluation may be attributable, in part, to a lingering bias that training is a delicate flower that cannot be "forced" or even aggressively managed in the way of other types of performance. For example, although forms of goal setting, incentive compensation, and "pay at risk" are now common in other areas of organizational life, there has been a curious reluctance to implement such strategies in conjunction with training and development.

Aside from providing no evidence to facilitate program improvement and redesign, the typical absence of specific objectives and measurement may be perceived by trainees as a signal of the low importance of training to the organization. Organizations today generally pronounce that training is vital to their mission and future, and there is no question that development expenditures have risen dramatically. But given that research has shown that neither management pronouncements nor resources expended are among the most salient signals of the organizational importance of training and development, it seems plausible that trainees often have not perceived that their learning and development were as important as the pronouncements would suggest (Baldwin & Magjuka, 1991).

With respect to outcome expectancies, it is suspected that trainees often perceive that they share no real responsibility for learning and will face no posttraining evaluation regarding the application of their skills. The result is a decline in motivation and a low yield from development initiatives. To reiterate a point made earlier, training success will be maximized when trainees perceive that desirable outcomes (or avoidance of undesirable outcomes) are attained as a result of completing a program satisfactorily and having their intellect, beliefs, and emotions engaged. There must also be some risk of failure. This is of particular concern in cooperative learning contexts, where trainees are in a position to cooperate, but may choose not to do so because they see no personal benefit or risk.

Finally, one exciting stream of research is that initiated by Rouiller and Goldstein (1993). These authors identified a set of supervisory and organizational characteristics they termed *transfer climate*. They classified the terms into situational cues and consequences, based on an organizational behavior model proposed by Luthans and Kreitner (1985). Surveys were developed that individually measured the transfer climate of each of 102 fast-food franchise locations. The trainees were assistant managers who completed a 9-week training program and then were randomly assigned to 1 of the 102 organizational units. Results indicate that trainees assigned to units that had a more positive transfer climate demonstrated more trained behavior on the job (Rouillier & Goldstein, 1993).

Unlike most prior research, Rouiller and Goldstein (1993) have begun to achieve a new level of operational specificity. Ultimately, it will be instrumental to providing prescriptive information to training professionals concerned with creating "training-friendly" environments that will maximize returns on training dollars.

Research Implications

An episodic perspective emphasizes that employees will be very cognizant of factors in the organizational climate that relate to transferring learned skills to the job. Prior to participating in any training experience, participants implicitly (in recent years, more explicitly) ask questions such as: (a) Is this training relevant to job performance and/or career progression? (b) Is this a job priority for me right now? (c) What do others who have attended report about the training? (d) Is my job secure? (e) What will enhance or block my use of learned skills? and (f) Are there punishments for not embracing the training? Positive training outcomes will be enhanced to the extent that the answers to those questions are clear and explicit.

For example, a trainee could be scheduled to attend a total quality management (TQM) training module and already have a well-formed set of expectancies about: (a) the current and future value of TQM to the firm, (b) the potential benefit of TQM in the trainee's work area, and (c) the scuttlebutt provided by those who have already completed the TQM training. There is no reason to anticipate a tidy separation of training and organizational experience. If an organizational initiative is a disaster, one can expect that a negative self-fulfilling cycle is established before trainees attend a session.

Put another way, trainees, like all human beings, are expected to jumble things up when interpreting their surroundings. In the traditional "positivist" research paradigm, any information concerning the reports on the training from prior participants would be treated as a variable exogenous to experimental design. Failure to control for this information would represent a contamination of the design, biasing the results obtained and clouding the interpretation of data. Our view is that the influence of social cognitions held by present and future trainees cannot be controlled when assessing the effect of training in practice, except in the rare situation when employees have no prior experience with the training content or training outcomes, and have no opportunity to examine the anticipated effects of training in the workplace. Although the research literature on transfer climate is in its infancy, the following propositions are offered based on our experience and the limited empirical evidence.

> Proposition 1: Transfer climate favorability will vary within and across organizations, and will be related to trainee self-efficacy and outcome expectations.
>
> Proposition 2: Explicit supervisor expectations and presence in the training process will positively influence trainee motivation.
>
> Proposition 3: Peer reports of training will significantly influence trainee self-efficacy and outcome expectations.

Proposition 4:   Explicit linkages of training performance to any meaningful
                 organizational reward (e.g., performance evaluation, pay,
                 career development) will positively influence trainee
                 motivation.

Proposition 4a: Linking managerial rewards to training outcomes
                  (learning) of subordinates will positively influ-
                  ence trainee motivation.

Proposition 5:   Pronouncements of training importance will have far
                 less influence on outcome expectations than behavioral
                 supervisor support.

Proposition 6:   Perceptions of situational constraints will negatively
                 influence trainee motivation.

CONCLUSION

Most research on training in industry has taken an "all things equal" perspective, which suggests that employees enter training under roughly the same
conditions. This chapter argued that trainees experience individual episodes,
and how they make sense of episodes will differ. This is true even among those
from the same organizational unit entering the same training experience.
Organizational contextual factors can easily overwhelm the effects of the best
planned and delivered training. A favorable context can enhance even subop-
timal training interventions. It is suspected that much prior training research
would be subject to reinterpretation if contextual factors and trainee perceptions had been measured and reported.

The lesson for researchers is that it is time to explicitly address the social
environment and organizational context of training activities. This does not
mean abandoning the core of training research. Rather, it means more careful
attention to variables that have been ignored or controlled. Rather than
generating additional ways to exclude these questions from study, training
research needs to explicitly explore how these context factors interact with
training design elements to help or hinder individual learning. The accumulated
experience in an organization concerning these design elements provides the
context within which training design practices are interpreted and given
meaning (Boobar, 1971). Each will be tagged or labeled by organizational
members as an effective or ineffective practice. As this chapter suggested, it is
incumbent on training researchers to gather more information from the perspective of the trainee, lest the results of training initiatives be misinterpreted.
Unfortunately, studying many of the contextual influences on trainee motivation may not be readily amenable to traditional experimental research.

In terms of data gathering, most organizations rely solely on reaction forms
to evaluate their training programs, yet such forms do not ask trainees anything
about contextual issues. Therefore, organizations that use standard reaction

measures to revise their training may make fruitless improvements to a training program if the actual source of discontent lies outside the instructional period context. Expanding the domain of evaluation information to include contextual information is an important direction—and one Rouiller and Goldstein (1993) have pioneered.

With respect to future research designs, the training literature would benefit enormously from more qualitative data, such as observations, open-ended interviews, and even participant observation (Conger, 1992). Qualitative research would be useful in discovering how informal networks form and modify, and reinforce or counteract the influence of different training elements. A useful general strategy is to move the focus away from microinstructional design issues and toward consideration of the larger context within which training programs reside.

On the practical side, although it is recognized that the meaning of an episode emerges through the interplay between initiator and respondent, this does not imply that the initiator cannot increase his or her ability to control that interpretation (Zurcher, 1979). A primary objective for a training administrator is to intentionally shape and control training design to affect trainee motivation and performance. The interrelationships among different factors are not well defined or easily observable. Therefore, the challenge for practitioners and researchers alike is to search for those factors that combine to increase training effectiveness. Keys to this search are the criteria of robustness, parsimony, and designability.

A robust design yields the highest level of predictable outcomes reliably and over time. In today's training contexts, cooperative learning characterized by group rewards and individual accountability has the potential to become a robust design element. A parsimonious design includes the fewest design elements. For example, if goal setting is shown to overwhelm other motivational influences in training designs, then simply using goal setting to induce motivation would be the most parsimonious strategy. Designability refers to the ease with which a training administrator can adopt recommendations for training design within existing budgetary and time constraints. It appears that certain labeling strategies may be exceptionally high in designability. A significant change in company reward or evaluation systems would be a less designable change.

Given the continuing challenge to realize greater gains from organizational training initiatives, further understanding of how one may best "prime" participants entering training programs (i.e., in a way that enhances their subsequent learning and transfer) is important for researchers and professional trainers alike (Campbell, 1989). Although the amount of variance potentially explained by contextual variables is yet undetermined, it is important to recall that effects do not need to be large in an absolute sense to produce meaningful economic consequences (Zedeck & Cascio, 1984).

The guiding premise here is that future training research can no longer focus narrowly on what occurs during a training session. It is more likely that the greatest contributions to increased trainee motivation and performance will be generated by effectively designing either the pretraining or posttraining stages of the training process. The view of training design adopted in this chapter is more closely aligned to the perspective on design incorporated in the literature on organizational development (Huse & Cummings, 1985). That is, design is systemic and intentional, and implemented to attain strategic organizational objectives while relying heavily on the perceptions, needs, and motives of employees to reach those objectives.

REFERENCES

Anderson, R. C. (1959). Learning in discussions: A review of the authoritarian-democratic studies. *Harvard Education Review, 29,* 201–215.

Baldwin, T. T., & Ford, J. K. (1988). Transfer of training: A review and directions for future research. *Personnel Psychology, 41,* 63–105.

Baldwin, T. T., & Magjuka, R. J. (1991). Organizational training and signals of importance: Linking pretraining perceptions to intentions to transfer. *Human Resource Development Quarterly, 2,* 25–36.

Baldwin, T. T., Magjuka, R. J., & Fulford, M. (1990, August). *Who volunteers? Testing the congruence of stated organizational objectives and volunteer group composition in two settings.* Paper presented at the annual meetings of the National Academy of Management, San Francisco, CA.

Baldwin, T. T., Magjuka, R. J., & Loher, B. T. (1991). The perils of participation: Effects of trainee choice on motivation and learning. *Personnel Psychology, 44,* 51–66.

Baldwin, T. T., Magjuka, R. J., & Loher, B. T. (1992, August). *Contextual influences on training effectiveness: An empirical analysis.* Paper presented at the annual meetings of the National Academy of Management, Las Vegas, NV.

Bandura, A. (1986). *Social foundations of thought and action.* Englewood Cliffs, NJ: Prentice-Hall.

Barling, J., & Beattie, R. (1983). Self-efficacy beliefs and sales performance. *Journal of Organizational Behavior Management, 5,* 41–51.

Boobar, R. (1971). Meaning, rules, and behavior. *Mind, 80,* 29–40.

Broad, M., & Newstrom, J. W. (1992). *Transfer of training: Action packed strategies to ensure high payoff from training investments.* Reading, MA: Addison-Wesley.

Campbell, J. P. (1989). The agenda for training theory and research. In, I. L. Goldstein (Ed.), *Training & development in organizations* (pp. 469-486). San Francisco: Jossey-Bass.

Cohen, D. J. (1990). What motivates trainees. *Training & Development Journal, 36,* 91–93.

Conger, J. A., (1992). *Learning to lead.* San Francisco: Jossey-Bass.

Cottrell, N. B. (1972). Social facilitation. In C. G. McGlintock (Ed.), *Experimental social psychology* (pp. 185–236). New York: Holt, Rhinehart & Winston.

Dewar, D. L. (1984). *Quality circles.* Red Bluff, CA: Quality Circle Institute.

Dixon, N. M. (1993). Developing managers for the learning organization. *Human Resource Management Review, 3,* 243–254.

Dunnette, M. D. (1972). *Performance equals ability and what?* (Tech. Rep. 4009, ONR Contract #N00014-68-A-0141). Minneapolis: University of Minnesota, Center for the Study of Organizational Performance and Human Effectiveness.

Eden, D. (1984). Self-fulfilling prophecy as a management tool: Harnessing pygmalion. *Academy of Management Journal, 9,* 64–73.

Eden, D., & Ravid, G. (1982). Pygmalion vs. self-expectancy: Effects of instructor and self-expectancy on trainee performance. *Organizational Behavior and Human Performance, 30*, 351–364.

Eden, D., & Shani, A. B. (1982). Pygmalion goes to boot camp: Expectancy, leadership, and trainee performance. *Journal of Applied Psychology, 67*, 194–199.

Elliott, E. S., & Dweck, C. S. (1988). Goals: An approach to motivation and achievement. *Journal of Personality and Social Psychology, 54*, 5–12.

Feldman, D. C. (1989). Socialization, resocialization and training: Reframing the research agenda. In I. L. Goldstein (Ed.), *Training & development in organizations* (pp. 376–416). San Francisco: Jossey-Bass.

Ford, J. K., Quiñones, M. A., Sego, D. J., & Sorra, J. S. (1992). Factors affecting the opportunity to perform trained tasks on the job. *Personnel Psychology, 45*, 511–527.

Frayne, C. A., & Latham, G. P. (1987). Application of social learning theory to employee self-management of attendance. *Journal of Applied Psychology, 72*, 387–392.

Gist, M. E., Schwoerer, C., & Rosen, B. (1989). Effects of alternative training methods on self-efficacy and performance in computer software training. *Journal of Applied Psychology, 74*, 884–891.

Gist, M., Stevens, C. K., & Bavetta, A. G. (1990). Transfer training method: Its influence on skill generalization, skill repetition and performance level. *Personnel Psychology, 43*, 501–523.

Goldstein, I. L. (1992). *Training in organizations: Needs assessment, development, and evaluation* (3rd ed.). Monterey, CA: Brooks/Cole.

Hall, D. T. (1984). Human resource development and organizational effectiveness. In C. Fombrun, N. Tichy, & M. Devanna (Eds.), *Strategic human resource management* (pp. 159–181). New York: Wiley.

Harkins, S. G., & Szymanski, K. (1989). Social loafing and group evaluation. *Journal of Personality and Social Psychology, 56*, 934–941.

Hicks, W. D., & Klimoski, R. J. (1987). The process of entering training programs and its effect on training outcomes. *Academy of Management Journal, 30*, 542–552.

Huse, E. F., & Cummings, T. G. (1985). *Organization development and change.* St. Paul, MN: West.

Jackson, S. E., Schuler, R. S., & Rivero, J. C. (1989). Organizational characteristics as predictors of personnel practices. *Personnel Psychology, 42*, 727–785.

Johnson, D. W., & Johnson, R. (1984). *Cooperative learning.* New Brighton, MN: Interaction.

Johnson, D. W., Maruyama, G., Johnson, R., Nelson, D., & Skon, L. (1981). The effects of cooperative, competitive, and individualistic goal structures on achievement: A meta-analysis. *Psychological Bulletin, 89*, 47–62.

Kanfer, R., & Ackerman, P. (1989). Motivation and cognitive abilities: An integrative/aptitude-treatment interaction approach to skill acquisition. *Journal of Applied Psychology, 74*, 657–690.

Kanter, R. M. (1986). The new workforce meets the changing workplace: Strains, dilemmas, and contradictions in attempts to implement participative and entrepreneurial management. *Human Resource Management, 25*, 515–538.

Kerr, N., & Bruun, S. (1981). Ringelmann revisited: Alternative explanations for the social loafing effect. *Personality and Social Psychology Bulletin, 1*, 224–231.

Knowles, M. (1984). The adult learner: A neglected species. Houston, TX: Gulf.

Langer, E. J. (1979). The illusion of incompetence. In L. Perlmutter & R. Monty (Eds.), *Choice and perceived control* (pp. 301–313). Hillsdale, NJ: Lawrence Erlbaum Associates.

Latane, B., Williams, K., & Harkins, S. G. (1979). Many hands make light the work: The causes and consequences of social loafing. *Journal of Personality and Social Psychology, 37*, 823–832.

Latham, G. P. (1988). Human resource training and development. *Annual Review of Psychology, 39*, 545–582.

Latham, G. P., & Crandall, S. (1991). Organizational and social factors. In J. Morrison (Ed.), *Training for performance: Principles of applied human learning* (pp. 259–285). Chichester, England: Wiley.

Latham, G. P., & Frayne, C. A. (1989). Self-management training for increasing job attendance: A follow-up and a replication. *Journal of Applied Psychology, 74*, 411–416.

Latham, G. P., Winters, D. C., & Locke, E. A. (1992, August). *Cognitive vs. motivational effects of participation: A mediator study*. Paper presented at the annual meetings of the National Academy of Management, Las Vegas, NV.

Lawler, E. E. (1986). *High involvement management*. San Francisco: Jossey-Bass.

Lighthall, F. F. (1989). *Local realities, local adaptations*. Philadelphia, PA: Falmer.

Locke, E. A., & Latham, G. P. (1990). *A theory of goal setting and task performance*. Englewood Cliffs, NJ: Prentice-Hall.

Locke, E. A., & Schweiger, D. M. (1979). Participation in decision-making: One more look. In B. M. Staw (Ed.), Research in organizational behavior (Vol. 1, pp. 265–339). Greenwich, CT: JAI.

Lookatch, R. P. (1989). Options for interactive video. *Training and Development Journal, 35*, 65–67.

Luthans, F., & Kreitner, R. (1985). *Organizational behavior and beyond*. Glenview, IL: Scott, Foresman.

Martocchio, J. J. (1992). Microcomputer usage as an opportunity: The influence of context in employee training. *Personnel Psychology, 45*, 529–552.

Mathieu, J., Martineau, J., & Tannenbaum, S. (1993). Individual and situational influences on the development of self-efficacy: Implications for training effectiveness. *Personnel Psychology, 46*, 125–148.

Mathieu, J., Tannenbaum, S., & Salas, E. (1990, April). *A causal model of individual and situational influences on training effectiveness measures*. Paper presented at the 5th annual conference of the Society for Industrial and Organizational Psychology, Miami, FL.

Meyer, J. W., & Rowan, B. (1977). Institutional organizations: Formal structures as myth and ceremony. *American Journal of Sociology, 83*, 340–363.

Mohrman, S. A., & Ledford, G. E. (1985). The design and use of effective employee participation groups: Implications for human resource managers. *Human Resource Management, 24*, 413–428.

Mullen, B., & Baumeister, R. F. (1987). Group effects on self-attention and performance: Social loafing, social facilitation, and social impairment. In C. Hendrick (Ed.), *Review of personality and social psychology* (pp. 189–206). Beverly Hills, CA: Sage.

Newstrom, J. W., & Lilyquist, J. M. (1979). Selecting needs analysis methods. *Training & Development Journal, 33*, 52–56.

Noe, R. A. (1986). Trainees' attributes and attitudes: Neglected influences on training effectiveness. *Academy of Management Review, 11*, 736–749.

Penner, L. A., & Craiger, J. P. (1992). The weakest link: The performance of individual team members. In E. Salas & R. Swezey (Eds.), *Teams: Their training and performance* (pp. 57–73). Norwood, NJ: Ablex.

Peters, L. H., O'Connor, E. J., & Eulberg, J. R. (1985). Situational constraints: Sources, consequences, and future considerations. In K. Rowland & G. Ferris (Eds.), *Research in personnel and human resource management* (pp. 79–114). Greenwich, CT: JAI.

Pfeffer, J. (1981). Management as symbolic action: The creation and maintenance of organizational paradigms. In L. L. Cummings & B. M. Staw (Eds.), *Research in organizational behavior* (pp. 1–52). Greenwich, CT: JAI.

Premack, S. L., & Wanous, J. P. (1985). A meta-analysis of realistic job preview experiments. *Journal of Applied Psychology, 70*, 706–719.

Robinson, D. G., & Robinson, J. C. (1989). *Training for impact: How to link training to business needs and measure the results*. San Francisco: Jossey-Bass.

Roethlisberger, F. J., & Dickson, W. J. (1939). *Management and the worker*. Cambridge, MA: Harvard University Press.

Rouiller, J. Z., & Goldstein, I. L. (1993). The relationship between organizational transfer climate and positive transfer of training. *Human Resource Development Quarterly, 4*(4), 377–390.

Saari, L. M., Johnson, T. R., McLaughlin, S. D., & Zimmerle, D. M. (1988). A survey of management training and education practices in U.S. companies. *Personnel Psychology, 41*, 731–743.

Salinger, R. D. (1973). *Disincentives to effective employee training and development*. Bureau of Training: U.S. Civil Service Commission.

Sashkin, M. (1984). Participative management is an ethical imperative. *Organizational Dynamics*, 12, 5–22.

Saxe, S. (1988). Peer influence and learning. *Training and Development Journal*, 42, 40–53.

Slavin, R. (1983). When does cooperative learning increase student achievement? *Psychological Bulletin*, 94, 429–445.

St. John, W. D. (1980). The complete employee orientation program. *Personnel Journal*, 59, 373–378.

Sundstrom, E., DeMeuse, K. P., & Futrell, D. (1990). Work teams: Applications and effectiveness. *American Psychologist*, 45, 120–133.

Tannenbaum, S. I., Mathieu, J. E., Salas, E., & Cannon-Bowers, J. A. (1991). Meeting trainees' expectations: The influence of training fulfillment on the development of commitment, self-efficacy, and motivation. *Journal of Applied Psychology*, 76, 759–769.

Tannenbaum, S. I., & Yukl, G. (1992). Training and development in organizations. *Annual Review of Psychology*, 43, 399–441.

Van Maanen, J. (1978). People processing: Strategies of organizational socialization. *Organizational Dynamics*, 7, 18–36.

Van Maanen, J., & Schein, E. H. (1979). Toward a theory of organizational socialization. In B. M. Staw (Ed.), *Research in organizational behavior* (pp. 209–264). Greenwich, CT: JAI.

Wagner, J. A. III, & Gooding, R. Z. (1987). Shared influence and organizational behavior: A meta-analysis of situational factors expected to moderate participation-outcome relationships. *Academy of Management Journal*, 30, 524–541.

Wlodkowski, R. J. (1985). *Enhancing adult motivation to learn*. San Francisco: Jossey-Bass.

Zedeck, S., & Cascio, W. (1984). Psychological issues in personnel decisions. *Annual Review of Psychology*, 35, 461–518.

Zurcher, L. (1979). The influence of internalized vocabularies of motive. *Symbolic Interaction*, 2, 45–62.

6

Unstructured Training and Development: The Role of Organizational Socialization

Georgia T. Chao
Michigan State University

Unstructured training and development is generally described as informal on-the-job instruction when an experienced worker serves as a model and teacher to a new employee (Goldstein, 1993). Despite the ad hoc nature of this mode of instruction, informal training is generally recognized as the most popular training method in organizations, with estimates that it is three to six times more common than formal training (Carnevale & Gainer, 1989). Rothwell and Kazanas (1990) reported that informal, on-the-job training costs ranged between $90 and $180 billion a year for employers, versus a $30 billion cost for formal training. The widespread use of informal training necessitates scientific understanding of it and practical applications to improve its effectiveness.

Whereas the U.S. Department of Labor (1989) defines *structured work-based learning* as formal training programs at the job site, *unstructured training and development* is characterized by two distinctions. First, the unstructured component describes an unplanned training and development intervention that often has an ill-defined beginning and end. Without a formal beginning, it may be problematic for an individual to recognize unstructured training as a valuable learning experience. The trainer may not have the formal authority to convince the trainee that he or she should pay attention and learn from the trainer. Furthermore, an ambiguous end may make it difficult for trainer and trainee to identify when learning needs are met. For example, it may be difficult to identify at what point a senior employee mentors a junior person or when that special tutelage ends. Problems arise when one person perceives the mentor–protégé relationship to be strong while the other perceives it to be over.

129

A second distinction is that unstructured training and development inter-ventions are not designed, directed, or evaluated by the organization. Neither the human resources department nor direct-line supervisors formally assess specific needs for unstructured training. Consequently, control over these learning experiences is indirect at best, and little is known about their impact on organizational outcomes.

Although the prevalence of informal training is obvious, it has largely been neglected in organizational study and research (Wexley & Latham, 1991). Perhaps one explanation for the limited amount of empirical research on informal training is the wide variety of organizational experiences that qualify as examples of it. Unstructured training and development include many forms of on-the-job training, as well as a wealth of information that is absorbed by observation and interaction with others that may or may not be sanctioned by the organization. Together, these unstructured training and development expe-riences represent a powerful process by which an individual learns about the job, work unit, and organization. This learning process is generally termed *organizational socialization*. Although some socialization tactics are formalized programs in the organization, the impact of informal tactics is generally viewed as more powerful than formal tactics (Feldman, 1989), and they represent a primary means by which most employees learn about their jobs.

The relationship between informal organizational socialization and un-structured training, and its effect on learning and career development, comprise the focus of this chapter. A brief overview of organizational socialization is presented, followed by discussions of how it is related to training and development and to implicit and explicit learning modes. Next, a model describing the relationships among socialization, training, learning, and changes in organizational roles is presented to provide a theoretical framework for future research. The model is followed by descriptions of how change can be recognized by the individual and/or the organization, and possible consequences of different change scenarios. Finally, a specific form of organizational socialization—mentorship—is presented to illustrate the link between informal socialization and training and development.

OVERVIEW OF ORGANIZATIONAL SOCIALIZATION

Organizational socialization is often identified as the fundamental process by which an individual learns how to adjust to the performance demands of the job and the culture of the organization (Chao, 1988). This process encompasses the learning of organizational goals and values, job-specific duties and expected behaviors, and the social skills needed to establish positive and productive relationships with other organizational members. If the lessons are well learned and regarded as positive experiences, the individual "fits in," is likely to develop a successful career, and makes a positive contribution to the organization. Conversely, if these lessons are not mastered or are regarded as negative experiences, the individual fails to "fit in" and is likely to leave the organization (Louis, 1980).

Early research was process-oriented, identifying different phases of socialization. Typical stages of this process are: (a) anticipatory socialization—formed expectations prior to job entry; (b) the encounter stage—reality shock of organizational entry and adjustment to the new situation, and (c) the insider stage—completed socialization, acceptance as a full organizational member, and settling into the organizational role (Feldman, 1988). Socialization is a dynamic process that occurs throughout the individual's career (Hall, 1980; 1986). As people change jobs, organizations, and/or careers, a new cycle of the socialization process occurs, with new situations that require learning and additional adjustments.

Socialization is a naturally occurring phenomenon in organizations (Van Maanen & Schein, 1979). The extent to which it occurs is determined by interactions among organizational members. From the group or organizational perspective, several studies on newcomer socialization have documented organizational influences on a newcomer's values (Enoch, 1989; Lachman, 1988), attitudes (Allen & Meyer, 1990; Chao, O'Leary-Kelly, Wolf, Klein, & Gardner, 1994; Jones, 1986), performance (Berlew & Hall, 1966) and work expectations (Major, Kozlowski, Chao, & Gardner, 1995; Nicholson & Arnold, 1991). The extent to which a work unit is characterized by a particular climate will affect how proactive and persistent organizational members will socialize a newcomer. An organization with strong values and a distinct culture is more likely to have members who will informally train newcomers into well-defined roles. It should be noted here that socialization is a process that helps shape and maintain an organization's culture. The learning process is value-neutral, whereas culture may be assessed for their value to the organization. Organizations with strong countercultures could be just as effective as organizations with strong positive cultures in shaping newcomers within these cultural molds. An organization with unclear values and ill-defined roles may be more likely to have newcomers take a proactive role in their adjustment.

The socialization process is most evident at a point of change, such as entry to a new job or organization. Hence, most of the research is focused on job change (Chao et al., 1994; Nicholson, 1984; Nicholson & West, 1988). However, the socialization process does not end once the individual is no longer a newcomer and has gained insider status. Recognition of the continued learning and role-definition process for insiders fully extends the conceptualization of organizational socialization. Many factors prompt role changes for insiders. Levinson (1986) and Neugarten (1975) described personality changes that can occur as an adult develops over the life course. These changes may affect how the individual values different aspects of life or how he or she interacts with others. For example, nonwork life transitions may prompt an insider to redefine work role relationships with other life roles, or relationships with coworkers may significantly improve or deteriorate. External conditions, such as a poor economy, new technology, or new personnel, may also demand change to an insider's role. Because these changes are often not formally initiated or controlled by the organization, there are no formal mechanisms to assess the need or direction for change. These learning demands created by a need to change an organizational role are best met by informal socialization and development practices.

Recent research has examined specific content areas that are learned during the socialization process. Chao et al. (1994) identified six dimensions for socialization learning: performance proficiency, language, people, politics, organizational goals and values, and history. These content areas are generally within the realm of organizational influence. Other learning dimensions related to socialization include individual aspects that often lie outside an organization's authority. For example, Feldman's (1988) encounter stage includes learning behaviors that better manage conflicts between work and nonwork. Fisher (1986) identified personal change related to identity and self-image as an important content area for socialization. Thus, the lessons learned during the socialization process not only shape the individual's identity at work, but also his or her total identity and self-concept.

Recognizing the variability among socialization levels and evolving changes for resocialization can help one understand the constant need for employee development. If people are very different in how they regard their roles within the organization, new socialization may offer opportunities to redefine roles that are more consistent with organizational goals. Furthermore, improved socialization of insiders enables a newcomer to more easily recognize which insider would be an appropriate role model. Sutton and Louis (1987) noted that there are situations where the organization would benefit from newcomers resocializing insiders, as opposed to the more traditional case of insiders socializing newcomers. An insider who is low in organizational commitment or who is a mediocre performer may be rejuvenated in these areas as he or she takes responsibility in shaping the role of a newcomer. Organizational strategies to pair these insiders with the newcomer socialization process may be an effective method of insider socialization.

This overview of socialization identifies many parallels with the introduction on unstructured training and development. Informal socialization strategies and unstructured training are each believed to be more prevalent and more influential than their formal counterparts. Both share general goals in helping employees adapt to their jobs. Both rely heavily on an individual's colleagues and supervisors to provide the necessary instruction. Finally, both are characterized as dynamic relationships between individuals who provide or receive the informal lessons. Given these similarities, one can readily see how many informal instruction experiences could be described as unstructured training and informal socialization.

Perhaps the greatest distinction between informal socialization and unstructured training and development concerns the range of activities. Informal socialization encompasses many aspects of work adjustment that include work-related, personal, and social issues. In contrast, unstructured training and development is generally restricted to activities directly related to work performance.

The degree of overlap between informal socialization and unstructured training and development can be great, reducing the two concepts as labels for the same experiences. However, differences between informal socialization and highly structured, formal training programs are much greater. Although both may share goals of employee adjustment, differences between them are evident when informal socialization can be used to complement, substitute for, or hinder formal training and development.

ORGANIZATIONAL SOCIALIZATION AND ITS RELATIONSHIP TO FORMAL TRAINING AND DEVELOPMENT

Socialization as a Complement to Formal Training

The transfer of an off-site formal training program can be facilitated by a supplemental learning environment on the job. Socialization tactics can be used to reinforce the new knowledge, skills, and attitudes that were acquired in formal training programs. Lewin's (1951) three-step model for change illustrates how socialization can complement training goals before, during, and after the formal program's implementation. First, socialization can help people unfreeze current work roles and recognize a need for change. Learning why new knowledge, skills, or abilities is required for their jobs or careers would help motivate trainees to learn the material presented in a formal training program. Second, while formal training is conducted, interactions among trainees or between trainees and coworkers outside the training classroom can help individuals learn or clarify training material. If employees are socialized to help one another, this could counteract training deficiencies in the formal program. Third, after trainees are back on the job, socialization can help refreeze the newly trained material and maximize their positive transfer to the changed work roles.

Socialization as a Substitute for Formal Training

Organizational socialization often can be an effective substitute for formal training programs. An example of this situation was found in a former office of this author, when it was introducing word-processing microcomputers to the secretarial staff. A senior secretary with over 20 years of experience did not want a computer, was frustrated during the formal training program, and insisted that she was more effective with a typewriter than with the computer. A faculty member observed this and spent 30 minutes with the secretary, showing her how to compose a simple letter using the computer and identifying key pages in the word-processing manual. After that impromptu, unstructured training, the secretary was convinced that the computer could help her do her work, and thus sought additional coaching from the other secretaries.

In other cases, unstructured training can be a less costly alternative to formal programs. Thayer and McGehee (1977) described how one organization was faced with the task of teaching its foremen the details of the latest labor contract. Before designing a formal training program for this task, a pretest was developed to determine how much information the foremen already knew. As an inducement for taking the test, the foreman who scored the highest grade would be rewarded with a steak dinner. The winning foreman's manager would also be similarly rewarded. Managers worked informally with their foremen to prepare for the test under a climate of friendly competition. The results from the unstructured learning experiences showed all exams were perfect or nearly so. The company rewarded all these foremen and managers, and concluded that a formal program would not have been able to achieve the results obtained under the informal learning environment.

There are two main advantages to the unstructured socialization approach when compared with formal training programs. First, the relationship between the trainer and trainee is already established within the work unit. Ideally, this relationship familiarizes the trainer with the trainee's current knowledge, skills, and abilities, as well as style of learning. In addition, the trainee is also familiar with the trainer's expertise and teaching style. Together, both individuals are able to gauge how well they complement each other in a learning context and can select each other for the socialization process.

The second advantage is the individual attention to the trainee. The learning experience can be tailored to a particular trainee, making the training more efficient than a typical formal program, which may not account for individual differences. Furthermore, the individual attention to shape a trainee's behavior or role in the organization often exceeds organizational boundaries. Organizational members socialize one another in a variety of contexts. On-the-job socialization is frequently accompanied by learning in nonwork settings. Organizational members often interact with each other in social situations, and these environments may provide a more relaxed or candid climate for learning.

In contrast to the advantages offered by organizational socialization, the disadvantages of informal on-the-job learning include: lack of control for what actually gets learned, lack of uniform training across trainees, problems with incompetent trainers, and hidden costs of informal training. Costs are especially difficult to assess. The ambiguous beginnings and ends of informal training make it impossible to estimate how many hours are devoted to organizational socialization. It is often impossible to estimate the amount of work that suffers, is delayed, or is ignored when people are engaged in informal training.

Socialization as a Barrier to Formal Training

Baldwin and Ford (1988) identified the work environment as a key factor influencing how much training content is learned, retained, and transferred to the job. When employees have been socialized to mistrust management and change, they create a negative climate that can be a strong barrier to formal training. Surveys by Kotter (1988) and Newstrom (1986) identified specific aspects in the environment that inhibited successful training transfer. Kotter's survey with executives found a lack of top management support was most frequently cited as a barrier, whereas Newstrom found trainers most often cited a general lack of reinforcement for the trained material. Both barriers could be minimized if managers and employees were socialized to take a more proactive interest and involvement in how newly trained content would be positively transferred to the work setting.

Broad and Newstrom (1992) described a number of strategies that the manager, trainer, and trainee can perform to maximize positive transfer of training. Linking with a buddy, forming support groups, and finding a mentor are three examples of trainee strategies to maximize transfer. These examples overlap with socialization tactics, either in the trainee's work environment or in the training environment. Failure to engage in these tactics may lower the probability of successful training transfer. However, implicit in these strategies is the assumption that the buddy, support group, and mentor would support the application of trained material to the trainee's job performance. Undoubtedly, there are cases where trainees are discouraged by others from applying the trained material. Within a training program, informal groups may form and rebel against the training program. Likewise, a mentor's reservations about a training program may decrease a trainee's motivation to learn.

In summary, the socialization process shapes how an individual views his or her role in the organization. Individuals who are well socialized perceive a good fit between themselves and the organization. The fit is often not based on formal organizational structure and espoused values, but is based on personal relationships with others and the organization's applied values. A growing number of psychologists believe these relationships and values are learned through explicit and implicit learning modes.

IMPLICIT AND EXPLICIT LEARNING: THEIR RELATIONSHIPS WITH ORGANIZATIONAL SOCIALIZATION AND TRAINING

Recent research in cognitive psychology has focused on the theoretical development of implicit learning and its relationship with explicit learning (Reber, 1993). The more generally accepted models of explicit learning argue that learning is a conscious process based on attention to selected stimuli in the individual's environment. The assumption of conscious learning is inherent in traditional operant conditioning paradigms, as well as recent models of knowledge compilation (cf. Anderson, 1983).

In contrast, implicit learning theory posits that learning can occur nonconsciously. Reber (1993) defined *implicit learning* as; "the acquisition of knowledge that takes place largely independently of conscious attempts to learn and largely in the absence of explicit knowledge about what was acquired" (p. 5). Knowledge gained from implicit learning is generally unavailable to conscious awareness and is known as *tacit knowledge* (Polanyi, 1969; Reber, 1993). Although some researchers include a conscious component of tacit knowledge (Wagner & Sternberg, 1985), the nonconscious base of tacit knowledge is emphasized here to distinguish it from consciously acquired knowledge and attitudes. Implicit learning and tacit knowledge are important to organizational socialization because they recognize that individuals may not be aware of the entire socialization learning process. Furthermore, tacit knowledge can influence an individual's reactions to socialization attempts and, subsequently, leave the individual unable to articulate or justify these actions.

The laboratory research programs of Arthur Reber, Donald Broadbent, and Pawel Lewicki have produced substantial evidence for implicit learning. An example of this research is found in a series of laboratory studies by Hayes and Broadbent (1988). Subjects were required to interact with a computer and attempt to get it to respond in a specific manner. Twelve decisions arrayed in a continuum were available to the subject and computer. Two conditions were established to compare decision-making rules that may be easy or difficult for a subject to detect. For one group, the computer's response was partially based on the subject's latest response and partially on random effects. For the second group, the computer's response was based on similar random effects and on the subject's response that was previous to his or her last response. Comparable levels of performance were observed when the first group completed 30 trials and the second group completed 50 trials. Upon completion of the task, subjects were required to provide verbal protocols to assess their knowledge of their decision-making strategies. Subjects in the first group were able to articulate some relationship between their decisions and the computer responses. However, subjects in the second group were generally unable to identify this relationship and based their decisions on intuition. Variations of the task, measures, and instructions were conducted to strengthen the evidence that some learning is inaccessible to conscious evaluation and verbal communication.

Lewicki, Hill, and Czyzewska (1992) reviewed the empirical literature on implicit learning, and concluded that nonconscious information acquisition is much faster and more complex than consciously controlled learning. Implicit learning is not confined to the limited number of variables that a person can consciously attend to. Consequently, implicit learning may involve all variables exposed in a person's environment. Covariations among these variables are encoded into algorithms of learning. An example of implicit learning occurs when there is nonconscious processing of a relationship between specific personality and physical characteristics. Although the individual may consciously believe there is no relationship, the encoding algorithm can affect how the individual behaves with people who share certain physical attributes.

Research reviewed by Lewicki et al. (1992) demonstrated that highly complex covariations can be nonconsciously processed. This complexity may lead to early associations among certain stimuli that are not truly represented in a person's objective environment. Preexisting algorithms based on limited exposure may be used to help interpret ambiguous stimuli, leading to discrepancies between processed covariations and true covariations. Thus, groundless biases, inexplicable preferences, and irrational behaviors may be consequences of nonconscious learning.

In summary, research on implicit learning or nonconscious information acquisition has recently gained more prominence in cognitive psychology. Nonconscious controlled aspects of human cognition are believed to be more complex and faster than consciously controlled functions. Although the full impact of implicit learning remains unknown, researchers in this area have concluded that nonconscious information acquisition directly affects interpretive schema, emotional reactions, and behaviors traditionally linked with conscious thinking.

The factors associated with implicit learning, (i.e., unawareness that learning is occurring, potential input of a large number of stimuli in the person's environment, and interpretations of that environment) are also key characteristics of the socialization process. Informal socialization can provide powerful lessons without necessarily specifying the objectives or identifying experiences as lessons to the newcomer. In addition, the lessons learned during socialization encompass a wide variety of topics, including how to perform one's duties, who to seek help from, and what to believe. Interpretations of work experiences often involve sense-making processes, which constitute a key aspect of socialization (Louis, 1980). Thus, much of the knowledge gained from socialization experiences may occur at nonconscious levels of information processing.

A heuristic model is presented in Fig. 6.1 to illustrate how informal socialization and unstructured training and development may influence change efforts initiated by the organization or the individual. Boxes in boldface identify basic relationships among socialization, training, and learning. Boxes in regular typeface identify important constructs related to change.

Basic Relationships Among Training, Socialization, and Learning

The literature on training and development presumes explicit learning as the mode of instruction. Structured training programs define relevant stimuli in the trainee's environment based on training needs assessment and objectives. The

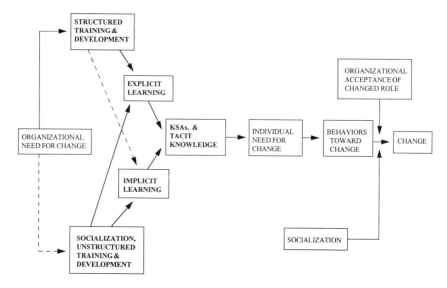

FIG. 6.1. Heuristic model for training and organizational socialization relationships with change (boldface = training and socialization links with learning process).

stimuli or training content is presented to trainees by instructional methods that would maximize most trainees' knowledge, skills, or abilities. These links are generally built into the design of structured training programs.

In addition to explicit learning of structured training, a weaker link between structured training/development programs and implicit learning is presented in the model. This relationship is based on research suggesting that the implicit learning mode functions as a default process (Reber, 1993). Nonconscious processing of information or development of implicit learning algorithms can occur regardless of whether an individual is consciously attending to relevant stimuli. These implicit lessons may be limited due to the relatively short duration of structured training and development programs. In addition, the environment of structured training often differs from the actual work environment, raising problems of transfer for tacit knowledge.

In contrast, unstructured training and development and informal socialization experiences generally occur on the job with colleagues and supervisors who are in constant contact with the individual. The knowledge gained from implicit learning of these unstructured experiences has more potential to be important lessons than those from off-the-job formal programs. Furthermore, training objectives from unstructured methods may be clearly communicated to trainees to guide their attention during explicit learning. Thus, implicit and explicit learning modes have strong links to unstructured training and informal socialization.

Change Within an Organizational Role

Generally, change in an individual's career may be initiated by the individual or by the organization. An individual's need for change can be based on conscious decisions about his or her lifestyle, family needs, career ambitions, qualifications, and so forth. In addition, the need for change can be based on nonconscious preferences for new directions or inexplicable dissatisfaction with current situations. These needs prompt behaviors that attempt change. Efforts toward change may be reinforced or discouraged by the organization's acceptance of the changed role and/or the prevailing work climate, which is shaped by socialization processes.

An organization's need for change may be initiated by a variety of causes, ranging from general conditions (new technology or global competition) to specific demands (new supervisor restructures work within one department). Formal change programs can be implemented, and employees can learn about the proposed changes through explicit learning mechanisms. Formal change programs can also be reinterpreted to fit historical trends or organizational values, and different lessons are learned through unstructured, informal communications and explicit and implicit learning mechanisms.

The heuristic model in Fig. 6.1 describes how implicit learning theory may be used to link structured and unstructured training experiences, organizational socialization, and organizational role change efforts. Implicit learning theory recognizes that people often learn without conscious effort to acquire knowledge. Many socialization experiences can shape an individual's adjustment to the organization in subtle ways that do not identify the experiences as formal or structured lessons. Likewise, unstructured training can provide implicit learning opportunities that far exceed the specific task that is taught. Attitudes and behaviors that are implicitly learned contribute to a wealth of knowledge that is used to evaluate and make sense of new information acquired by implicit or explicit means. An individual's decision to change his or her organizational role is influenced by this knowledge, and efforts to change are affected by formal and informal organizational reactions.

Although the model recognizes organizational and individual needs to change, it does not specify how an organization persuades an individual to accept a change strategy, or vice versa. Organizations and individuals often do not recognize or accept role changes simultaneously, nor do they always agree on the direction or magnitude of change. Four cases for recognizing role changes are presented and integrated with socialization processes.

RECOGNIZING ROLE CHANGES

Generally, role changes may be initiated by the organization or the individual. The extent to which role changes are successful would depend on how well the proposed change is accepted by both parties. Change efforts are usually successful when both parties agree on the direction and process for change. In these cases, socialization processes can facilitate change. When there is a lack of acceptance, or disagreement on change, organizations and individuals use socialization processes to reinforce their positions regarding the individual's role. In these cases, a two-step process is likely when change is attempted by one party and the other party initially does not recognize this change. Following the initial change attempt, socialization processes can be used to persuade the reacting party to accept the need for change. Likewise, socialization processes can be used by the reacting party to reject the change and reinforce the status quo. Acceptance of the new role would moderate the relationship between attempted and actual role change.

Four situations are described in Fig. 6.2 to illustrate the change process when (a) the organization and individual both recognize a need for change, (b) only the individual or the organization recognizes a need for change, or (c) neither recognizes a need for change.

Change Recognized by Both Parties

When both the individual and organization recognize that the employee's role is evolving, change may be anticipated and planned for. In this situation, the individual and organization can cooperate with one another to ensure that the changed role benefits both parties. When a planned change effort is supported by both, the rewards may be substantial. Proactive efforts to accommodate new organizational roles can place the organization in the most flexible position to meet future needs. Weick and Berlinger (1989) described how self-designing organizations continually redesign their processes and innovate new jobs and career paths to react quickly and effectively to uncertain and dynamic environ-

<table>
<tr><td></td><td colspan="2">ORGANIZATION</td></tr>
<tr><td></td><td>Role change is recognized</td><td>Role change is not recognized</td></tr>
<tr><td>Role change is recognized</td><td>The organization and individual can plan a change program. Socialization can reinforce formal change and may even compensate for any training deficiencies.</td><td>Two-step process is most likely. Individual initiates change and organization adapts if the change is accepted. Socialization can facilitate or impede change and adaptation processes.</td></tr>
<tr><td>Role change is not recognized</td><td>Two-step process is most likely. Organization initiates change and the individual adapts if the change is accepted. Socialization can facilitate or impede change and adaptation processes.</td><td>Unrecognized change may create future problems if it intensifies. Poor socialization or negative climate may contribute to failure in recognizing need for change.</td></tr>
</table>

INDIVIDUAL

FIG. 6.2. Recognizing role changes.

ments. Employees of self-designing organizations view changing roles as a constant phenomenon, and are expected to provide input and direction in shaping new roles.

In cases where the individual and organization agree on the direction and type of change, organizational socialization can support a positive change environment. Supportive relationships among organizational members can help raise awareness for the need to change, facilitate transfer of any formal training, and reinforce new knowledge, skills, and attitudes on the job. Informal networks provide additional resources for people to learn outside formal organizational programs. Organizational socialization that teaches employees to value change and to support one another would be an ideal environment to support formal change programs. In contrast, if employees learn to be rigid and competitive, formal change programs are less likely to be successful.

When the organization and individual do not agree on how the new role should evolve, the resulting actions may not benefit either party. Planned change programs may not be successfully designed, and the result may be uncontrolled and chaotic actions that result in an unstable organization. For example, organizational restructuring due to downsizing can lead to redesigned jobs that create role overload and stress for the surviving employees (Kozlowski, Chao, Smith, & Hedlund, 1993). If employees learned explicitly and/or implicitly to mistrust management, formal programs may be doomed from the start unless they can prove themselves credible and valid.

Positive or negative outcomes could be derived from a situation where both the individual and organization recognize changing roles. Positive outcomes are characterized by mutual support from formal and informal learning experiences, and negative outcomes are described by instability from unresolved differences in how the role should be changed.

Change Recognized by the Individual

When only the individual recognizes a need for change, the causes for change are most likely to be subtle and personal. Role changes initiated by the individual can benefit both the individual and the organization (Schein, 1971). Attempts to reverse a career plateau and rejuvenate a career have been documented (Bardwick, 1986), but they are rare. Efforts to redefine the individual's role may force the organization to recognize the change and adapt to the new role. This cell describes a two-step process, with the individual trying on new roles and the organization reacting and adapting to them.

Perhaps the most visible example of this process is when family priorities force individuals to redefine their work roles and organizations adopt plans to accommodate these nonwork needs. Studies at Johnson & Johnson and AT&T concluded that organizational programs designed to help employees resolve conflicts between work and nonwork resulted in increased morale and productivity (Galen, 1993). However, progressive programs offering flextime, telecommuting, and job sharing may also require training for successful implementation.

Galen (1993) described how employees at Corning Inc. were not taking advantage of these progressive programs because they believed management did not really endorse their use. Managers were originally socialized to believe that dedicated, high-performing employees put in long hours at the office. Resocialization was necessary for managers to learn how to assess job performance by criteria other than number of hours worked. Resocialization was also necessary for employees to learn that they can take advantage of these programs without jeopardizing their careers. This highlights the conclusion that attitudes fostered during the socialization process are important in sensitizing others for the need to change and for supporting specific change programs.

Change Recognized by the Organization

This case occurs when the organization recognizes that the employee's role has changed. New technology, organizational restructuring, and new management induce changes in an employee's job without prior agreement or acceptance by the employee. The organization must then socialize employees to accept these changes.

For example, the previous case of the secretary unwilling to accept new technology in her job was quickly remedied by informal, one-on-one training that was sensitive to the particular concerns of that person. A formal training program may not have the resources to identify trainee concerns, or the unique problems of a particular trainee may not warrant incorporation into a formal program for all trainees. Relationships formed during the socialization process can help coworkers identify training deficiencies, correct these deficiencies, and foster a supportive climate to reinforce change.

Previously socialized values can prevent or delay employee acceptance of new policies that reflect changing values. IBM's long-held tradition of no layoffs left many employees in disbelief when personnel cuts began (Goldberg, 1993). Schneider (1987) argued that "people make the place," and that new roles created by structural or process innovations may not be successfully implemented if the employees hold onto old values and roles. New equipment sabotage (Sullivan, 1982) or job transfer requests illustrate the problems facing organizations that are trying to change people who do not want change. Thus, like the previous analysis, this cell can describe a two-step process, with the organization identifying new roles and then socializing individuals to recognize and adapt to them.

Unrecognized Role Change

The last cell of the matrix describes a changing situation that is recognized by neither the organization nor the individual. Essentially no change is perceived and no adaptation is made by either party. Loyal employees who value their role in the organization may protect that role from job and individual factors that change over time. Organizations may treat changing situations as temporary aberrations and ignore signs of change in favor of maintaining the status quo. However, the failure to recognize how roles within the organization are changing or should be changed can result in stagnation for both the individual and organization. Argyris (1976) described this as the dry rot that characterizes unresponsive organizations and their propensity toward organizational entropy.

One socialization tactic—mentorship—is discussed in detail to illustrate how socialization can provide unstructured training and development to enhance an individual's career. A brief background of the mentorship literature is presented, followed by a process to utilize mentorships to maximize successful training and development.

A SPECIFIC FORM OF INDIVIDUAL SOCIALIZATION—MENTORSHIP

Mentorship is often defined as an intense work relationship between senior and junior organizational members (Kram, 1985). The mentor provides personal guidance and support to the protégé's career that goes beyond any formal supervisory requirements. Although mentorships can trace their origins to ancient Greek mythology, most of the empirical research on mentorships has been conducted only within the past decade. Current studies have explored mentorships in several directions, including the phases of mentorships (Kram, 1983), functions served by the mentor (Carden, 1990; Noe, 1988a; Scandura, 1992; Tack & Tack, 1986), and outcomes of the mentorship (Chao, Walz, & Gardner, 1992; Dreher & Ash, 1990; Riley & Wrench, 1985).

Mentoring Phases

Kram (1983) described four distinct phases of mentorship. The first phase, the initiation phase, is the time period when the mentorship forms. A prospective protg begins to respect the potential mentor as a competent individual and a person from whom the protégé would like to receive support and guidance. At the same time, the mentor begins to recognize the protégé as someone who deserves special attention and coaching within the organization. The initiation stage is typically followed by the cultivation phase, in which the mentorship partners learn more about each other's capabilities and optimize the benefits of participating in the mentorship. Kram noted that the cultivation phase would be the period in which the protégé benefits most from interactions with the mentor. The third phase involves a structural and psychological separation between the mentorship partners when the functions provided by the mentor decrease and the protégé acts with more independence and autonomy. Last, the redefinition phase terminates a mentorship, and the partners evolve the relationship to one of informal contact and mutual support.

Mentoring Functions

The literature reveals many functions that mentorships are expected to serve. The bulk of this research has focused on the functions that the mentor performs for the protégé, although Noe (1988b) proposed the need for research concerning functions served by the protege for the mentor.

Kram (1985) delineated two categories of functions served by mentors for their protégés: career and psychosocial. Career functions include providing sponsorship, exposure, visibility, coaching, protection, and challenging assignments—activities that directly relate to the protégé's career advancement. Psychosocial functions include providing role modeling, acceptance, confirmation, counseling, and friendship—activities that influence the protégé's self-image and competence. Kram found that different phases were associated with different developmental functions, with career functions emerging first, psychosocial functions becoming more important in the cultivation phase, and both functions declining in importance in the later stages.

Mentoring Functions and Outcomes

Most of the empirical research on mentoring outcomes has focused on comparing mentored versus nonmentored people, or examining the relationship between mentoring activities and outcomes. At a theoretical level, Hunt and Michael (1983) described three types of mentorship outcomes: those for the mentor, the protégé, and the organization. According to their model, mentors get satisfaction and confirmation from providing assistance to junior members, protégés develop a secure and positive self-image, and organizations obtain an improved pool of managerial talent. Negative outcomes for the protégé are also recognized in Hunt and Michael's model. They proposed that a mismatch between protégé and mentor, or a premature end of the mentorship, may produce feelings of betrayal and self-doubt for the protégé. Kram (1985) described how mentors may suffer from association with an unsuccessful protégé. Chao and O'Leary (1990) speculated that organizational problems can occur if employees outside a mentorship view the relationship with jealousy and take actions to thwart the mentorship.

Fagenson (1988) proposed a type of function–outcome link through her focus on protégé power as an outcome of the mentoring relationship. Protégés were believed to have greater influence on policy decisions, closer relationships with key organizational players, and more control over resources than nonmentored individuals by virtue of the special opportunities and treatment they received from mentorships. Fagenson's results support a link between protégé status and their degree of perceived power in terms of influence, access, and control.

Riley and Wrench (1985) classified women lawyers into groups of truly mentored protégés and those whose relationships did not conform to a strict definition of mentorship. They found the truly mentored group reported significantly higher levels of career success and satisfaction than the group that was not mentored. Dreher and Ash (1990) found mentoring was related to promotions and satisfaction with pay and benefits for business school graduates. Whitely, Dougherty, and Dreher (1991) found mentoring was related to early promotions and compensation. Ostroff and Kozlowski (1993) found that mentoring had an impact on the learning process during early socialization for organizational newcomers. In particular, newcomers with mentors were more sensitive to learning about the organization's features (culture, goals, power) from all possible learning sources.

Scandura (1992) used three factors to describe mentoring functions. The vocational function was similar to Kram's (1985) career-related function, whereas the role modeling and social support functions tapped aspects of Kram's psychosocial function. When examining their relationships with career mobility outcomes of managers, Scandura found the vocational and social support functions to be significantly related to promotions and salary, respectively.

Chao et al. (1992) also examined the relationship between mentoring functions and career outcomes for engineers and managers. Using Noe's (1988a) scale, they found a significant canonical correlation among the two functions and job/career satisfaction, socialization, and salary. Protégés who reported their mentors provided more career-related support also reported higher intrinsic job satisfaction and better socialization on organizational goals, politics, and history. The results also support mentorship as a socialization tactic because protégés in informal mentorships reported significantly higher levels of socialization than non-mentored employees.

Improving Mentorship Effectiveness

Recognition of the advantages of mentorships have spurred many organizations to formalize this socialization tactic by designing and managing mentorship programs. Generally, formal mentorship programs are minimally structured: They focus on assigning people to a mentor–protégé dyad and providing some coaching advice for the mentors. Most formal mentorships are also unstructured in the day-to-day interactions between the mentor and protégé. The concept of formal mentorship programs has been hailed as an innovative career development tool by some (Gray & Gray, 1990) and as an oxymoron by others (Levinson, Darrow, Klein, Levinson, & McKee, 1978). Critics of formal mentorship programs point out that the initiation stage is subverted by a managed matching process, and that such relationships are a far cry from true mentorships.

Chao et al. (1992) provided the only empirical comparison of protégés in formal and informal mentorships. Their results found that protégés in informal mentorships reported significantly higher career-related support from their mentors. These protégés reported significantly higher salaries than protégés in formal programs. However, there were no significant differences in these two groups on their perceived organizational socialization or job satisfaction.

Formal mentorship programs may be able to achieve some, but not all, of the benefits of informal mentorships. If organizations want to maximize the advantages of informal, unstructured training and development techniques, perhaps a training approach, instead of a management approach, may be best. Instead of formalizing the entire mentoring intervention, gains may be better achieved by training people to use unstructured training techniques. For example, training people on mentorship would focus on teaching people how to mentor. In contrast, a formal mentorship program typically matches mentors and protégés, but provides little direction for each.

Training content for potential mentors could include topics such as: (a) how to identify a protégé for yourself, (b) the phases of mentorship and learning when to let go, (c) how to coach and provide direction without being overbearing, (d) the rewards of being a mentor, (e) how to reinforce company goals and values, and (f) how to work with a protégé who is different from you (age, race, gender). In addition, training for mentors can include knowledge about implicit and explicit learning processes. This information can help mentors to be aware of their actions and influence on protégés. Not only is a mentor's conscious lesson important, it is also relevant for the mentor to know how that lesson is sensed, interpreted, and evaluated by the protégé. The tacit knowledge learned from a mentorship can be critical in guiding future interactions and gauging mentorship's effectiveness.

If senior organizational members are knowledgeable on how to conduct successful mentorships, they may be more likely to engage in these relationships through the informal socialization process. The organization may be able to maximize the benefits of informal mentorships by investing in a training program that teaches people how to mentor on their own. Because many mentorships offer rewarding experiences for the mentor, as well as the protégé, the training program may be one component of the mentor's own career development program.

RESEARCH DIRECTIONS

Research on socialization as an unstructured training and development process should take an interactional psychology framework (Reichers, 1987). An interactional view emphasizes that work roles must be defined in terms of the particular individual's perceptions and experiences (Bowers, 1973; Pervin, 1989). Thus, organizational socialization practices cannot uniformly shape people into a homogeneous group of employees. The unique combinations of personality and past experiences affect how people respond to socialization efforts. In addition, the changing conditions of work, and the physical and psychological development of adults influence how work roles change as people mature on the job. These changes spark the following research questions.

Given that the impetus for role change is not always salient to the individual or organization, the identification of socialization needs for established employees should be the focus of early research in this area. Research is needed to determine how organizational, job, and individual factors are perceived to be triggers for role change. Future research should also examine the extent to which socialization practices can facilitate or impede the recognition of the need to change and the implementation of those changes. Results can help establish theoretical groundwork for understanding the transfer of formal training programs, and for the promotion of unstructured learning on the job.

Research on individual differences should also be integrated with the concept of organizational socialization to identify characteristics that predispose people to socialization pressures. Katz and Kahn (1978) described research that identified a generalized aptitude for role taking, where some people are more adaptable to role changes than others. These differences may help an organization identify who may be most receptive to organizational and job changes. These differences may also predict who is most likely to initiate changes on the job. It is speculated here that these differences are related to tacit knowledge and implicit learning. What people learn from observation and general exposure to change situations can influence their reactions to change and their explicit learning.

The study of organizational socialization is one that should be extended to all phases of an individual's job tenure and career. Longitudinal research that examines these changes over a life course may reveal patterns of change that can provide direction for future career development programs. How organizational roles are shaped and constantly changed by organization, job, and/or individual factors can help human resource practitioners anticipate changes and better manage career concerns of established employees.

Research is also needed to determine which training and development areas can benefit most from the application of informal socialization tactics. Perhaps organizational changes that involve a value or attitude component can best take advantage of the unstructured learning experiences. Already there are examples of organizations that have trained employees to instruct their coworkers on workforce diversity (Johnson & O'Mara, 1992) and quality performance (Rothenberg & Drye, 1991). These train-the-trainer programs provide technical expertise to key employees who conduct training within their work unit and serve as readily available resources to ensure everyone has learned the training material. However, there are no empirical evaluations of these programs. Thus, research is needed to determine the utility of these programs as compared with more traditional formal programs.

CONCLUSION

Unstructured training relies on relationships between trainers and trainees to create a learning environment for the less experienced trainees. Informal organizational socialization is a prime example of unstructured training, and most people are exposed to one or more socialization tactics as they learn about their jobs and their roles in the organization. Hall (1980) described how socialization processes are pervasive throughout an individual's career. Although most of the research focuses on newcomer socialization, the personal and career changes that individuals encounter present continuing demands for learning and relearning how one fits into the organization.

As a link with formal training programs, informal organizational socialization can help create a work environment that supports or opposes formal training goals, as well as compensates for training deficiencies. Socialization provides implicit learning experiences that affect how formal training and change are perceived and valued by the individual. Employees who are socialized to cooperate with one another and experiment with change create a climate conducive to learning on and off the job. Conversely, employees who are socialized to mistrust one another and resist change create a climate that would minimize any transfer of formal training.

In addition to the relationship between formal training programs and informal socialization on the job, the socialization process within a formal training program can also affect a program's success. Feldman (1989) described how training programs can formally and informally socialize people during the learning process, and how it may also spill over into the individual's job after the program is completed. Lessons learned from previous socialization episodes, regardless of context, may influence nonconscious interpretative schemata. In turn, the tacit knowledge gained through implicit learning may affect expectations for subsequent learning.

As a specific socialization tactic, mentorship was presented to illustrate how informal work relationships help an individual learn and develop one's career. Although the literature typically describes benefits of mentoring, several problems could arise when the relationship fails to address the needs of both mentor and protege. Rather than manage the relationship in formal mentoring programs, it is suggested that the benefits of mentorships may be best achieved by providing training to guide senior employees on how to mentor others, but still preserving the informal nature of the relationship. Problems may be avoided when potential mentors are trained in the mentorship process, but the actual initiation, cultivation, separation, and redefinition of the relationship is left to the discretion of the trained mentor.

Formal organizational guidance on the learning process can also be extended to other socialization tactics. Training programs that focus on individual learning can capitalize on implicit and explicit learning modes to guide the individual's socialization into the larger organization. Formal training and socialization practices can set a foundation for informal socialization to provide a positive work and learning environment. This environment can promote career development that benefits the individual and the organization.

REFERENCES

Allen, N. J., & Meyer, J. P. (1990). Organizational socialization tactics: A longitudinal analysis of links to newcomers' commitment and role orientation. *Academy of Management Journal*, 33 (4), 847–858.

Anderson, J. R. (1983). *The architecture of cognition*. Cambridge, MA: Harvard University Press.

Argyris, C. (1976). Problems and new directions for industrial psychology. In M. D. Dunnette (Ed.), *Handbook of industrial and organizational psychology* (pp. 151–184). Chicago: Rand McNally.

Baldwin, T. T., & Ford, J. K. (1988). Transfer of training: A review and directions for future research. *Personnel Psychology*, 41, 63–105.

Bardwick, J. M. (1986). *The plateauing trap*. New York: AMACOM.

Berlew, D. E., & Hall, D. T. (1966). The socialization of managers: Effects of expectations on performance. *Administrative Science Quarterly*, 11, 207–223.

Bowers, K. S. (1973). Situationism in psychology: An analysis and a critique. *Psychological Review*, 80, 307–336.

Broad, M. L., & Newstrom, J. W. (1992). *Transfer of training*. Reading, MA: Addison-Wesley.

Carden, A. D. (1990). Mentoring and adult career development: The evolution of a theory. *The Counseling Psychologist*, 18, 275–299.

Carnevale, A. P., & Gainer, L. J. (1989). *The learning enterprise*. Washington, DC: American Society for Training and Development and Department of Labor.

Chao, G. T. (1988). The socialization process: Building newcomer commitment. In M. London & E. M. Mone (Eds.), *Career growth and human resource strategies* (pp. 31–47). New York: Quorum.

Chao, G. T., & O'Leary, A. M. (1990). How others see same- and cross-gender mentoring. *Mentoring International*, 4 (3), 3–12.

Chao, G. T., O'Leary-Kelly, A. M., Wolf, S., Klein, H. J., & Gardner, P. D. (1994). Organizational socialization: Its content and consequences. *Journal of Applied Psychology*, 79, 730–743.

Chao, G. T., Walz, P. M., & Gardner, P. D. (1992). Formal and informal mentorships: A comparison on mentoring functions and contrast with nonmentored counterparts. *Personnel Psychology*, 45, 619–636.

Dreher, G. F., & Ash, R. A. (1990). A comparative study of mentoring among men and women in managerial, professional, and technical positions. *Journal of Applied Psychology*, 75, 539–546.

Enoch, Y. (1989). Change of values during socialization for a profession: An application of the marginal man theory. *Human Relations*, 42 (3), 219–239.

Fagenson, E.A. (1988). The power of a mentor. *Groups & Organization Studies*, 13, 182–194.

Feldman, D. C. (1988). *Managing careers in organizations*. Glenview, IL: Scott, Foresman.

Feldman, D. C. (1989). Socialization, resocialization, and training: Reframing the research agenda. In I. L. Goldstein (Ed.), *Training and development in organizations* (pp. 376–416). San Francisco: Jossey-Bass.

Fisher, C. D. (1986). Organizational socialization: An integrative review. In G. R. Ferris & K. M. Rowland (Eds.), Research in personnel and human resources management (Vol. 4, pp. 101–145). Greenwich, CT: JAI.

Galen, M. (1993, June 28). Work and family. *Business Week*, pp. 80–88.

Goldberg, A. (1993, April). Organizational downsizing at IBM. In S. Kozlowski & G. Chao (Chairs), *Organizational downsizing*. Symposium conducted at the eighth annual conference of the Society for Industrial/Organizational Psychology, San Francisco, CA.

Goldstein, I. L. (1993). *Training in organizations* (3rd ed.). Pacific Grove, CA: Brooks/Cole.

Gray, M. M., & Gray, W. A. (1990). Planned mentoring: Aiding key transitions in career development. *Mentoring International*, 4(3), 27–32.

Hall, D. T. (1980). Socialization processes in later career years: Can there be growth at the terminal level? In C. B. Derr (Ed.), *Work, family, and the career: New frontiers in theory and research* (pp. 219–233). New York: Praeger.

Hall, D. T. (1986). Breaking career routines: Midcareer choice and identity development. In D. T. Hall (Ed.), *Career development in organizations* (pp. 120–159). San Francisco: Jossey-Bass.

Hayes, N. A., & Broadbent, D. E. (1988). Two modes of learning for interactive tasks. *Cognition*, 28, 249–276.

Hunt, D. M., & Michael, C. (1983). Mentorship: A career training and development tool. *Academy of Management Review*, 8, 475–485.

Johnson, R. B., & O'Mara, J. (1992). Shedding new light on diversity training. *Training & Development Journal*, 46(5), 44–52.

Jones, G. R. (1986). Socialization tactics, self-efficacy, and newcomers' adjustments to organizations. *Academy of Management Journal*, 29, 262–279.

Katz, D., & Kahn, R. L. (1978). *The social psychology of organizations* (2nd ed.). New York: Wiley.

Kotter, J. P. (1988). *The leadership factor*. New York: The Free Press.

Kozlowski, S. W. J., Chao, G. T., Smith, E. M., & Hedlund, J. (1993). Organizational downsizing: Strategies, interventions, and research implications. *International Review of Industrial and Organizational Psychology*, 8, 263–332.

Kram, K. E. (1983). Phases of the mentor relationship. *Academy of Management Journal*, 26, 608–625.

Kram, K. E. (1985). *Mentoring at work*. Glenview, IL: Scott, Foresman.

Lachman, R. (1988). Factors influencing workers' orientations: A secondary analysis of Israeli data. *Organization Studies*, 9(4), 497–510.

Levinson, D. J. (1986). A conception of adult development. *American Psychologist*, 41, 3–13.

Levinson, D. J., Darrow, C. N., Klein, E. B., Levinson, M. H., & McKee, B. (1978). *The seasons of a man's life*. New York: Knopf.

Lewicki, P., Hill, T., & Czyzewska, M. (1992). Nonconscious acquisition of information. *American Psychologist*, 47, 796–801.

Lewin, K. (1951). *Field theory in social science* (pp. 228–229). New York: Harper & Row.

Louis, M. R. (1980). Surprise and sense-making. *Administrative Science Quarterly*, 25, 226–251.

Major, D. A., Kozlowski, S. W. J., Chao, G. T., & Gardner, P. D. (1995). A longitudinal investigation of newcomer expectations, early socialization outcomes, and the moderating effects of role development factors. *Journal of Applied Psychology*, 80, 418–431.

Neugarten, B. L. (1975). Adult personality: Towards a psychology of the life cycle. In W. C. Sze (Ed.), *The human life cycle* (pp. 379–394). New York: Aronson.

Newstrom, J. W. (1986). Leveraging management development through the management of transfer. *Journal of Management Development*, 5(5), 33–45.

Nicholson, N. (1984). A theory of work role transitions. *Administrative Science Quarterly*, 29, 172–191.

Nicholson, N., & Arnold, J. (1991). From expectation to experience: Graduates entering a large corporation. *Journal of Organizational Behavior*, 12, 413–429.

Nicholson, N., & West, M. A. (1988). *Managerial job change: Men and women in transition*. New York: Cambridge University Press.

Noe, R. A. (1988a). An investigation of the determinants of successful assigned mentoring relationships. *Personnel Psychology*, 41, 457–479.

Noe, R. A. (1988b). Women and mentoring: A review and research agenda. *Academy of Management Review*, 13, 65–78.

Ostroff, C., & Kozlowski, S. W. J. (1993). The role of mentoring in the information gathering processes of newcomers during early organizational socialization. *Journal of Vocational Behavior*, 42, 170–183.

Pervin, L. A. (1989). Persons, situations, interactions: The history of a controversy and a discussion of theoretical models. *Academy of Management Review, 14*, 350–360.

Polanyi, M. (1969). *Knowing and being.* London: Routledge & Kegan Paul.

Reber, A. S. (1993). *Implicit learning and tacit knowledge: An essay on the cognitive unconscious.* New York: Oxford University Press.

Reichers, A. E. (1987). An interactionist perspective on newcomer socialization rates. *Academy of Management Review, 12*, 278–287.

Riley, S., & Wrench, D. (1985). Mentoring among women lawyers. *Journal of Applied Social Psychology, 15*, 374–386.

Rothenberg, R. G., & Drye, T. R. (1991). Train 700 people in quality? No problem. *Training & Development Journal, 45*(12), 43–46.

Rothwell, W. J., & Kazanas, H. C. (1990). Planned OJT is productive OJT. *Training & Development Journal, 44*(10), 53–56.

Scandura, T. A. (1992). Mentorship and career mobility: An empirical investigation. *Journal of Organizational Behavior, 13*, 169–174.

Schein, E. H. (1971). Occupational socialization in the professions: The case of the role innovator. *Journal of Psychiatric Research, 8*, 521–530.

Schneider, B. (1987). The people make the place. *Personnel Psychology, 40*, 437–454.

Sullivan, M. J. (1982). Managing to mismanage robot productivity programs (MS82–137). SME Technical Paper, Dearborn, MI

Sutton, R. I., & Louis, M. R. (1987). How selecting and socializing newcomers influences insiders. *Human Resource Management, 26*, 347–361.

Tack, W. L., & Tack, L. (1986). Don't ignore seasoned mangers—The case for management cycling. *Sloan Management Review, 27*, 63–70.

Thayer, P. W., & McGehee, W. (1977). On the effectiveness of not holding a formal training course. *Personnel Psychology, 30*, 455–456.

U.S. Department of Labor (1989). *Work-based learning: Training America's workers.* Washington, DC: U.S. Government Printing Office.

Van Maanen, J., & Schein, E. H. (1979). Toward a theory of organizational socialization. In B. M. Staw (Ed.), *Research in organizational behavior* (pp. 209–264). Greenwich, CT: JAI.

Wagner, R. K., & Sternberg, R. J. (1985). Practical intelligence in real-world pursuits: The role of tacit knowledge. *Journal of Personality and Social Psychology, 49*, 436–458.

Weick, K. E., & Berlinger, L. R. (1989). Career improvisation in self-designing organizations. In M. B. Arthur, D. T. Hall, & B. S. Lawrence (Eds.), *Handbook of career theory* (pp. 313–328). New York: Cambridge University Press.

Wexley, K. N., & Latham, G. P. (1991). *Developing and training human resources in organizations* (2nd ed.). New York: Harper Collins.

Whitely, W., Dougherty, T. W., & Dreher, G. F. (1991). Relationship of career mentoring and socioeconomic origin to managers' and professionals' early career progress. *Academy of Management Journal, 34*, 331–351.

7

Employee Development: Issues in Construct Definition and Investigation of Antecedents

Raymond A. Noe
Michigan State University

Steffanie L. Wilk
University of Pennsylvania

Ellen J. Mullen
Iowa State University

James E. Wanek
Boise State University

Traditionally, U.S. companies lag behind Asian and European competitors in providing training and development once employees qualify for their jobs (Carnevale & Goldstein, 1990). However, employee development is a necessary component of U.S. companies' efforts to improve quality, meet the challenges of global competition, use new technologies in producing products and services, and capitalize on the strengths of a diverse workforce. Many companies have adopted a continuous learning philosophy as a means to facilitate employee development. One of the major tenets of a continuous learning philosophy is that employees at all levels of the company must actively pursue training and development activities. Continuous learning also requires employees to understand the relationship between their jobs and work units and the company's mission.

To advance research and practice of employee development practices, one needs to understand what types of activities are considered to be developmental, how development activities should be measured, how development activities facilitate learning, and what individual and organizational characteristics influence the amount and type of development activities that employees participate in.

153

This chapter attempts to increase our understanding of these issues. The conceptual model that serves as an organizing framework for this chapter is presented in Fig. 7.1. The figure describes the process through which development activities result in the attainment of cognitive, affective, and skill-based learning outcomes. According to Kraiger, Ford, and Salas (1993), cognitive outcomes include verbal knowledge, how knowledge is organized, and the development and application of strategies for problem solving. Skill-based outcomes relate to the development of technical or motor skills. Affective outcomes include attitudes (such as self-awareness or values) and motivational outcomes (including motivational disposition, self-efficacy, and goal setting). Individual and organizational antecedents affect individuals' decisions regarding the type and amount of participation in development activities. Each development activity affects one or more cognitive, skill-based, or affective learning outcomes. Each type of development activity requires a specific type of learning environment for the learning outcomes to be achieved.

This chapter discusses the theoretical and empirical literature supporting the linkages shown in Fig. 7.1. The first section discusses issues concerning the construct validity and measurement of employee development. Next, a typology of development activities (assessment, job experiences, relationships, and formal courses) and a review of the current research conducted on each of the types of development activity are provided. The first section concludes with a discussion of how different types of development activity influence learning processes and outcomes. In the second section, the individual and organizational antecedents of employee development are discussed, as well as several different theoretical frameworks that might be useful for understanding individuals' decisions regarding participation in development activities. Directions for future research on employee development are provided at the end of each part.

UNDERSTANDING THE CONSTRUCT
OF EMPLOYEE DEVELOPMENT

To understand the construct of employee development, it is necessary to differentiate *employee development* from *training*, identify dimensions on which development activities might differ, and identify the types of development activities. Issues related to how developmental activity is measured, the validity and reliability of the source of information regarding development activity, and the temporal dimensionality of development activity must also be considered.

Differentiating Employee Development
From Training

Most attempts at defining *employee development* focus on how it differs from training (Fitzgerald, 1992; Pace, Smith, & Mills, 1991). *Training* refers to a planned effort by a company to facilitate the learning of specific knowledge,

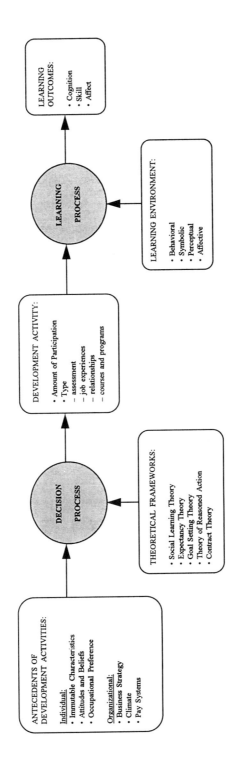

FIG 7.1. A conceptual model of the relation between antecedents, development activity, and learning outcomes.

155

skills, or behaviors that employees need to be successful in their current job (Goldstein, 1993). The objectives of employee development are not necessarily tied to a specific job. For example, London (1989) defined *development* as courses, workshops, seminars, and assignments that influence personal and professional growth. Development opportunities are likely less focused on skills or behaviors tied to a certain position, but instead on skills, behaviors, and abilities that are necessary for long-term personal effectiveness, and that contribute to the company's ability to remain competitive by providing high-quality goods and services to its customers.

Dimensionality of Development Activity

Development activities can be defined along several dimensions. Some of the possible dimensions that are useful for understanding the construct of *employee development* include voluntary versus involuntary, informal versus formal, current versus future oriented, incremental versus framebreaking, and introspective versus interactive.

Voluntary Versus Involuntary. Employee participation in development activities might be dictated by organizational policy or prescription. For example, many employees are asked to participate in job-rotation programs, in which the length and function involved in job assignments have been predetermined by the organization. Also, employees who have been identified by the organization as having high management potential often participate in a prescribed set of courses related to the development of management skills. Employees may also participate in development activities simply because of a personal interest in acquiring knowledge or skills in a particular area, or an interest in confirming (or disconfirming) their interest in gaining knowledge, skills, or behaviors in a ceratin area. These development activities are not formally prescribed by the organization. For example, employees in the accounting department may decide to apply for a job assignment in human resources or take a class in leadership skills to confirm their interest in working with people.

Informal Versus Formal. Employees can develop skills, knowledge, or behavior through a variety of means, such as courses or job experiences. Formal development activities are sponsored by the organization, usually to target the development of specific skills, knowledge bases, or behaviors. For example, employees might be rotated from the marketing to finance function to improve their understanding of financial practices in the organization. Informal development activities are not sponsored by the organization. Employees might actively try to develop new skills and knowledge bases by deciding to participate in extracurricular activities (such as coaching a soccer team), which can help develop skills (sensitivity and providing feedback, for the coaching example) that may be transferable to the workplace.

Current Versus Future Oriented. This dimension deals with the degree to which the development activity is related to the knowledge, skills, abilities, or attitudes that employees need to be successful in their current job versus preparing them for a future assignment or anticipated changes to their current job. For example, employees might chair a task force designed to understand work and family issues to develop leadership and organizational ability that might not be applicable for their current job assignment (engineer), but that helps them develop the skill base needed to move into another position. In many organizations, participation in development activities has been linked with employees enhancing their salary or their chances for achieving promotions. One of the dilemmas of organizations that hope to facilitate a continuous learning environment is how to persuade employees to participate in development activities that are not immediately rewarded.

Incremental Versus Framebreaking. London (1989) distinguished incremental learning from framebreaking situations. Incremental situations are those in which time to clarify role expectations is provided and flexibility for self-paced learning is available. Framebreaking learning experiences place individuals in difficult positions, requiring the acquisition of a large number of skills to be successful. Framebreaking experiences require considerable individual investment with a high potential for learning, but also a high risk for failure. Giving employees the opportunity to develop skills or experiences through enlarging the domain of their current job might be considered incremental learning. Activities such as temporary project assignments, switching roles within a team, or researching new ways to serve clients and customers might "stretch" the employees' current skill base, but not create a situation where the risk for failure is high.

Introspective Versus Interactive. Development activities also differ in the extent to which they require the individual to interact with other persons and the work environment. In one type of development activity (i.e., assessment), individuals are involved in exploring their own values, interests, attitudes, career goals, or learning style preferences. The personal insights gained occur without any assistance from supervisors, peers, or subordinates. In other types of development activity, such as mentoring and job experiences, the individual acquires skills or experiences attitude and behavior changes directly through interacting with others or the work experience.

Operationalization of Development

Various operationalizations of development activity are possible, including development plans, historic developmental records, and number of hours spent in development activities. Researchers must identify the operationalization of development activity that is relevant to the purpose of the study (Does the research question involve trying to predict the rate of participation in development activity or predicting the type of development activities that persons with certain characteristics will participate in?). A key issue is to decide what development means. As noted earlier, there are several dimensions that the researcher needs to consider in defining the domain of development activities: Are mandatory activities considered to be development activities? Does development activity include just formal courses and seminars? Are work experiences such as job rotation also considered to be developmental assignments?

Sources of Information Regarding Development Activity. Self-report data using employee surveys and objective data from information systems or personnel records are potential sources of information regarding development activity. Recently, Noe and Wilk (1993) found a lack of convergence between self-report and objective measures of development activity. Data collected from personnel files may appear to be the most valid and reliable source of information regarding development activities. However, many employees may not report participation in development activities if involvement in courses, seminars, and programs is not reimbursed or rewarded, or if development activities are informal. Organizations may not systematically collect this information. Also, organizational records may not differentiate between formal and informal or voluntary and involuntary development activities. As a result, researchers collecting archival development information need to make sure that the data collected match the types of development activity they are interested in studying.

Temporal Dimensionality. Researchers must determine whether study hypotheses have to do with predicting future versus current rates of participation in development activity. The expectancy model (which is often used as the theoretical basis for understanding participation in development activity) focuses on predicting future effort levels. As a result, longitudinal studies that investigate the relationship between attitudes and perceptions and development activity participation rate are required at a later point in time.

Potential Covariates. Individual- and organizational-level characteristics may artificially influence employees' participation in development activity. Employees may have more opportunities to participate in development activities simply as a result of organizational tenure. Carnevale, Gainer, and Villet (1991) reported that there are large differences across positions in the degree to which employees are provided with development opportunities. In many organizations, managerial-level employees have a larger menu of development activities to choose from, and more discretion regarding the types of formal programs and experiences they want to participate in than nonmanagerial employees.

Types of Development Activity

Our review of the practitioner and academic literature suggests that there are four types of development activities: employee assessment, job experiences, formal courses and seminars, and relationships.

Employee Assessment.   Assessment involves collecting information and providing feedback to employees about their behavior, communication style, or skills (Bolt, 1989; Hinrichs & Hollenbeck, 1991; Howard & Bray, 1988). Self-report information as well as information from peers, managers, and customers can be collected. Although an individual's awareness of their strengths and weaknesses can be considered developmental, assessments typically stimulate a person to engage in other types of developmental activities designed to strengthen skills, behaviors, or attitudes. Typically, employees are provided with a summary of their strengths and weaknesses, as seen by the different rating groups, which they can use to direct development activities. The organization can also use assessment information to determine what other types of development activities might benefit the employee. Several different types of professionally developed, as well as "home-grown," measures are available for assessment purposes. Because of page limitations, this chapter cannot possibly discuss all available assessment measures that might be used for development purposes. Hence, this chapter discusses Benchmarks, Myers–Briggs Type Inventory, assessment centers, performance appraisals, and programs designed to improve dysfunctional managers.

Benchmarks is designed to assess managerial skill strengths and weaknesses. The Benchmarks instrument includes a series of items designed to measure managers' skills in dealing with subordinates, acquiring resources, and creating a productive work climate (McCauley, Lombardo, & Usher, 1989).

Research studies comparing Benchmarks to other assessment tools (such as the Myers–Briggs Type Inventory and the California Psychological Inventory) have provided evidence of the construct validity of the instrument (McCauley & Lombardo, 1990). Validity studies have shown that the ratings managers receive on the various Benchmarks scales are related to independent assessment of the managers' promotion potential and job performance.

The most popular psychological test for employee development is the Myers–Briggs Type Indicator (MBTI; some estimates are that 2 million people take the MBTI in the United States each year). Based on the work of Carl Jung, the MBTI identifies individual preferences for energy (introversion vs. extroversion), information gathering (sensing vs. intuition), decision making (thinking vs. feeling), and lifestyle (judging vs. perceiving; Hummer, 1993). Sixteen unique personality types result from the combination of the four MBTI preferences. The MBTI has been used for understanding such things as communication, motivation, teamwork, workstyles, and leadership. The MBTI can

purportedly help develop teams by matching team members with job assignments that allow them to capitalize on their preferences, and to help employees
understand how the different personality types of team members can lead to
useful problem solving (Hirsch, 1992).

Research on the validity, reliability, and effectiveness of the MBTI is incon-
clusive (see Druckman & Bjork, 1991). Individuals react positively to taking
the MBTI, and report that it helps them change their behavior. One concern
with the MBTI is that personality types may not be stable over time. Test–retest
reliability analyses of the MBTI have found that as few as 24% of individuals
who took the MBTI were classified as the same type at a later time. Validity
studies of the MBTI conducted to date have examined the relationship between
MBTI scores and behavior in experimental situations, differences in MBTI
profile by occupation, relationship between instrument and self-typing, and
correlations with other instruments. The validity of the MBTI has been questioned for several reasons. First, although there appears to be some relationship
between type preference and different occupations (sales persons have higher
percentages of extraverts than introverts), no evidence has indicated a relationship between type and performance in an occupation. Second, comparisons of
judgments made by analysts who are familiar with the Jungian philosophy
underlying the instrument, with the personality typing determined by the
MBTI, show varying degrees of agreement depending on the preference being
considered. Third, the sensing-intuition and thinking-feeling dimensions do not
correlate with measures designed to assess similar constructs.

The research base supporting the validity of assessment centers for employee
selection is well established (see Gaugler, Rosenthal, Thornton, & Bentson,
1987). Besides selection, assessment centers are believed to serve an important
development function by providing assesses with feedback on administrative
and interpersonal skills believed to be related to managerial success. However,
participation in assessment centers has been shown to be related only to changes
in self-perceptions and intentions to develop, but not to development activities
completed, behavior change, or performance improvement (Noe & Schmitt,
1986; Schmitt, Ford & Stults, 1986; Jones & Whitmore, 1995).

Performance appraisals can be useful for employee development under
certain conditions. Silverman (1991) suggested that performance appraisal
that stimulates employee development includes five steps: (a) clarifying the
employee's major job responsibilities, (b) developing performance standards,
(c) providing periodic performance feedback, (d) diagnosing and coaching
employee performance, and (e) reviewing overall performance. In the typical
performance appraisal system, the manager provides ratings of employees'
behavior, performance, or competencies. The manager and employees jointly
discuss the appraisal results and develop an action plan. The use of only one
source of ratings—the manager—assumes that the manager is aware of each
employee's behavior and competencies. Many employees may question the

validity of appraisal information collected from only one source because peers, subordinates, or customers may interact with the employee and see their work products more frequently than does their manager. Therefore, employees may not be motivated to develop weaknesses identified through the appraisal process.

An innovation in the use of performance appraisals for employee development has been the development of 360-degree feedback systems. There are several excellent discussions of practical and theoretical issues related to 360-degree feedback systems (e.g., see the Summer and Fall 1993 volumes of *Human Resource Management*). London and Smither (1995) have developed the most comprehensive model of the effects of multisource feedback on perceptions of goal accomplishment, re-evaluation of self-image, and changes in outcomes such as development, goals, behavior, and performance. Many organizations use some type of 360-degree assessment inventory, in which the employee is provided with feedback information from persons with whom they come in contact with at the workplace, including managers, peers, subordinates, and customers (Nowack, 1992). These 360-degree feedback systems would be expected to motivate more development activity than traditional appraisal systems for several reasons. First, employees are more likely to feel the appraisal information is valid because it comes from multiple perspectives. Second, in many cases, along with a report summarizing self, peer, and manager evaluations, employees are provided with normative information summarizing the best, typical, and worst scores for each appraisal dimension. As Festinger (1954) noted in his theory of social comparison, people need to compare themselves to others to evaluate their abilities. Differences between one's abilities and those of others create pressure to reduce the discrepancy. The 360-degree feedback provides employees with credible information regarding differences in self- and others' perceptions of strengths and weaknesses. As a result, employees involved in 360-degree feedback systems would be expected to be more motivated to develop weaknesses than employees in traditional appraisal systems.

A special type of assessment program involves helping managers who are otherwise good performers, but who have dysfunctional behaviors, such as insensitivity, inability to be a team player, arrogance, and poor conflict-management skills (see Hellervik, Hazucha, & Schneider, 1992). One example of this type of program is the Individual Coaching for Effectiveness (ICE) program. In the ICE program, psychologists conduct the diagnosis, coach and counsel the manager, and assist in the development of action plans for implementing new skills on the job. Diagnosis involves collecting information related to the manager's interests, skills, and personality. Interviews and assessments completed by the manager, peers, and supervisor are used to gather this information. The coaching phase of the program involves presenting the manager with information gathered in the assessment phase, participation of the manager in behavior modeling training designed to improve skill deficiencies identified in the assessment phase, and psychological counseling. The support phase of the program involves creating conditions under which the manager is able to use new behaviors on the job. The manager's supervisor is asked to provide feedback to the manager and the psychologist overseeing the manager's development. The psychologist and manager also develop action plans that outline how the manager should try to use new behavior in his or her daily work activities.

Job Experiences. Most employee development is believed to occur through job experiences (McCall, Lombardo, & Morrison, 1988). Job experiences can be used for employee development through enlarging the job, job rotation, transfers, promotions, downward moves, and employee exchanges. A major assumption of using job experiences for development is that development is most likely to occur when there is a mismatch between employees' skills and experience base and the skills required for the job. To be developmental, a job experience must require employees to stretch their skills(i.e., they must be forced to learn new skills, apply their skills and knowledge in a different way, and master new experiences; London, 1989).

An important issue in the use of job experiences for employee development is the need to identify the developmental potential of jobs. The Development Challenge Profile (DCP) was created to identify the developmental components of managerial jobs (Ruderman, Ohlott, & McCauley, 1990). The DCP has been found to have solid psychometric characteristics (internal consistency, construct validity of the factor structure, test–reset reliability) as well as being related to reports of on-the-job learning, job transitions, and objective features of jobs (McCauley, Ruderman, Ohlott, & Morrow, 1994). Experiencing job transitions and task-related characteristics (creating change, high levels of responsibility, and nonauthority relationships) were found to be related to learning. Obstacles (adverse business conditions, lack of top management support, lack of personal support, having a difficult boss) were negatively related to learning.

Job rotation involves providing employees with a series of assignments in various functional areas of the organization or movement among jobs in a single functional area or department (Wexley & Latham, 1994). In one of the few studies to investigate the effectiveness of job rotation for employee development, Campion, Cheraskin, and Stevens (1991) found a positive relationship between rates of job rotation and self-reported benefits, including stimulating work and a greater understanding of the relationship between jobs in the organization.

A relatively new approach to employee development is for two organizations to exchange employees. The exchange typically occurs between companies that are customers for each others' products or services. First Chicago National Bank and Kodak have participated in an employee-exchange program. The employee from First Chicago helped the business-imaging division of Kodak to identify applications for computer disc technology. The Kodak employee helped First Chicago understand areas within the bank that could benefit from imaging technology (Gunsch, 1992).

Formal Courses and Programs. Formal education programs include off- and on-site programs designed specifically for the organization's employees, short courses offered by consultants or universities, executive Master's of Business Administration (MBA) programs, and university programs in which participants are housed at the university while taking classes. These programs may involve various types of activities, such as lectures by business experts, business games and simulations, adventure learning, and meetings with customers. There are usually separate education programs offered for supervisors, middle managers, and executives (Bolt, 1989; Hinrichs & Hollenbeck, 1991; Saari, Johnson, McLaughlin, & Zimmerle, 1988; Tichy, 1989).

There has been little research on the effectiveness of formal education programs for employee development. In a study of Harvard University's Advanced Management Program, Hollenbeck (1991) found that participants reported that they had acquired valuable knowledge from the program. They also reported that the program helped them gain a broader perspective on issues facing the company, increased their self-confidence, and helped them learn new ways to think about and look at problems.

Adventure learning continues to be a popular development activity either by itself or in conjunction with other educational activities. Adventure learning involves groups who are exposed to difficult and unfamiliar physical and mental challenges in an outdoor environment (Wagner, Baldwin, & Rowland, 1991). Both individual and group problem-solving challenges are used. These activities are designed to stimulate participants' use of teamwork, trust, risk-management strategies, and support networks.

Evidence supporting the effectiveness of adventure learning is based on self report data and positive testimonials. For example, Ewert (1988) and Marsh, Richards, and Barnes (1987) found that participation in adventure learning resulted in a true reduction of anxiety and improvements in self-concept. Studies have not yet addressed whether the experiences influence individuals' use of new skill sets in the work setting or stimulate the development of skill weaknesses realized during the exercises.

Relationships. Interactions with other members of the organization, including mentors, sponsors, and peers, can influence employee development. Most of the research regarding developmental relationships has focused on mentoring relationships. A mentoring relationship involves a more experienced employee (mentor) and a less experienced employee (protégé) who interact with the primary purpose of promoting the personal and professional development of the protégé. Most of the research regarding mentoring relationships has focused on the development of the relationship, the benefits that the protégé receives from the relationship, and the functions that the mentor serves (Chao, Walz, & Gardner, 1992; Dreher & Ash, 1990; Noe, 1988; Ostroff & Kozlowski, 1993).

Although mentoring has historically been viewed as only valuable to the protégé, mentors might also receive benefits from the relationship. Serving as a mentor might be useful for stimulating plateaued employees to develop their skills and feel that they make a contribution to the organization's mission. Although most of the research regarding developmental relationships has focused on mentoring relationships, it is clear from the literature that mentors might not be available for all organizational members (Noe, 1988; Ragins & Cotton, 1991). Peer relationships are more accessible to most employees, and research indicates that individuals receive the same types of vocational and psychological benefits (Kram & Isabella, 1985). With the movement toward work designs involving teams, peers are often called on to provide training to other team members. Also, group mentoring is becoming popular. Groups can provide the same type of support to their members as is found in traditional one-on-one mentoring relationships through communications of social norms, providing valuable information, and access to social networks. Individuals who are active participants of professionally oriented groups are likely to experience outcomes that are similar to career and psychosocial mentoring functions (Dansky, 1996).

Relationships Among Development Activity, Learning Environment, and Learning Outcomes

Table 7.1 highlights the relationship among development activities, learning outcomes, and learning environments. As Table 7.1 indicates, each type of development activity has the potential for individuals to achieve one or more of the learning outcomes.

TABLE 7.1
Relationship's Among Development Activity, Learning Environment, and Learning Outcomes

Development Activity	Learning Environment	Primary Outcome
Assessment	Affective	Affective
		self-awareness, changing values
		Cognitive
		problem-solving strategies
Courses	Perceptual/Symbolic	Cognitive
		knowledge organization
		problem-solving strategies
		verbal knowledge
Relationships and job experiences	Perceptual/behavioral	Affective
		attitudinal and motivational
		Cognitive
		problem-solving strategies
		knowledge organization

Relationships Between Learning Environments and Development. Research suggests that the environment plays an important role in learning, particularly if the individuals are self-regulated learners who are motivationally, behaviorally, and cognitively active in the learning process (see Zimmerman, 1989). Each development activity needs to occur in a specific type of learning environment for the learning outcomes to be realized. Kolb and Lewis (1986) suggested that there are four types of learning environments: affective, perceptual, symbolic, and behavioral. Each learning environment has unique characteristics that facilitate the attainment of one or more of the learning outcomes.

An affectively oriented environment is characterized by activities designed to help learners realize their opinions, feelings, and values, as well as receive feedback. This type of environment is necessary for assessment activities to meet affective outcomes. Individuals must be willing to be open, truthful, and unbiased toward the feedback they receive.

A perceptually oriented environment involves activities focused on understanding a concept or a relationship between events. This environment encourages the learner to experiment with new perspectives or ways of thinking. A perceptually oriented environment is critical for relationships, job experiences, and courses to be successful.

A symbolically oriented environment is characterized by activities designed to help the learner master a skill or concept to solve a problem. Theories, examples, key behaviors, or principles are provided to the learner. A symbolically oriented environment is especially important for formal courses to be effective. Learners need to receive appropriate theory and principles within a meaningful framework (such as job-related problems).

A behaviorally oriented environment is characterized by having learners apply knowledge and skills to solve work-related problems. Learners are forced to take responsibility for their actions. Managers need to provide expertise and coaching as desired by the employee, but responsibility for learning is completely up to the learner. This type of learning environment is needed for job experiences to be effective. Managers need to be sure to not tell employees how to solve work-related issues they may be unfamiliar with. Managers should provide advice and resources, and should refer the employee to sources that might be useful.

Link Between Development Activity and Learning Outcomes. Given the appropriate learning environment, each development activity will result in specific learning outcomes. None of the development activities likely influence motor skill development. Assessment through participating in assessment centers, receiving performance feedback, or completing instruments designed to assess interpersonal style, values, or personality type likely result in an increase in awareness of attitudes, interaction styles, competencies, and skill strengths and weaknesses. Courses and programs are usually targeted at developing specific cognitive skills or attitudes. For example, executive development

programs might involve developing executive skills in managing change, valu-
ing diversity, or thinking strategically. Relationships primarily relate to motivational outcomes. As Kraiger et al. (1993) noted, mentors help provide an
interpersonal environment (i.e., provide advice, visibility, coaching) that helps
employees develop a mastery orientation toward work. Employees with a
mastery orientation are more likely to take responsibility for learning, view
learning as a continuous process, and take responsibility for success and failure.
Mentors may also provide employees with information needed to understand
acceptable patterns of behavior in the organization (how to deal with vendors),
and effective problem-solving strategies. Similarly, as a result of a new job,
addition of new responsibilities to the current job, or committee assignment,
employees may be forced to acquire new skills, apply current skills and competencies in a different way, or improve problem-solving skills or interpersonal
strategies. Job assignments likely involve interacting with persons from different
technical or cultural backgrounds (particularly for international assignments).
As a result, job assignments may increase employees' awareness of their personal
values and affect their concern and tolerance for others. Job experiences may
also affect motivational outcomes, such as a person's self-efficacy. Job experiences provide employees with challenges, that if met, increase their beliefs that
they can be successful in similar situations.

Directions for Future Research

Understanding the Construct of Employee Development.   To better understand the antecedents of employee development, one needs to have a better
understanding of the characteristics of developmental activities. Currently,
what is known about the use of job experiences for employee development is
based on research using the interview methodology developed by the Center
for Creative Leadership (McCall et al., 1988; Valerio, 1990). The experiences
identified were based on this process: Mid- to upper level managers were asked
to identify events that led to a lasting change in their approach to management,
and then the categories of developmental experiences were constructed. It
might be useful to see if research utilizing a deductive approach would lead to
similar conclusions regarding the importance and types of job experiences
related to development. A deductive approach would involve identifying critical categories of learning experiences (such as job assignments, coursework, or
interpersonal relationships), developing items related to each category, and
evaluating the construct validity of the categories.
    It was noted earlier that one dimension that development activities might
vary on is the extent to which they involve framebreaking versus incremental
learning. According to London (1989), framebreaking learning experiences
place individuals in difficult positions requiring the acquisition of a large number

of skills to be successful. Framebreaking experiences require considerable individual investment with a high potential for learning, but also a high risk for failure. Research needs to identify the characteristics of framebreaking experiences and the types of persons most likely to respond positively from them. For example, individuals with high levels of self-efficacy may respond more positively to framebreaking experiences than individuals with low self-efficacy.

Assessment as Development Activity. More than 10 years ago, Thornton and Byham (1982) published a critical evaluation of assessment center theory, research, technology, and practice. They identified several research questions regarding the use of assessment centers for employee development that remain unanswered, but need to be investigated. These questions include: (a) What are the assessor behavior and skills required for developmental assessment centers? (b) Does participation in an assessment center lead to more accurate self perceptions of ability? (c) Which individual characteristics influence participants' use of feedback for development? (d) What types of development activities do individuals participate in as a result of assessment? (e) For established assessment centers that supposedly involve assessment and development, does development really occur?

For example, considerable research has investigated the role of learning orientation and feedback-seeking orientation on behavior. Persons with a feedback-seeking orientation are more likely to detect discrepancies between self-perceptions and others' perceptions of behavior and subsequently correct behavior others believe needs improvement (Ashford & Tsui, 1991: Tsui, Ashford, St. Clair, & Xin, 1995). Dweck and Leggett (1998) proposed that persons have either a learning or performance orientation. Persons with a learning orientation are more concerned with increasing their competence and less concerned with others' evaluations of them. Persons with a performance orientation are more concerned with gaining favorable judgments of their competence, not necessarily with improving their competence. This suggests that managers with a learning orientation or who actively seek feedback may demonstrate higher levels of development activity (e.g., meet with raters to clarify weaknesses they identified, enroll in courses and seminars) following participation in a 360-degree feedback system than persons with a performance orientation or low feedback-seeking orientation.

Multirater feedback systems have been shown to have a positive impact on managerial behavior and performance (Atwater, Roush, & Fischthal, 1995; Smither et al., 1995). However, few studies have addressed the relationship between participation in multirater feedback systems (like 360-degree feedback) and development. Research investigating the relationship between the sigh, specificity, and consistency of feedback that managers receive and participation in development activity is needed. Bernardin, Dahmus, and Redmon (1993) suggested that managers' acceptance of subordinate feedback is enhanced when managers receive feedback from both their managers and subordinates. Several studies suggest that positive feedback provides less of an incentive for persons to change behavior than negative feedback because positive feedback focuses attention on the self-concept rather than on the task (Kluger & DeNisi, 1996; Taylor, 1991).

MBTI preferences might have some relationship to development activity preferences. A useful area of research would be to investigate whether persons with introversion personality types learn more in structured (courses) rather than unstructured (committee work) experiences. Self-report data regarding behavior change resulting from receiving MBTI feedback need to be verified by collecting behavior change data from supervisors and peers, and documenting activities that people engage in to bring about change.

Experiences as Development Activity.   More needs to be known about how job experiences can be beneficial for nonmanagerial employees. Most of the work on job experiences for development has utilized managers or white-collar employees. Burgoyne and Hodgson (1983) provided an example of how qualitative methodology might be used to understand the characteristics of job experiences that employees consider to be developmental. Their method included: (a) conducting general interviews exploring the managers' work, activities, role, and use of time; (b) having the managers observe and record actual incidents from their work lives and recall their thoughts and feelings during the incident; and (c) following up with interviews regarding the actions that managers took, the choices they made, or the orientations they adopted as a result of the incidents. The researchers evaluated "learning" as occurring when the managers qualitatively changed the way they conceived something. Although researchers have found relationships between job demands and learning, there has not been a direct test of the assumptions underlying this relationship. The major assumptions are that job demands create challenge for the job incumbent, and a "stretched" or challenged incumbent will learn and develop in response to the challenge provided. Empirical research needs to investigate if challenge mediates the relationship between job demands and development. That is, do job demands have a direct effect on development, or do job demands only influence development indirectly through the amount of challenge that the job incumbent perceives?

Relationships as a Developmental Activity.   It might be useful to view the mentoring relationship from an information-exchange perspective. Protégés receive information from the mentor regarding the organizational norms, role expectations, and behaviors needed to be rewarded and promoted in the organization. Mentors also have the opportunity to obtain information from the protégés. Such information might include current technical information related to their job, information regarding how they are perceived by others in the organization (social feedback), and feedback from the protégés regarding ideas and rough drafts of projects (performance feedback). Morrison (1993) provided a typology of information that might be useful in pursuing research that views mentoring from an information-exchange perspective.

Research is needed to investigate the types of benefits that employees obtain from peer and group relationships, the characteristics of a developmental peer relationship, and what organizations can do to facilitate the development of effective peer relationships. This type of developmental relationship is probably critical for the success of teams. One potentially useful study would be to identify teams that are known to be successful, and collect information regarding the development activities that the team members provide for each other.

Influence of the Learning Environment on the Development Activity–Learning Outcome Relationship. Several issues need to be examined regarding the relationship between development activity and learning outcomes. For example, are certain types of developmental experiences (i.e., job experiences) more conducive for attitudinal and motivational changes than others? Kolb (1984) suggested that an effective learner needs four capabilities: concrete experience skills, reflective observation skills, abstract conceptualization skills, and active experimentation skills. That is, the individual must be able to be fully involved in the activity, reflect on and interpret experiences, create concepts that integrate observations gained from the activity into a theory, and use theories to make decisions and solve problems. Protocol analysis might be useful to gain a better understanding of how development experiences influence learning and vary in the degree to which they require the learners to utilize Kolb's four capabilities. Employees who are participating in development activities could be required to keep a diary or record on audiotape the types of cognitive activities they are engaging in. These protocols could be analyzed looking for evidence of Kolb's four learning capabilities. This type of study would allow for a comparison of individual differences in learning skills both within and across development activities.

ANTECEDENTS OF PARTICIPATION IN DEVELOPMENT ACTIVITIES

This section begins with a brief overview of the individual and organizational antecedents of development activity. It then examines how the antecedents are hypothesized to influence participation in development activity via various theoretical frameworks. It concludes with directions for future research.

Individual Antecedents

Many proposed models focus on individual-level characteristics believed to influence participation in development. Research focusing specifically on participation in formal developmental courses has examined the effects of choice of training course on trainee motivation (Baldwin, Magjuka, & Loher, 1991), and of trainee motivation and perceived pressure from supervisors on training session attendance (Fishbein & Stasson, 1990). In addition, the effect of perceived climate (Kozlowski & Farr, 1988; Kozlowski & Hults, 1987) and age and commitment level (McEnrue, 1989) on attitudes regarding participation in development activities has been examined.

Because of the diversity of factors that fall under the guise of "individual-level characteristics," they are organized into the following groups. First, this section examines the role of immutable individual characteristics, such as age, race, and gender, on participation in development. Second, it discusses the influence of individual attitudes and beliefs on participation. Third, using Holland's (1973) typology, the role of occupational choice on the type of development activity a person participates in is discussed.

Immutable Characteristics.   Given the rapidly changing makeup of today's workforce (Johnston & Packer, 1987), it is important to examine the role, if any, of workplace diversity on development participation. Immutable charac-teristics, such as age, race, gender, and even cognitive ability, may play a role in an individual's level of participation in development activities. Certain groups are not less able to participate in development. However, certain groups (White males) may receive more encouragement and opportunities to partici-pate in development than others.

Little research has been done in this area, with most focusing on the older worker. Cleveland and Shore (1992) found a negative relationship between age and participation in development activity. Chronological age was the most consistent predictor of both self ratings and managers' ratings of participation in development activity. Similarly, McEnrue (1989) found that younger workers were more willing to engage in self development than older workers to prepare for increased levels of organizational responsibility. It may be that the climate for development for older workers is different than that for younger workers, making it easier for younger workers to develop. Sterns and Doverspike (1989) pointed out that motivating older workers to engage in development activities may require special efforts, including changing the attitudes of managers or supervisors about the training and development of older workers, as well as older workers' attitudes about themselves (fear of failure). As London and Bassman (1989) stated: "Many organizations do not view older workers as able to learn or accept new technologies and function in an increasingly competitive envi-ronment" (p. 358). Negative perceptions may inhibit older persons' confidence in their ability to handle new challenges and, subsequently, decrease active participation in development opportunities.

Absent from most of the employee development literature is the role of both race and gender on development program participation. Most of the current research focuses on the potential bias that exists in terms of the career development processes of women. Powell and Mainiero (1992) observed that women's career patterns are much more complex and do not follow the traditional (male) models. Additionally, Stroh, Brett, and Reilly (1992) pointed out that, even when women do "all the right stuff" (e.g., similar career patterns as men), their career progression lagged behind that of men. The differences observed in career progression could be influenced by a lack of support for women's development program participation. A potentially important emerging area of research is attempting to identify the extent to which persons from different demographic groups value similar (and different) aspects of a development climate. Maurer and Tarulli (1994) found that African Americans placed less value on social support (peer and manager) for development in comparison to Whites. Older employees placed slightly greater value on social support as well as on having access to a career counselor than younger employees.

The U.S. Department of Labor (1991) defined a glass ceiling as "artificial barriers based on attitudinal or organizational bias" (p. 1) that serve to inhibit the advancement of minorities and women. The glass ceiling has been offered as a reason that the career patterns of minorities and women do not follow those of White men. A study conducted by the U.S. Department of Labor observed that the glass ceiling seems to occur after the first levels of management, with few minorities or women making it into mid- to senior-level management. One explanation offered for this phenomena is that minorities and women were not offered the same opportunities to develop within the organization. Development opportunities, including education and special projects and assignments, "which are traditional precursors to advancements—were often not as available to minorities and women" (U.S. Department of Labor, 1991, p. 5).

An additional individual characteristic that may influence development program participation is cognitive ability. Unlike age, race, or gender, which may influence participation because of the perceptions of others, cognitive ability may influence individuals' own perceptions of their development needs and/or capabilities to develop. Some empirical support has been found for the latter. Hunter (1986) found that cognitive ability predicted training success across a wide spectrum of jobs. Looking specifically at flight attendants, Ferris, Bergin, and Gilmore (1986) found that mental ability was a predictor of training program success. Peters and O'Connor (1980) suggested that situational constraints may be more detrimental to the job performance of high-ability rather than low-ability employees. That is, cognitive ability may be a moderator between an employee's attitudes and perceptions and participation in development activities. Current empirical research has not simultaneously investigated the influence of ability and other antecedents (attitudes) on participation in development activities.

Attitudes and Beliefs. An individual's attitudes and beliefs regarding development activities is believed to be an important determinant of participation. Although many things affect an individual's attitudes, researchers have examined the role of past experiences in development activities on beliefs and attitudes toward future participation (Noe, 1986; Noe & Schmitt, 1986). The assumption is that individuals who have had positive experiences in development activities are more likely to participate in the future than individuals who have had negative experiences. Noe and Wilk (1993) found that individuals' perceptions of constraints on their participation in development activities influenced their future plans to participate. Individuals who had negative development experiences were less likely to participate in development activities in the future. This section focuses on two types of attitudes and beliefs. One group includes those attitudes and beliefs that are more directly related to decisions to participate in development activities—namely, motivation to learn, motivation to transfer, and self-efficacy. The second group includes attitudes and beliefs that are tied to the individual's present organization, namely job satisfaction and organizational commitment.

Motivation to learn, defined as employees' desire to learn the content of the developmental program, may be an important factor for training participation and effectiveness (Noe, 1986). Studies have shown that motivation to learn is related to learning and program completion (Baldwin et al., 1991; Hicks & Klimoski, 1987). These findings have resulted in a variety of organizational models intended to increase the effectiveness of developmental activities (Keller, 1987; Yelon, 1992). For example, Keller developed the attention, relevance, confidence, and satisfaction (ARCS) model to help organizations and designers of developmental programs stimulate employees' motivation to learn.

Motivation to transfer involves employees' desire to use the knowledge and skills acquired in development activities on the job (Noe, 1986). Motivation to transfer requires confidence in the new skill, belief in applicability of the new skill on the job, and support on the job to use the new skill. If individuals believe that the content of the development activity is important for their job, they may be more likely to participate in order to learn and, subsequently use the new skill(s). Yelon (1992) proposed a model to promote the transfer of training that incorporates these aspects. The motivation, awareness, skills, and support (MASS) model involves the following steps: (a) increase employees' motivation to learn, (b) teach employees when and how to use the new skill, (c) enable employees to master and apply the new skill, and (d) give employees support on the job. However, it is unclear how such a model would work in situations where the new "skill" is more ambiguous (a challenging job assignment during which an employee is expected to "develop").

Self-efficacy is defined as individuals' confidence that they can cope with challenging situations (Bandura, 1977). Self-efficacy could potentially impact motivation to learn, motivation to transfer, and, subsequently, participation in development. Gist and Mitchell (1992) listed mobilization as one of the components of the construct of self-efficacy. They concluded that self-efficacy is an important part of motivation through its influence on choice of task, effort toward the task, and persistence in achievement of the task. Therefore, individuals with high levels of self-efficacy are more likely to participate in new and challenging situations than individuals with low levels of self-efficacy. Previous research has identified self-efficacy as an important determinant of an individual's motivation to participate in development activities (Gist, 1987; Noe, 1986; Noe & Schmitt, 1986).

Although the three previous attitudes and beliefs are those that employees may have developed before entering their present organization, the next two—job satisfaction and organizational commitment—are more reflective of employees' current situation. Individuals' attitudes toward an organization may also impact their participation in development. Although researchers have used participation in development activities as an indicator of organizational commitment (Meyer & Allen, 1984), little research has looked at the role of organizational commitment on development program participation. In one study, McEnrue (1989) found that employees' level of organizational commitment correlated positively with their willingness to self-develop. Individuals who expressed higher levels of organizational commitment were more likely to also express a desire to voluntarily participate in development activities.

Researchers often look at training and development activities as antecedents to job satisfaction (cf. Mathieu, 1991; Roznowski & Hulin, 1992). Job satisfaction models assume that certain behavior changes are influenced by current levels of satisfaction. Outcomes most often associated with low levels of job satisfaction are withdrawal behaviors, such as slacking off, absenteeism, and turnover. In an overview of new job satisfaction research, Fisher and Locke (1992), provided results from studies that attempt to go beyond the typical job satisfaction outcomes. One study they examined labeled a category of job satisfaction outcomes *constructive protest or problem solving*, which includes participation in training as one way for employees low in job satisfaction to act in a positive manner. Employees' participation in development activities may be influenced by their level of job satisfaction in several additional ways. Individuals with high job satisfaction may be inclined to participate in development activities to increase the probability of retaining their current job or remaining a member of the organization. If job satisfaction is low, employees may either: (a) reduce development program participation because of a lack of desire to remain in their current situation, (b) increase development program participation if they see it as a chance to avoid regular work activities, or (c) increase development program participation to improve their opportunities to change jobs or occupations.

Occupational Preference.   Unlike the other individual-level antecedents of participation in development activities, occupational preference influences both the type of development activities employees participate in, as well as their rate of participation. Research on the type of development activity chosen by employees is limited. In one of the few articles examining choice in participation, the focus was on the effect of choice on motivation to learn. Baldwin et al. (1991) found that those who had choice, but who were told they did not receive their choice of training, were less motivated to learn than either those with no choice or those who received their choice. But what determines the type of development program an employee chooses to participate in?

It may be that individuals' choice of what type of development activity to participate in is based on their occupational preference. Holland's (1973) model of vocational choice argued that individuals can be characterized into six different personality types: realistic, investigative, artistic, social, enterprising, and conventional. Likewise, environments can be categorized by the same six types, and individuals search for an environment that is most congruent to their own personality. One of the outcomes of this pairing of individuals and environments is the development of individuals' vocational choice or preference. Individuals will most prefer an occupation (environment) that best matches their own interests and competencies.

This "theory of careers" might also be extended to explain choice of development activities. Individuals who are congruent in their occupation may choose development activities that will improve their competencies in and chance to remain in that occupation. However, individuals who are not congruent with their occupation may choose development activities that improve their chance of moving into an occupation or situation that allows them to use preferred competencies and skills. No research has directly examined the link between occupational preferences and choice of development activity.

Organizational Antecedents

Because development activities often occur in the organizational context, the characteristics of the organization likely impact participation in development activities. An organization's strategy or philosophy regarding development, the climate for development (or at least perceived climate), and the structure of pay and benefit systems may influence the level of participation in development activities. A discussion of these firm-level characteristics follows.

Business Strategy.   Firms in high-technology fields, such as those in the computer industry, may place a higher priority on development behaviors and may encourage their employees to participate. This is supported by the fact that many studies on participation in development have focused on employees in technical occupations (DeMeuse, 1985; Kaufman, 1972, 1975). For example, using a sample of engineers, Kozlowski and Farr (1988), developed and tested a model of updating behavior. They found that the effect of the organizational environment or context on performance and participation in development activities was mediated by job and climate perceptions.

The emphasis in many of these studies was on ways to combat obsolescence. Dubin (1990) defined *technical obsolescence* as the difference between what a professional should know and an individual's capabilities to perform tasks both now and in the future. Given that an individual's knowledge can become obsolete in anywhere from 1 year (computers) to approximately 8 years (business management), the importance of updating may vary by field (Dubin, 1990). Keeping up to date on new technological advances requires individual's to access the work of others in their field (courses, professional journals). Therefore, organizations involved in more technical fields with a shorter "shelf life" of knowledge may make updating behaviors a priority.

Likewise, an organization may have a philosophy regarding entry into the organization, making development either more or less important to success in the company. Some organizations prefer to hire individuals who already possess the requisite skills and abilities needed to succeed in their job. Others prefer to hire less experienced and less skilled workers and develop them in-house. Miles and Snow (1980) referred to these two types of organizations as the "buy"-oriented versus the "make"-oriented.

Progression patterns in the organization, as set up by the internal labor market, may also influence the strategic role of development. For those organizations that fill vacancies in upper level positions from an internal pool of applicants, development may be important to facilitate a fluid change in position. Sonnenfeld and Peiperl (1988) suggested that firms that are considered the dominant competitor in their market—so called "academy" firms—often restrict organizational entry to early career and emphasize promotion from within. They indicated that, in these types of firms, the training and development function is valued by top management, and extensive development opportunities are available to employees.

Climate. Research has shown that the perceived presence of supports and constraints to develop what are collectively referred to as the development "climate " impact employees' development program participation (Kozlowski & Farr, 1988; Kozlowski & Hults, 1987; Noe & Wilk, 1993). Constraints like lack of money, equipment, or time are believed to inhibit individuals' participation in development activities. However, supports, including supervisor or manager encouragement and feedback, are believed to promote participation in development activities.

Research has looked at constraints' effects on various types of behaviors, such as performance. Peters, O'Connor, Eulberg, and Watson (1988) found that constraints present in the workplace resulted in decreased satisfaction, increased frustration, and increased thoughts of leaving. Situational constraints have also been used in training and development research as a predictor of participation. Noe and Wilk (1993) found that employees' perceptions of the supportiveness of their work environment influenced their rate of participation in development activities. A supportive climate positively influenced participation, whereas situational constraints negatively influenced future plans to participate in development activities.

A supportive environment for participation in development activities is often characterized in terms of social support, where employees are encouraged to participate, are given regular feedback regarding development needs, or are encouraged to implement behavior, knowledge, or skills acquired in development activities from their supervisor or peers. Dubin (1990) also included such things as salary and promotion recommendations as examples of managerial support. Dubin argued that a work environment that involves manager and peer support better facilitates updating behavior than one that lacks such support.

Pay Systems.   The compensation system of an organization reflects the various strategic objectives of the firm with regard to labor (Milkovich, 1988; Milkovich & Boudreau, 1994; Milkovich & Newman, 1993). These pay systems are expected to do many different things, often with competing goals (e.g., attract and retain qualified workers; motivate high individual performance; encourage teamwork; reduce turnover, absenteeism, and shirking; increase job satisfaction and organizational commitment). Pay system attributes may also be used to influence employee development activities. The key components of an organization's compensation system—pay structure, pay level, and pay mix—can either directly (pay for skill acquisition) or indirectly (pay for promotion attained through skill development) encourage employees' development activities.

"Pay structure refers to the array of pay rates for different work or skills within a single organization. It focuses attention on the levels, differentials, and criteria used to determine those pay rates" (Milkovich & Newman, 1993, p. 35). Structures can be job evaluation-based, which is the traditional approach, or individual- or skill-based. Job evaluation-based structures are believed to induce job- or promotion-seeking behaviors, which may indirectly encourage skill development to gain future promotions or job opportunities (Dufetel, 1991; Gerhart & Milkovich, 1992). Although this influence is not as direct as specifically paying for skill acquisition, it may be as effective. Clear communication of skills required for promotions and higher paying jobs can direct the employee into developmental channels.

However, individual- or skill-based structures signal employees about the importance of skill acquisition and directly reward the development of those skills. These skill-based structures either link pay to the breadth of a set of skills an employee can perform, or to the depth of knowledge possessed in a specific occupation or field of expertise (Luthans & Fox, 1989).

An example of a job evaluation structure acting like a skill-based structure is the dual-career ladder or path. Instead of forcing technically skilled employees into managerial positions to obtain promotions and pay increases, a dual-career ladder with wide pay ranges allows technical personnel to move up in their position and receive higher pay for their growing expertise (Farr & Middlebrooks, 1990; Milkovich & Newman, 1987).

Pay level refers to the average wage paid by a firm in relation to its competitors. The developmental influence of pay level has not been explored. Although it is difficult to imagine examples of pay level directly encouraging employee development activities, several indirect influences of pay level on participation in development activities can be suggested, some based on efficiency wage models. (For a general discussion of efficiency wage models, see Gerhart & Milkovich, 1992.) An efficiency wage model contends that employers realize higher levels of efficiency and productivity by paying above the average market rate. This is accomplished because the higher pay (a) attracts higher ability individuals, and (b) reduces shirking behaviors and turnover because individuals fear losing their high-paying job (see Rynes & Barber, 1990: Yellen, 1984). Two indirect influences on development can be hypothesized from the attraction ability and the fear of job loss components of the model. First, Noe (1991) makes the point that higher ability individuals are more likely to recognize the need for, and thus seek out, development activities. Second, individuals receiving efficiency wages should be more willing to pursue opportunities to develop skills and knowledge in order to keep their current job.

Pay mix (also known as *pay form*) refers to the relative proportion of compensation made up of base pay, incentives, and benefits. Base pay is the wage or salary an employee receives in return for the labor he or she provides. Incentives are specified rewards for specific performance outcomes, and can be given on an individual or group basis. Benefits, which now make up about a third of the typical employee's compensation, are those mandatory payments (such as Social Security, unemployment insurance, workers compensation) and discretionary payments and services (such as insurance, child care, tuition reimbursement, paid time off) provided by an employer conditional on employment. Heavy reliance on annual increases to base pay, often called a *merit increase*, is evident in many traditional pay systems. Much discussion has centered around whether merit increases actually link pay to performance (and therefore serve a motivational function), or whether merit increases reward organizational commitment (Gerhart, Milkovich, & Murray, 1992; Lawler, 1989). Although increases to base pay can be considered a reward for cumulative past performance, evidence linking base pay directly to employee motivation or development activities is lacking. Base pay increases tied to promotions could indirectly influence employees to develop new skills to secure a position in the next level of the hierarchy. However, base pay increases that are not tied to specific performance outcomes, or that are tied to outcomes that do not require development of new skills, seem unlikely to encourage employee development.

The link between incentive portions of the pay mix and employee development is more clearly defined than that of base pay. Individual incentives, such as lump sum payments or bonuses, commissions, or piece-rate payments, link recent performance to the rewards received. These may induce employees to pursue development activities that will make goal attainment (and reward acquisition) more likely in the future. As noted by Lawler (1989), "Effective pay for performance systems motivate learning and development because individuals perceive that they must develop their skills in order to perform effectively. Of course, if individuals feel they already have the requisite skills, then a pay for performance system may not have this impact" (p. 143).

However, when new skills are not directly related to the performance of the current job for which individuals receive incentive pay, the system may actually discourage employees from learning new skills (Lawler, 1989). For example, in a piece-rate system, the cost of time away from the job to pursue developmental activities reduces current income for employees. If employees perceive the potential pay-back of development activities to be risky or far in the future, they may be less likely to pursue development opportunities.

Interest in group incentives has grown as teamwork, total quality management (TQM), and worker participation strategies have been adopted by more organizations. The three general types of group incentives are profit sharing, gain sharing, and stock ownership plans. Of the three, gainsharing plans may have some direct influence on employees' participation in development activities by fostering participation and information exchange among work group members (Hatcher & Ross, 1991). However, there is no indication that the development activities the work group members participate in extends their knowledge and skills beyond those required for the group's assignments.

The final type of incentive is retirement incentives. In the wake of mergers, downsizing, and restructuring, the developmental aspects of early retirement plans cannot be ignored. Early retirement packages may encourage employees to pursue developmental opportunities not related to their current position or current employer. Employees may develop hobbies into a career opportunity (e.g., bait-and-tackle shop, consulting), completely retrain for a new career, or remain retired and develop nonwork goals (Colarelli & Beehr, 1993).

One of the most frequently noted benefits that directly influence employees' participation in development activities is tuition reimbursement. However, other benefits can directly encourage employees to make use of developmental opportunities, such as paid time off to attend developmental seminars and events travel stipends subscriptions to professional/industrial journals and corporate sponsorship of membership in professional organizations. Benefits can indirectly influence employee development when eligibility for certain benefits is tied to a job or employment level. For example, part-time employees who need health insurance may seek to develop firm-specific skills and knowledge to compete and obtain full-time employment, which includes health insurance benefits. Anecdotal evidence supporting this example comes from retailing, where a frequent port of entry is the part-time job, but where most benefits are tied to full-time employment.

Useful Theoretical Frameworks for Studying Development Activities

Social learning theory, expectancy theory, goal setting theory, theory of reasoned action, and contract theory are frameworks used to better understand individuals' decision to participate in development activities. These theories can be differentiated from one another on how each would answer the following question: Given a set of individual and organizational antecedents, how does an individual decide to participate in development activities? Some emphasize the role of external or organizational characteristics, and others emphasize the internal or individual characteristics in employees' choice to participate in development activities. A brief description of each theory's tenets regarding participation decisions follows.

Social Learning Theory. According to social learning theory, participation in development activities is the result of employees mimicking the behavior of an organizational agent (i.e., a model; Bandura, 1986). An individual observes the behavior of the agent(s) of the organization and the subsequent outcomes that result from the behavior. The employee mimics the model's behavior, expecting the same or similar outcomes—which serve as reinforcers of the behavior. These reinforcers can encourage or discourage the behavior, and provide valuable information on which the individual can modify his or her behavior. For example, employees who observe their peers receiving interesting and challenging job assignments as a result of their development participation may be influenced to participate if such an outcome is desired. One way internal labor market structures may influence participation decisions is through modeling behavior. If an organization hires externally for low-level positions and promotes from within for higher level positions, a newcomer may observe others to see what warrants a promotion to higher levels. If the organization rewards those who are actively developing, a newcomer may mimic that behavior to advance.

Expectancy Theory. According to expectancy theory, participation in development is dependent on an individual's beliefs regarding effort-performance and performance-outcome relationships, as well as the value placed on outcomes related to participation in development (Farr & Middlebrooks, 1990).

The catalyst for an individual to choose to participate in development activities is motivation through expectation. If the expectations of the linkages between effort-performance and performance-outcome are positive, and if the outcome has value, an individual will be motivated.

One potential reason that perceptions of supervisor or peer support are important to participation decisions is that it may impact individuals' expectations and beliefs regarding the value of updating behavior. Using an expectancy theory framework, Farr and Middlebrooks (1990) suggested that supervisor and peer support may positively influence motivation because it positively impacts expectancies, instrumentalities, and valences. Employees who perceive a supportive climate for development may be more apt to believe that their participation will result in increased competence (expectancy), and that increasing competencies will result in outcomes such as promotions and salary increases (instrumentalities).

Goal Setting Theory. According to goal setting theory, the impetus to participate in development activities is motivation to achieve a goal. By definition, a *goal* is something individuals desire and strive for. It requires commitment on the part of the individual holding it for any action toward goal attainment to take place (Locke & Latham, 1990). Individuals must invest effort now in the hopes that their behavior will lead to goal achievement. Individuals may participate in development activities if they believe that this will increase their chances of achieving personal goals. This framework may help explain how occupational preference may influence decisions to participate in development activities. For example, if individuals are not well matched to their current occupation or job, their goal may be to attain a different job. One way to accomplish that goal is to participate in development activities that may increase the probability of goal achievement.

Theory of Reasoned Action. Fishbein and Ajzen's (1975) theory of reasoned action proposes that both an individual's attitude toward a behavior (development) and perceptions of the wants and wishes of important others (supervisor or peers) determine behavioral intentions. The theory of reasoned action explains participation behavior by both the wishes of others and by the strength of the individual's intention to develop. Fishbein and Stasson (1990) hypothesized that the wishes or wants of the important others would be mediated by the intentions of the individual. The intentions, then, would be directly related to the behavior.

The theory of reasoned action may help explain how social support in organizations influence's an individual's decision to participate in development activities. Research showing a positive relationship between social support and participation decisions has been well documented (Dubin, 1990; Kozlowski & Farr, 1988). In studying training session attendance, Fishbein and Stasson

(1990) found a direct relationship between both an individual's motivation or intention to attend and supervisory influence and actual attendance. It may be that the support of important others (supervisors and peers) influences an individual's own intentions to develop, tipping the scale as to whether an individual will develop.

Contract Theory. Psychological contracts explain an individual's participation in development primarily as a fulfillment of an obligation. Rousseau (1989) characterized a psychological contract as individual beliefs in reciprocal obligations between the individual and the organization. According to Rousseau: "It is an individual's belief that promise of future return has been made, a consideration or contribution has been offered (and accepted), and an obligation to provide future benefits exists" (p. 126). Because psychological contracts are a relatively new research area, little is known about their effects on organizational behaviors (performance, participation in development). Primarily, behavior will be related to the terms and conditions of the contract. The incentive to perform these contract-related behaviors, then, is the perceived obligation to the other party of the contract. Individuals' perceptions of reciprocity between themselves and their employer regarding development create a responsibility to fulfill the terms of the contract that exists between them. Employees may perceive an obligation to develop in exchange for rewards that they perceive the organization is obligated to supply.

The obligations regarding issues of training and development that exist between an employee and employer have been included in previous research as part of the psychological contract (Robinson, Kraatz, & Rousseau, 1994; Robinson & Rousseau, 1994). Sims (1992) examined the role of psychological contracts in developing a learning climate to facilitate the development of a shared responsibility for training and learning. Additionally, Scott and Meyer (1991) argued that training is becoming institutionalized as employees acquire certain "membership rights" or contractual rights from organizations. After gaining an "elite" position in the organization, for instance, rights that serve to legitimize the employee's new standing in the hierarchy are conferred. These rights may include increased training and development opportunities.

Directions for Future Research

Individual Antecedents. The influence of age, race, and gender should be examined in future research on participation in development activities. Certain groups may have different opportunities or different perceptions of opportunities to develop, which may directly limit their actual rate of participation. Further, this may limit the advancement opportunities of these group members. These characteristics may work with other antecedents to limit participation decisions.

Looking at developmental job experiences, Ohlott, Ruderman, and McCauley (1994) found gender differences in perceived personal support (networks, relationships). Women reported having less support from others in the work environment than men. They argued that this type of obstacle may actually serve as a developmental experience. Research has identified self-efficacy—belief in one's ability to handle challenging situations (Bandura, 1977)—as an important determinant of an individual's participation in development activities (Gist, 1987; Noe & Schmitt, 1986; Noe & Wilk, 1993; Wilk & Noe, 1993). Future research should examine the relationship between an individual's self-efficacy and perceived obstacles for development. It may be that women with high self-efficacy are more able to turn an obstacle into a developmental experience than women with low self-efficacy.

Current empirical research has not simultaneously investigated the influence of ability and attitudes on development activities. Given the importance of awareness of development needs in participation in development activities (McEnrue, 1989; Noe, 1986; Noe & Schmitt, 1986), future research should examine the effect of cognitive ability on individuals' awareness of their own development deficiencies, as well as on their beliefs about solving them through development programs. The Baldwin et al. (1991) model of trainee choice includes ability, but only as a factor in training outcomes. They also statistically controlled for ability to assess the impact of trainee choice on pretraining motivation and training outcomes. In the future, research should examine how ability is related to an individual's awareness of developmental needs, as well as participation choice. Expectancy theory may provide the proper framework for examining this question. Individuals' perceptions of their own ability and training needs may impact effort-performance perceptions, thus influencing future behavior.

Research on participation in development activities often focuses on the role of individuals' attitudes and beliefs that are specific to development participation—namely, motivation to learn, motivation to transfer, and self-efficacy. Specifically, researchers often look for ways to increase these attitudes and beliefs with the assumption that they will translate into higher participation rates. However, the type of skill(s) to be developed may influence this attitude–behavior relationship. Future research should examine how the characteristics of the skill to be developed (ambiguity) impact an individual's perception of transfer and, subsequently, interest in participation in development activities. A highly ambiguous skill (managerial leadership) versus a more concrete skill (handling customer complaints) may appear to be more difficult for an employee to transfer, and may reduce not only motivation to transfer, but motivation to learn and, subsequently, attendance in those types of courses.

There has been less focus on the role of job- and organization-specific attitudes—namely, job satisfaction and organizational commitment on participation in development activities. Research often looks at opportunities to develop as an antecedent to job satisfaction, but neglect's to look at participation in development activities as an outcome of it. Future research should take into account both the antecedent and outcome role of development activities on job satisfaction. As the presence of and importance of development opportunities change over the course of an individual's tenure with an organization, a longitudinal study could best capture these changes and the changes in both participation rates and job satisfaction over time. A contract theory perspective may provide a framework for examining the perceived obligations of an employer to provide development opportunities to a newcomer. Perceived violations of the contract may help explain changes in job satisfaction and participation rates over time.

An individual's occupational preference and perceived match with their occupation may influence participation in development activities. Research should examine the relationship between congruence of the type of development activities an individual participates in and the individual's current occupation and tenure in that occupation. Research often focuses on employees in certain occupational types. For example, Kaufman (1972) and Kozlowski and Farr (1988) both examined updating activities of specifically technical employees (engineers). Research is needed for employees in more varied occupational categories.

A goal setting framework may be used to examine these issues. Individuals' current fit with their occupation may impact the type of career goals set and the methods by which they attempt to achieve them. Specifically, a study that measures employees' occupational match and their career goals would be able to test: (a) if fit impacts the career goal set, and (b) if development participation is used as a means to improve their chances of goal attainment.

Organizational Antecedents.   The type of field or industry and the internal labor market of an organization likely impact both the opportunities and encouragement given to employees to participate in development activities. These types of macro, organizational-level characteristics are not regularly examined as antecedents of development program participation. Future research needs to move beyond the individual level to include organizational strategy antecedents of development activity participation.

Certain types of organizational policies may impact an individual's beliefs that development activities are worth the time and effort. If an organization's policy or norms regarding entry and promotion are to hire low and promote from within, employees may believe that development activities are an important way to increase promotability. A researcher may want to gather information on these types of policies or norms that exist within an organization from individuals of varying tenure levels. For example, an individual who is plateaued may believe that participation in development is futile for promotion, whereas an individual who is new may see participation as a worthwhile endeavor.

Employees' perceptions of the organization's development "climate" (con-straints and supports) may impact their development program participation (Kozlowski & Farr, 1988; Kozlowski & Hults, 1987; Noe & Wilk, 1993). In their study of the influence of organizational climate and culture on the transfer of supervisory behaviors learned in a training program, Tracey, Tannenbaum, & Kavanagh (1995) developed a reliable and valid measure of continuous learning culture. Although the construct of continuous learning has been fashionable in the practitioner literature, until this instrument was developed there were no measures available with acceptable psychometric characteristics. Tracey et al. argue that a continuous learning culture is based on an organizational frame of reference, and such a culture demonstrates the importance of the acquisition and application of new knowledge and skills gained in many ways, not just through formal training programs. Because of the pervasive effect that the organizational culture can have on employees' behavior, future research on employee development needs to assess continuous learning culture and other macro level variables.

One important issue for future research may be to examine whether the constraints or supports perceived to be present in the environment are actually present. Research that surveys both employees and other organizational repre-sentatives (supervisors, managers, and executives) at various levels and areas in the organization may be useful to determine whether there is congruence between perceived and actual constraints and supports. If not, certain worker (race or gender) or departmental characteristics may be examined as influenc-ing the discrepancy. Additionally, future research needs to examine the rela-tionship between these perceptions and both attitudes toward development activities and actual participation in development activity.

Pay systems in organizations perform many functions, often with competing priorities and goals. In addition to serving to attract, retain, motivate, and reward employees, pay systems may encourage or discourage employee devel-opment. Theories of motivation, such as expectancy theory and efficiency wage theory, can provide a framework for future research investigating the impact that pay systems may have on employees' decisions to pursue development activities based on rewards and labor market conditions. Future research should include basic descriptive information on both the explicit and incidental use of pay systems as a driving force behind employee development.

REFERENCES

Ashford, S. J., & Tsui, A. S. (1991). Self-regulation for managerial effectiveness: The role of active feedback-seeking. *Academy of Management Journal, 34*, 251–280.

Atwater, L., Roush, P., & Fischthal, A. (1995). The influence of upward feedback on self- and follower ratings of leadership. *Personnel Psychology, 48*, 35–59.

Baldwin, T. T., Magjuka, R. J., & Loher, B. T. (1991). The perils of participation: Effects of choice of training on trainee motivation and learning. *Personnel Psychology, 44*, 51–66.

Bandura, A. (1977). *Social learning theory.* Englewood Cliffs, NJ: Prentice-Hall.

Bandura, A. (1986). *Social foundations of thought and action: A social cognitive theory.* Englewood Cliffs, NJ: Prentice-Hall.

Bernardin, H. J., Dahmus, S. A., & Redmon, G. (1993). Attitudes of first-line supervisors toward subordinate appraisals. *Human Resource Management, 32*, 315–324.

Bolt, J. F. (1989). *Executive development.* New York: Harper Business.

Burgoyne, J. G., & Hodgson, V. E. (1983). Natural learning and managerial action: A phenomenological study in the field setting. *Journal of Management Studies, 20*, 387–399.

Campion, M. A., Cheraskin, L., & Stevens, M. J. (1994). Career-related antecedents and outcomes of job rotation. *Academy of Management Journal, 37*, 1518–1542.

Carnevale, A. P., Gainer, L. J., & Villet, J. (1991). *Training in America.* San Francisco: Jossey-Bass.

Carnevale, A. P., & Goldstein, H. W. (1990). Schooling and training for work in America: An overview. In L. A. Ferman, M. Hoyman, M. J. Cutcher-Gershenfeld, & E. J. Savoie (Eds.), *New developments in worker training: A legacy for the 1990s* (pp. 25–54). Madison, WI: Industrial Relations Research Association.

Chao, G. T., Walz, P. M., & Gardner, P. D. (1992). Formal and informal mentorships: A comparison on mentoring functions and contrast with nonmentored counterparts. *Personnel Psychology, 45*, 619–636.

Cleveland, J. N., & Shore, L. M. (1992). Self- and supervisory-perspectives on age and work attitudes and performance. *Journal of Applied Psychology, 77*, 469–484.

Colarelli, S. M., & Beehr, T. A. (1993). Selection out: Firings, layoffs, and retirement. In N. Schmitt & W. C. Borman (Eds.), *Personnel selection in organizations* (pp. 341–384). San Francisco: Jossey-Bass.

Dansky, K. H. (1996). The effect of group mentoring on career outcomes. *Group & Organization Management, 21*, 5–21.

DeMeuse, K. P. (1985). Employees' responses to participation in an in-house continuing education program: An exploratory study. *Psychological Reports, 57*, 1099–1109.

Dreher, G. F., & Ash, R. A. (1990). A comparative study of mentoring among men and women in managerial, professional, and technical positions. *Journal of Applied Psychology, 75*, 539–546.

Druckman, D., & Bjork, R. A. (Eds.). (1991). *In the mind's eye.* Washington, DC: National Academy Press.

Dubin, S. S. (1990). Maintaining competence through updating. In S. L. Willis & S. S. Dubin (Eds.), *Maintaining professional competence* (pp. 9–43). San Francisco: Jossey-Bass.

Dufetel, L. (1991, July/August). Job evaluation: Still at the frontier. *Compensation and Benefits Review*, pp. 53–67.

Dweck, C. S., & Leggett, E. L. (1988). A social-cognitive approach to motivation and personality. *Psychological Review, 95*, 256–273.

Ewert, A. (1988). Reduction of trait anxiety through participation in Outward Bound. *Leisure Sciences, 10*, 107–117.

Farr, J. L., & Middlebrooks, C. L. (1990). Enhancing motivation to participate in professional development. In S. L. Willis & S. S. Dubin (Eds.), *Maintaining professional competence* (pp. 195–213). San Francisco: Jossey-Bass.

Ferris, G. R., Bergin, T. G., & Gilmore, D. C. (1986). Personality and ability predictors of training performance for flight attendants. *Group and Organization Studies, 11*, 419–435.

Festinger, L. (1954). A theory of social comparison processes. *Human Relations, 7*, 117–140.

Fishbein, M., & Ajzen, I. (1975). *Belief, attitude, intention, and behavior: An introduction to theory and research. Reading*, MA: Addison-Wesley.

Fishbein, M., & Stasson, M. (1990). The role of desires, self-predictions, and perceived control in the prediction of training session attendance. *Journal of Applied Social Psychology, 20*, 173–198.

Fisher, C. D., & Locke, E. A. (1992). The new look in job satisfaction research and theory. In C. J. Cranny, P. C. Smith, & E. F. Stone (Eds.), *Job satisfaction: How people feel about their jobs and how it affects their performance* (pp. 165–194). Lexington, MA: Lexington.

Fitzgerald, W. (1992). Training vs. development. *Training and Development, 5*, 81–82, 84.

Gaugler, B. B., Rosenthal, D. B., Thornton, G. C., & Bentson, C. (1987). Meta analysis of assessment center validity. *Journal of Applied Psychology, 72*, 493–511.

Gerhart, B., & Milkovich, G. T. (1992). Employee compensation: Research and practice. In M. D. Dunnette & L. M. Hough (Eds.), *Handbook of industrial and organizational psychology* (Vol. 3, pp. 481–569). Palo Alto, CA: Consulting Psychologists Press.

Gerhart, B., Milkovich, G. T., & Murray, B. (1992). Pay, performance, and participation. In D. Lewin, O. S. Mitchell, & P. D. Sherer (Eds.), *Research frontiers in industrial relations and human resources* (pp. 193–238). Greenwich, CT: JAI.

Gist, M. E. (1987). Self-efficacy: Implications for organizational behavior and human resource management. *Academy of Management Review, 12*, 472–485.

Gist, M. E., & Mitchell, T. R. (1992). Self-efficacy: A theoretical analysis of its determinants and malleability. *Academy of Management Review, 17*, 183–211.

Goldstein, I. L. (1993). Training in organizations (3rd ed.). Pacific Grove, CA: Brooks Cole.

Gunsch, D. (1992, October). Customer service focus prompts employee exchange. *Personnel Journal*, pp. 32, 34–36, 38.

Hatcher, L., & Ross, T. L. (1991). From individual incentives to an organization-wide gainsharing plan: Effect on teamwork and product quality. *Journal of Organizational Behavior, 12*, 169–183.

Hellervik, L. W., Hazucha, J. F., & Schneider, R. J. (1992). Behavior change: Models, methods, and a review of the evidence. In M. D. Dunnette & L. M. Hough (Eds.), *Handbook of industrial & organizational psychology* (2nd ed., Vol. 3, pp. 823–896). Palo Alto, CA: Consulting Psychologists Press.

Hicks, W. D., & Klimoski, R. J. (1987). Entry into training programs and its effects on training outcomes: A field experiment. *Academy of Management Journal, 30*, 542–552.

Hinrichs, J. R., & Hollenbeck, G. P. (1991). Leadership development. In K. N. Wexley (Ed.), *Developing human resources* (pp. 221–258). Washington, DC: Bureau of National Affairs.

Hirsch, S. K. (1992). *MBTI Team Building Program*. Palo Alto, CA: Consulting Psychologists Press.

Holland, J. L. (1973). *Making vocational choices: A theory of careers*. Englewood Cliffs, NJ: Prentice-Hall.

Hollenbeck, G. P. (1991). What did you learn in school? Studies of a university executive program. *Human Resource Planning, 14*, 247–260.

Howard, A., & Bray, D. W. (1988). *Managerial lives in transition*. New York: Guilford.

Hummer, A. L. (1993). *Introduction to types and careers*. Palo Alto, CA: Consulting Psychologists Press.

Hunter, J. E. (1986). Cognitive ability, cognitive aptitude, job knowledge, and job performance. *Journal of Vocational Behavior, 29*, 340–362.

Johnston, W. B., & Packer, A. H. (1987). *Workforce 2000*. Indianapolis, IN: Hudson Institute.

Jones, R. G., & Whitmore, M. D. (1995). Evaluating developmental assessment centers as interventions. *Personnel Psychology, 48*, 377–388.

Kaufman, H. G. (1972). Relations of ability and interest to currency of professional knowledge among engineers. *Journal of Applied Psychology, 56*, 495–499.

Kaufman, H. G. (1975). Individual differences, early work challenge, and participation in continuing education. *Journal of Applied Psychology, 60*, 405–408.

Keller, J. M. (1987). Strategies for stimulating the motivation to learn. *Performance and Instruction, 26*, 1–7.

Kluger, A. N., & DeNisi, A. (1996). The effects of feedback interventions on performance: A historical review, a meta-analysis, and a preliminary feedback intervention theory. *Psychological Bulletin, 119*, 254–284.

Kolb, D. (1984). *Experiential learning*. Englewood Cliffs, NJ: Prentice-Hall.

Kolb, D., & Lewis, L. H. (1986). Facilitating experiential learning: Observations and reflections. In L. H. Lewis (Ed.), *Experiential and simulation techniques for teaching adults. New Directions for Continuing Education,* No. 30 (pp. 99–107). San Francisco: Jossey-Bass.

Kozlowski, S. W. J., & Farr, J. L. (1988). An integrative model of updating and performance. *Human Performance, 1,* 5–29.

Kozlowski, S. W. J., & Hults, B. M. (1987). An exploration of climates for technical updating and performance. *Personnel Psychology, 40,* 539–564.

Kraiger, K., Ford, J. K., & Salas, E. (1993). Application of cognitive, skill-based, and affective theories of learning outcomes to new methods of training evaluation. *Journal of Applied Psychology, 78,* 311–328.

Kram, K. E., & Isabella, L. A. (1985). Mentoring alternatives: The role of peer relationships in career development. *Academy of Management Journal, 28,* 110–132.

Lawler, E. E. III. (1989). Pay for performance: A strategic analysis. In L. R. Gomez-Mejia (Ed.), *Compensation and benefits* (pp. 3.136–3.181). Washington, DC: Bureau of National Affairs.

Locke, E. A., & Latham, G. P. (1990). *A theory of goal setting and task performance.* Englewood Cliffs, NJ: Prentice-Hall.

London, M. (1989). *Managing the training enterprise.* San Francisco: Jossey-Bass.

London, M., & Bassman, E. (1989). Retraining midcareer workers for the future. In I. L. Goldstein & Associates (Eds.), *Training and development in organizations* (pp. 333–375). San Francisco: Jossey-Bass.

London, M., & Smither, J. W. (1995). Can multi-source feedback change perceptions of goal accomplishment, self-evaluations, and performance-related outcomes? Theory-based applications and directions for research. *Personnel Psychology, 48,* 803–839.

Luthans, F., & Fox, M. L. (1989, March). Update on skill-based pay. *Personnel,* 26–31.

Marsh, H. W., Richards, G. E., & Barnes, J. (1987). A long-term follow-up of the effects of participation in an Outward Bound program. *Personality and Social Psychology Bulletin, 12,* 475–492.

Mathieu, J. E. (1991). A cross level nonrecursive model of the antecedents of organizational commitment and satisfaction. *Journal of Applied Psychology, 76,* 607–618.

Maurer, T. J., & Tarulli, B. A. (1994)). Investigation of perceived environment, perceived outcome, and person variables in relationship to voluntary development activity by employees. *Journal of Applied Psychology, 79,* 3–14.

McCall, M. W., Lombardo, M. M., & Morrison, A. M. (1988). *The lessons of experience.* Lexington, MA: Lexington.

McCauley, C. D., & Lombardo, M. M. (1990). Benchmarks: An instrument for diagnosing managerial strengths and weaknesses. In K. E. Clark & M. B. Clark (Eds.), *Measures of leadership* (pp. 535–545). West Orange, NJ: Leadership Library of America.

McCauley, C. D., Lombardo, M. M., & Usher, C. J. (1989). Diagnosing management development needs: An instrument based on how managers develop. *Journal of Management, 15,* 389–403.

McCauley, C. D., Ruderman, M. N., Ohlott, P. J., & Morrow, J. E. (1994). Assessing the developmental components of managerial jobs. *Journal of Applied Psychology, 79,* 544–560.

McEnrue, M. P. (1989). Self-development as a career management strategy. *Journal of Vocational Behavior, 34,* 57–68.

Meyer, J. P., & Allen, N. J. (1984). Testing the "side-bet theory" of organizational commitment: Some methodological considerations. *Journal of Applied Psychology, 69,* 372–378.

Miles, R. E., & Snow, C. C. (1980). Designing strategic human resource systems. *Organizational Dynamics, 13,* 36–52.

Milkovich, G. T. (1988). A strategic perspective on compensation management. In G. R. Ferris & K. M. Rowland (Eds.), *Research in personnel and human resources management* (Vol. 6, pp. 263–288). Greenwich, CT: JAI.

Milkovich, G. T., & Boudreau, J. W. (1994). *Human resource management* (7th ed.). Homewood, IL: Irwin.

Milkovich, G. T., & Newman, J. M. (1987). *Compensation* (2nd ed.). Plano, TX: Business Publications, Inc.

Milkovich, G. T., & Newman, J. M. (1993). *Compensation* (4th ed.). Homewood, IL: Irwin.

Morrison, E. W. (1993). Newcomer information seeking: Exploring types, modes, sources and outcomes. *Academy of Management Journal, 36,* 557–589.

Noe, R. A. (1986). Training attributes and attitudes: Neglected influences of training effectiveness. *Academy of Management Review, 11,* 736–749.

Noe, R. A. (1988). An investigation of the determinants of successful assigned mentoring relationships. *Personnel Psychology, 41,* 457–479.

Noe, R. A. (1991, October). *Motivational, personal, and organizational determinants of participation in development activities.* Paper presented at Training Effectiveness conference, Michigan State University, East Lansing.

Noe, R. A., & Schmitt, N. (1986). The influence of trainee attitudes on training effectiveness: Test of a model. *Personnel Psychology, 39,* 497–523.

Noe, R. A., & Wilk, S. L. (1993). Investigation of the factors that influence employees' participation in development activities. *Journal of Applied Psychology, 78,* 291–302.

Nowack, K. M. (1992). 360-degree feedback: The whole story. *Training and Development, 1,* 69–72.

Ohlott, R. J., Ruderman, M. N., & McCauley, C. D. (1994). Gender differences in managers' developmental job experiences. *Academy of Management Journal, 37,* 46–67.

Ostroff, C., & Kozlowski, S. W. J. (1993). The role of mentoring in the information gathering processes of newcomers during early organizational socialization. *Journal of Vocational Behavior, 42,* 170–183.

Pace, R. W., Smith, P. C., & Mills, G. E. (1991). *Human resource development.* Englewood Cliffs, NJ: Prentice-Hall.

Peters, L. H., & O'Connor, E. J. (1980). Situational constraints and work outcomes: The influence of a frequently overlooked construct. *Academy of Management Review, 5,* 391–397.

Peters, L. H., O'Connor, E. J., Eulberg, J. R., & Watson, T. W. (1988). An examination of situational constraints in Air Force work settings. *Human Performance, 1,* 133–144.

Powell, G. N., & Mainiero, L. A. (1992). Cross-currents in the river of time: Conceptualizing the complexities of women's careers. *Journal of Management, 18,* 215–237.

Ragins, B. R., & Cotton, J. L. (1991). Easier said than done: Gender differences in perceived barriers to gaining a mentor. *Academy of Management Journal, 34,* 939–951.

Robinson, S. L., Kraatz, M., & Rousseau, D. M. (1994). Changing obligations and the psychological contract. *Academy of Management Journal, 37,* 137–152.

Robinson, S. L., & Rousseau, D. M. (1994). Violating the psychological contract: Not the exception but the norm. *Journal of Organizational Behavior, 15,* 245–259.

Rousseau, D. M. (1989). Psychological and implied contracts in organizations. *Employee Responsibilities and Rights Journal, 2,* 121–139.

Roznowski, M., & Hulin, C. (1992). The scientific merit of valid measures of general constructs with special reference to job satisfaction and job withdrawal. In C. J. Cranny, P. C. Smith, & E. F. Stone (Eds.), *Job satisfaction: How people feel about their jobs and how it affects their performance* (pp. 123–163). Lexington, MA: Lexington.

Ruderman, M. N., Ohlott, P. J., & McCauley, C. D. (1990). Assessing opportunities for leadership development. In K. E. Clark & M. B. Clark (Eds.), *Measures of leadership* (pp. 547–562). West Orange, NJ: Leadership Library of America.

Rynes, S. L., & Barber, A. E. (1990). Applicant attraction strategies: An organizational perspective. *Academy of Management Review, 15,* 286–310.

Saari, L. M., Johnson, T. R., McLaughlin, S., & Zimmerle, D. M. (1988). A survey of management training and education practices in U.S. companies. *Personnel Psychology, 41,* 731–743.

Schmitt, N., Ford, J. K., & Stults, D. M. (1986). Changes in self-perceived ability as a function of performance in an assessment center. *Journal of Occupational Psychology, 59,* 327–335.

Scott, W. R., & Meyer, J. W. (1991). The rise of training programs in firms and agencies: An institutional perspective. In L. L. Cummings & B. M. Staw (Eds.), *Research in organizational behavior* (Vol. 13, pp. 297–326). Greenwich, CT: JAI.

Silverman, S. B. (1991). Individual development through performance appraisal. In K. N. Wexley (Ed.), *Developing human resources* (pp. 5120–5151). Washington, DC: BNA Books.

Sims, R. R. (1992). Developing the learning climate in public sector training programs. *Public Policy Management, 21,* 335–346.

Smither, J. W., London, M., Vasilopoulos, N. L., Reilly, R. R., Millsap, R. E., & Salvmini, N. (1995). An examination of the effects of an upward feedback program over time. *Personnel Psychology, 48,* 1–34.

Sonnenfeld, J. A., & Peiperl, M. A. (1988). Staffing policy as a strategic response: A typology of career systems. *Academy of Management Review, 13,* 588–600.

Sterns, H. L., & Doverspike, D. (1989). Aging and the training and learning process. In I. L. Goldstein & Associates (Eds.), *Training and development in organizations* (pp. 299–332). San Francisco: Jossey-Bass.

Stroh, L. K., Brett, J. M., & Reilly, A. H. (1992). All the right stuff: A comparison of female and male managers' career progression. *Journal of Applied Psychology, 77,* 251–260.

Taylor, S. E. (1991). Asymmetrical effects of positive and negative events: The mobilization minimization hypothesis. *Psychological Bulletin, 110,* 67–85.

Thornton, G. C. III., & Byham, W. L. (1982). *Assessment centers and managerial performance.* New York: Academic Press.

Tichy, N. M. (1989). GE's Crotonville: A staging ground for a corporate revolution. *Academy of Management Executive, 3,* 99–106.

Tracey, J. B., Tannenbaum, S. I., & Kavanagh, M. J. (1995). Applying trained skills on the job: The importance of the work environment. *Journal of Applied Psychology, 80,* 239–252.

Tsui, A. S., Ashford, S. J., St. Clair, L., & Xin, K. R. (1995). Dealing with discrepant expectations: Response strategies and managerial effectiveness. *Academy of Management Journal, 38,* 1515–1543.

U.S. Department of Labor. (1991). *A report on the glass ceiling initiative.* Washington, DC: Author.

Valerio, A. M. (1990). A study of developmental experiences for managers. In K. E. Clark & M. B. Clark (Eds.), *Measures of leadership* (pp. 521–534). West Orange, NJ: Leadership Library of America.

Wagner, R. J., Baldwin, T. T., & Rowland, C. C. (1991, March). Outdoor training: Revolution or fad? *Training and Development,* pp. 51–57.

Wexley, K. N., & Latham, G. P. (1991). *Developing and training human resources in organizations* (2nd ed.). New York: HarperCollins.

Wilk, S. L., & Noe, R. A. (1993). *The role of psychological contracts in determining employees' participation in development activities.* Unpublished manuscript, Industrial Relations Center, University of Minnesota, Minneapolis.

Yellen, J. (1984). Efficiency wage models of unemployment. *American Economic Review, 74,* 200–205.

Yelon, S. (1992). M.A.S.S.: A model for producing transfer. *Performance Improvement Quarterly, 5,* 13–23.

Zimmerman, B. J. (1989). A social cognitive view of self-regulated academic learning. *Journal of Educational Psychology, 81,* 329–339.

III

Understanding How Context Affects Training Evaluation and Transfer

8

Individual and Situational Influences on Training Motivation

John E. Mathieu
Pennsylvania State University
Jennifer W. Martineau
Center for Creative Leadership

Researchers and practitioners in the field of training evaluation have long used Kirkpatrick's (1976) fourfold criteria typology for assessing the effectiveness of training programs. Kirkpatrick's framework suggests that training should be evaluated in terms of its effects on trainees': (a) reactions to the program and its content, (b) learning—acquisition of knowledge and/or skills, (c) behavior—changes in the extent to which trainees can execute desired training-related behaviors, and (d) results—extent to which job behaviors change and yield increased organizational effectiveness. Recently there has been a call for an expanded view of training effectiveness. Campbell (1988, 1989), Tannenbaum and Yukl (1992), and others have argued that the role of variables such as trainees' motivation and attitudes, both before and after training, should be investigated more thoroughly. Other authors (Fleishman & Mumford, 1989; Noe, 1986) have argued that training must be viewed in the context of ongoing organizational processes. Effects beyond the immediate training program, such as individual and situational influences, should be considered if a more complete understanding of what makes for effective training is to be developed. This chapter is designed to help sculpt that larger framework.

The guiding conceptual framework for this chapter is presented in Fig. 8.1. It illustrates the general relationship between trainees' motivation and traditional training criteria. Training programs are viewed as existing in a larger organizational context, subject to the influences of individual and situational factors. For example, organizational selection and socialization systems will

193

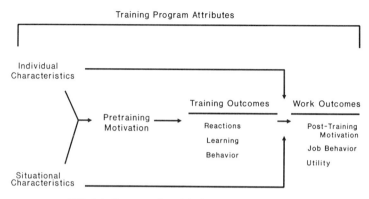

FIG. 8.1. Conceptual model of training motivation.

determine, in large part, the kinds of individuals who will be trained. Trainees come to programs with a history of organizational experiences and a knowledge of what they will confront when they return to their jobs. In short, participants enter and leave training with varying levels of motivation that will likely influence how much they learn, whether they transfer learning to the job, and ultimately how successful the program is. It is important to consider the roles of individual and situational influences on trainees' motivation.

Before proceeding, one important caveat is offered. The panel running along the top of Fig. 8.1 implies that the nature of the training program may have a direct impact on the effectiveness of training and/or interact with the other factors depicted. Different training forms (lecture vs. behavioral modeling) and purposes (developing psychomotor skills vs. introducing a total quality management [TQM] philosophy) will likely have differing effects on traditional training criteria, as well as trainees' motivation. The specific role's of various individual or situational influenc5 on trainees' motivation are also likely to differ depending on the form and purpose of training. Explication of these more subtle relationships is beyond this chapter. However, it does offer a few detailed propositions to illustrate the importance of these considerations. Ultimately, practitioners and researchers must consider aspects of their specific circumstances to decide how the design of the training program interfaces with what is discussed here.

First, the conceptual model of training motivation and effectiveness in context is developed. Second, a representative review of how trainee motivation has been considered and studied in previous research is provided. Third, the chapter outlines how individual and situational influences are likely to impact the effectiveness of training through their impact on trainees' motivations. Finally, the chapter concludes with some suggestions for future research and application, with particular emphasis on the role of training needs analysis in a systematic view of training effectiveness.

TABLE 8.1

Measures of Training Motivation

Definition	Sample Items	Studies
Motivation for training		
The extent to which trainees are stimulated to attend training, learn from training, and use the skills and/or knowledge obtained in training after returning to the job.	I will try to learn as much as I can from this program. I am motivated to learn the skills emphasized in the training program. The skills I learn in this program will be helpful in solving work-related problems.	Baldwin, Magjuka, & Loher (1991); Clark (1990); Eden & Shani (1982); Facteau, Dobbins, Russell, Ladd, & Kudisch (1992); Hicks & Klimoski (1987); Martocchio & Webster (1992); Noe & Schmitt (1986); Ryman & Biersner (1975)
Self-efficacy		
"... people's judgments of their capabilities to organize and execute courses of action required to attain designated types of performances." (Bandura, 1986, p. 391).	I have confidence in my ability to do the job. There is a ___ % chance that I can score at least a (69, 79, 89, 99, etc.) on this test.	Ford, Smith, Sego, & Quiñones (1993); Martocchio & Webster (1992); Mathieu, Martineau, & Tannenbaum (1993); Sparks (1988)
Valence-instrumentality-expectancy		
A combination of confidence in acquiring a given skill, the perception that skill acquisition leads to specific outcomes, and the values placed on those outcomes.	I am willing to exert considerable effort to improve my skills in the training program. Increasing your skills in the training program will help you to obtain a salary raise.	Mathieu, Tannenbaum, & Salas (1992); Noe & Schmitt (1986); Ralls & Klein (1991); Ryman & Biersner (1975)

The model depicted in Fig. 8.1 suggests that individuals enter training with differing levels of motivation due to personal characteristics and the work environment. The model also predicts that trainees who are motivated to do well in training will learn the content or principles of the program better than will less motivated participants. Pretraining motivation may prepare trainees to learn by heightening their attention and increasing their receptivity to new ideas. Motivated trainees should be more "primed" or ready to learn. Several studies have found empirical support for a linkage between trainees' motivation and learning (cf. Baldwin et al., 1991; Hicks & Klimoski, 1987; Martocchio, 1992).

Notice, too, that Fig. 8.1 adopted Cannon-Bowers, Salas, Tannenbaum, and Mathieu's (1993) distinction between training behavior versus job behavior changes. The logic here is that trainees may be able to exhibit the appropriate behaviors in the training context (simulate appropriate responses to a problem employee situation during a leadership skills training program), yet not demonstrate the same behaviors back on the job. As developed further later, if trainees are not motivated to actually use what they have learned back on the job, the program will ultimately fail. Individuals who are motivated to learn initially (pretraining motivation) are also likely to be motivated to apply the skills they develop during training once back on the job. The next section reviews the different ways that training motivation has been conceptualized and measured to provide a template for exploring the different influences on training motivation.

TRAINING MOTIVATION

Research has shown that trainees who are motivated on entry into a training program clearly have an advantage from the beginning (Goldstein, 1993). In a review, Tannenbaum and Yukl (1992) stated that, the less likely an individual is to have basic skills and motivation prior to training, the more likely that person is to require remedial preparation prior to the beginning of the actual training program. For example, Ryman and Biersner (1975) found that pretraining motivation predicted eventual graduation from training. Participants whose training-related attitudes and expectations are positive and supportive of the activities initially should be more ready for, and perform better in, training than others (Sanders & Yanouzas, 1983).

Alternative Conceptions of Training Motivation

Given the role that trainee motivation is likely to play in the ultimate effectiveness of the program, it is important to consider the different ways it has been conceptualized and measured. Essentially, three different approaches have been followed: (a) summative measures of training motivation, (b) self-efficacy, and (c) valence-instrumentality-expectancy formulations. A representative list of studies that have adopted each approach appears in Table 8.1. Also included in the table are representative items that have been used to assess each strategy.

Direct Summative Measures. In his 1986 model, Noe discussed the importance of measuring "motivation to learn" and "motivation to transfer" when examining training effectiveness. The most direct way to assess trainees' motivation is to collect self-ratings of how motivated they are before entering training, as well as how motivated they are to apply what they have learned back on the job. In terms of face validity, this approach makes a lot of sense and should allow researchers to rank order trainees on motivation. Alternatively, this approach is likely to be susceptible to response acquiescence and social desirability effects. These measures say little about why some trainees are motivated more than others. Nevertheless, the summative approach provides a relatively simple and direct way to gauge the role of motivational processes in training effectiveness studies.

Self-Efficacy.   *Self-efficacy*, defined as "people's judgments of their capabilities to organize and execute courses of action required to attain designated types of performance" (Bandura, 1986, p. 391), has also been shown to be significantly related to training effectiveness. In terms of training, self-efficacy measures usually require trainees to rate the extent to which they believe they can master training-related functions along a continuum of performance levels. For example, Mathieu, Martineau, and Tannenbaum (1993) had respondents rate the extent to which they believed they could accomplish eight different levels of performance in a physical education course. Sparks (1988) had teachers rate their confidence that they could handle challenging classroom situations. At their core, self-efficacy perceptions reflect the extent to which trainees have a "can do" attitude about their training performance. Gist and her associates (Gist, 1989; Gist, Schwoerer, & Rosen, 1989) found that trainees who had higher self-efficacy before and at the midpoint of the training program performed better on assessments at the completion of training than did those with lower self-efficacy. Similarly, Mathieu et al. (1993) reported that self-efficacy significantly predicted subsequent training performance and reactions to training.

Efficacy measures are perhaps best viewed in terms of individuals' self-perceptions of trainability. In other words, these measures are well suited for predicting how well individuals are likely to perform during training. If collected at the end of training and framed in terms of job performance, efficacy measures may be quite predictive of training transfer. We are not aware of any applications of self-efficacy measures in this manner. Used in either fashion, efficacy measures would likely be sensitive to the four general sources of influence described by Bandura (1982, 1986): (a) individuals' experiences in the same or similar circumstances, (b) normative effects, (c) modeling and encouragement, and (d) physiological reactions. Efficacy measures are far more focused than the summative indices described earlier, and they are likely to be more predictive of specific training outcomes. Alternatively, these measures do not address other aspects of the training or organizational contexts, such as how important performance is to different individuals.

Valence-Instrumentality-Expectancy.   The third category of training motivation measures follows from the body of literature on valence-instrumentality-expectancy (VIE) theory (Vroom, 1964). *Expectancy* refers to one's personal belief concerning whether one can acquire a given skill, *instrumentality* concerns the perception that acquisition of that skill will lead to specific outcomes, and *valence* is the relative desirability of those outcomes for each individual. The expectancy portion of this model is similar to the efficacy measures discussed previously, although the latter tends to be a more encompassing construct (Gist, 1989). The unique features of a VIE approach is the linkages to outcomes. For example, Mathieu, Tannenbaum, and Salas (1992) used a VIE composite measure that assessed the extent to which individuals perceived that increased job performance attributable to training would yield a variety of outcomes, including feelings of accomplishment, higher pay, and enhanced promotion potential. Thus, the VIE approach places the role of training into a large motivational framework rooted in individuals' work roles. Although the resulting composites should appropriately tap the resulting motivational force or perceived consequences of doing well in training for different individuals, disaggregating the various components may also prove useful from a diagnostic standpoint. In other words, should trainees report low training-related motivation, examination of the component scores should reveal whether the root cause stems from (a) low expectancy (or efficacy type) perceptions—E, (b) perceptions that performing well in training is not related to various job outcomes—I (perhaps because the training program is not particularly job related), and/or (c) the fact that individuals do not value outcomes associated with successful performance in training—V.

Conclusion

Each of the three approaches outlined earlier have various strengths and weaknesses. The direct measures provide a quick, straightforward method of gauging how trainees view their participation. These qualities are also their biggest drawback: They are very transparent and provide little diagnostic information. The efficacy measures are particularly well suited for predicting how well individuals will perform in training (or, if framed properly, how well they will transfer training). Bandura's (1986) typology of antecedents provides a useful guide for identifying different sources of influence on training-related motivation. However, these measures fall short in terms of viewing training motivation in the larger organizational context.

The VIE approach best captures the contextual features of trainees' perceptions of the overall utility of performing well in training. Whereas effort-performance expectancies are akin to efficacy perceptions, instrumentality and valence estimates tie individuals' motivation bases to the perceived rewards available in their organizational contexts. Unfortunately, VIE composites have not proved to be highly predictive of performance outcomes in previous research (Schwab, Olian-Gottlieb, & Heneman, 1979). The VIE approach is better suited for predicting choices between discrete alternatives, such as whether to participate in a voluntary training program. Perhaps the clearest lessons to be learned are that (a) researchers should choose an approach based on the criteria they are most interested in predicting, and (b) the simultaneous use of multiple approaches should prove fruitful for both research and practice.

Proposition 1: The manner in which training motivation is defined and measured will influence its relationship with other variables of interest.

Proposition 1a: Efficacy-based measures will likely relate more directly to pretraining motivation.

Proposition 1b: VIE-based measures will likely relate more directly to work outcome measures.

INDIVIDUAL INFLUENCES ON TRAINING MOTIVATION

Individuals possess certain characteristics that differentiate them from others. They are male or female, old or young, have ethnic affiliations, and different personalities. Trainees bring varying degrees of job experience, participation in development activities, and work-related attitudes to the training setting. Some may enjoy the challenge of learning, others may prefer to think of training as an opportunity to achieve their goals, whereas others may view the experience as a total waste of time. In short, different people will want different things from training, and thus react differently to the same program. In fact, Fleishman and Mumford (1989) stated that individual attributes are among the most important determinants of training outcomes. There are several different categories of individual differences that have been shown to influence training effectiveness and/or training motivation, including: (a) demographics; (b) knowledge, skills, abilities, and experiences; (c) personality and needs; and (d) work-related attitudes.

Demographic Variables

Variables in this category refer to enduring and distinguishable characteristics of individuals. Although commonly used in research as explanatory variables in and of themselves, it is perhaps more informative to view trainees' demographic characteristics as surrogate measures of some common experiences that certain groups of people have likely had. It is with this viewpoint that this chapter reviewed some of the relationships found in previous research.

Recent research suggests that older people have more difficulty in learning new technologies than younger people (Elias, Elias, Robbins, & Gage, 1987; Gist, Rosen, & Schwoerer, 1988; Gomez, Egan, & Bowers, 1988; Hartley, Hartley, & Johnson, 1984; Ralls & Klein, 1991). However, the evidence for the influence of age on training motivation is not consistent. Rosen and Jerdee (1976) argued that older workers are less likely to receive support for retraining as compared with younger, equally qualified workers. Thus, the instrumentality of training is likely to be lower for older employees, possibly resulting in negative effects on their motivation for training.

Men and women may react differently to training programs. For example, Gattika and Hlavka (1992) found gender differences in attitudes toward a computer training program, whereas Goldstein and Gilliam (1990) reported that there is no evidence that women need special training different from that offered to males to succeed in work organizations. There has also been no consistent trend between trainees' race and training outcomes. For example, race was not a significant predictor of posttraining skill levels for a group of juvenile delinquents participating in a cognitive-behavioral skills program (Hawkins, Jenson, & Catalano, 1991). However, race did play a role in the prediction of success in an Air Force mechanical skills training program (Houston & Novick, 1987).

Research Implications.   The most consistent findings concerning demographic variables and training outcomes are their inconsistencies. This is perhaps the clearest example of the importance of considering both the form and purpose of the training program. For example, because men, in general, tend to hold more positive attitudes toward computers, they also tend to respond to computer training better than do women. However, this does not mean that men are "more trainable" than women. The influence of age and racial differences among trainees would also likely shift depending on the training content.

Women would be expected to have more positive attitudes toward, and would likely perform better in, training programs designed to alter organizational cultures that promote sexual harassment. Similarly, minority trainees would likely react more positively than would White males to diversity training. Rather than looking for uniform effects of trainee demographic characteristics, their potential influences should be considered in the context of the specific training programs in question.

> Proposition 2: Trainees' demographic characteristics are not likely to demonstrate uniform (i.e., linear) effects on training-related motivation. However, they may interact with the nature of the training program to impact training-related motivation.

Knowledge, Skills, Abilities, and Other Influences

Ghiselli (1973) summarized a number of studies showing that trainees' motivational, aptitude, interest, and previous work histories influenced their performance in training as well as attrition rates. Mumford, Weeks, Harding, and Fleishman (1988) concluded that student characteristics, such as aptitude, motivation level, and reading level, were among the most powerful determinants of performance in U.S. Air Force training programs. These factors exhibited stronger effects on performance than did any of the training content variables. The next section considers the potential effects that trainee differences—in terms of abilities, education, and experiences—have on training motivation. These factors typically have been considered predictors of "trainability," in that individuals who do not possess the requisite background would not be seen as benefitting much from training. The emphasis in this chapter is more in terms of how these factors influence individuals' motivation to do well in training.

Ability. Indicators of abilities include scholastic aptitude, spatial aptitude, verbal reasoning, intelligence, deductive/inductive reasoning, and mathematical ability (Howard, 1971). The evidence for the influence of trainee ability or aptitude on training performance and motivation is mixed. Schmitt, Gooding, Noe, and Kirsch (1984) reported that ability is a strong predictor of learning in a training program and subsequent performance on the job. Elsewhere, Ralls and Klein (1991) predicted that trainee ability would moderate the relationship between trainee motivation and performance (i.e., the stronger one's ability, the more influence motivation would have on performance). This hypothesis was not supported.

If a relationship does exist between ability and motivation, it may be fairly complex. Intelligence and other abilities have been found to be related to trainability in some cases (Bale, Rickus, & Ambler, 1973; Gill, 1982; Williams, Sauser, & Kemery, 1982), and this relationship may be nonlinear. Gill (1982) reported that when a task requires participants to determine whether the ordering of certain priorities is correct, the relationship between intelligence and gain in performance is positive and linear. However, when the task requires the establishment of these priorities, the relationship is positive and slightly curvilinear, and is stronger than the former relationship. This study suggests that there may be an optimum range of intelligence for decision-making potential. As related to training, it is possible that trainees with either very high or very low intelligence may perform differently than those with moderate levels, unless the program is designed to simply promote rote memorization of material.

Education. Education has been considered a predictor of individuals' trainability. The assumption is that individuals with higher education levels are more likely to benefit from training than are less educated trainees. Mathieu et al. (1992) found that trainees' previous education levels exhibited a positive influence on a learning measure. Alternatively, managers' education levels did not have any significant effect on their attempts to transfer skills learned in training to the job (Baumgartel & Jeanpierre, 1972). Similarly, education level did not affect the participation rates of unemployed individuals in a job training program (Grisez & Ryan, 1993). Taken together, it seems that there may be some truth to the perception that "more is better" in terms of the effect of education level on training. However, education level may affect training outcomes differentially depending on the type of outcomes examined. For example, education level may relate to training criteria, such as tests or behavior practice sessions, whereas it may be unrelated to motivational criteria, such as participation and intent to transfer training. Multifaceted studies of this type are needed.

Work Experience.   Ford et al. (1993) examined the impact of individual and task experience factors on Air Force mechanics' task-analysis ratings. Airmen whose breadth of task experience increased over time tended also to increase their ratings of training emphasis. In other words, as individuals gained greater experience in the job, they began to value training more highly. Baumgartel and Jeanpierre (1972) examined the impact of job level (a surrogate measure of work experience) on transfer processes and found no significant results. However, Ford and Noe (1987) reported that job level has also been related to the types of training individuals desire. They argued that lower level managers desired more technical supervisory training, whereas managers in materials handling desired more training in quality control skills.

Research Implications.   The influence of trainees' abilities, education, and work experience on training motivation are best viewed in terms of their impact on effort-performance expectancies or efficacy perceptions. To the extent that individuals have the requisite backgrounds to do well in training, they are likely to perceive that their efforts will yield higher performance in training. This is not likely to be a perfectly linear relationship. If individuals already possess the skills that are targeted in training, they are unlikely to be motivated to learn much from the program, nor are they likely to exhibit much improvement as compared with others who do not yet possess those skills. Alternatively, if trainees perceive that there is no possibility that they can master the training content, they are likely to mentally or even physically disengage from the program. The highest training motivation is likely to occur when individuals believe that they have the appropriate foundation on which to build skills that they do not yet possess, but can gain if they exert themselves.

> Proposition 3: Trainees who possess important content-related knowledge, skills, and abilities (KSAs) are likely to perform better in training than are those with lower requisite KSAs.
>
> Proposition 4: Training-related KSA levels will exhibit a curvilinear relationship with individuals' training motivation. Specifically, the highest motivation will be reported by individuals who have yet to develop the skills targeted in training, but believe that they can learn them, as

compared with individuals who believe that they already possess such skills or who believe that they do not have the
capability to develop such skills.

Personality and Needs

Beyond various demographics, individuals have enduring features that influence how they approach various experiences. One can categorize these
predispositions loosely in terms of needs, personality, or orientations. This
chapter considers these effects on training motivation in terms of (a)
Murray's manifest needs, (b) the "Big Five" personality dimensions, and (c)
learning orientations.

Manifest Needs. Murray (1938) developed an extensive list of individual
needs that, when proper situational opportunities avail themselves, influence
individuals' actions. Of the more than two dozen needs that Murray discussed,
the achievement, affiliation, and dominance motives have received the greatest
attention. Individuals high in achievement motivation generally aspire to
accomplish difficult tasks and to maintain high standards of performance. They
prefer performance to depend on their efforts, and generally like to receive a
great deal of feedback about their progress toward goals. Mathieu (1988) found
that ROTC cadets with high achievement motivation reported their training
environment had more positive group relationships and less role stress than did
cadets with lower levels of achievement motivation. Achievement motivation
was also correlated positively with cadets' commitment to the ROTC program.
In addition, achievement motivation demonstrated a significant positive influence on the development of self-efficacy in the context of skill acquisition in a
physical education course (Mathieu et al., 1993). Sharpley and Pain (1987)
found that achievement motivation evidenced a positive effect on individuals'
performance beyond that attributable to previous performance. These studies
provide strong evidence that achievement motivation plays a significant role in
training effectiveness.

In the studies cited earlier, achievement motivation exhibited positive
influences on training-related outcomes in competitive settings. It is argued
here that other needs are likely to be important, depending on training program
attributes. The need for *affiliation*—defined as the desire to be with other people,
to make friends, and to prefer cooperative environments—would likely have a
positive influence on trainees' motivation and performance in sensitivity training. Alternatively, the need for *dominance*—defined as a preference for leading
others, controlling one's environment, and assuming leadership roles—would
likely have positive effects on trainees' motivation and performance in a
leadership skill training program, particularly those in military settings. Thus,
needs should not be viewed in isolation or as necessarily having uniform positive

or negative effects on training outcomes. Needs must be considered in terms of how they predispose individuals to react to the training program and use what they learn back on the job setting.

Personality.   There has been an increased interest recently in the role of personality variables in applied psychology, generally in terms of the "Big Five" framework that includes: (a) extraversion, (b) emotional stability, (c) agreeableness, (d) conscientiousness, and (e) openness to experience (Digman, 1990; Norman, 1963; Tupes & Christal, 1961). Barrick and Mount (1991) found that the dimensions of *conscientiousness, openness to experience,* and *extraversion* are all predictive of training proficiency. The dimensions that are associated with being outgoing, having a stronger sense of purpose and persistence, and a willingness to take risks and try new things seem to lead individuals to high levels of training performance. Given that training is often a new experience that involves taking risks in front of other people who may not be familiar to the trainee, these findings are intuitively appealing.

Goal Orientation.   There is a growing body of research (Dweck, 1986; Dweck & Leggett, 1988) on the topic of goal orientation. Goal orientation concerns whether individuals perceive situations as opportunities to learn (mastery orientation) or opportunities to demonstrate their capabilities (performance orientation). Farr and his colleagues (Farr, Hofmann, & Ringenbach, 1993; Farr & Middlebrooks, 1990) reported that performance-oriented individuals may interpret being sent to training as a message from management that their performance is subpar. This could cause a decrease in their motivation to attend, or to do well in, training. Elsewhere, junior high school students with performance goal orientations reported negative attitudes toward their classes, whereas those with mastery goal orientations had positive attitudes (Ames & Archer, 1988). Furthermore, those with a mastery orientation used more effective learning strategies and preferred challenging situations more so than did those with a performance orientation. These studies suggest that goal orientation is related to training motivation, in that trainees who approach task situations as learning opportunities will be more motivated and will enjoy training more than will those with performance goal orientations.

Research in this area has sometimes treated goal orientation as an attribute of situations, and sometimes has viewed it as an individual-difference variable. Although there is empirical support for both strategies, the consequences of adopting either approach are not yet clearly understood. This raises a question concerning the compatibility between individual and situational orientations. Research has yet to examine the consequences of placing learning oriented-individuals into a highly competitive training program versus, say, placing a performance-oriented individual into a self-paced mastery program.

Proposition 5: Trainees' predispositions will interact with the nature of the training program to influence individual training motivation. For example, highly achievement-oriented individuals are likely to be more motivated to perform well in a military leadership training program, as compared to individuals with a high need for affiliation. Alternatively, the latter individuals would likely be more motivated in a sensitivity training program than would the achievement-oriented individuals.

Work-Related Attitudes

Tannenbaum, Mathieu, Salas, and Cannon-Bowers (1991) provided an example of the complex nature of the relationship between work-related attitudes and training effectiveness. They suggested that attitudes such as organizational commitment would influence how trainees perceived their training experiences and how they would likely react to the program. They also suggested that changes in work-related attitudes are important outcomes of training. This study underscores the important role of work-related attitudes in effective training programs. Two representative attitudes are considered here as exemplars of this larger issue: job involvement and career attitudes.

Job Involvement. *Job involvement* is defined as the extent to which people are psychologically attached to their jobs. Highly job-involved individuals participate actively in the job, view their jobs as a central interest in their lives, and perceive their job performance as central to their self-concepts (Kanungo, 1982; Lodahl & Kejner, 1965). Noe and Schmitt (1986) found that job involvement was positively and significantly related to the acquisition of key job behaviors in the context of a skills training program for educators. Clark (1990) found that job involvement related positively to training motivation across a diverse set of training programs. In a training program designed to improve the productivity levels of two maintenance districts, Hensey (1987) found that training was less successful in the district in which workers were less involved with their jobs. There is also evidence that job involvement does not predict training effectiveness; job involvement was not found to predict either training motivation (Facteau et al., 1992; Mathieu et al., 1992) or transfer of training to the job (Facteau et al., 1992). Considering the previous findings, perhaps job involvement relates most positively to training-related outcomes when the program is designed to improve performance on central aspects of their current job, and is less influential when the program is targeted toward more peripheral aspects of trainees' current jobs.

Career-Related Attitudes.   When employees undertake exploratory behavior in terms of determining the status of their own strengths and weaknesses,
career values, interests, goals, and plans, they are participating in the activity
known as *career planning* (Noe, 1986). Career planning serves to help individuals prepare for their work-related futures by assessing current status and comparing it to future desires. In terms of training effectiveness, one study indicated
that managers and supervisors who had completed a management training
curriculum reported a higher motivation to learn the training content if they
had previously considered a strategy for their careers (Facteau et al., 1992).
Similarly, Noe suggested that individuals involved in career planning would be
motivated to learn the content of training because they are aware of their
strengths and weaknesses. In contrast, Mathieu et al. (1992) failed to find
the hypothesized positive relationship between career planning and training-
related motivation. The authors questioned whether their results may have
been due to the nature of the training program investigated—one that was
targeted toward activities that trainees performed in their current jobs.

Research Implications.   This chapter has commented on just two of the
myriad of potentially relevant work-related attitudes. The point here is that
different attitudes are likely to play important roles in different training
situations.

> Proposition 6:   The anchoring or focal entity of work-related attitudes
>   will interact with the nature of the training content to
>   influence trainees' motivation.

One would expect that attitudes such as organizational commitment and
organizational citizenship would exhibit positive influences on training
effectiveness in most situations. The impact of other attitudes may depend
more on the particular form and purpose of training. As suggested earlier,
highly job-involved employees may only respond positively to training if it is
designed to enhance performance on central aspects of their current job.
Alternatively, individuals with well-articulated career plans may only value
training programs that help them move along their personal ladders. Changes
in such work-related attitudes should perhaps be viewed as an added criteria
set for evaluating the effectiveness of training (cf. Tannenbaum et al., 1991).

Implications of the Role of Individual Variables

To summarize what is known about the influence of individual variables on
training motivation, it appears that their influence is likely to be stronger on
pretraining motivation processes than on motivation to transfer processes. The

findings indicate that differences, such as gender, work experience, achieve-ment motivation, job involvement, and career attitudes, contribute to a desire to participate in training, a desire to do well in training, and the selection of the training program content. These characteristics seem to predispose certain people to being "ready" for training; that is, they consider their interests, skills, and abilities prior to training, along with the training content, and determine that they do want to succeed in training.

These studies also indicate that individuals' "trainability," or their propensity toward success in training, is influenced not only by their KSAs, but also by their motivation. Many of these variables, such as achievement motivation, goal orientation, or job involvement, are not likely to be highly correlated with KSA measures. This suggests that training effectiveness can be improved by attend-ing to such individual differences. For example, increasing the degree to which individuals identify with their jobs can improve the chances that their partici-pation in training results in positive outcomes. This creates numerous oppor-tunities for helping individuals achieve in training-oriented situations. Improving work-related attitudes is not an easy task. Yet if these attitudes are likely to have an effect on the success of training, they should be addressed before the training is even introduced. Otherwise, one runs the risk of investing a great deal of time and money into a program that is doomed because individuals are predisposed to reject it.

Finally, the effect of many of these individual influences on training motiva-tion depends on the form and purpose of training. Later it is argued that the interface between individual characteristics and the form and purpose of training should be thoroughly investigated during the needs analysis phase of training. If researchers and practitioners attend to these potential effects initially, they can harness the positive effects and minimize the negative effects of individual influences by properly designing and executing training programs.

SITUATIONAL INFLUENCES ON TRAINING MOTIVATION

No doubt the type of program implemented and participants' characteristics influence the effectiveness of training. However, to fully appreciate the array of influential factors, training must be viewed in the context of ongoing organiza-tional processes. Tannenbaum and Yukl (1992) argued that "elements of the posttraining environment can encourage (e.g., rewards, job aids), discourage (e.g., ridicule from peers), or actually prohibit the application of new skills and knowledge on the job (e.g., lack of necessary equipment)" (p. 240). This suggests that if the need for a particular training program was not well specified in advance, if successful completion of training is not reinforced, or if participants are not given the opportunity to use and hone the new skills they developed, one could hardly claim that "the training was ineffective."

As outlined in Fig. 8.1, trainees' awareness of their organizational realities are likely to influence their motivation for learning before they enter the program. Further, after returning from training, their motivation to apply what they have learned is shaped, in large part, by the opportunities they have to use their newly developed skills and whether they are rewarded for doing so. Thus, examination of the organizational context from which trainees come and will return is an important ingredient for successful training programs.

Before discussing some of the specific aspects of situations that likely affect trainees' motivation, it is important to note that situational characteristics cut across various levels of influence or analysis. Individual effects are tied uniquely to individual trainees, whereas situational influences may vary from one trainee to another, or be common to all or subsets of participants. For example, at the individual level, varying time pressures and the nature of work that different trainees perform would likely affect their opportunities to implement TQM principles. At the group level, some trainees may come from departments where management supports and encourages TQM principles, whereas others may come from areas where TQM is not held in high regard. One would expect that participants from the first department would, as a group, report greater motivation to learn and to use the principles of the program as compared with the latter group. Finally, there may be a pervasive climate or culture throughout the organization suggesting that TQM is either a "valuable and powerful management tool" or simply a "silly waste of time." Obviously the likelihood of successful TQM training would be enhanced in the former setting and ill-fated in the latter.

The previous example highlights that one must adopt a multilevel perspective when examining the potential impact of situational factors on training effectiveness (Kozlowski & Salas, this volume; Ostroff & Ford, 1989; Rousseau, 1985). Such a perspective enables practitioners to determine, for example, whether certain individuals need added release time to practice what they have learned, if certain groups or departments need additional preparation or follow-up efforts, or whether larger organizational factors need to be addressed before a training program is initiated. These multilevel effects present a particularly difficult challenge for researchers: Specifying multi- and cross-level models of training effectiveness demand complex theoretical orientations and sophisticated methodological and statistical skills. For example, multilevel approaches demand that researchers identify, a priori, the nature and level of constructs that they believe to influence the criteria measures of interest. Further, scaling aggregate environmental features, such as subunit processes or organizational characteristics, require sophisticated measurement strategies. Nevertheless, ignoring the complexity of levels issues will likely lead to simplistic and misguided models of training effectiveness (Ostroff & Ford, 1989). Aspects of trainees' work environments that are likely to have an impact on their motivation and training effectiveness include: (a) situational constraints, (b) social psychological factors, and (c) training maintenance systems. Recently, there have been efforts to develop and test integrated models of training motivation that include individual and situational variables (Baldwin et al., 1991; Facteau et al., 1992; Mathieu et al., 1992, 1993; Noe & Schmitt, 1986; Quiñones, 1994). However, the variables that have been included in these studies, as well as the purposes and forms of training that have been sampled, have varied so widely that researchers are far from developing any taxonomic views of important antecedents. The next section provides a brief overview of the types of situational variables that have been considered as antecedents of training motivation. Thus, the review provides a framework for considering the different potential sources of influence.

Situational Constraints

Situational constraints can be defined as characteristics of the environment that interfere with or restrict individuals' performance (Peters & O'Connor, 1980; Peters, O'Connor, & Eulberg, 1985). These would include such tangible factors as: (a) adequacy of job-related information, (b) tools and equipment, (c) materials and supplies, (d) financial and budgetary support, and (e) time availability. Because the focus of employee training is typically on behavior change, the desired and expected outcome of training is increased performance. Trainees' willingness and ability to perform may not translate into performance improvements if the situation inhibits their efforts. For example, Kopelman, Brief, and Guzzo (1990) suggested that having sufficient supplies, materials, equipment, services, and resources necessary to perform one's job will yield higher employee motivation, whereas a lack of the same would create frustration. Guzzo and Gannett (1988) suggested that "inhibitors" (situational constraints) could affect performance both directly and indirectly through the mediating effects of motivation. Several authors have found support for a negative relationship between situational constraints and individuals' affective reactions (Gist & Mitchell, 1992; Peters et al., 1985; Phillips & Freedman, 1984).

More specifically, in terms of training-related motivation, Mathieu et al. (1992) found some support for a negative relationship between perceptions of situational constraints and a VIE composite. In contrast, Mathieu et al. (1993) found individual-level constraints to have a negative impact on both the development of self-efficacy during training and affective reactions to training. Noe and Wilk (1993) found that constraints inhibited managers' participation in development activities. Ford, Quiñones, Sego, and Sorra (1992) found that situational factors significantly affected trainees' opportunity to perform trained skills on the job, which in turn moderated the extent to which training effects transferred.

Although the presence of constraints reduces the likelihood that training will be successful, the impact of constraints is likely to be twofold. First, the Mathieu et al. (1992, 1993) findings suggest that trainees' foreknowledge of constraints will likely reduce their motivation to perform well in training. Situational constraints may operate as negative antecedents of training motivation. Second, the Noe and Wilk (1993) and Ford et al. (1992) findings indicate that, even if trainees prevail and learn the training material, it will not likely transfer to the job setting if they are not given the opportunity to perform such skills. Thus, situational constraints may also function as a moderator of the transfer process, and this may operate through lower motivation to transfer.

Proposition 7:   Situational constraints may operate in a twofold fashion: (a) initially, constraints may inhibit individuals' pretraining motivation if they do not believe that they will be able to use what they are being taught; and (b) constraints will be likely to moderate the extent to which what was learned in training will transfer to the job setting.

Social-Psychological Influences

Although situational constraints describe physical aspects of the work environment that should be considered, interpersonal or social psychological forces also operate and influence training effectiveness. Whether these effects are referred to as *climate, culture, interpersonal relations,* or other labels is not important here. (See Schneider, 1990, for a review. Note also that issues of level have been widely debated in this area.) What is important is that trainees' interactions with others will likely influence their motivation both going into training programs and when back on the job. For example, Salinger (1973) relayed an instance where top management failed to set aside adequate time for employee training. As a result, participants felt penalized for attending training because the importance of the program was not clear and their normal work was piling up while they were away from the job. Similarly, Baumgartel and his colleagues (Baumgartel & Jeanpierre, 1972; Baumgartel, Reynolds, & Pathan, 1984) found that managers reported greater transfer in organizations that supported training both informally in terms of approval and support and formally in terms of willingness to spend money on training.

Rouiller and Goldstein (1993) examined the impact of an organization's climate for *transfer of training,* defined as "those work group policies, practices, and procedures that affect how trainees perceive the worthiness of utilizing their new skills" (p. 5) on training effectiveness. They identified a number of different aspects of climate for training, including situational cues and consequences. The results of their empirical investigation indicate that climate for transfer related significantly to training transfer beyond the influence of individual learning and unit performance. Similar findings were obtained by Russell, Terborg, and Powers (1985); Kozlowski and Hults (1987); and Tracey (1992). The results of these studies, while varying in specifics, yield a consistent picture—that when the work environment is supportive of training outcomes, transfer is enhanced.

> Proposition 8: Trainees who come from work environments that are supportive of what is targeted in training will likely: (a) report greater pretraining motivation; and (b) evidence greater transfer of training, as compared with trainees who come from less supportive environments.

A specific facet of the social psychological environment that has received some scrutiny, as related to training motivation, is whether participants choose to enroll in the training. In general, it has been argued that trainees who volunteer for training are likely to be more motivated to learn than are individuals who are assigned to training. The logic here is twofold. First, the fact that volunteers sought out the program suggests that they perceive some value in it. Second, individuals who are forced into training may well experience some reactance and respond negatively to their assignment. But choice of whether to attend training may be a double-edged sword. On the one hand, there is some empirical support for the notion that forcing individuals to attend training may reduce their motivation to learn and perform, as well as relate negatively to training reactions (cf. Baldwin et al., 1991; Hicks & Klimoski, 1987; Mathieu et al., 1992, 1993). On the other hand, the results are far from consistent or compelling, and the strongest effects have occurred in studies conducted in nontraditional work settings.

Accurate deciphering of the effects of choice on trainees' motivation requires an analysis of how participants perceive their enrollment in the program. No doubt forcing people to be in situations they do not value will not generate motivation to learn. However, demanding that certain individuals or all employees successfully complete a given program will likely send out a clear message that training is important. For example, the first author recently developed a "safety-climate" training program with a diverse team of employees from a nuclear power plant. These programs notoriously receive giggles and smirks from seasoned employees "who are wasting their time in touchy feelie exercises." When the participants found themselves participating in full-day sessions that they could not get out of, working through videotaped scenarios shot professionally using respected company employees and managers, and interacting with executive-level managers in open discussions, there was no mistake that training was viewed as important by the company.

> Proposition 9:   The influence of making training voluntary versus mandatory on trainees' motivation will depend on the perceived "message" of the program. Specifically, when a lack of choice is perceived as a manipulative force, trainees will likely have little motivation to learn. Alternatively, when mandated training is perceived as a real commitment by the organization to emphasize new skills and/or move in a different direction, employees will likely be highly motivated to learn.

Maintenance Systems

Other factors in the work environment may be targeted specifically at enhancing training transfer and ensuring its longevity. Marx (1982) emphasized the identification of high-risk situations that trainees might face and the need for appropriate coping skills for those situations. At issue here is that organizations might employ additional interventions aimed specifically at facilitating and maintaining transfer of training. These specific efforts are referred to as *maintenance systems for training*.

Perhaps the most encompassing strategy for developing training motivation, as well as enhancing motivation for transfer, is to adopt a skill-based pay system (Lawler, 1981). Essentially, skill-based pay systems first compensate employees with a set wage based on the general classification of jobs they perform, hours worked, and tenure with the organization. Second, employees may earn more by developing additional job-related skills through formal and on-the-job training experiences. The logic of this approach is that, overall, the organization benefits from a more fully trained and flexible workforce. For employees, skill-based pay systems reward them for developing new skills and having the opportunity to perform a wider variety of jobs.

The first author recently worked with a production company that utilized a skill-based pay system. The climate at the plant was markedly different than those of more traditionally designed organizations, and a continuous learning environment was clearly evident. However, these benefits do come with costs. The company needed a separate facility where it continually offered training programs, and it was invested heavily in a video library of self-paced programs. The training overhead was tremendous as compared with more traditional training departments, and coordination challenges were evident. These included managing a fairly elaborate job-rotation scheme and an ever-changing payroll program. To enhance the effectiveness of training, the company also incorporated an on-the-job training or apprenticeship element that complemented the formal training, yet it presented further coordination problems. Finally, skill-based pay systems run the risk of "overmotivating" employees to fly through training programs as quickly as possible just to reach the next pay grade. Clearly, this approach places a premium on conducting well-designed evaluation studies to ensure that trainees are actually learning what is intended.

> Proposition 10: Trainees will likely be more motivated to attend, learn, and apply training when doing so is consistent with the overall organizational reward system.

The skill-based pay approach represents a large-scale organizational intervention, whereas more targeted maintenance interventions may be adopted. Wexley and Baldwin (1986) tested the effectiveness of assigned- and participatively set goal setting interventions, along with a self-management approach, on the maintenance of transfer over time. They concluded that the two goal setting conditions enhanced the maintenance of transfer, as compared with self-management or a control condition. Frayne and Latham (1987) demonstrated that training in self-management targeted toward absence reduction not only can have immediate effects on job behaviors, but also sustained effects over time (Latham & Frayne, 1989). At issue here is that organizations may want to introduce other interventions that complement the design of training. Regardless of whether these efforts are aimed at moving the entire organization toward a more continuous learning culture, or more focused on reinforcing transfer for trainees who work in nonsupportive environments, they are likely to pay dividends in terms of enhanced training effectiveness.

Implications of the Role of Situational Variables

Situational characteristics, whether they be physical, social-psychological, or maintenance systems, are critical when designing and evaluating the effectiveness of training programs. Research needs to take a multilevel view of these effects. Although it is clear that situational constraints have many detrimental effects on trainees' motivation, previous research has been unclear as to what level(s) these constraints operate. If a trainee is unmotivated to learn a new work process because he or she is under too many time pressures, what should be done? This question cannot be answered adequately until the nature of the time pressure is deciphered. Is it that the person has too many job responsibilities, or that his or her department is not managed effectively, or perhaps that the organization is short staffed overall? Determining the source(s) at which the time constraints emanate will clarify what needs to be done and how many trainees will be influenced by any changes that are introduced. In short, it is not enough to determine simply that time constraints reduce trainees' motivation.

In terms of the nature of situational influences on trainees' motivation, usually they have been viewed as moderators of the transfer process. In other words, attention is typically given to situational facilitators or inhibitors as boundary conditions for the application of newly developed skills. We concur with this viewpoint, but further believe that the impact of situational factors are much more pervasive than has previously been appreciated. As a field, little is known about the individuals who decide not to attend training. Also, little is known about those who enter training unmotivated to learn because they perceive that they would not have the opportunity to use the training, or because management or their coworkers do not value the results of training. Traditional research designs would not even consider those who do not participate in the training (or, worse yet, assign the disenchanted to a quasi-control group), and would likely attribute the unmotivated trainees' lack of learning to a poor training program. Clearly a more systems-oriented perspective is warranted.

NEEDS ANALYSIS
AND TRAINING MOTIVATION

The key to simplifying the complexity of factors that should be considered in any particular circumstance rests with a thorough needs analysis. The importance of needs analysis for effective training programs has been discussed extensively. We endorse a blending of the perspectives introduced by McGehee and Thayer (1961) and advanced by Goldstein (1993) in the context of the framework articulated by Ostroff and Ford (1989).

McGehee and Thayer (1961) and Goldstein (1993) argued that a thorough needs analysis will include a(n): (a) organizational analysis, (b) task analysis, and (c) person analysis. At the risk of oversimplifying, these amount to identifying the most pressing organizational needs and determining whether training is a reasonable solution, determining what specifically needs to be trained, and identifying who needs the training. Ostroff and Ford (1989) applied a multilevel perspective to needs analysis, and noted that the previous three facets may reside at different, or even multiple, levels of analysis.

We concur with both the content and multilevel perspectives. However, most needs analyses tend to be targeted toward what should constitute the training program. In other words, the de facto reason for conducting a needs analysis is to design the training and determine who will participate. We believe that needs analysis should be conducted more as a general organizational diagnosis and assessment process, where training is viewed as simply one of many options for developing an organization. This orientation may help to identify when training should occur in the sequence of organizational processes.

The organizational analysis is typically focused on macrostrategic issues about the future direction of the organization. If viewed as an option, training needs analysis in this case is essentially the same as any other strategic diagnosis. The analysis will indicate which type of intervention is required, rather than immediately jumping into determining training design and types of participants to include. Training is often viewed as the "cure all" for many organizational ills. Undoubtedly, some form of training is involved in almost all organizational change efforts. However, when training becomes the answer to all problems, it is doomed to failure. Employees will quickly develop the attitude that they have to attend yet another training session that has little to do with their job. When training is seen in more of a supplemental role, such as when a new technology is introduced in the workplace, it is often relegated to such a subordinate role that it is given little attention and typically introduced late in the development sequence. It is little wonder that trainees become disenchanted with programs that are repeatedly thrown together at the last minute when their need was evident long ago.

> Proposition 11:   The timing of training programs, relative to other organizational changes, will have significant influences on trainees' motivation. Programs that are introduced late and/or rushed and thrown together at the last minute will not likely motivate employees, and may even become points of contention.

Although the organizational analysis is typically concerned with overall organizational goals and needs, it and the task-analysis phase are also likely to be important at one or more subunit levels of analysis (Ostroff & Ford, 1989). It is quite likely that the most pressing organizational needs and methods of accomplishing work will differ from one organizational subunit to another, and that a failure to appreciate these differences will likely generate negative attitudes toward a training program. For example, assume that it is determined that an organization, as a whole, is in need of supervisory skills training. Often a single training program will be designed to address these needs and to capitalize on economy of scale. If the ideal supervisory styles for, marketing, production, sales, design, and so forth differ appreciably (and we suspect they do), the uniform program is likely to leave many trainees disenchanted.

> Proposition 12:   Although uniform training programs are likely to be the most cost-efficient from a delivery standpoint, they will likely decrease trainees' motivation if they fail to address the differing needs of employees from different subunits.

At the individual level, where the person analysis is focused, individuals differ in terms of their trainability. Trainability has typically been discussed in terms of requisite trainee KSAs. As outlined earlier, there are a variety of individual needs, attitudes, and so forth that will likely impact their readiness to learn. For example, if employees hold negative attitudes toward some new technology (robotics or computer systems), efforts designed to address their concerns first, before entering training, are critical if training is to have a chance at being effective. It makes little sense to train employees how to use new technology that is threatening to them, or during hostile union negotiations that are designed to block the introduction of the new methods.

In summary, the training system must be viewed in the context of ongoing organizational processes, and the effectiveness of training depends on the program as well as relevant individual and situational factors. A systematic, multilevel needs analysis should be employed to help: (a) researchers identify the critical variables that should be incorporated in studies of training effectiveness; and (b) practitioners consider what other aspects of the organizational environment need to be addressed, as well as to determine the ideal sequencing of training and other organizational interventions to realize the greatest organizational effectiveness.

IMPLICATIONS FOR RESEARCH
AND PRACTICE

Scientist/practioners have the exciting opportunity to study training motivation in field settings, and to integrate the results into training needs assessment, design, delivery, and evaluation. Although there is a preponderance of studies indicating the relationship of certain individual influences to training motivation and training effectiveness, other areas have not yet been fully confirmed. More attention is needed in the following areas:

1. Consider the question "Efficacy for what?" Self-efficacy measures can be framed in terms of job performance levels and/or efficacy to learn. The former would ask how well respondents feel they can perform their jobs, whereas the latter would query how well they can master the training content. Are these different? What are the implications of assessing efficacy for different training-related outcomes? What difference does this make for the design of training programs?

2. Are trainees predisposed to react to training in a particular way and to use what they learn back on the job based on their manifest needs (achievement motivation, need for affiliation)? Is successful training performance dependent on one's predisposition for being outgoing, willing to take risks, and having a stronger sense of purpose and persistence? If so, should we select individuals for

training who match need patterns and/or personalities? What implications might this have on employee development efforts, and in terms of fairness?

3. What are the consequences of mismatching goal orientations and training emphases? Will a learning-oriented trainee become frustrated in a highly competitive program? If so, will the results be so detrimental as to lead us to pretest for goal orientations, or are there other options for maintaining high training motivation?

In addition to individual influences, certain situational factors warrant further research. Among these are:

1. What are the situations that drive employees to avoid training? What factors encourage employees to participate in voluntary training programs?

2. Skill-based pay systems and other types of maintenance systems have not yet been fully investigated in terms of their effect on training motivation and training effectiveness. What are the influences of formal and informal organizational reward systems on trainees' motivation?

Finally, the entire field of training research and implementation should recognize the importance of focusing on the complete context of training when evaluating the effectiveness of training programs. It needs to employ multilevel and multifaceted needs analyses before designing new programs. We should also use a systems-oriented approach when designing training research so that researchers can study not only trainees, but also those who opted out of training.

REFERENCES

Ames, C., & Archer, J. (1988). Achievement goals in the classroom: Students' learning strategies and motivation processes. *Journal of Educational Psychology*, 80, 260–267.

Baldwin, T. T., Magjuka, R. J., & Loher, B. T. (1991). The perils of participation: Effects of choice of training on trainee motivation and learning. *Personnel Psychology*, 44, 51–65.

Bale, R. M., Rickus, G. M., Jr., & Ambler, R. K. (1973). Prediction of advanced level aviation performance criteria from early training and selection variables. *Journal of Applied Psychology*, 58, 347–350.

Bandura, A. (1982). Self-efficacy mechanism in human agency. *American Psychologist*, 37, 122–147.

Bandura, A. (1986). *Social foundations of thought and action*. Englewood Cliffs, NJ: Prentice-Hall.

Barrick, M. R., & Mount, M. K. (1991). The "Big Five" personality dimensions and job performance: A meta-analysis. *Personnel Psychology*, 44, 1–26.

Baumgartel, H. J., & Jeanpierre, F. (1972). Applying new knowledge in the back-home setting: A study of Indian managers' adoptive efforts. *Journal of Applied Behavior Science*, 8, 674–694.

Baumgartel, H. J., Reynolds, M. J. I., & Pathan, R. 7 (1984). How personality and organizational climate variables moderate the effectiveness of management development programs: A review and some recent research findings. *Management Labor Studies*, 9, 1–16.

Campbell, J. P. (1988). Training design for performance improvement. In J. P. Campbell, R. J. Campbell, & Associates (Eds.), *Productivity in organizations* (pp. 177–215). San Francisco: Jossey-Bass.

Campbell, J. P. (1989). The agenda for theory and research. In I. L. Goldstein (Ed.), *Training and development in organizations* (pp. 469–486). San Francisco: Jossey-Bass.

Cannon-Bowers, J. A., Salas, E., Tannenbaum, S. I., & Mathieu, J. E. (1993). Toward theoretically-based principles of training effectiveness: A model and initial empirical investigation. *Military Psychology, 7*, 141–164.

Clark, C. (1990). *Social processes in work groups: A model of the effect of involvement, credibility, and goal linkage on training success.* Unpublished doctoral dissertation research, University of Tennessee, Knoxville.

Digman, J. M. (1990). Personality structure: Emergence of the five-factor model. *Annual Review of Psychology, 41*, 417–440.

Dweck, C. S. (1986). Motivational processes affecting learning. *American Psychologist, 41*, 1040–1048.

Dweck, C. S., & Leggett, E. L. (1988). A social-cognitive approach to motivation and personality. *Psychological Review, 95*, 256–273.

Eden, D., & Shani, A. B. (1982). Pygmalion goes to boot camp: Expectancy, leadership, and trainee performance. *Journal of Applied Psychology, 67*, 194–199.

Elias, P. K., Elias, M. F., Robbins, M. A., & Gage, P. (1987). Acquisition of work-processing skills by younger, middle-aged, and older adults. *Psychology and Aging, 2*, 340–348.

Facteau, J., Dobbins, G., Russell, J., Ladd, R. T., & Kudisch, J. (1992, April). *Noe's model of training effectiveness: A structural equations analysis.* Paper presented at the 7th annual conference of the Society of Industrial and Organizational Psychology, Montreal, Canada.

Farr, J. L., Hofmann, D. A., & Ringenbach, K. L. (1993). Goal orientation and action control theory: Implications for industrial and organizational psychology. *International Review of Industrial and Organizational Psychology, 8*, 193–232.

Farr, J. L., & Middlebrooks, C. L. (1990). Enhancing motivation to participate in professional development. In S. L. Willis & S. S. Dubin (Eds.), *Maintaining professional competence* (pp.195–213). San Francisco: Jossey-Bass.

Fleishman, E. A., & Mumford, M. D. (1989). Individual attributes and training performance. In I. L. Goldstein (Ed.), *Training and development in organizations* (pp. 183–255). San Francisco: Jossey-Bass.

Ford, J. K., & Noe, R. (1987). Self assessed training needs: The effects of attitudes toward training, managerial level, and function. *Personnel Psychology, 40*, 39–53.

Ford, J. K., Quiñones, M. A., Sego, D. J., & Sorra, J. (1992). Factors affecting the opportunity to perform trained tasks on the job. *Personnel Psychology, 45*, 511–527.

Ford, J. K., Smith, E. M., Sego, D. J., & Quiñones, M. A. (1993). Impact of task experience and individual factors on training emphasis ratings. *Journal of Applied Psychology, 78*, 583–590.

Frayne, C. A., & Latham, G. P. (1987). The application of social learning theory to employee self-management. *Journal of Applied Psychology, 72*, 387–392.

Gattika, U., & Hlavka, A. (1992). Computer attitudes and learning performance: Issues for management education and training. *Journal of Organizational Behavior, 12*, 89–101.

Ghiselli, E. E. (1973). The validity of aptitude tests in personnel selection. *Personnel Psychology, 26*, 461–477.

Gill, R. W. T. (1982). A trainability concept of management potential and an empirical study of its relationship with intelligence for two managerial skills. *Journal of Occupational Psychology, 55*, 139–147.

Gist, M. E. (1989). The influence of training method on self-efficacy and idea generation among managers. *Personnel Psychology, 42*, 787–805.

Gist, M. E., & Mitchell, T. R. (1992). Self-efficacy: A theoretical analysis of its determinants and malleability. *Academy of Management Review, 17*, 183–211.

Gist, M. E., Rosen, B., & Schwoerer, C. (1988). The influence of training method and trainee age on the acquisition of computer skills. *Personnel Psychology, 41*, 255–265.

Gist, M. E., Schwoerer, C., & Rosen, B. (1989). Effects of alternative training methods on self-efficacy and performance in computer software training. *Journal of Applied Psychology, 74*, 884–891.

Goldstein, I. L. (1993). *Training in organizations* (3rd ed.). Belmont, CA: Brooks/Cole.

Goldstein, I. L., & Gilliam, P. (1990). Training systems in the year 2000. *American Psychologist, 45*, 134–143.

Gomez, L. M., Egan, D. E., & Bowers, C. (1988). Learning to use a text editor: Some learner characteristics that predict success. *Human-Computer Interaction, 2*, 1–23.

Grisez, M. L., & Ryan, A. M. (1993, April). *Motivation to seek training: Explaining training participation among the unemployed.* Paper presented at the 8th annual conference of the Society of Industrial and Organizational Psychology, San Francisco, CA.

Guzzo, R. A., & Gannett, B. A. (1988). The nature of facilitators and inhibitors of effective task performance. In F. D. Schoorman & B. Schneider (Eds.), *Facilitating work effectiveness* (pp. 21–50) Lexington, MA: Lexington.

Hartley, A. A., Hartley, J. T., & Johnson, S. A. (1984). The older adult as computer user. In P. K. Robinson, J. Livingston, & J. E. Birren (Eds.), *Aging and technological advances.* New York: Plenum.

Hawkins, J. D., Jenson, J. M., & Catalano, R. F. (1991). Effects of a skills training intervention with juvenile delinquents. *Research on Social Work Practice, 1*, 107–121.

Hensey, M. (1987). Commitment as an aspect of leadership. *Organization Development Journal, 5*, 53–55.

Hicks, W. D., & Klimoski, R. J. (1987). Entry into training programs and its effects on training outcomes: A field experiment. *Academy of Management Journal, 30*, 542–552.

Houston, W. M., & Novick, M. R. (1987). Race-based differential prediction in Air Force technical training programs. *Journal of Educational Measurement, 24*, 309–320.

Howard, A. (1971). *Training for individuals and individual differences.* Unpublished manuscript, University of Maryland.

Kanungo, R. N. (1982). Measurement of job and work involvement. *Journal of Applied Psychology, 67*, 119–138.

Kirkpatrick, D. L. (1976). Evaluation. In R. D. Craig (Ed.), *Training and development handbook* (pp. 301–319). New York: McGraw-Hill.

Kopelman, R. E., Brief, A. P., & Guzzo, R. A. (1990). The role of climate and culture in productivity. In B. Schneider (Ed.), *Organizational climate and culture* (pp. 282-318). San Francisco: Jossey-Bass.

Kozlowski, S. W. J., & Hults, B. M. (1987). An exploration of climates for technical updating and performance. *Personnel Psychology, 40*, 539–563.

Latham, G. P., & Frayne, C. A. (1989). Self-management training for increased job attendance: A follow-up and replication. *Journal of Applied Psychology, 74*, 411–416.

Lawler, E. E. III. (1981). *Pay and organizational development.* Reading, MA: Addison-Wesley.

Lodahl, T., & Kejner, M. (1965). The definition and measurement of job involvement. *Journal of Applied Psychology, 49*, 24–33.

Martocchio, J. J. (1992). Microcomputer usage as an opportunity: The influence of context in employee training. *Personnel Psychology, 45*, 529–552.

Martocchio, J. J., & Webster, J. (1992). Effects of feedback and cognitive playfulness on perform-ance in microcomputer software training. *Personnel Psychology, 45*, 553–578.

Marx, R. D. (1982). Relapse prevention for managerial training: A model for maintenance of behavior change. *Academy of Management Review, 7*, 433–441.

Mathieu, J. E. (1988). A causal model of organizational commitment in a military training environment. *Journal of Vocational Behavior, 32*, 321–335.

Mathieu, J. E., Martineau, J. W., & Tannenbaum, S. I. (1993). Individual and situational influences on the development of self-efficacy: Implications for training effectiveness. *Personnel Psychology*, 46, 125–147.

Mathieu, J. E., Tannenbaum, S. I., & Salas, E. (1992). Influences of individual and situational characteristics on measures of training effectiveness. *Academy of Management Journal*, 35, 828–847.

McGehee, W., & Thayer, P. W. (1961). *Training in business and industry*. New York: Wiley.

Mumford, M. D., Weeks, J. L., Harding, F. D., & Fleishman, E. A. (1988). Measuring occupational difficulty: A construct validation against training criteria. *Journal of Applied Psychology*, 72, 578–587.

Murray, H. (1938). *Explorations in personality*. New York: Oxford University Press.

Noe, R. A. (1986). Trainees' attributes: Neglected influences on training effectiveness. *Academy of Management Review*, 11, 736–749.

Noe, R. A., & Schmitt, N. (1986). The influence of trainee attitudes on training effectiveness: Test of a model. *Personnel Psychology*, 39, 497–523.

Noe, R. A., & Wilk, S. L. (1993). Investigation of the factors that influence employees' participation in development activities. *Journal of Applied Psychology*, 78, 291–302.

Norman, W. T. (1963). Toward an adequate taxonomy of personality attributes: Replicated factor structure in peer nomination personality ratings. *Journal of Abnormal and Social Psychology*, 66, 574–583.

Ostroff, C., & Ford, J. K. (1989). Assessing training needs: Critical levels of analysis. In I. L. Goldstein (Ed.), *Training and development in organizations* (pp. 25–62). San Francisco: Jossey-Bass.

Peters, L. H., & O'Connor, E. J. (1980). Situational constraints and work outcomes: The influences of a frequently overlooked construct. *Academy of Management Review*, 5, 391–397.

Peters, L. H., O'Connor, E. J., & Eulberg, J. R. (1985). Situational constraints: Sources, consequences, and future considerations. In K. M. Rowland & G. R. Ferris (Eds.), *Research in personnel and human resources management* (Vol. 3, pp. 79–114). Greenwich, CT: JAI.

Phillips, J. S., & Freedman, S. M. (1984). Situational performance constraints and task characteristics: Their relationship to motivation and satisfaction. *Journal of Management*, 10, 321–331.

Quiñones, M. A. (1994, April). *Pre-training context effects: Training assignment as feedback*. Paper presented at the 9th annual conference of the Society of Industrial and Organizational Psychology, Nashville, TN.

Ralls, R., & Klein, K. J. (1991). *Trainee cognitive ability and motivation: Effects on computer training performance*. Poster presented at the 6th annual conference of the Society of Industrial and Organizational Psychology, St. Louis, MO.

Rosen, B., & Jerdee, T. H. (1976). The nature of job-related stereotypes. *Journal of Applied Behavioral Psychology*, 61, 180–183.

Rouiller, J. Z., & Goldstein, I. L. (1993). The relationship between organizational transfer climate and positive transfer of training. *Human Resource Development Quarterly*, 4, 377–390.

Rousseau, D. M. (1985). Issues of level in organizational research: Multi-level and cross-level perspectives. In L. L. Cummings & B. M. Staw (Eds.), *Research in organizational behavior* (Vol. 7, pp. 1–38). Greenwich, CT: JAI.

Russell, J. S., Terborg, J. R., & Powers, M. L. (1985). Organizational performance and organizational level training and support. *Personnel Psychology*, 38, 849–863.

Ryman, D. H., & Biersner, R. J. (1975). Attitudes predictive of diving training success. *Personnel Psychology*, 28, 181–188.

Salinger, R. D. (1973). *Disincentives to effective employee training and development*. Washington, DC: U.S. Civil Service Commission, Bureau of Training.

Sanders, P., & Yanouzas, J. N. (1983). Socialization to learning. *Training and Development Journal*, 37, 14–21.

Schmitt, N., Gooding, R. Z., Noe, R. A., & Kirsch, M. (1984). Meta-analysis of validity studies published between 1964 and 1982 and the investigation of study characteristics. *Personnel Psychology, 37,* 407–422.

Schneider, B. (1990). *Organizational climate and culture.* San Francisco: Jossey-Bass.

Schwab, D., Olian-Gottlieb, J., & Heneman, H. III. (1979). Between subjects expectancy theory research: A statistical review of studies predicting effort and performance. *Psychological Bulletin, 86,* 139–147.

Sharpley, C. F., & Pain, M. D. (1987). Self-motivation vs. previous grades as predictors of success in counsellor training. *Canadian Journal of Counselling, 21,* 200–206.

Sparks, G. M. (1988). Teachers' attitudes toward change and subsequent improvements in classroom teaching. *Journal of Educational Psychology, 80,* 111–117.

Tannenbaum, S. I., Mathieu, J. E., Salas, E., & Cannon-Bowers, J. (1991). Meeting trainees' expectations: The influence of training fulfillment on the development of commitment, self-efficacy, and motivation. *Journal of Applied Psychology, 76,* 759–769.

Tannenbaum, S. I., & Yukl, G. (1992). Training and development in work organizations. *Annual Review of Psychology, 43,* 399–441.

Tracey, J. B. (1992). *The effects of organizational climate and culture on the transfer of training.* Unpublished doctoral dissertation, State University of New York at Albany.

Tupes, E. C., & Christal, R. E. (1961, May). *Recurrent personality factors based on trait ratings* (ASD-TR-61-97). Lackland Air Force Base, TX: Aeronautical Systems Division, Personnel Laboratory.

Vroom, V. H. (1964). *Work and motivation.* New York: Wiley.

Wexley, K. N., & Baldwin, T. T. (1986). Posttraining strategies for facilitating positive transfer: An empirical exploration. *Academy of Management Journal, 29,* 503–520.

Williams, B. B., Sauser, W. I., Jr., & Kemery, E. R. (1982, April). *Intelligence and physical fitness as predictors of success in early infantry training.* Paper presented at the annual meeting of Southeast American Psychological Association, New Orleans, LA.

9

When Training Affects Variability: Beyond the Assessment of Mean Differences in Training Evaluation

George M. Alliger
State University of New York

Steven Katzman
City University of New York

Generally speaking, the literature on methods and issues in training evaluation focuses on the assessment of mean group differences. Because of many thorough discussions of training evaluation measures, design, and statistical analyses, it is likely that training evaluation is approached in a way that assures valid conclusions about changes in the means of dependent variables. Very often, the observation of changes in means from pretraining to posttraining is the most appropriate way to address hypotheses of interest regarding training effectiveness.

There are at least two other important ways to consider the effectiveness of training. One alternative is the analysis of individual change over a long period of time. In this approach, the group of trainees as a whole is often not of essential interest. Rather, the attempt to model individual "growth" curves is central (Rogosa, 1988; Rogosa, Brandt, & Zimowski, 1982; Willet, 1988). This literature most appropriately addresses long-term training (perhaps better called *education*), when a many occasion measurement plan is both appropriate and feasible. When a typical organizational training evaluation is considered, however, a second alternative way to address the question of training effectiveness becomes attractive. This approach would consider the effect of training on between-person variability—the focus of this chapter.

Whether and how training might affect variability in posttraining scores relative to pretraining measures has received sparse attention. This lack of attention is perhaps natural given that changes in group means due to training provide simple important proof of training effectiveness: The trained group as a whole has changed its position on some relevant dependent variable(s). Assessment of changes in variability may also reveal important benefits (or drawbacks) of training that should not be overlooked. Indeed, a change in variability, in addition to a change in group means, could be an important goal of training. There may even be cases where it is the only goal, and where a change in the group mean is not important (Howell, 1982; Olejnik, 1988). As an example of this, consider training designed to inculcate group consensus: A reduction in opinion variation might be the only desired outcome.

This chapter stresses the potential interest that an examination of variability changes may have for training. It delineates potential problems that may occur when simply comparing mean differences between experimental and control groups in training research. Situations are described where changes in experimental group variability may be expected. These changes in variability may affect testing for mean differences. Examples are provided for test score reliability, effect size calculations, statistical power, and regression to the mean. A five-factor model is proposed for the prediction of variability effects due to training, and research propositions based on the model are advanced. First, however, the historical background in this area is discussed.

PREVIOUS RESEARCH AND THEORY
ON VARIABILITY EFFECTS

Although the literature dealing with training effects on variability is somewhat limited, several individuals have made important contributions to the beginnings of a theory in this area. Thorndike (1908, 1910, 1916) suggested that the effect of training on variability was an important research topic. In his studies examining the influence of "equal practice on individual differences," he posited that general intelligence (what is now often termed g) would predict rate of change due to training more for complex than for simple tasks (Thorndike, 1910).

Other early studies explicitly considered change in variability as a measure of practice effects (Anastasi, 1934; Chapman, 1925; Kincaid, 1925; Reed, 1931). Generally, these articles investigated the effects of practice (often termed *training* in these articles) on the variability of performance of simple tasks in laboratory studies. Much of this early research was designed to examine the relative importance of heredity and environment in learning. If practice decreased the variability of a group of individuals performing the same task, the inference was that initial ability (as reflected by initial status on the task) was primarily determined by environment (in fact, by some kind of previous training)—because everyone approached equal task facility after practice. If practice increased the variability in a group of individuals, it was believed that this result was due to inherited abilities—these innate abilities playing a greater role as practice proceeded.

Recently, Ackerman (1987) reviewed this literature and reanalyzed data from Kincaid (1925). Drawing on the automatic–controlled information-processing perspective (Fisk & Schneider, 1981; Shiffrin & Schneider, 1977), previous theory in skill acquisition (Anderson, 1982), and Norman and Bobrow's (1975) performance-resource function, Ackerman proposed an intriguing theory regarding "skill learning." *Skill learning* was operationalized as increasing task proficiency over repeated trials for relatively simple tests, such as canceling "A"s, addition, mental multiplication, and memory scanning. Ackerman posited that the demands that many such simple, consistent tasks make on people can change with practice. He defined tasks in terms of whether they required consistent or inconsistent demands on a person's cognitive resources. Specifically, individuals need to exert less and less conscious effort on performing tasks requiring consistent demands as practice proceeds. A slightly different way to say this is that the task changes with practice from resource-dependent to resource-independent—although tasks themselves do not become automatized, but processes may (Lord & Maher, 1991). The important point is that performance on such tasks may, with practice, show a decrease in variability among people. This may be the case because, although differences in cognitive ability cause initial differences in task performance, the decreasing demand placed on those abilities with practice permits similar performance attainment for most people. However, tasks that place inconsistent demands on cognitive resources may not show this convergence of performance, because the process will remain controlled, and initial individual differences should remain or even increase.

Ackerman's (1987) theory furnishes one basis for the prediction of change in variability due to practice and pinpoints the nature of the task as an important parameter in understanding variability effects. It would appear useful to further develop the theoretical bases for understanding the conditions under which change in variability will be a useful indicator of learning or change, not only for laboratory studies, but for the study of organizational training effectiveness. For tasks typically trained in organizations, one might expect either no change, a decrease in variability, or an increase in variability. Which outcome would be predicted would vary by circumstance. Stoddard (1925) cogently argued that virtually any prediction regarding change in variability could be appropriate under different circumstances. The identification of these circumstances (or boundary conditions) seems critical to a complete understanding of variability effects. This chapter presents an initial model that stipulates such boundary conditions.

Prior to model specification, some of the previous research on change assessment is integrated into the framework of a discussion of variability effects.

This includes: (a) a discussion of the reasons for believing that an assessment of variability changes will be useful to organizational researchers, and (b) a discussion of the heretofore unexamined effects of such training caused differences in variability on traditional assessments of training effectiveness.

RESEARCH ON THE MEASUREMENT OF CHANGE AND THE ASSUMPTION OF HOMOGENEITY OF VARIANCE

The measurement of change has received considerable attention over the past several decades (Cohen & Cohen, 1983; Cronbach & Furby, 1970; Maxwell & Howard, 1981; Overall & Woodward, 1975; Rogosa, 1988). A substantial portion of this attention has focused on assessing mean change in a variable measured at two points in time. This body of literature seems to have settled on the conclusion that, although simple change or difference scores can be less reliable than the corresponding pre- and postmeasures (Cronbach & Furby, 1970), this is by no means necessarily true (Rogosa, 1988). In any case, change score unreliability is not a problem for testing the usual hypothesis of interest that the mean change is zero (Maxwell & Howard, 1981; Nicewander & Price, 1978; Overall & Woodward, 1975). Some have argued that simple change scores, because of the common occurrence of correlation between change and initial status, may not be as appropriate as change scores with pretest differences partialed out (Cohen & Cohen, 1983; Linn & Slinde, 1977). This position on regressed change is sharply contested by others (Rogosa, 1988; Willet, 1988). Still other research has presented useful comparisons in statistical power between simple change score analysis and regressed change (Arvey & Cole, 1989; Arvey, Cole, Hazucha, & Hartanto, 1985; Arvey, Maxwell, & Salas, 1992). However, this literature on change has not addressed changes in variability, despite the implications that a change in variability may have for assessing mean differences, and the importance of variability effects per se for understanding the effects of organizational training.

Some of the literature discussing change has focused on one group of pre- and posttest designs, where the computation of change scores seems a natural thing to do (Cohen & Cohen, 1983). Often this is extended to the case of a control- and experimental-group design (Arvey & Cole, 1989; Arvey et al., 1985; Overall & Woodward, 1975). It is this latter and frequently employed case on which the present chapter elaborates. Consider, for simplicity, a 2×2 mixed design (one within-groups factor, pre- and posttest; one between-groups factor, assignment to control or experimental group). This design is commonly used by researchers interested in examining the effects of almost any type of intervention, whether this be training, psychological or drug therapy, or persuasion. It is certainly typical of many training situations where an experimental method of training might be compared with a control group that would receive no training.

A Debatable Assumption: Homogeneity of Variance

One assumption that has apparently been nearly universal in the change literature is that of homogeneity of variance. That is, in discussing the various issues surrounding change scores, it has been assumed that all design cells are drawn from populations with equal variance. In calculating the power of t tests for assessing posttest differences, it has typically been assumed that the variances of the posttest scores (Y) are equal for both the control (C) and experimental (E) groups—that is, $\sigma_{Y_C}^2 = \sigma_{Y_E}^2$. For similar examinations of analyses of variance (ANOVA) and analyses of covariance (ANCOVA), homogeneity for the pretest scores (X) are also assumed: $\sigma_{X_E}^2 = \sigma_{X_C}^2 = \sigma_{Y_E}^2 = \sigma_{Y_C}^2$ (Arvey & Cole, 1989; Overall & Woodward, 1975).

This assumption of variance homogeneity may be a faulty one in many actual training cases. It is reasonable to assume that, in particular, $\sigma_{Y_E}^2$, the variance of the posttest measure in the trained group, will sometimes have a substantially smaller or larger population value than will that of the control posttest.

Why Posttraining Variability
May Be Smaller in the Trained Group

Assume an organization wants to test the effectiveness of a stress-reduction program. Two randomly selected groups of employees are chosen, and a measure of experienced stress is taken (i.e., reasonable reliability). One group participates in the program. The other group, the control, receives no special attention. After a time, both groups are again measured for stress. In the case of the control group, it is reasonable to assume equal variances in the pre- and post-measures. In fact, the correlation between the two administrations of the stress measure in the control group can be taken as a coefficient of test–retest reliability, recognizing of course the various threats typical to test–retest reliabilities, such as "maturation" or "history" (Cook & Campbell, 1979). Given some real effectiveness of the intervention, not only will the mean of the postmeasure for the experimental group differ from its pretest level, but the variance could well be less. This should be the case because people in the experimental group with initial greater levels of stress are likely to experience greater raw change in their status than are those who are less stressed to begin with. In other words, the individuals in the experimental group who are not stressed initially cannot experience much reduction in this variable. As one example, Zalesny and Farace (1986) predicted, based on social information-processing theory, a decrease in between-person variance in attitudes toward an organizational intervention for a group of individuals provided information about the intervention (rendering it non-novel), as opposed to a group that received no such information (and for whom the intervention was therefore novel). Such reductions in variability can be illustrated by graphing individual change from pre- to posttest as in Fig. 9.1a. In this figure, both the mean and variance of the dependent measure decrease from Time 1 to Time 2.

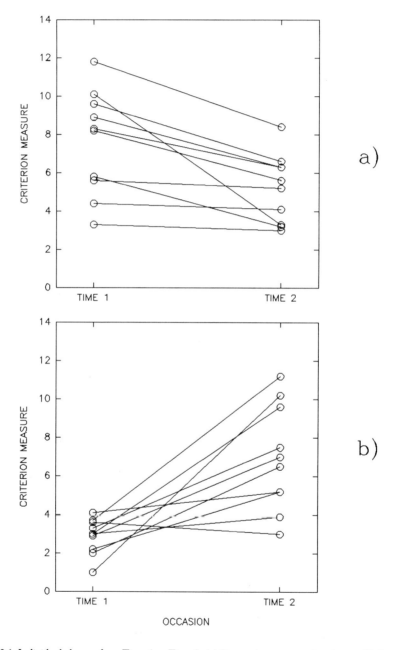

FIG. 9.1. Individual change from Time 1 to Time 2. (a) Decreasing mean and variance. (b) A "spreading fan" pattern resulting in greater posttest variance as well as greater mean.

A reduction in range and variance from pre- to postmeasures is also likely in many educational situations. As Micceri (1989) suggested, those students who do well on a knowledge pretest cannot gain much on a parallel posttest. Rather, it is those students who know little initially who can gain substantially. Equal gains in achievement are simply less possible when starting at a higher level (just as it may be harder for students to go from a grade of B to one of A than from a C to a B). Learning curves, after all, invariably show a decrease in slope at the upper levels. Individuals starting out at different points in a learning curve will not be expected to have equal gains over equal intervals of time. As an organizational example, pre- and posttest distributions for a large sample of managerial trainees are shown in Fig. 9.2. The pretest standard deviation for these data is 17.4; for the posttest, 9.9—a difference significant at p < .001, using the Snedecor and Cochran (1980) test for variance differences from dependent samples. Micceri provided a similar example of a decrease in variance in an educational setting. This leads to an interesting research question: If some trainees have experience in the training material before training and can do well on a pretest measure, will variability necessarily decrease in this group at posttest?

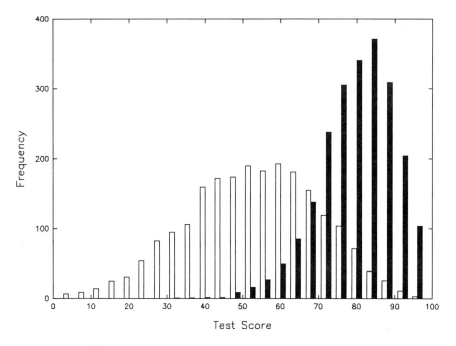

FIG. 9.2. Pre- and posttest distributions for a sample of managerial trainees (n_{pre}=2210, n_{post}=2226; Alliger & Horowitz, 1989).

Note that in the previous examples, a reduction in variance occurs from pretraining to posttraining, but this is not necessarily because the task that is learned becomes resource-independent. In the stress-reduction example, reduction in variability is due to some individuals already residing at some low base level and being joined by others after training. In the knowledge training examples, reduction in variance could occur either because some individuals already know the material while others do not (this view is argued by Micceri, 1989), or because of differential difficulty in gain at the upper levels of achievement. In these cases of knowledge gain, we have an example of reduction of variability after training for a task that could be considered resource-dependent. In any case, traditional classroom training would appear to include much that is different from those simple constant-mapping tasks for which automaticity has been demonstrated (Shiffrin & Schneider, 1977).

Why the Posttest Variability
May Be Larger in the Trained Group

Range enhancement, or an increase in variance, can occur due to training, just as a decrease in variance can occur. Such an increase in variability may be seen whenever individuals differ in rate of learning in such a way that a "spreading fan" pattern of data, such as depicted in Fig 9.1b, results. It was Thorndike's (1908) belief that this effect would be common in learning studies—underlying individual differences in ability expressing themselves more after than before training. This type of increasing variability effect can be considered an aptitude-treatment interaction (ATI). Individuals higher in initial aptitude may benefit more from training than other individuals, thereby increasing the variability of the group as a whole.

An example of an increase in variance, likely due to an ATI, is reported in Gordon and Cohen (1973):

> [T]he standard deviations [in time to completion from the beginning of the course] for each of the three groups and the combined sample steadily increased in magnitude from task 1 through task 14. This finding indicates that the trainees became increasingly dissimilar in terms of the amount they had progressed the longer they were in the program. This steadily increasing dispersion suggested that those trainees who learned the first few tasks more quickly than their classmates continued to master each subsequent task at a faster pace than the slow learners and, therefore, continued to outdistance the latter. (p. 266)

This example presumably represents what might be called *Thorndike's effect*. Underlying ability becomes more manifest as training continues—in this case, on the dependent variable, which indicates time to task completion.

EFFECTS OF CHANGE IN VARIANCE
DUE TO TRAINING ON THE EXAMINATION
OF CHANGE IN MEANS

Effects of Decreased Variance in Posttest

To discuss the implications for variance effects due to training, the case of decreased variability is considered. An increase in variability, however, will have effects that can be readily understood as analogous to those for decreased variability.

Decreased variability in experimental-group posttraining measures relative to control measures will have at least three effects. First, these posttraining measures will tend to be less reliable than postmeasures in the control group, or premeasures in either group. Second, change scores in the experimental group will also be less reliable than those in the control group. Third, the appropriate indices of effect size for comparisons of interest, such as the difference between posttest measures, will be somewhat different than those for the case where all variances are assumed to be homogeneous. This change in effect sizes will have implications for the power of tests for mean change. Each of these effects is looked at briefly.

Lesser Posttest Score Reliabilities.   The lesser reliability of the postmeasures in the experimental group is automatic if the posttest variability of the measure in that group is less. The degree of reduction in posttest reliability is given by:

$$\rho_{YY_E} = 1 - \left[(\frac{\sigma_{X_E}}{\sigma_{Y_E}})^2 (1 - \rho_{XX_E}) \right] \qquad (1)$$

(Ghiselli, Campbell, & Zedeck, 1981). Hence, if the observed pre- and posttest variances in the experimental group, $\sigma^2_{X_E}$ and $\sigma^2_{Y_E}$ are 1 and .81, respectively, and $\rho_{XX_E} = .8$, then $\rho_{YY_E} = .753$. James, Demaree, Mulaik, and Ladd (1992) noted that this process of decreasing the reliability of measures through variance reduction could occur in organizations with restrictive climates. James et al. pointed out that this would also restrict predictor correlations with performance measures (validities). In a sense, some organizational training is designed to restrict climate in the sense of promoting homogeneity of performance. It would be ironic if training would, through its effect on posttraining measure variability, inadvertently thwart the search for substantial predictor test validity.

Lesser Change Score Reliabilities.   Change score reliabilities are notoriously low (Cronbach & Furby, 1970). The fact that these change score reliabilities will be even less in the experimental group, when posttest variability is less
for the experimental than for the control group, is clear from the equation for
the reliability of change scores (Overall & Woodward, 1975):

$$\rho_{cc} = \frac{(\rho_{XX} + \rho_{YY} - 2\rho_{XY})}{2(1 - \rho_{XY})} \tag{2}$$

where ρXX and ρYY are the pre- and postmeasure reliabilities (presumably some
good internal consistency estimate; cf. Cohen & Cohen, 1983, p. 414), and ρXY
the pretest–posttest correlation. But, because ρ_{Y_E} will be less than ρ_{Y_C}
—because $\sigma^2_{Y_E} < \sigma^2_{Y_C}$ (see Equation 1)—the value for ρCC should be calculated
within groups. For example, if internal-consistency reliabilities in both pre- and
postmeasures in the control group are .8, but in the experimental group the
analogous reliabilities are .8 and .7, and if ρXY in both cases is .4, then the
reliability of the gain scores in the control group is .67, but in the experimental
group it is .58.

In the control group, which receives no treatment, ρXY could be considered
a reliability estimate. However, the pretest–posttest correlation in the experimental group, ρXY_E, cannot be assumed to be a reliability estimate. This is
because ρXY_E will be reduced not only by unreliability, but also influenced by
individual differences in the effects of the intervention (Cohen & Cohen,
1983). The effect of individual differences in change will either increase or
decrease ρXY_E, and this change may then either increase or decrease the
reliability of the difference scores in the experimental group.

The difference between ρXY_C and ρXY_C, which is due to unreliability, can
be estimated: ρXY_C is, as an estimate of ρXY_E, attenuated by the square root
of the ratio of ρXY_E to ρXY_C. Specifically,

$$\rho_{XY_E} = \rho_{XY_C} \sqrt{\frac{\rho_{YY_E}}{\rho_{YY_C}}} \tag{3}$$

So, for example, if ρYY_C is .8, ρYY_E is .7, and $\rho XY_C = .4$, as before, Equation
3 estimates ρXY_E now as .37. The difference of .03 between the pretest–posttest
correlations for the experimental and control groups is due to the lower
reliability of the posttest measure in the experimental group, which, in turn,
reflects the lower variability of that measure. Substituting this value of .37 for
ρXY_E into Equation 2, the estimate for ρCC_E is reduced slightly less (.60 instead
of .58).

It is important to recall that this or any difference between experimental and control group change or gain score reliabilities is not important for a test of the hypothesis that the treatment will have some effect (Huck & McLean, 1975). However, it is important for correlations between change scores and outside variables of interest. These correlations will be differentially reduced for the experimental and control groups.

Effect Size Calculations.   There are three typical approaches to analyzing the effect of training using the pre- and postmeasure experimental- and control-group design. These are: to assess group difference on the posttest only, to test the group difference on the change or gain scores, or to use an ANCOVA approach—testing for group differences on posttest scores adjusted for pretest scores. Arvey and colleagues have several examinations of the power of these three approaches to detect mean differences (Arvey & Cole, 1989; Arvey et al., 1985, 1992). The following section adopts their terminology and presents formulas for effect sizes for each of the three designs, but under the condition of unequal posttest variances, for which case effect size estimates have not been examined.

The sample effect size for a posttest-only design with equal variances is:

$$d_p = \frac{(\mu_{Y_E} - \mu_{Y_C})}{\sigma_{Y_C}} \tag{4}$$

(Cohen, 1969; the denominator could also be σ_{Y_E}). But for unequal variances, the denominator of Equation 4 is:

$$\sigma_{Y_{pooled}} = \sqrt{\frac{\sigma_{Y_C}^2 + \sigma_{Y_E}^2}{2}} \tag{5}$$

(Cohen, 1969, p. 42). This root mean square term for posttest variance is represented as σ_{Y_P} in the following equations. For gain scores, the appropriate effect size for unequal posttest variance is:

$$d_g = \frac{(\mu_{Y_E} - \mu_{Y_C})}{\sigma_{Y_P} \sqrt{2(1 - \rho_{XY})}} \tag{6}$$

(Arvey et al., 1985). For ANCOVA, when posttest variances are unequal, the effect size is:

$$d_a = \frac{(\mu_{Y_E} - \mu_{Y_C})}{\sigma_{Y_P} \sqrt{1 - \rho_{XY}^2}} \tag{7}$$

(Arvey et al., 1985).[1]

Figure 9.3 presents a comparison of the effect of reduction of variability on the effect size in each of the three cases: the posttest-only design, the gain score design, and the ANCOVA design, assuming equal sample sizes in experimental and control groups. As Fig. 9.3 shows, reduction in variability always increases the nominal effect size. The ANCOVA design retains its general superiority in effect size over the other methods. These changes in nominal effect size create analogous changes in power, as pointed out later.

Power.   Equations 5, 6, and 7 permit the calculation of sample sizes necessary to detect statistical significance for given effect sizes. This chapter presents a single example (see Table 9.1)—for power = .8, effect size = .2 (a "small" effect size; Cohen, 1969). Although only the case for the small effect size (.2) is presented here, a computer program is available from the authors, which permits a wide range of power analyses for the case of experimental-group posttest variance reduction.

The assumptions are random assignment, equal sample size, and equal regressions in the case of ANCOVA (Keppel & Zedeck, 1989). When the ratio of posttest standard deviations, $\sigma_{Y_E}/\sigma_{Y_C}$ (or the ratio of variances $\sigma_{Y_E}^2/\sigma_{Y_C}^2$), is equal to one, then the appropriate (bottom) row in Table 9.1 presents results equivalent to the analogous table in Arvey et al. (1985). Table 9.1 shows that the equivalence of the posttest-only and gain score approaches when pre- and

---

[1]See Arvey et al. (1985) for derivations of Equations 6 and 7 under the assumption of homogeneity. It should also be noted that, in Arvey et al. (1985) p. 497 and Arvey and Cole (1989) p. 99, the "r" is not squared in what is here Equation 7. The values in the tables in Arvey et al. (1985) and Arvey and Cole (1989), however, appear to use Equation 7 as it appears here, and are hence correct. One problem that may be noted with Equation 7 is that unequal posttraining variances will automatically mean that the assumption for ANCOVA of equal homogeneity of residual variation is violated (cf. Dretzke, Levin, & Serlin; 1982, Equation 2), even if an additional ANCOVA assumption of equality of regression slopes (assumed here) is not. Thus, the considerations presented here on the impact of training-caused heterogeneity of variance effects on the power of the three training evaluation designs should be taken only as illustrative, not conclusive, particularly in the case of ANCOVA. Nonetheless, for all three designs, previous research indicating that *t* tests and ANCOVA *F* tests are robust to violations of the homogeneity of variance assumption if sample sizes are equal (Huitema, 1980) provides some level of confidence that the values in Fig. 9.3 and Table 9.1 are acceptably accurate.

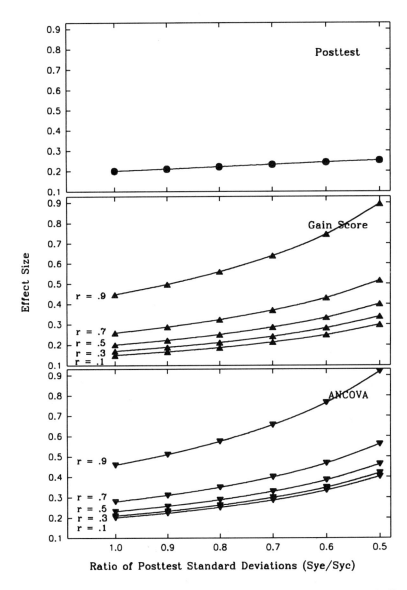

FIG. 9.3. The relation between effect size and variability. In Fig. 9.3, the nominal effect size was .2 for the posttest-only design when the ratio of variances was one. Equations 5, 6, and 7 were used to generate the other effect sizes.

postmeasure correlate at .5 (cf. Arvey et al., 1985) only holds when $\sigma^2_{Y_E} = \sigma^2_{Y_C}$, otherwise the gain score approach is more powerful at this correlation. The gain score analysis is more powerful than the posttest-only analysis for correlations

TABLE 9.1

Sample Sizes Required for Power = .80 for Three Tests of Control versus
Experimental Training Effects, for Various Correlations Between Pre-
and Posttest Scores and Various Ratios of Posttest Standard Deviations
Where Nominal Effect Size = .2

			Test Used to Detect Effect of Training									
σ_{Y_E}	$\sigma^2_{Y_E}$	Posttest Only	Gain Score					ANCOVA				
σ_{Y_C}	$\sigma^2_{Y_C}$		ρ_{xy}					ρ_{xy}				
			.1	.3	.5	.7	.9	.1	.3	.5	.7	.9
0.5	(.25)	194	140	109	78	47	16	77	71	59	40	15
0.6	(.36)	211	201	157	112	67	23	111	102	84	57	22
0.7	(.49)	231	273	213	152	92	31	151	139	114	78	29
0.8	(.64)	254	357	278	199	119	40	197	181	149	102	38
0.9	(.81)	281	452	351	251	151	51	249	229	189	128	48
1.0	(1.0)	310	557	434	310	186	63	307	282	233	158	59

of .7 and .9 for all ratios of $\sigma^2_{Y_E}$ to $\sigma^2_{Y_C}$, but inferior when the correlation is less than .5 and the ratio of $\sigma^2_{Y_E}$ to $\sigma^2_{Y_C}$ is greater than .7. In general, the Arvey et al. (1985) conclusion that the ANCOVA analysis will be the best choice as far as power goes still holds. Also of interest is the fact that reduction in pooled posttest variability increases power in all cases. This may appear counterintuitive, because, as was pointed out, reduction in variance decreases change score reliabilities. As Sutcliffe (1980) has stated, "One does not achieve greater power by realizing less reliable difference scores; it is rather that power will be greater (and [change score reliability] will be numerically smaller) if subjects happen to be less heterogeneous in their differential response to treatment independently of the measuring procedure" (p. 513).

Other Effects. There are probably many implications of a reduction in $\sigma^2_{Y_E}$, worth considering other than those for reliabilities, effect sizes, and power computations. For example, consider that regression to the mean, so often considered inevitable when measuring at two points in time, is based precisely on the premise of equal variances at Time 1 and Time 2 (Rogosa, 1988). Although variability of population measures of the control group at both times may rationally be assumed to equal those of experimental pretest measures ($\sigma^2_{X_E} = \sigma^2_{X_C} = \sigma^2_{Y_C}$), the variance of the experimental group post-measures, $\sigma^2_{Y_E}$, may often be expected to be smaller or larger than these. This has an impact on various points of interest to researchers in organizational training, including the assessment of mean differences.

Up to this point, this chapter has discussed why heterogeneity of variance is a reasonable expectation in many training evaluation situations, and how that heterogeneity can affect testing for mean differences. Because the assessment of variance effects may be desirable (may be used to test an hypothesis of interest), we need to be able to suggest conditions under which predictions of variance effects may accurately be made.

To understand, in a given training situation, whether and how training can be expected to affect variability on measures of interest, two pieces of information are needed. First, the initial variability between individuals on the measure must be known or assumed. Second, whether and in what direction change in this initial variability can be expected must be known. The following section describes an initial model to assist in the intelligent prediction of variability effects due to training.

A FIVE-FACTOR MODEL

There are at least five parameters that characterize circumstances under which predictions about variability could be made. These are: (a) degree to which stable individual differences in abilities relevant to performance and learning on task(s) to be trained are present among trainees, (b) degree of initial true differences among individuals on dependent variable(s), (c) characteristics of task(s) to be trained, (d) type of training, and (e) characteristics of measure(s) used. Figure 9.4 shows the posited relationships among these parameters.

Individual Differences in Relevant Predictive Variables

The first parameter of this model is the extent to which individuals to be trained differ in stable and relevant underlying or latent abilities. Consider general intelligence, or g. Some have argued that g is the major predictor of training

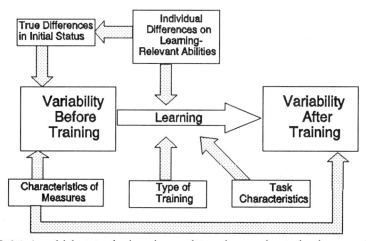

FIG. 9.4. A model depicting five boundary conditions that must be stipulated to correctly predict the effect of training on variance.

success (Ree & Earles, 1991). If individuals differ substantially in *g* and training success requires *g*, one may predict that, everything else being equal in the case of a controlled task, increased variability among individuals may be expected after training. This would be the case because those higher in *g* would gain more than those low in *g*. This was Thorndike's (1908) argument. A potential ATI may occur in which high- and low-ability people benefit differently from the training. The complexity of the training may play an important interacting role. In a review of instructional learning studies, Snow and Lohman (1984) concluded that high-ability students benefit more from less structured, highly complex programs, whereas the reverse is true for low-ability students. Abilities specifically important to training can also be important determinants of training success, such as mechanical aptitude for mechanical training or spatial judgment aptitude for training in tasks with a spatial component (Fleishman & Mumford, 1989).

There may be many other individual-difference predictors of "trainability" besides the measurement of general or specific aptitudes or abilities, including early training and past performance (Gordon, Cofer, & McCullough, 1986; Gordon & Cohen, 1973), trainee attitudes (Noe & Schmitt, 1986), experience (Schmidt, Hunter, Outerbridge, & Goff, 1988), or chance to practice on the job (Ford, Quiñones, Sego, & Speer, 1991). The assessment of each of these, in conjunction with the other factors in the model, could be important in determining whether training can be expected to affect variability.

Initial True Differences Among Individuals on Dependent Variable(s)

True initial differences on dependent variables are important because these will be reflected, to a large degree, in the measures used (assuming valid and reliable measures). Where substantial initial differences exist, convergence from pre- to postmeasures is more likely than if small initial differences exist. Indeed, if one were able to select trainees with identical or near identical initial true scores on some performance measure, then it would be virtually impossible to see any decrease in variability due to training, even for tasks where this might otherwise be predicted. Similarly, in the case where trainees have great initial differences, whether by researcher's intent or happenstance, it would be difficult to increase that variability through training. It would be interesting for researchers to examine the extent to which organizational structure or job formalization plays a role in these initial differences, thereby affecting variability changes. Other variables that may affect true initial differences among trainees include differences in ability or in previous training and experience.

One important reason for including "true" initial differences in the model is to underscore the fact that the researcher is, in most cases, examining *measures* of pre- and poststatus. It is certainly possible to assess change in variance in the latent variable underlying this measured status. This can be done, for example, using ANCOVA (cf. Meredith, 1991; Schmitt, 1982; Sorbom, 1974). A covariance structure analysis would also permit the examination of the variability of several latent variables pre- and posttraining. A change in factor structure from pre to post would be possible, but not necessarily a result of a change in variance in latent variables due to training.

Characteristics of Task(s) to Be Trained

The nature of a task may reasonably be expected to affect performance variability (Jackson & Zedeck, 1982). There are different views from which the characteristics of the tasks or subject matter to be trained might be considered. Ackerman's (1987) model of resource-dependence suggests that a task can be consistent in its demands for resources (simple task) or inconsistent (complex). The reason that the simplicity or complexity of the task to be trained is important is that a simple task may be more likely to lead to behavior that is automatized (becomes resource-independent) than one that is complex. Resource-independent tasks will show less variability across people after practice (Ackerman, 1987; Weiss, 1990), given, of course, sufficient initial variability. Howell and Cooke (1989) suggested that most tasks begin in a controlled state. If this is true, the amount of practice (a variable discussed in a later section) and the degree of task demand consistency may determine the extent of automaticity, which in turn should affect variability.

Placing a task along a single dimension of mapping, such as degree of resource-dependence, however, is probably too coarse. There are other suggested task taxonomies that may help. Norman and Shallice (1980) suggested that there are several important task characteristics that will force "willed," rather than automatic, control of behavior. These characteristics include the degree to which tasks: (a) require decision making or planning, (b) include troubleshooting components, (c) are unlearned or novel to begin with, (d) are judged to be dangerous or technically difficult, or (e) require overcoming strong habitual response(s).

In this context of considering the nature of tasks, a caveat offered by Lord and Maher (1991) is important:

> One critical distinction that is often not acknowledged is that it makes sense only to speak in terms of automatic or controlled processes, but many industrial and organizational psychologists imply that entire tasks are performed in either an automatic or controlled manner. That is, tasks are comprised of many specific processes, each of which may be characterized along a continuum. Therefore, it is misleading to characterize an entire task as either automatic or controlled. (p. 50)

Howell and Cooke (1989) clearly agreed when they argued for "identifying task *elements* that involve consistent stimulus-response mapping and then providing intensive (*part-task*) training on them" (pp. 163–164, italics added). Because tasks typically have many elements, some of which may favor automatic processes and others controlled processes, the researcher interested in making predictions of variability effects might have to either make a judgment about which type of element predominates a task or use measures on a task-element level. This would require a careful task-element analysis, which is difficult enough under any circumstances (Annett & Duncan, 1967). The guidelines for a task analysis that will enable identification of elements by their probable susceptibility to automatization have yet to be written, although task analysis is becoming more scientific (Fleishman & Quaintance, 1984). In any case, issues of automaticization are clearly important in understanding variability effects. Indeed, Jacoby, Lindsay, and Toth (1992) argued that individuals may be particularly prone to implicit processes when these are part of a larger "flow of ongoing activity" (p. 807), such as work presumably is.

Type of Training

The type of training is important because, to the extent that it is effective, it will facilitate either a dispersion or collapsing of individual differences. Olejnik (1988) presented a cogent statement in this regard, highlighting the importance of how the teacher directs his or her attention:

> In the case of student achievement, teacher behavior could reduce the variability of student achievement by focusing attention and instructional time on those students at the lower end of the achievement distribution. On the other hand, teacher behavior could increase the variability of student achievement within a class by focusing attention at the higher end of the ability distribution and letting the lower ends fall farther and farther behind. (pp. 193–194)

The extent to which the training program involves "mastery training" will have a similar effect. For example, intelligent tutoring systems, (ITSs), or computer-assisted instruction, often allows individuals to master training material at their own pace. Training to mastery would likely result in initial increases in variability because initial individual differences would play a larger role. Decreases in variability would likely follow when all students approach mastery of the training material.

Practice is also important for automaticization of resource-independent tasks (Shiffrin & Schneider, 1977). When practice is encouraged on such tasks where there is sufficient initial variability, the result should be a reduction in that variability. However, when the task is more resource-dependent, it would seem important only that the training be effective—and an increase in variability, when other initial conditions are met, may be one measure of such effectiveness. Unfortunately, researchers are only on the frontier of what they know about training when they discuss how to match training to task characteristics to obtain the best results, although there are clear signs of progress in this regard (Kraiger, Ford, & Salas, 1993).

Characteristics of Measures

Measurement characteristics such as reliability, validity, sensitivity (Poulton, 1965), and capacity to assess relatively high or low values will be important to correctly assessing change in variability. Floor and ceiling effects, which are due to faulty instruments (Reichardt, 1979), could obviously lead to spurious variability reduction (for a general discussion of floor and ceiling effects on variability, see Alliger, Hanges, & Alexander, 1988). The parsing of spurious variability change and actual variability change is a problem to be tackled by careful psychometric research.

Ackerman (1987) pointed out the importance of *what* is measured when examining hypotheses about changes in variability due to practice on simple tasks. Specifically, he distinguished between attainment (such as number of items solved in a given time period) and reaction time (RT; time to solve an item) measures. He concluded, from his own data and reanalyzed data from other researchers, that RT measures clearly display the predicted decrease in variability due to practice for consistent tasks. Attainment and RT although related, may provide different answers to the question, "Did variability decrease with practice?" (cf. Table 9.1 in Ackerman, 1987). The conclusion here would seem to be that RT is the appropriate measure of performance for testing variance hypotheses on simple, consistent tasks, whereas other traditional measures of learning (knowledge test, successful task performance) are more appropriate for complex tasks. But it does not seem possible at this time to place the discussion of variability into a simple context like that of Kirkpatrick's taxonomy of criteria (Alliger & Janak, 1989; Kirkpatrick, 1959).

CONCLUSION

The organizational training literature to date has not considered the issue of variability as a dependent measure of interest. Goldstein's (1992) classic text on training addresses this issue only obliquely, in a discussion of the "erasing individual differences" approach to training. This discussion focused on how one might tailor computer-assisted instruction "to minimize individual differences by offering remedial branches" (p. 263). This is not too different from the concerns of educators who advocate "mastery" training, which was touched on earlier. In these cases, training designers are indirectly looking for reduction in variability on outcome measures. A direct discussion of the effects of such a variability reduction on traditional training evaluation has been lacking. Specifically, a consideration of the likelihood of variance change in traditional pretest–posttest control- and experimental-group designs, and the effect of that reduction on statistical power or on the choice of appropriate tests for change, appears not to have been formally addressed in the literature to date. Researchers should take into consideration when planning such studies whether a change in experimental group variance is to be expected, whether that may influence their approach to the analysis of the data that eventuate, and whether such a change in variation might be of interest in determining the impact of the training.

The foregoing discussion may have implications for organizations beyond training. Performance appraisal data usually represent mean performance across time. Variability of that performance is not usually assessed or estimated, and little is known about just how work performance really distributes across people (Alliger & Hosoda, 1992). Information on mean performance, it is true, is probably sufficient for many purposes, because it can be said that the organization is most interested in average or typical employee performance. Mean performance level would appropriately be used, for example, as one input on which to make organizational decisions, such as those concerning wages or promotions, or in estimating the utility of an individual's contribution (Schmidt, Hunter, McKenzie, & Muldrow, 1979). But if one draws on the quality-control analogy, variation of performance across people should be kept within "control limits." It is interesting to note that intervening to reduce variation is precisely the *modus operandi* of the statistical methods of quality control popularized by Deming (1986) and others.

There are several points that are germane to the topic of training variability effects that have not been covered here. First, this chapter did not review the statistical methods whereby differences in variance may be tested (i.e., how to best test statistically whether variability has been affected by training). Generally speaking, it appears that the researcher is best advised to retain the raw data and use a method that transforms the data (Howell, 1982; O'Brien, 1981). There is also the issue of power to detect variance differences (as opposed to the impact of variability effects on the power to detect mean differences). In an attempt to understand whether training studies typically have sufficient power in this regard, we examined 20 training articles that employed the 2 × 2 mixed design yielding 83 dependent measures. The average power to detect differences in variance between the groups on the posttest measure across 83 possible tests was only .29, using the F test for variance ratios for independent samples (Kraemer & Theimann, 1987). This would seem to suggest that many studies would lack sufficient power for detection of variance differences. However, we could not use a raw score transformation with these data because only variances were reported. Therefore, advice is needed on what sample sizes would provide sufficient power using the various methods available to analyze variance differences.

This chapter also has not discussed the many ways in which between-person variability may be operationalized. This chapter has assumed that the standard deviation or its square—variance—is the most common metric for variability, and thus has focused on this measure. However, the ratio of the standard deviation to the mean (coefficient of variation), the range, or some absolute variation index can also capture variability, although in somewhat different ways. The advantages of any of these measures over the more common standard deviation is not obvious. Before a definitive choice of metric is made for examining variability effects, other measures of variability need to be carefully examined for benefits and drawbacks.

This chapter pointed out the potential importance of variability effects for organizational training, both through the possible impact of such effects on traditional approaches to training evaluation and through the development and testing of training variance effects in their own right. An initial model was presented describing the parameters that need to be taken into consideration in any viable examination of variance effects. It is hoped that this addition to the literature will assist the organizational researcher in understanding if and how training may affect variability, and to spur research on this topic.

ACKNOWLEDGMENT

The authors thank Scott E. Maxwell for comments on a previous version of this manuscript.

REFERENCES

Ackerman, P. L. (1987). Individual differences in skill learning: An integration of psychometric and information processing perspectives. *Psychological Bulletin, 102*, 3–27.

Alliger, G. M., Hanges, P. J., & Alexander, R. A. (1988). A method for correcting parameter estimates in samples subject to a ceiling. *Psychological Bulletin, 103*, 424–430.

Alliger, G. M., & Horowitz, H. M. (1989). IBM takes the guessing out of testing. *Training & Development Journal, 43*, 69–73.

Alliger, G. M., & Hosoda, M. (1992). The distribution of objective measures of work performance. In K. P. Carson (Chair), *Research on job criteria meets total quality management*. Symposium presented at the 7th annual conference of the Society of Industrial and Organizational Psychology, Montreal, Canada.

Alliger, G. M., & Janak, E. A. (1989). Kirkpatrick's levels of training criteria: Thirty years later. *Personnel Psychology, 42*, 331–342.

Anastasi, A. (1934). Practice and variability: A study in psychological method. *Psychological Monographs, 45* (Whole No. 204).

Anderson, J. R. (1982). Acquisition of cognitive skill. *Psychological Bulletin, 89*, 369–406.

Annett, J., & Duncan, K. D. (1967). Task analysis and training design. *Occupational Psychology, 41*, 211–221.

Arvey, R. D., & Cole, D. A. (1989). Evaluating change due to training. In I. L. Goldstein & Associates (Eds.), *Training and development in organizations* (pp. 89–117). San Francisco: Jossey-Bass.

Arvey, R. D., Cole, D. A., Hazucha, J. F., & Hartanto, F. M. (1985). Statistical power of training evaluation designs. *Personnel Psychology, 38,* 493–507.

Arvey, R. D., Maxwell, S. E., & Salas, E. (1992). The relative power of training evaluation designs under different cost configurations. *Journal of Applied Psychology, 77,* 155–160.

Chapman, J. C. (1925). Statistical considerations in interpreting the effect of training on individual differences. *Psychological Review, 32,* 224–234.

Cohen, J. (1969). *Statistical power analysis for the behavioral sciences.* New York: Academic Press.

Cohen, J., & Cohen, P. (1983). *Applied multiple regression/correlation analysis for the behavioral sciences.* Hillsdale, NJ: Lawrence Erlbaum Associates.

Cook, T. D., & Campbell, D. T. (1979). *Quasi-experimentaion: Design and analysis issues for field settings.* Chicago: Rand McNally.

Cronbach, L. J., & Furby, L. (1970). How we should measure "change" — or should we? *Psychological Bulletin, 74,* 68–80.

Deming, W. E. (1986). *Out of the crisis.* Cambridge, MA: MIT Press.

Dretzke, B. J., Levin, J. R., & Serlin, R. C. (1982). Testing for regression homogeneity under variance heterogeneity. *Psychological Bulletin, 91,* 376–383.

Fisk, A. D., & Schneider, W. (1981). Controlled and automatic processing during tasks requiring sustained attention: A new approach to vigilance. *Human Factors, 23,* 737–750.

Fleishman, E. A., & Mumford, M. D. (1989). Individual attributes and training performance. In I. L. Goldstein & Associates (Eds.), *Training and development in organizations* (pp. 183–255). San Francisco: Jossey-Bass.

Fleishman, E. A., & Quaintance, M. K. (1984). *Taxonomies of human performance: The description of human tasks.* Orlando, FL: Academic Press.

Ford, J. K., Quiñones, M., Sego, D., & Speer, J. (1991, April). *Factors affecting the opportunity to use trained skills on the job.* Presented at the 6th annual conference of the Society of Industrial and Organizational Psychology, St. Louis, MO.

Ghiselli, E. E., Campbell, J. P., & Zedeck, S. (1981). *Measurement theory for the behavioral sciences.* New York: Freeman.

Goldstein, I. L. (1992). *Training in organizations: Needs assessment, design, and evaluation* (2nd ed.). Monterey, CA: Brooks/Cole.

Gordon, M. E., Cofer, J. L., & McCullough, P. M. (1986). Relationships among seniority, past performance, interjob similarity, and trainability. *Journal of Applied Psychology, 71,* 518–521.

Gordon, M. E., & Cohen, S. L. (1973). Training behavior as a predictor of trainability. *Personnel Psychology, 26,* 261–272.

Howell, D. C. (1982). *Statistical methods for psychology.* Boston: PWS-Kent.

Howell, W. C., & Cooke, N. J. (1989). Training the information processor: A review of cognitive models. In I. L. Goldstein & Associates (Eds.), *Training and development in organizations* (pp. 121–182). San Francisco: Jossey-Bass.

Huck, S., & McLean, R. (1975). Using a repeated-measures ANCOVA to analyze data from a pretest-posttest design: A potentially confusing task. *Psychological Bulletin, 82,* 511–518.

Huitema, B. E. (1980). *The analysis of covariance and alternatives.* New York: Holt, Rhinehard & Winston.

Jackson, S. E., & Zedeck, S. (1982). Explaining performance variability: Contributions of goal setting, task characteristics, and evaluative contexts. *Journal of Applied Psychology, 67,* 759–768.

Jacoby, L. L., Lindsay, D. S., & Toth, J. P. (1992). Unconscious influences revealed: Attention, awareness, and control. *American Psychologist, 47,* 802–809.

James, L. R., Demaree, R. G., Mulaik, S. A., & Ladd, R. T. (1992). Validity generalization in the context of situational models. *Journal of Applied Psychology, 77,* 3–14.

Keppel, G., & Zedeck, S. (1989). *Data analysis for research designs: Analysis of variance and multiple regression/correlation approaches.* New York: Freeman.

Kincaid, M. (1925). A study of individual differences in learning. *Psychological Review, 32,* 34–53.

Kirkpatrick, D. L. (1959). Techniques for evaluating training programs. *Journal of American Society of Training & Development, 13,* 3–9.

Kraemer, H. C., & Theimann, S. (1987). *How many subjects?* Newbury Park, CA: Sage.

Kraiger, K., Ford, J. K., & Salas, E. (1993). Application of cognitive, skill-based, and affective theories of learning outcomes to new methods of training evaluation. *Journal of Applied Psychology, 78*, 311–328.

Linn, R. L., & Slinde, J. A. (1977). The determination of the significance of change between pre- and posttesting periods. *Review of Educational Research, 47*, 121–150.

Lord, R. G., & Maher, K. J. (1991). Cognitive theory in industrial and organizational psychology. In M. D. Dunnette & L. M. Hough (Eds.), *Handbook of industrial & organizational psychology* (Vol. 2, pp. 1–62). Palo Alto, CA: Consulting Psychologists Press.

Maxwell, S. E., & Howard, G. (1981). Change scores—necessarily ANATHEMA? *Educational and Psychological Measurement, 41*, 747–756.

Meredith, W. (1991). Latent variable models for studying differences and change. In L. M. Collins & J. L. Horn (Eds.), *Best methods for the analysis of change: Recent advances, unanswered questions, future directions* (pp. 149–163). Washington, DC: American Psychological Association.

Micceri, T. (1989). The unicorn, the normal curve, and other improbable creatures. *Psychological Bulletin, 105*, 156–166.

Nicewander, W. A., & Price, J. M. (1978). Dependent variable reliability and the power of significance tests. *Psychological Bulletin, 85*, 405–409.

Noe, R. A., & Schmitt, N. (1986). The influence of trainee attitudes on training effectiveness: Test of a model. *Personnel Psychology, 39*, 497–523.

Norman, D. A., & Bobrow, D. B. (1975). On data-limited and resource-limited processes. *Cognitive Psychology, 7*, 44–64.

Norman, D. A., & Shallice, T. (1980). *Attention to action: Willed and automatic control of behavior* (Tech. Rep. 8006). San Diego: University of California, Center for Human Information Processing.

O'Brien, R. G. (1981). A simple test for variance effects in experimental designs. *Psychological Bulletin, 89*, 570–574.

Olejnik, S. F. (1988). Variance heterogeneity: An outcome to explain or nuisance factor to control. *Journal of Experimental Education, 56*, 193–197.

Overall, J. E., & Woodward, J. A. (1975). Unreliability of difference scores: A paradox for measurement of change. *Psychological Bulletin, 82*, 85–86.

Poulton, E. C. (1965). On increasing the sensitivity of measures of performance. *Ergonomics, 8*, 69–76.

Ree, M. J., & Earles, J. A. (1991). Predicting training success: Not much more than g. *Personnel Psychology, 44*, 321–332.

Reed, H. B. (1931). The influence of training on changes in variability in achievement. *Psychological Monographs, 41* (Whole No. 185).

Reichardt, C. S. (1979). The statistical analysis of data from nonequivalent group designs. In T. D. Cook & D. T. Campbell (Eds.), *Quasi-experimentaion: Design and analysis issues for field settings*. Chicago: Rand McNally.

Rogosa, D. (1988). Myths about longitudinal research. In K. W. Schaie (Ed.), *Methodological issues in aging research* (pp. 171–209). New York: Springer.

Rogosa, D. R., Brandt, D., & Zimowski, M. (1982). A growth curve approach to the measurement of change. *Psychological Bulletin, 92*, 726–748.

Schmidt, F. L., Hunter, J. E., McKenzie, R., & Muldrow, T. (1979). The impact of valid selection procedures on workforce productivity. *Journal of Applied Psychology, 64*, 609–626.

Schmidt, F. L., Hunter, J. E., Outerbridge, A. N., & Goff, S. (1988). Joint relation of experience and ability with job performance: Test of three hypotheses. *Journal of Applied Psychology, 73*, 46–57.

Schmitt, N. (1982). The use of analysis of covariance structures to assess beta and gamma change. *Multivariate Behavioral Research, 17*, 343–358.

Shiffrin, R. M., & Schneider, W. (1977). Controlled and automatic human information processing: Perceptual learning, automatic attending, and a general theory. *Psychological Review, 84*, 127–190.

Snedecor, G. W., & Cochran, W. G. (1980). *Statistical methods*. Ames, IA: Iowa State University Press.

Snow, R. E., & Lohman, D. F. (1984). Toward a theory of cognitive aptitude for learning from instruction. *Journal of Educational Psychology, 76*, 347–376.

Sorbom, D. (1974). A general method for studying differences in factor means and factor structure between groups. *British Journal of Mathematical and Statistical Psychology, 27*, 229–239.

Stoddard, G. D. (1925). The problem of individual differences in learning. *Psychological Review, 32*, 479–485.

Sutcliffe, J. P. (1980). On the relationship of reliability to statistical power. *Psychological Bulletin, 88*, 509–515.

Thorndike, E. L. (1908). The effect of practice in the case of a purely intellectual function. *American Journal of Psychology, 19*, 374–384.

Thorndike, E. L. (1910). Practice in the case of addition. *American Journal of Psychology, 21*, 483–486.

Thorndike, E. L. (1916). Notes on practice, improvability, and the curve of work. *American Journal of Psychology, 27*, 550–565.

Weiss, H. M. (1990). Learning theory and industrial and organizational psychology. In M. D. Dunnette & L. M. Hough (Eds.), Handbook of industrial & organizational psychology (Vol. 1, pp. 171–221). Palo Alto: Consulting Psychologists Press.

Willet, J. B. (1988). Questions and answers in the measurement of change. In E. Z. Rothkopf (Ed.), *Review of research in education* (pp. 345–422). Washington, DC: American Educational Research Association.

Zalesny, M. D., & Farace, R. V. (1986). A field study of social information processing: Mean differences and variance differences. *Human Communication Research, 13*, 268–290.

10

A Multilevel Organizational Systems Approach for the Implementation and Transfer of Training

Steve W. J. Kozlowski
Michigan State University

Eduardo Salas
Naval Air Warfare Center Training Systems Division

Training activities are embedded within the context of the organization as a dynamic, multilevel system. Interestingly, training research has largely neglected the research and practical implications of this theoretical perspective. Indeed, one of the more consistent criticisms of the field has been its insular nature and the relative lack of emphasis on theory development (Campbell, 1971; Goldstein, 1980; Latham, 1988; Wexley, 1984). Training has generally been slow to integrate theoretical concepts from other research areas. In addition, the training literature is characterized by a micro orientation. Linkages among training activities, the organizational system, and its processes have received little attention.

There are indications that this state of affairs is changing. Training research has begun to draw heavily on theory from related research domains (Tannenbaum & Yukl, 1992). Influences from cognitive and differential psychology are having a significant impact on training research. This recent work is extending the conceptualization of learning and individual change beyond the prescriptions of classic principles of learning, which have dominated training design for over three decades (Ackerman, Sternberg, & Glaser, 1989; Howell & Cooke, 1989; Kanfer & Ackerman, 1989). This integration is encouraging. It promises to revolutionize conceptualization of the process by which expertise develops. However, this work continues to reflect the dominant individual-level orientation of training.

Training can also significantly benefit from an integration with concepts drawn from organizational theory. The training function is bound by the contextual constraints of the organizational system and its defining features. Recent theory has begun to consider the interface between the organizational system and training (Goldstein, 1991; London, 1989). Training is being conceptualized as integral to the strategic goals of the organization (Schuler & Walker, 1990), as a component of the human resource planning process (Jackson & Schuler, 1990), and as an activity that is constrained by organizational environment features (Baldwin & Ford, 1988). This broader perspective on training has theoretical implications for all phases of the training process, including needs analysis, instructional design, and transfer.

The purpose of this chapter is to extend and more fully elaborate this evolving perspective. This chapter develops a conceptual framework that integrates training with concepts drawn from organizational systems theory. This model represents an effort to move beyond simple metaphorical references to the organization as a system; the goal is to derive conceptual themes that have substantive implications for training research and application. The model is used to make explicit several issues that must be addressed if training interventions are to yield tangible impacts on organizational effectiveness.

AN OVERVIEW: TRAINING FROM
AN ORGANIZATIONAL PERSPECTIVE

The Traditional Perspective

Training has typically been micro in its orientation, with a focus on individual learning, development, and change. This is true despite the fact that, at least at a conceptual level, training needs assessment (McGehee & Thayer, 1961), evaluation (Kirkpatrick, 1967), and instructional design models (Goldstein, 1992) assert that training should be designed to support and contribute to clearly articulated organizational goals. In practice, however, training activities are generally focused at the individual level, including needs analysis (Ostroff & Ford, 1989), delivery programs (Salas, Dickinson, Converse, & Tannenbaum, 1992), and evaluation criteria (Alliger & Janak, 1989). This can be attributed to the dominance of instructional theory in training, which is based on individual-level models of change. An inherent assumption is that the individual level is the source of organizational-level change.

Although it is axiomatic that psychological change is rooted in individuals, this narrow orientation neglects the constraining influence of contextual factors at higher levels of the organizational system. The need for change, the implementation of interventions, and the transfer of trained skills are embedded within the context of work team, subunit, and organizational levels (Roberts, Hulin, & Rousseau, 1978; Sundstrom, DeMeuse, & Futrell, 1990). These contextual features and processes ultimately facilitate or inhibit the expression of trained skills.

The neglect of the organizational system and its processes has implications for training effectiveness, particularly in those instances when training content or its level of delivery does not align well with contextual constraints. This chapter takes the position that the incorporation of a systems perspective identifies issues that must be addressed to ensure that training contributes to desired changes. Trained knowledge, skills, and attitudes (KSAs) at the individual level are embedded in team- or unit-level technology, coordination processes, and social system contexts, with broader contextual constraints originating at higher system levels. From this perspective, preparing individuals to accept training-induced change, and encouraging them to express their new capabilities in the work environment, require training that is delivered at the appropriate level and is congruent with contextual supports. It is clear that training shares themes with other research domains that also address the problem of organizational change. Yet, these themes have rarely been systematically applied to issues in training.

Toward an Integrative Perspective

This overview suggests an approach to integrate traditional training concerns with concepts derived from organizational theory. This approach must incorporate more explicit recognition of the individual, team/unit, and organizational levels inherent in the organization system. This approach must also specify the process linkages among organizational levels in terms of their relevance to training activity. The general systems paradigm (Von Bertalanffy, 1975, 1980) provides principles relevant to differentiating levels of analysis (Rousseau, 1985), and can provide a conceptual foundation for specification of the process linkages that permeate the system.

To accomplish this integration, one must pull together common themes from research on organizational change and relate them to neglected problems in training. The different research domains have tended to be insular, not only because of disciplinary origin and evolution, but also because they have as their primary focus different levels of analysis and, to some extent, different content as well. For example, organizational development (OD), although it originally grew out of individual-change efforts, takes as its focus the entire organizational system. OD efforts regard change as best leveraged at the organizational level, with a focus on changing the culture of the system (Beer & Walton, 1990). Sociotechnical systems theory (SST) takes as its primary focus the subunit, team, or group that comprise a technology system (Walton, 1977). Change is focused on aligning the technological system with the needs, expectations, and norms of its human resources. SST has served as a dominant model for implementing advanced manufacturing technologies (AMT; Majchrzak, 1988) and other forms of innovation. Organizational training, in contrast, focuses on individual change in knowledge, behavioral skills, attitudes, and other characteristics (Goldstein, 1992). Each of these approaches recognizes that change must move across levels in the organizational system. Each domain specifies change processes most completely at a particular level; linkages to other levels are not well specified. Thus, effects originating from other levels are often not made salient.

Three common themes unite these different approaches to individual and organizational change: levels of analysis, content focus, and congruence. They comprise the conceptual dimensions for this integrative model. The levels of analysis theme provides the theoretical foundation for specifying the target level for training delivery and identifying the process linkages to other levels implicated in change. It provides the principles for articulating the linkages between the target level and levels above and below it. The content theme provides the rationale for specifying the training focus on techno-structural versus enabling process factors. Technostructural factors implicate technical knowledge and skills, whereas enabling processes reference the human interactions, perceptions, and shared expectations that allow the technical knowledge to be usefully applied in work settings. Content is not only relevant to the training target, but also implicates related content at different levels in the organizational system. The congruence theme helps specify requisite alignments across technostructural and enabling process content within levels. It also specifies alignments within each content domain from higher to lower levels of analysis; it provides a basis for identifying relevant features of the embedding context that must be consistent with training content for change to occur. A brief listing of the implications of these themes is found in Table 10.1. These issues are further elaborated with respect to training transfer once the foundation and rationale for the framework have been developed.

This framework is used to identify organizational factors and processes that may bear on the implementation and transfer of training interventions. This indicates the supports at the individual, team/unit, and organizational levels that must be properly aligned with the objectives underlying the training for the intervention to be effective. Thus, the framework helps make salient the organizational infrastructure that should be in place to support training. In addition, the framework allows identification of those areas where the organizational literature provides little theoretical or empirical guidance; it provides a basis to identify avenues for further conceptual development and directions for research and practice.

Chapter Organization

This chapter develops the rationale for an integrative approach. First, it examines training system linkages to the context defined by the organizational

TABLE 10.1
Issues of Level, Content, and Congruence

Theme	Issue
Level	Level issues determine how much of the entire organizational system is implicated in the training and change effort.
	Level issues specify the theoretical and methodological questions that must be resolved for training effects to compose or transfer "upwards," such that training targeted at lower levels aggregates to accomplish higher level objectives.
Content	Content issues are defined by the particular "problem" of interest and the unique characteristics of the organization in question.
	Focal content provides the basis for operationalizing specific constructs that are implicated in a particular training situation; it is central for establishing congruence.
Congruence	Congruence issues are concerned with the creation of contextual consistency across levels and content areas.
	The target levels and content areas for training will implicate required system consistencies: within content, within level; across content, within level; and across content and levels (contextual alignment).

system. The purpose is to identify limitations in existing conceptualizations that the integrative model addresses. Second, it derives, explains, and illustrates the three unifying themes from organizational research: levels of analysis, content focus, and congruence. Third, it develops a model to apply the integrating themes to training, with a particular emphasis on the identification of processes and factors at higher levels of analysis that are likely to set constraints on the effective implementation and transfer of training interventions. It makes explicit the expanded perspective on transfer offered by this model. Finally, it demonstrates the theoretical utility of this approach by identifying research propositions. Because team-based work systems are at the intersection of the individual and organizational levels, teams are used as a central focus of this presentation. This serves to illustrate the limitations of the strictly individual-level perspective and to provide a vehicle for posing research questions.

TRAINING IN ORGANIZATIONS

Classic models of organizational training highlight two key areas of linkage between training activity and the organizational system. McGehee and Thayer (1961) emphasized the organizational goals and objectives derived through *needs assessment* that drive the determination of training content. They defined training as, " ... the formal procedures which a company uses to facilitate employees' learning so that their resultant behavior contributes to *the attainment of the company's goals and objectives*" (p. 3; italics added). Goldstein (1992) incorporated this linkage, but emphasized *transfer*. He defined training as " ... the systematic acquisition of skills, rules, concepts, or attitudes that results in *improved performance in another environment*" (p. 3; italics added); trained KSAs cannot affect organizational goals if they are not expressed in the work environment. Needs analysis is traditionally regarded as a diagnostic process that occurs prior to training. The purpose of needs analysis is to identify what is to be trained, training content, and who is to receive training—training targets. Transfer is traditionally regarded as a posttraining outcome and a key indicator of training effectiveness (Kirkpatrick, 1967).

Each of these linkages between training activity and the organizational system is considered. The purpose here is to identify important theoretical issues that emerge when the linkages are considered from an organizational systems perspective—issues that this model addresses. This approach is consistent with the classic perspective, but attempts to more fully elaborate linkages to the organizational context. It assumes that needs analysis has its primary impact on training design and delivery, or what is referred to as *implementation issues*, whereas transfer implicates *contextual issues*—the alignment between trained skills and the context in which they are to be expressed. Thus, needs analysis must be sensitive to the level at which trained skills are to have their intended impact. For example, training that is intended to affect team performance must consider the form of composition by which individual skills aggregate to the target level—the team. These considerations affect the design and implementation of training delivery systems. Similarly, transfer processes implicate characteristics of the work context that facilitate or inhibit the expression of newly trained skills. This necessitates consideration of alignment across levels—between the training target and the higher level context.

Organizational Goals and Training

Training is predicated on meeting organizational goals and objectives. Classic models of training emphasize needs assessment as the means by which these goals exert an influence on training design, although they do not link this process directly to transfer. Needs assessment incorporates three principal activities: organizational analysis, operations or task analysis, and person analysis. All three activities are relevant to the implementation issues identified earlier (specifying the target level for training delivery and deriving training content). The following identifies neglected issues that necessitate elaboration and extension of the traditional perspective to link it more directly to transfer.

Organizational Analysis.   The major aspect of organizational analysis involves the broad-based determination of organizational goals, objectives, and resources; their time frames; and likely future states (McGehee & Thayer, 1961). There is resurgent interest in the strategic, forward-looking, and dynamic aspects of organizational analysis (Tannenbaum & Yukl, 1992). Many researchers have indicated the need to devise training and human resource systems that are driven by the strategic requirements of the organization (Jackson & Schuler, 1990; Schuler, 1987; Schuler & Jackson, 1987). The primary issue has been that training policies need to be linked to organizational business strategy (Brown & Read, 1984), that changes in the strategic plan should be reflected in revised training objectives for personnel development (Hussey, 1985), and that needs assessment must incorporate a future orientation (Schneider & Konz, 1989). For example, an organization planning to implement advanced manufacturing technology will need to identify the kinds of technical skills, managerial skills, and supporting processes necessary to operationalize the innovation well in advance of its implementation (Kozlowski, 1987; Majchrzak, 1988). This calls for planning techniques that are not well represented in conventional needs assessment procedures (Kraut, Pedigo, McKenna, & Dunnette, 1989).

This renewed interest in the dynamic, system character of organizational analysis forces a consideration of the multilevel linkages inherent in each of the three needs analysis activities. For example, organizational analysis cannot be considered in isolation of the other levels comprising the organizational system (Ostroff & Ford, 1989). Inasmuch as organizational analysis should drive the determination of training objectives, the level at which organizational analysis targets training affects the implementation of the intervention and has a profound impact on the effectiveness of transfer as well. Linkages between organizational goals and training interventions designed to meet them must be considered at each level in the system. A levels perspective requires specification or mapping of contextual relations during the assessment process to enhance transfer.

A key implication of the levels perspective is that it highlights an aspect of organizational analysis that is frequently overlooked—the necessity of organizational supports for training. These supports include both tangible (policies, procedures, and reward systems) and intangible (leadership, socialization, and climate) factors. In a classic study, Fleishman (1953) demonstrated that the transfer of leadership behaviors acquired in training was constrained by the "leadership climate" of the unit to which the trainees returned. In essence, support by the trainees' superior for the new leadership concepts was the primary determinant of transfer. This is an example of a contextual constraint that directly determines the extent to which the training can be transferred. Organizational analysis needs to consider additional interventions beyond training to create contexts supportive of the trained behaviors. One critical conceptual issue is the need for a model to help specify the important contextual factors and their linkages across levels prior to implementation.

Operations Analysis. The primary purpose of operations analysis is to identify the functional content of training. McGehee and Thayer (1961) selected the term *operations analysis* to explicitly differentiate it from conventional job analysis because the latter is historical and static. *Job analysis* describes jobs as they currently exist, with no provision for improvement or reconfiguration as organizational goals, technology, structure, or conditions change over time (Kozlowski, 1987). This distinction between *operations analysis* and *job analysis* has been largely neglected.

The traditional focus of operations analysis is on the individual job or clusters of similar jobs. It abstracts jobs from their context and considers them in isolation. This focus is rapidly becoming outmoded as organizations move beyond functional work structures (Sundstrom et al., 1990). The emphasis has begun to shift to focus on teams of people with differentiated and distributed skills. In this perspective, jobs are embedded in a technical system (Rousseau, 1978a, 1978b), connected through work flow interdependencies (Comstock & Scott, 1977) and facilitated by interpersonal communication and coordination processes within the work team (Hackman & Morris, 1975; Morgan, Glickman, Woodard, Blaiwes, & Salas, 1986).

At the team level, individual jobs are contextually bound by subunit constraints, including technology (Kozlowski & Farr, 1988, Rousseau, 1978a, 1978b), structure (Brass, 1981; Kozlowski & Farr, 1988; Oldham & Hackman, 1981), and interpersonal climates (Jones & James, 1979). Subunits are bound by higher level system constraints (Perrow, 1967; Thompson, 1967). Moreover, many contextual factors (leadership, group processes) have a developmental dimension, such that linkages among variables within and across levels evolve over time (Kozlowski, Gully, McHugh, Salas, & Cannon-Bowers, 1996).

An implication of this perspective is that the failure to consider trained skills in the job context, within which they must be integrated, is likely to inhibit their expression. This requires attention to training implementation and transfer issues early in the program design process. However, theoretical frameworks and methodologies for conceptualizing training at the team level of analysis are not well represented in the training literature (Salas et al., 1992).

Person Analysis. Person analysis is directly concerned with individuals in terms of their level of performance and the aspects of performance that may require improvement. Although the classic orientation of person analysis is at the individual level, individual performance is contextually bound by contextual constraints at higher levels, as previously noted. When considered within the team level, for example, the focus of person analysis shifts to include those individual skills that are necessary to define, create, and maintain the higher level entity called the *team*. What individual factors influence the creation of cohesion, consensus, and the kind of performance coherence that is the hallmark of team effectiveness? Questions of this sort are not derived from conventional approaches to person analysis.

In addition, recent research in training has begun to focus on "trainability" issues, which are primarily motivational, as opposed to ability based (Mathieu, Tannenbaum, & Salas, 1992; Noe & Schmitt, 1986; Tannenbaum, Mathieu, Salas, & Cannon-Bowers, 1991). A key implication of this perspective is that individual-level factors can interact with the training context or situation. Individual-difference characteristics must be aligned with the defining features of the embedding context.

Conclusion. The development of training interventions to satisfy organizational goals implicates complex linkages across levels of the organizational system. Although existing frameworks acknowledge the necessity of these connections, they are not specific about the implications for training implementation and the consequences for transfer. Organizational goals are bounded by dynamic environment and strategic considerations. Organizational goals drive the determination of training needs, but the link between goals and the targeted KSAs of training is mediated by contextual features at multiple levels in the organizational system. Current models of training are deficient with respect to these issues.

Training Transfer

There is high consensus that the acquisition of knowledge, skills, behaviors, and attitudes in training is of little value if the new characteristics are not generalized to the job setting and are not maintained over time. Transfer is the core issue with respect to linking individual change to the requirements of the organizational system.

Traditional approaches to transfer in industrial and organizational psychology tend to consider it as a horizontal linkage that connects training and performance environments. A comprehensive review (Baldwin & Ford, 1988) classified factors affecting transfer into three categories: (a) training inputs, including trainee, training design, and work environment characteristics; (b) training outputs, composed of learning and retention; and (c) conditions of transfer, which focus on the generalization and maintenance of training. All three sets of training input features are seen as affecting learning and retention, which directly influence generalization and maintenance. Trainee characteristics and work environment features are also regarded as influencing generalization and maintenance, outside of any influence from the training per se. The implications of these factors begin to push the conceptualization of transfer beyond the traditional environment to environment link. The next section considers the implications of these input factors for transfer from an organizational systems perspective.

Training Design.   The individual-level perspective of classic transfer theory is represented within training design. Identical elements theory (Thorndike & Woodworth, 1901) maintains that transfer is improved by increasing the degree of correspondence between training setting stimuli, responses, and conditions, and those related factors operative in the performance setting. General principles theory indicates that transfer is facilitated by provision of the general rules that underlie the use of trained skills (Judd, 1908). The notion of stimulus variability asserts that transfer is positive when many different forms of relevant training stimuli are employed (Ellis, 1965). Finally, conditions of practice concern several different learning principles, including massed versus spaced practice (Briggs & Naylor, 1962), whole versus part training (Naylor & Briggs, 1963), feedback (Wexley & Thornton, 1972), over learning (Hagman & Rose, 1983), and the constraints under which each principle contributes to positive transfer.

Principles of training design are undergoing significant evolution, primarily due to the influence of cognitive theory. Cognitive concepts—including knowledge organization structures, mental models, metacognition, learning strategies, and self-regulation—are believed to improve the acquisition and retention of declarative knowledge. Appropriate use of sequencing and variability of practice opportunities and feedback are thought to enhance skill acquisition and proceduralization. This influence from cognitive psychology represents a significant advance in the development of training theory. However, the focus remains at the individual level (Kozlowski, Ford, & Smith, 1993).

When considered from a higher level perspective, different and more complex issues of training design emerge. For example, most training for team-based tasks is designed for delivery at the individual level, with faith that the individual skills will somehow combine to yield more effective teams (Salas et al., 1992). For the technical skills that comprise the differentiated tasks of team members, this individual delivery may be appropriate initially. However, for training the coordination and adaptation skills that underlie effective teamwork, training design and delivery oriented toward intact teams may be more effective. When training teams, several questions become relevant: (a) What specific KSAs are most appropriate for individual-versus team-level training delivery? (b) What is the appropriate sequence of individual versus team training? and (c) What time frames are relevant for coordinating training delivery at more than one level?

Trainee Characteristics.   Of the various trainee ability, personality, and motivational factors likely to affect the transfer process, the motivational factors have provided the most consistent positive effects (Baldwin & Ford, 1988).

Factors including trainee confidence (Ryman & Biersner, 1975), job involvement (Noe & Schmitt, 1986), self-expectancies (Cannon-Bowers & Salas, 1990; Eden & Ravid, 1982; Tannenbaum et al., 1991), self-efficacy, attitudes (Cannon-Bowers & Salas, 1990; Tannenbaum et al., 1991), and other motivational features (Baumgartel, Reynolds, & Pathan, 1984; Hicks & Klimoski, 1987) have been positively associated with transfer. From an expectancy theory perspective (Mathieu et al., 1992; Noe, 1986), trainee motivation before, during, and after training is likely to be linked to contextual features. It is argued here that the identification of the individual-difference characteristics likely to be important in a given situation requires an understanding of contextual congruence.

Work Environment. Training research has tended to focus on the notion of "supervisor support" as the critical work environment factor affecting training transfer (Baldwin & Ford, 1988). Positive findings have been cited for the influence of goal setting freedom and support (Baumgartel & Jeanpierre, 1972; Baumgartel, Sullivan, & Dunn, 1978), supporting organizational reward systems (Hand, Richards, & Slocum, 1973), and supporting management styles (Huczynski & Lewis, 1980) for the transfer of human resource skills.

Although there is broad endorsement for the idea that the work environment is critical to transfer, Baldwin and Ford (1988) reproached existing research because it revealed little about the specific work environment factors involved in constraining transfer. They noted that the evidence was limited by the use of self-report measures of transfer, typically given immediately after the completion of training. In addition, the conceptual specification of "supporting work environment" has not been seriously addressed. In many instances, it has been operationalized as the global interpersonal relationship with the supervisor (Russell, Terborg, & Powers, 1985). This vague definition of *support* lacks specificity with respect to training content, and makes it difficult to identify more tangible, higher level contextual influences that may be mediated by the supervisor relationship (Kozlowski & Doherty, 1989). The transfer environment literature reviewed by Baldwin and Ford (1988) is indicative of the limited conceptualization of the organizational context in training research. A theoretically based, methodologically sound, and empirically supported framework is needed to specify contextual effects on transfer.

Conclusion. Emerging perspectives on training transfer are extending conceptualization of the process. They explicitly recognize that transfer is contingent on interactions with trainee characteristics and work environment features (i.e., on alignment between the work context and individual KSAs). This conceptualization is reflected in recent research on trainability, which hypothesizes that trainee characteristics (motivation) and work environment features (supervisor support) moderate the training to work setting linkage. As initial efforts, however, the higher level constructs are not yet well defined (What is meant by the work environment?), and their derivation is not theory-driven. An integration with organizational theory can create a fuller articulation of the higher level constructs and elaboration of their linkages to factors at different levels in the organizational system.

ORGANIZATION THEORY

Toward a Broader Perspective

There is broad support for the notion that organizational context factors affect the implementation and transfer of training (Fleishman, 1953; McGehee & Thayer, 1961; Marx, 1982). The major impediments preventing the application of this perspective have been the lack of theory development and the failure to define constructs and relevant content. Theory development and construct specification can benefit from the application of concepts drawn from systems-oriented theories of organizational behavior. In addition to a broad theoretical foundation, these literatures have a substantial research base on which to draw inferences regarding the effects of contextual factors. This enhances the ability to identify tangible work environment characteristics, which are also implicated in training transfer situations.

Contemporary organizational theory indicates that contextual factors exert an influence on individual responses through perceptions of the organizational environment. These perceptions are conceptualized as cognitively based interpretations of salient contextual features, events, and processes (Kozlowski & Hults, 1987). In other words, important, tangible, and meaningful work environment factors (structure, reward systems, or decision autonomy) are stimuli that underlie perceptions of the context. These interpretive perceptions serve as mediating mechanisms to link salient contextual features to individual responses (Kozlowski & Farr, 1988). Interpretive perceptions are influenced by work environment factors at the team, unit, and organizational levels of analysis (James & Jones, 1974, 1976).

This theoretical perspective—regarding the organizational system, its contextual character, and its influence on behavior—has arguably been most highly developed in regard to the concept of climate. For example, Kozlowski and Hults (1987) showed that specific organizational climate factors significantly distinguished different organizational environments. The climate factors were consensual within organizations, thereby demonstrating a collective interpretation of the context, and were significantly related to behavior ratings of skill updating and job performance. Moreover, their results indicate that the strength of the relationship among the climate factors and behavioral responses increased over time. Thus, climate defined contexts that supported the expression of related skills and behaviors. In a more direct examination of the effects of climate on training transfer, Rouiller and Goldstein (1993) showed that work unit climate for transfer accounted for significant variance in behavior transfer above and beyond any effect due to learning. Contextual factors can either facilitate or inhibit training transfer.

Three theoretical concepts or themes—levels, content, and congruence—underlie conceptualization of the organizational context from the perspective of climate theory. These themes offer advantages absent in the training literature. First, the contemporary framework explicitly addresses the organization as a system represented at different levels of analysis (James & Jones, 1976; Kozlowski & Hults, 1987). It is well grounded theoretically (Forehand & Gilmer, 1964; James & Jones, 1974; Schneider, 1981), and has spurred the development of methodologies to address cross-level and multilevel composition (Dansereau, Alutto, & Yammarino, 1984; James, Demaree, & Wolf, 1984; Kozlowski & Hattrup, 1992).

Second, empirical research provides a solid basis for identifying contextual factors across multiple levels that may be critical to the transfer problem. Climate research has moved into the third stage of construct evolution (Reichers & Schneider, 1990), whereby the construct has been conceptually delineated, basic theoretical processes have been defined, and the construct has demonstrated applicability to understanding applied problems. Climate research findings provide a foundation for the development of a climate for transfer construct. Research by Kozlowski and Farr (1988), Kozlowski and Hults (1987), Rouiller and Goldstein (1993), Schneider and Bowen (1985), and Zohar (1980) represents useful examples that can be used to identify relevant facilitating and inhibiting contextual factors that have applicability for training and development situations. In addition, work by Peters and his colleagues (Peters & O'Connor, 1980; Peters, O'Connor, & Rudolf, 1980) has identified a broad array of situational constraints that may be considered in the specification of relevant contextual factors for a particular training situation.

The application of the contextual themes represented in climate theory and related research domains provides a conceptual foundation for a more integrative approach to the training implementation and transfer problem. These themes can be used to develop a framework that can guide the identification of training research issues, questions, and directions that follow from an explicit consideration of contextual effects. These issues have clear implications for practical considerations in the design, development, and implementation of training interventions.

Integrating Themes

This view of the organization as a contextual system has emerged from the literature of several related, but conceptually distinct, research domains in organizational science. Variations on these themes distinguish different research domains from one another, yet they also provide a common framework for pulling the disparate pieces back together. The three critical integrating themes include: (a) systems framework, with particular emphasis on a levels of analysis perspective; (b) congruence of constructs and processes both within and across levels of analysis; and (c) focus on technostructural versus human process content.

Systems and Levels of Analysis. Use of the systems framework in organizational research is ubiquitous. The integrative aspects of the systems approach, however, have tended to play more the role of heuristic or metaphor in theory, with less direct impact on actual research. Key concepts that underlie the systems framework include: organizations are open to external environmental influences (Katz & Kahn, 1978), subsystem events are embedded in the larger systems context or network of relations (Lewin, 1951), and it is impossible to understand complex events in systems by reducing them to their individual elements (Von Bertalanffy, 1975, 1980). Although the high degree of interrelatedness inherent in the systems framework is conceptually powerful, it has paradoxically made the general systems paradigm difficult to apply. Nothing can be tested without considering the entire system (Roberts et al., 1978).

Theoretical principles from the levels of analysis perspective allow the disentangling of this high degree of interrelatedness, making the research problem more tractable. A system can be decomposed into relatively independent subsystems that exist at different levels, and yet still maintain the characteristics of the larger system (Simon, 1973). Levels that are relevant in organizational research generally include the organization, the unit (subunit, group, or team), and the individual, although finer distinctions can also be made (Rousseau, 1985). Decomposition is possible because different levels operate according to different time frames, with processes at higher levels proceeding more slowly than processes at lower system levels (Simon, 1973). The linkage among levels can be considered separately, although those among levels are not negligible. Adjacent levels in the system tend to be the most meaningful for research because their time frames are more synchronous, and the higher system level provides the immediate embedding context for processes that unfold in the lower system level. In terms of the general systems paradigm, the "bond strength" of adjacent levels is much stronger than that of levels farther apart.

An explicit consideration of levels is first and foremost a theoretical issue. Models of the phenomenon of interest can be compositional, cross-level, or multilevel in nature, following the terminology specified by Rousseau (1985). *Composition models* are relevant when the interest is on forms of essentially the same construct that exist at different levels. For example, psychological climate represents individual-level perceptions of salient contextual characteristics, whereas subunit or organizational climate reference a collective, shared interpretation of the context (James & Jones, 1974). Although the constructs reference similar content, they exist at different levels of conceptualization. Moreover, the higher level construct is qualitatively distinct; it necessitates the specification of processes that yield group consensus (Kozlowski & Hattrup, 1992; Kozlowski & Hults, 1987). *Cross-level models* are relevant when the interest is on the relationships among different constructs that exist at different levels. For example, the correlation between subunit structural characteristics (functionalization, standardization, and centralization) and individual job satisfaction represent cross-level relations (Herman & Hulin, 1972). *Multilevel models* assume that *constructs* comprising a model, including antecedents, mediators or moderators, and responses, and the *causal processes* linking those constructs are functionally identical at multiple levels. This requires composition among the constructs across levels *and* process relations among constructs that are parallel across levels.

Once the levels model has been determined, several methodological issues become relevant for its operationalization. These issues include specification of the focal unit or unit of theory, the unit of measurement for model constructs, and the level at which data will be analyzed to examine hypotheses. The *focal unit* or unit of theory refers to the essential level of the phenomenon of interest. At what level do the factors or processes exist? To what level will generalizations be made? The *unit of measurement* refers to the level at which data are obtained for the phenomenon of interest. *Level of data analysis* refers to the level at which a given phenomenon is addressed in a model for hypothesis testing. The level of data and analysis should be compatible with the unit of theory to avoid misspecification error, which leads to spurious conclusions (Rousseau, 1985).

In conclusion, the levels of analysis approach requires that the focal unit, unit of measurement, and unit of analysis be made explicit. The specific constructs involved and the relevant levels incorporated in the model must be determined by (grounded in) the phenomenon of interest. Linkages among levels—compositional, cross-level, or multilevel—must be justified by clearly articulated theory, preferably with empirical support.

Congruence. A related theme inherent in several distinct organizational literatures is the concept of *congruence*. This theme further elaborates the theoretical processes in levels models. Congruence is readily apparent in macroorganization theory and in more microliteratures on person–environment fit. The notion of *congruence* asserts that systems must maintain a fit or alignment among factors and processes both within and across different levels of analysis.

For example, classic research by Burns and Stalker (1961) and Lawrence and Lorsch (1967) demonstrated that organizations adopted mechanisms for structuring activities among their functions that were appropriate for the type of environment the organizations inhabited. Similar adaptive linkages have also been identified in organizational theory for relations between technology and structure. Thompson (1967), Perrow (1967), and Galbraith (1973) each devel-oped typologies that specify the necessary adaptive linkages between organiza-tional technologies and structuring mechanisms.

This concept of congruence or alignment forms the basis for organizational contingency theory (Van de Ven & Drazin, 1985). More integrative expressions of this approach have been represented in the organizational adaptation litera-ture (Mealiea & Lee, 1979; Miles, Snow, Meyer, & Coleman, 1978; Randolph & Dess, 1984). For example, Miles et al. (1978) developed a typology that specifies the requisite alignments among organization strategy, goals, environ-ment, technology, and structure that are required for effectiveness. The typo-logy addresses the necessity for shifts in alignments as environmental and strategic dynamics force adaptation. It even goes so far as to indicate links between the strategic typology and human resource policies and practices—the situational factors implicated in climate theory—although these links are tentative and not well specified. Several tests of the model have been supportive (Shortell & Zajac, 1990).

An explicit consideration of congruence requires that the theoretical form of alignment or fit be specified. Van de Ven and Drazin (1985) described three forms of fit relevant to the congruence theme. In its simplest form, fit is represented by the significant correlation between variables. A more complex form of fit includes the specification of outcome relations. Van de Ven and Drazin defined this form of fit as a moderator relationship, such that fit yields effectiveness and lack of fit yields ineffectiveness. Although not discussed by Van de Ven and Drazin, we would argue that mediation relations are also relevant because they can serve as cross-level links that represent contextual embeddedness (Kozlowski & Farr, 1988). The most complex conceptualization of fit references the internal consistency among multiple contingencies within the organizational system. In this form, a finite set of equally effective configu-rations of fit are possible. Deviations from the ideal configurations (lack of fit) negatively affect outcomes of interest.

Congruence can be conceptualized both within and across levels. Although this creates methodological complexity, analytical techniques are available to address congruence from a levels perspective (see Edwards, 1994). In compo-sition theory terms, within-level congruence references interoceptive con-straints(i.e., constraining relations among different constructs at the same level of analysis). These congruence relations are most relevant for content consis-tency within a single level. As is explained here, this is most important for training design and delivery—to ensure that the content of training fits within level constraints(e.g., that trained teamwork skills fit the requirements of the technical system). Alignment is also represented in the cross-level relations among different constructs at different levels of analysis. Exteroceptive constraints at higher levels of analysis influence variables at a lower level in the system. Research examining cross-level relations has generally focused on the subunit and individual levels. This is illustrated by the theory and research that link subunit technology and structure to individual-level responses, such as attitudes or performance (Herman & Hulin, 1972). Additional research has shown that this relationship between subunit contextual factors and individual responses is mediated by individual-level job characteristics (Brass, 1981; Oldham & Hackman, 1981) and climate perceptions (Kozlowski & Farr, 1988). Exteroceptive constraints are most important to transfer, ensuring that the training is consistent with the context factors originating at higher levels in the system.

In conclusion, the concept of congruence shows considerable generalizability across different levels of the organizational system, as well as across different organizational research domains. Congruence is a theoretical process that aids in the fuller articulation of relations among key constructs defining the organizational system. The form of congruence is relevant for the determination of consistencies among factors within a particular level, and for specifying context configurations and their effects on outcomes across levels.

Content Focus. Both the levels and congruence themes reference abstract processes that bind contextual factors together within and across levels of the organizational system. To be meaningful, these processes must be grounded in specific content. A third theme that cuts across different research domains is the focus on *technostructural* versus *human process* content (Friedlander & Brown, 1974; Roethlisberger & Dickson, 1939). *Technostructural* approaches tend to focus on the more concrete, tangible, and visible aspects of the system. Strategy, goals, technology, hierarchical structure, and organizational control systems represent the content of this approach. *Human process* approaches emphasize the less concrete, but no less important, aspects of the organization. The emphasis is on mutual interdependencies, normative expectations, and shared perceptual interpretations, that is, on the culture, climate, and social processes that constitute the tacit, informal constraints on the dynamics of human behavior in organizational settings. Although these content areas are not mutually exclusive, different research domains tend to emphasize one more than the other. The point to be made here is not which one is most important—they both are—but rather that they need to be compatible. The emphasis is on integrating the formal and informal aspects of organizational processes (Homans, 1950; Likert, 1967).

This form of compatibility between the technostructural and human process aspects of the organizational system is present in several research domains. The macroadaptation literature is most concerned with the alignment among technostructural factors, but also regards organizational technostructure as constraining appropriate human resource management policies (Miles et al., 1978). The OD literature focuses on human process interventions, but recognizes that these interventions must be compatible with the technostructural characteristics of the system. Beer and Walton (1990) stated, "Changes in structures and systems demand new behaviors by individuals and groups . . . .these changes must be accompanied by the development of leadership, human skills, and shared values that are consistent with the purpose of the structures and systems introduced" (p. 155).

SST, which takes more of a unit or team focus, asserts that technological systems should be designed for compatibility with human needs and require‐ ments. The hardware comprising a technology and the effective use of the hardware's capability by people are inexorably entwined (Brooks, 1982). A failure to plan for this compatibility leads to ineffectiveness. Like OD, however, SST approaches tend to emphasize human process content and regard certain types of processes as inherently more valued than others (autonomous work groups vs. assembly lines). The content distinction is also represented in the AMT implementation literature, which draws heavily on SST and OD, but in a more balanced approach. This literature has distinguished technological content and its embedding content (Kozlowski, 1987).

Finally, this distinction is also represented in training practice. Training can typically be clustered into two categories with distinctly different content orientations: (a) task‐, knowledge‐, and skill‐based training designed to provide the individual with the attributes necessary to effectively interact and utilize the hardware capabilities of a system; and (b) attitude‐, expectation‐, and perception‐based training designed to provide the individual with the attributes necessary with which to effectively interact and utilize the human and social attributes of a system. Morgan et al. (1986) refered to this content distinction as *taskwork* versus *teamwork*. They noted that the second content orientation is the most critical in interdependent task environments (team‐based systems).

In conclusion, several organizational literatures focusing on different levels of conceptualization have distinguished technostructural and enabling process content. All the literatures indicate the necessity for congruence between these content areas. This congruence has typically been conceptualized most clearly within a single level of analysis. However, content must be grounded in a more integrative, multilevel model of the organizational system.

A SYSTEMS APPROACH TO TRAINING IMPLEMENTATION AND TRANSFER

The theoretical themes derived previously represent central principles in the conceptualization of the organization as a dynamic, multilevel system. This section develops a framework that applies the themes to organizational training. The framework, in conjunction with the previous review of the research domains, can be used to identify research issues to improve the effectiveness of training implementation and transfer.

An Integrative Framework

The integrative framework is illustrated in Fig. 10.1. The external environment is acknowledged as a critical influence on the organization system. Environmental characteristics are directly relevant to organizational-level characteristics, generate the need for organizational change, and drive the determination of training requirements. However, the model is focused on internal characteristics and relations, and their relevance to implementation and transfer after training needs have been identified.

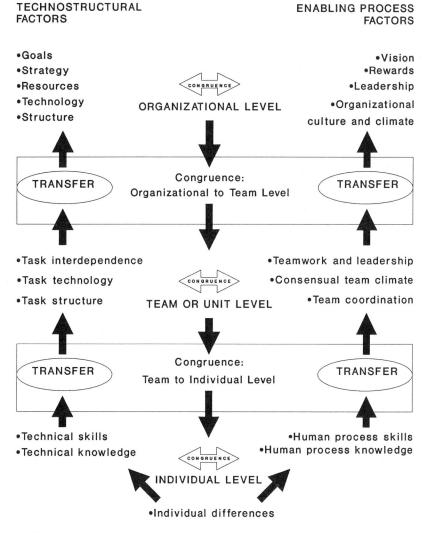

TECHNOSTRUCTURAL
FACTORS

ENABLING PROCESS
FACTORS

•Goals
•Strategy
•Resources
•Technology
•Structure

CONGRUENCE

ORGANIZATIONAL LEVEL

•Vision
•Rewards
•Leadership
•Organizational
culture and climate

TRANSFER

Congruence:
Organizational to Team Level

TRANSFER

•Task interdependence
•Task technology
•Task structure

CONGRUENCE

TEAM OR UNIT LEVEL

•Teamwork and leadership
•Consensual team climate
•Team coordination

TRANSFER

Congruence:
Team to Individual Level

TRANSFER

•Technical skills
•Technical knowledge

CONGRUENCE

INDIVIDUAL LEVEL

•Human process skills
•Human process knowledge

•Individual differences

FIG. 10.1. A multilevel model for training implementation and transfer.

First, the most dominant feature of the model is the distinction among the levels that comprise the organizational system—individual, team or unit, and organization. The levels theme is the primary source of theory specifying the process linkages that bind the system's different levels. It also provides a foundation for identifying important methodological issues. Second, the model distinguishes between technostructural and enabling process content. The primary function of this theme is to provide a means to identify relevant features that comprise contexts—it helps make salient the "stuff" underlying process linkages. The model is an abstraction; specific focal content must be operationalized with respect to a particular organization's training application. Third, the framework incorporates congruence as a critical mechanism for conceptualizing configurations or alignments among key variables comprising the organizational system. It addresses the connection of variables within content domains, between content domains, and between levels. The following sections further elaborate each of these features.

Levels. The model conceptualizes the organization as multilevel in nature, with higher levels in the system comprising embedding contexts for lower level phenomena. The general failure of training theory, research, and practice to look beyond the individual level was at the core of this critique. Although it is accepted that training-induced change is ultimately rooted within the individual, the manner in which training is implemented and the embedding context within which new skills, behaviors, and attitudes are to be expressed is critical to transfer and, ultimately, effectiveness.

The main advantage of the levels approach is that it forces consideration of issues that would otherwise be neglected. First, it requires explicit specification of the level at which training is to have its intended impact. Training targets beyond the individual level require consideration of system linkages that bind lower level factors and processes to the higher level. Second, as the target for training moves to a team level, issues related to the composition of the targeted behavior come forward. The manner in which individual-level skills and behavior compile to yield a collective outcome must be specified. Third, constraining contextual influences that originate at higher system levels (work environment factors) and linkages that originate at lower system levels (individual differences) also need to be considered for a team- or unit-level target. The framework requires explicit recognition of the relevant composition, cross-level, and, possibly, multilevel linkages that influence the target level for training.

Composition relations are relevant when the focus is on a higher level construct that is qualitatively similar to a lower level counterpart. The primary issue concerns the nature or form of the contribution of the lower level construct to the higher level representation. For example, except in restricted circumstances, team performance is not a simple additive function of individual performance. The form of individual contributions to this higher level construct of team performance will need to be explicitly specified through a composition model. As the target moves to higher levels of conceptualization (unit, division, or organization), additional issues of composition must also be considered. Composition has direct relevance to the aggregate effects of individual change on organizational training outcomes, one important aspect of transfer.

Cross-level relations are implicated when the focus is on qualitatively different constructs that exist at different levels. Linkages of this type are relevant when the focus is on identifying contextual factors at higher levels that may facilitate or inhibit the expression of trained behaviors. Leader support, organizational rewards, and coworker encouragement are all work environment supports when they are consistent with training content. Such relationships are cross-level in nature.

Multilevel models are relevant when similar content and processes are implicated at adjacent levels of analysis. Current theory suggests that work environment or climate perceptions at the individual level are likely to affect the expression of trained behaviors. This model may be extrapolated to the team level: Team-level climate is likely to affect the expression of team behaviors. When composition exists for the constructs of interest and the process linking the constructs is similar, multilevel models are appropriate.

Issues of level have direct implications for training delivery and transfer. In the simplest case of an individual-level focus (individual performance), cross-level linkages representing the context for the expression of trained behavior (i.e., transfer) will be implicated (unit climate). When the focal unit is at higher levels (team behavior), issues of composition, cross-level contextual linkages, and, possibly, multilevel linkages are also implicated.

Focal Content. The second dimension of the framework addresses the content orientation of the change or training effort. Technostructural factors refer to the concrete derivatives of technology and structure that exist at each level of the system. Enabling processes refer to the more ephemeral informal, social, and human interactional processes that operationalize a given technological system at each level. For purposes of illustration, Fig. 10.1 lists examples of both types of content. This listing is intended to be prototypic, not exhaustive. Content factors must be operationalized for a given organization and its specific training situation.

At the individual level, technostructural factors include the technical knowledge and skills needed to fill the requirements of a particular job. At the team level, these factors expand in scope, although the content remains conceptually similar. Team-level factors include the hardware system (technology), its configuration (structure), and its task-specified interdependence. At higher levels, technostructural factors approach macroconceptualizations of technology and structure (Perrow, 1967; Thompson, 1967). Here the emphasis is on the conversion process and its work-flow configuration across subunits within the organization.

Human or enabling process factors focus on different content. At the individual level, these factors refer to the social and interpersonal skills that allow individuals to fill the role requirements of jobs. At the team level, relevant human process factors include those capabilities that enable the team members to be integrated with the technology system. The system may require coordination and mutual adjustment among team members in real time (aircrews). The collective ability and willingness to scan the requirements of other team members, to anticipate adjustments, and to assist other members as needed would be critical enabling processes for system effectiveness. When these enabling processes are absent, the system will not be properly operationalized. Process skills of this type will need to be tightly coupled to the technical skills of the respective team members.

As noted, these two content areas need to be closely associated, and it may be difficult to distinguish their boundaries completely. The theoretical, methodological, and empirical research base required to specify linkages and alignments among technostructural factors is more highly developed than that for enabling processes (Hattrup & Kozlowski, 1993). Moreover, the forms of enabling process that fit a given technology system exhibit a range of diversity (Kozlowski, 1987). Thus, the identification of specific enabling processes and their linkage to technostructural factors represents the more problematic content focus.

Individual differences are regarded as independent of the content areas, although they may affect the acquisition or expression of content-relevant behavior. Differences in ability, for example, affect the acquisition of technical knowledge and skills (Kanfer & Ackerman, 1989). Similarly, differences in motivation and personality may affect the acquisition and expression of enabling skills (Noe, 1986). This model suggests that when wide variations of content-relevant individual differences exist within a work unit or team, discontinuities in the timing of skill acquisition and their expression may inhibit transfer to the setting.

Congruence.   Achieving an appropriate alignment among critical factors and processes constitutes the third dimension of the framework. Although congruence overlaps to some extent with the levels and content dimensions, it is so critical that its separate consideration is warranted. Three aspects of alignment are represented in the framework: (a) within focal content domains, within levels; (b) between focal content domains, within levels; and (c) the combination of the first and second aspects of congruence across levels.

The first and most elemental aspect of congruence deals with the fit of factors within a focal content area, within levels. This is most consistent with a correlational form of congruence (Van de Ven & Drazin, 1985). Aligning unit technology, work flows, and coordinating structure illustrates this aspect (Comstock & Scott, 1977). This is represented in Fig. 10.1 by congruence among task technology, structure, and interdependence at the team or unit level. Similarly, teamwork and leadership processes, team climate, and the normative expectations among team members must be consonant (Beer & Walton, 1990). For example, directive leadership is not consistent with the normative expectations of self-managing work teams.

The second aspect addresses the alignment of the technostructural factors and the enabling processes within levels. This form of congruence is interactional in nature; misalignments yield ineffectiveness. For example, highly uncertain, flexible, and reciprocally coordinated technostructural systems will be enabled by self-managing work teams (Slocum & Sims, 1980). The technology system represented by task technology, structure, and interdependence must be supported by the enabling processes inherent in the teamwork and leadership, team climate, and normative expectations of team members (Kozlowski, 1987). This form of congruence is signified by the horizontal double-headed arrows that link technostructural factors and enabling processes within each level.

The first two aspects of congruence are most relevant to appropriate system design prior to the implementation of any training. Misalignments within or across the content areas must be rectified by organizational redesign or development efforts. The introduction of training content must be consistent with existing content factors; attempts to introduce incongruent training content will likely fail.

The third aspect is concerned with the alignment of embedding content across levels. It is configural in nature—a combination of the first two aspects of congruence—with a cross-level influence. It is illustrated by the downward arrows that link embedding features at higher levels of conceptualization to lower, adjacent levels in the model. Embedding features set constraints on processes that unfold at the lower level in the system (James & Jones, 1974, 1976). This aspect of congruence is most concerned with cross-level effects, whereby contextual factors facilitate or inhibit the expression of newly trained skills (Rouiller & Goldstein, 1993).

Thus, congruence is a pervasive process inherent in the framework. Individual-level technical knowledge and skills need to be supported by corresponding human process knowledge and skills—within the constraints set by variations in ability, motivation, and personality—to achieve a fit between the individual and the job. Group technology, interdependence, and coordinating structures require corresponding team and leadership processes, climates, and shared interpretive systems (Kozlowski & Doherty, 1989). Organizational-level strategy, resources, technology, and structure must be aligned with the external environment (Miles et al., 1978), and must fit the organizational culture, leadership, vision, and reward processes operative in the system (Beer & Walton, 1990).

Congruence across the levels provides the glue that binds these aspects of fit together. A lack of alignment will preclude change. The model indicates that an organization characterized by rigid, predictable, routine technologies with congruent leadership and cultural processes—authoritarian, hierarchical, bureaucratic—will not be able to create decentralized, empowered, and self-managing work teams. Formal and emergent leaders at the team level will model the leadership and culture enacted in the embedding content of the higher level (Fleishman, 1953; Kozlowski & Doherty, 1989). If a shift to self-managing teams becomes a critical change—perhaps due to the investment in new technologies—corresponding changes in the embedding content of the higher level will be required.

Transfer. Traditional training research generally conceptualizes transfer as a horizontal process that links settings; learning acquired in the training environment must transfer to the performance environment. The focus is on stimulus–response fidelity and generalization across environments. We acknowledge this necessity, but argue that this perspective neglects level, content, and congruence influences from the organizational system. Key implications of this perspective are described in Table 10.2.

This framework expands the conceptualization of transfer by making salient additional dimensions. Changes in system functioning produced by training interventions are represented by arrows: (a) Horizontal arrows illustrate congruence between content areas within levels, (b) central downward arrows signify congruence between higher level embedding characteristics and lower level training targets, and (c) upward arrows within content areas represent composition processes that link training-induced change at lower levels to higher level change targets.

Training implementation, in terms of design and delivery, must consider more complex horizontal linkages than are considered by traditional models. The level at which training is intended to have its effects may necessitate a consistency in the level of training delivery relative to the target level. For example, improving team performance may necessitate training intact teams, rather than individuals drawn across different teams. Under different circumstances, cross-level horizontal links may be appropriate. Although Fig. 10.1 does not illustrate these linkages across environments, they are inherent in the theory. Another horizontal aspect of transfer that the model illustrates is the congruence between content areas within a level that supports the expression of trained skills.

In addition to an expanded view of horizontal connections, this model incorporates vertical linkages. Trained individual skills must be exhibited in a work context. This requires attention to higher level embedding characteristics that, when congruent, facilitate the expression of newly trained skills. When incongruent, the expression of new skills is inhibited. The embedding effects of

TABLE 10.2

Issues of Level, Content, and Congruence Applied to Training Transfer

Theme	Issue
Level	Level issues determine how much of the entire organizational system is implicated in the change effort. Level issues specify the theoretical and methodological questions inherent in the framework that must be resolved for training to be effective.
	• What is the level of analysis for training-induced change? At what level are the effects of change ultimately desired?
	• What is the focal unit? At what level will training be delivered to induce change?
	• A difference between the level of analysis and the focal unit will necessitate a theory of composition or a cross-level model to specify the form of the linkage across levels for transfer to occur.
Content	Content issues are defined by the particular "problem" of interest and the unique characteristics of the organization in question. These issues provide the basis for operationalizing specific constructs within the framework for a particular application.
	• What is the primary content focus for training induced change?
	• Where the primary emphasis is on upgrading technical skills, what are the enabling processes needed to apply the technical content? Are they already in place?
	• In situations where enabling factors are not in place, how will their provision be coordinated with technical training to facilitate transfer?
Congruence	Congruence issues are concerned with the creation of contextual consistency. The levels and content areas of interest for training will implicate system consistencies to facilitate both the implementation and transfer of training induced change.
	• Are the important factors aligned (correlated) within the target level and content focus? Misalignments should be corrected through redesign.
	• Is there alignment between the technostructural and enabling process content areas (interactional fit) within the target level? Misalignments should be corrected through redesign (technostructural content) or organizational development (enabling process content).
	• Is the context at the level above the target level aligned with the training content (mediation) to facilitate transfer?

contextual congruence are represented by downward, central arrows in the figure. A critical aspect of this perspective is to make explicit the "building-up" assumption inherent in training models. Training exerts influence through individual-level change, which aggregates to affect successively more molar organizational outcomes. Training that is intended to have impacts at higher levels in the system must specify the underlying composition linkages that reference that upward transfer.

The traditional focus of transfer is on the post training situation. The processes inherent in this model, however, implicate the pretraining environment as well. The motivation of trainees to learn trained skills is expected to be a function of trainee characteristics in interaction with the existing context (Mathieu et al., 1992). If the context does not support or discourages the use of new skills prior to the implementation of training, it is unlikely that trainees will be motivated to learn them. This would clearly also affect transfer. This model emphasizes a broader conception of the congruence between training and the organizational system.

The assertion that system congruence is essential for transfer is deceptively simple. In practice, it will be complex to achieve. Considerable planning will be required to identify the relevant factors, processes, levels, and linkages implicated by the targeted training. Establishing the requisite alignments may necessitate simultaneous or phased interventions across several different factors, processes, and system levels.

Implications for Training Research and Application

The framework developed here has heuristic value for posing questions and suggesting answers to key issues in training effectiveness—that is, how, where, and when to deliver different forms of training (Cannon-Bowers, Tannenbaum, Salas, & Converse, 1991), and how to ensure a congruent organizational system to support the expression of trained skills. The theoretical principles inherent in the framework are abstract. Although this gives the model generalizability, it makes it difficult to provide generic answers to questions without the grounding of a specific application. The framework can only be operationalized when it is mapped onto a particular training problem, which allows specification of levels, content, and congruence dimensions for the application in question.

Having noted that caveat, there are several propositions that can be drawn as a consequence of simply shifting the level of focus beyond the traditional individual level. A series of examples are used to develop propositions that illustrate the model's utility. The propositions are grounded theoretically and have practical implications for training effectiveness. The propositions represent research issues that require attention. They have not been constructed in the form of hypotheses, although the rationale supporting each proposition provides the basis for developing specific hypotheses. The team level is used as a primary vehicle in these examples because it fits at the juncture between the individual and higher levels of conceptualization.

This chapter focuses on two primary areas of interest. First, it addresses implementation issues—considerations regarding system design and delivery, and their impact on training transfer. Second, it examines the organizational context as a constraint for skill expression and maintenance in the performance environment. With respect to implementation, this chapter considers: (a) at what level training should be delivered—the individual, the team, or both; (b) the extent to which focal content (technostructural vs. enabling process) can be distinct or separable training issues; and (c) factors of timing and sequence that arise when either level of delivery or type of content are distinguished. With regard to contextual issues, this chapter considers (a) the development of a congruent contextual infrastructure to support trained skills, (b) the identification of relevant contextual factors, and (c) the implications of contextual boundaries and bond strengths. Although an attempt has been made to distinguish between issues of implementation and context for purposes of presentation, they are not always clearly distinguishable in their impact.

Implementation Issues and Transfer. This section addresses delivery issues that will have an impact on training transfer. This focus on design and delivery as a means by which to enhance transfer is consistent with prevailing views of transfer. The innovations of this orientation concern the delivery implications derived from the focus on the levels of the training targets and the composition of focal target skills, and from the concern with achieving congruence across content domains within persons and among team (or unit) members.

The first set of issues focuses on the level at which the training intervention should be delivered—the individual, the team, or some combination of both levels. It might be assumed that delivery should simply be determined by the level of analysis at which the trained KSAs are intended to have their ultimate impact (i.e., training targeted toward changing individual KSAs should be delivered at the individual level, team level change should implicate team-level training delivery). Although this is expected to hold when the focus is solely on the individual level, the problem is more complex at higher levels. When the team or higher levels are targeted, the form of composition for the higher level—the nature of individual KSA contributions to the higher level construct—becomes critical for resolving the delivery question.

> Proposition 1: When the target of training is higher than the individual level, training delivery should be determined by the composition model for the target behavior. Transfer will be facilitated when the level of training delivery is consistent with the underlying composition model.

When team performance is an additive function of individual performance—that is, when pooled coordination mechanisms (Thompson, 1967) are operative—it is appropriate to regard team performance as a simple aggregation of individual performances. Under pooled coordination, each element of task completion adds to the overall product, and there is virtually no required coordination among team members. Team members may interact, but it is incidental to the aggregate outcome. The contributions of members of a typing pool illustrate this type of situation. Performance is compensatory. Each member of the pool contributes incrementally to overall group performance. Training interventions designed to improve group productivity could be targeted at the individual level, given the additive composition of group performance.

When team members' task roles are highly differentiated and interdependent, requiring more complex forms of coordination (Thompson, 1967), team performance will not be well represented by a simple summation of members' performances (Fleishman & Zaccaro, 1992; Salas et al., 1992). Teams of this nature include sports teams, surgical staffs, aircrews, combat teams, and so forth—teams that Sundstrom et al. (1990) classified as *action–negotiation* teams. In teams of this type, the linkage between individual and team performance is not additive. Single-member actions may have dramatic impacts on overall team performance. For the team to be effective, differentiated team-member actions must fuse together into a seamless, synchronous, and coordinated performance sequence. Where member roles are critical and nonredundant, an error by a single team member may result in ineffectiveness for the team. The failure of a team member may not be compensated by better performance on the part of other members. Team members must be able to compile the specific task linkages, role expectations, and goals that determine the performance of all team members (Kozlowski et al., 1994). The composition of team performance in this example suggests that training may need to be delivered to the team as an intact group (Kozlowski et al., 1996).

> Proposition 2: When enabling process content is critical to the composition model of the training target, training delivery that integrates technical and process content for the team as a whole will help ensure congruence and enhanced transfer.

A second implementation issue concerns the extent to which target content (technostructural vs. enabling content) can be distinct in training delivery. It is useful here to build on the previous example. The performance of action–negotiation teams is critically dependent on the mutual adaptation and adjustment among team members in real time to shifting team task demands, uncertain cues, and time compression (Salas et al., 1992). This calls for a high degree of congruence between individual technical skill proficiency and collective enabling process skills required to ensure smooth, seamless, and coherent performance (Kozlowski et al., 1996).

Conventional approaches to training teams of this type tend to treat these content distinctions as separable issues. Training often focuses on individual technical proficiency, with the assumption that the required team-coordination processes will develop on their own (Morgan et al., 1986). In other instances, explicit efforts are made to enhance team process skills through the delivery of interpersonal skills training at the individual level. Again, this assumes a direct impact on team-level behavior.

An implication of this model, where tight coupling is required between technical and process skills, is that both types of content may need to be provided at the same time during training delivery. Enhancing the real-time coordination of individual technical skills is likely to require training that delivers advanced technical training to intact teams in the context of high-fidelity team simulations. Moreover, the high levels of proficiency required of such teams may require continued learning through structured experiences in the performance context. This places emphasis on the instructional skills of team-leaders and further blurs the traditional distinction between the training and performance environments (Kozlowski et al., 1996). This approach assumes some individual-level technical skill proficiency, followed by training at the team level that emphasizes coordinated task performance (Kozlowski, Ford, & Smith, 1993).

> Proposition 3: Transfer will be enhanced when individual-level technical skills are trained to proficiency prior to the delivery of training at the team level or for enabling content.

When training is to be targeted at more than one level, issues relating to the optimum allocation of individual-level versus team-oriented delivery, the sequence of individual versus team skill delivery, and the relative timing of individual versus team training arise. Similar issues arise when distinctions are made in the delivery of training content.

The model incorporates the assumption that individual technical skill proficiency is a fundamental building block for higher level composition models of performance. Individual performers must acquire some proficiency on their task before they can devote attention to process skills necessary to enable team performance (Kozlowski et al., 1996; Salas et al., 1992). Although there is some corroboration for this proposition (Denson, 1981; Johnston, 1966; Klaus & Glaser, 1970), research incorporating a true levels framework has yet to be undertaken.

> Proposition 4: Transfer will be enhanced when the shift from individual- to team-level training is predicated on the development of shared knowledge and understanding of the team and its task.

When training is to be delivered at mixed levels, the relative allocation of individual-versus team-level delivery becomes a concern primarily from the perspective of efficiency. Theory suggests that teams progress through a developmental sequence, moving from an orientation toward individual instrumentalities to a team orientation (Kozlowski et al., 1996; Kozlowski et al., 1994). An orientation to the team begins to form as members develop consensual interpretations of their context (James & Jones, 1974; Kozlowski & Hattrup, 1992) and shared mental models of their technology system (Cannon-Bowers, Salas, & Converse, 1990; Cannon-Bowers et al., 1991; Orasanu & Salas, 1993). The optimal shift from individual- to team-level training would occur after the team orientation develops. At that point, a more integrated team-level intervention is likely to enhance the development of shared, collective knowledge among team members.

> Proposition 5: Transfer will be enhanced when training that cuts across content domains appropriately times delivery *within* individuals.
>
> Proposition 6: Training delivery targeted at higher levels (teams) must be coincidental in time and space *across the individuals* that comprise the focal unit to facilitate transfer.

Training delivery that shifts across levels and/or content domains also implicates timing. Timing refers to the coordination of training interventions within and between persons, as well as among levels comprising the focal contexts. Although timing is a delivery issue, its effects would be exhibited primarily on transfer. For example, if technical knowledge and skills require the support of enabling processes—that is, if the task components among individuals are highly interdependent and must be coordinated—then both types of training will have to be coincidental within persons. This also implies that the expression of trained skills requires congruent responses from teammates and leaders. If so, all relevant parties need to receive the training within the same time frame.

In this situation, training that is not coincidental in time is likely to result in poor transfer. Technical skills trained in isolation of the enabling processes will already have decayed by the time the requisite supporting human process skills are trained at some later point. Individuals trained in isolation from their teammates will have extinguished the trained behaviors by the time the teammates receive training at some later point. By the time the entire team has been trained, the enabling skills may be inconsistent across the team, inhibiting transfer for later trainees.

For tasks that require reciprocal, nonrecursive responses among members—coordination by mutual adjustment (Thompson, 1967)—it may not be meaningful to train team members separately from one another, even if the timing is simultaneous. The problem is that tasks of this sort, requiring teamwork, joint problem solving, and joint decision making, are not operationalized via preprogrammed responses. Much of the coordination of effort is tacit (Dyer,

1984; Hackman & Morris, 1975). To maximize transfer of enabling skills, it may be necessary to train individuals as intact teams, even where their roles and contributing technical skills differ.

Contextual Issues and Transfer. This section focuses on contextual factors in the performance environment as facilitators or inhibitors of transfer. The approach moves beyond traditional approaches to transfer, where the primary focus is on stimulus–response fidelity and generalization to a different environment. Conventional approaches intervene during delivery (the training task) by attempting to simulate a narrowly defined context (the task or, perhaps, a larger man–machine system). This approach is more concerned with achieving congruence between training and relevant factors comprising the context within which the trained skills are to be expressed.

> Proposition 7: The congruence between relevant organizational context factors at the higher level and targeted training content will moderate training transfer.
>
> Proposition 8: The congruence of individual-difference factors with targeted training content will moderate training transfer.

Consider training targeted on individual-level KSAs that do not reference higher level constructs (e.g., team, unit, or organization). As shown in Fig. 10.1, the team or unit level provides the context for individual-level targets. It is expected that climate related factors relevant to the trained skills, such as positive feedback from leaders, encouragement from coworkers, and opportunities to use the new skills, will moderate transfer. When the contextual factors are congruent with the trained skills, transfer will be enhanced, whereas a lack of alignment with contextual supports will likely inhibit transfer (Fleishman, 1953; Rouiller & Goldstein, 1993). In addition, individual differences in ability, motivation, or personality are also expected to moderate the extent to which the skills transfer (Noe & Schmitt, 1986; Prince, Chidester, Cannon-Bowers, & Bowers, 1992).

> Proposition 9: When training is targeted at individual- or pooled group-level change (Thompson, 1967), transfer processes will be cumulative. Contextual supports will facilitate transfer, although congruence will not be as critical an issue.

The target level and composition model for the skills of interest have implications for the model of transfer. An individual-level focus does not require high coherence and integration of responses among persons in a setting. When the focus is truly on the individual level, or on pooled responses at the team/group level, individual change or change in a small critical mass may be sufficient for some transfer to occur. Some positive benefit will accrue to training objectives even when transfer is not uniform for all persons trained.

For example, consider stress-reduction training, where the goal is to reduce organizational health care costs by improving employees' well-being. Transfer for this type of training will be enhanced by supporting policies (opportunities to perform) and encouragement by key peers (coworkers, supervisor). The failure of some individuals to transfer the skills is not likely to inhibit all other trainees. Potential benefits for individuals and the organization can still be realized. Individual outcomes are linked to the use of the trained skills (better health, a sense of well-being). The impacts of these outcomes for the organization are cumulative (lower health care costs) because the individual effects are additive in their aggregation to the higher level.

> Proposition 10: When training is targeted at interdependent teams where sequential and/or reciprocal coordination is required (Thompson, 1967), transfer must be uniform across individual team members for training to be effective. Contextual congruence will play a more critical role in ensuring uniform transfer.

When team tasks are highly interdependent, coordinated, and yet differentiated, the composition of team performance will not be a simple aggregation of individual responses. Teams must adapt dynamically to the demands of the situation, often without explicit instruction or communication. This tacit adjustment process is a critical component of team effectiveness (Cannon-Bowers & Salas, 1990). Use of skills must be coherent and integrated across team members, although some of the skills are unique to individual roles. Transfer at the team level needs to be uniform across all team members. The failure of a single individual to transfer trained skills will jeopardize team performance. The performance failure of a single crew person in an aircraft cockpit can have disastrous consequences, even when all other crew members perform effectively. This highlights the importance of developing congruent contextual supports to help facilitate uniform transfer across all critical performers.

> Proposition 11: Contextual factors relevant to training transfer are determined by the focal content of training. Transfer will be enhanced when contextual factors at the higher level of the system are congruent to the specific content of the training.

It has been noted throughout this chapter that higher level contextual features operate to facilitate or inhibit the expression of trained skills. It has also been noted that the factors defining organizational contexts for training are not necessarily isomorphic across situations, although certain factors are likely to have some generalizability. Determination of the relevant factors that define particular transfer settings must be guided by training content. Content refers to the behavioral domain or criterion variables referenced by the training. What is to be changed? If one is interested in safety, then safety-related behaviors define the content domain and help guide the determination of related contextual factors. Research has repeatedly demonstrated that generic perceptions are not predictive of behavior, whereas perceptions specific to the dependent variable predicts behavior very well. This has been shown for the topics of skill updating (Kozlowski & Hults, 1987), customer service (Schneider & Bowen, 1985), and safety-related behaviors (Zohar, 1980). Cross-level influences from constructs at higher levels (the embedding context) can then be identified through theory, empirical findings, and logic (Brass, 1981; Kozlowski & Farr, 1988; Rousseau, 1978a, 1978b). The key issue is to clearly specify the link between the content of contextual influences and the focal phenomenon.

This suggestion may appear obvious, yet training research has rarely studied contextual factors that are relevant to training content. Of the few studies that have examined work environment supports for transfer, most have operationalized some form of general "supportive climate," regardless of the nature of the training content. An example of this weak methodology is provided by Russell et al. (1985), who reported no significant effects for the work context on transfer. Although this study is limited in many respects (post hoc construction of constructs, misspecification error), the critical limitation is the use of global "supervisor support" as a contextual influence for specific sales skills in a retail setting. The support measure bore no content relation to sales behavior, and none was found. Had supervisor support been operationalized in terms relevant to the use of sales skills, the results might well have been different.

In contrast, Fleishman (1953) found contextual effects because the content of his perceptual measure matched the trained behavior of interest. Recent research by Rouiller and Goldstein (1993) provided strong support for this assertion. Their development of content for a climate for transfer construct was grounded by the content of the trained KSAs. Consequently, unit-level transfer climate accounted for significant variance in transfer behavior, even after the effects of learning during training and unit performance were controlled. It is the content domain—with its theoretical and empirical base—that provides the foundation for establishing the composition specifications needed to address contextual influences. The importance of this issue cannot be overemphasized.

Proposition 12: Training content must be consistent with central, pivotal contextual values that define the culture and climate of the organization. Inconsistent content will have little likelihood for expression and transfer unless the entire system is radically transformed.

Another issue to consider when attempting to identify contextual constraints and their potential impact on transfer is the centrality of the content. The more related training content is to strongly held beliefs and values, shared perceptions of the climate, and the organizational culture, the more difficult it will be to transfer skills that are inconsistent with those pivotal contextual norms and values (Schein, 1968). Pivotal values are represented in the cultural traditions, beliefs, and assumptions that define life in an organization, and in the human processes that are enacted within groups. They can be identified by examining the knowledge that is emphasized to newcomers during the socialization process (Chao, O'Leary-Kelly, Wolf, Klein, & Gardner, 1994; Ostroff & Kozlowski, 1992).

Training that is inconsistent with central embedding features will be much more difficult to transfer than training that addresses neutral or peripheral issues. Moreover, it will be more difficult to modify contextual features that are linked to central embedding factors than to develop a supportive infrastructure for less pivotal factors. For example, individual-level training aimed at technical skills may be much more easily transferred than training targeted toward human process skills. Human process skills are often more tightly bound to the pivotal cultural values that define the organization (Schein, 1968). These pivotal values tend to be deeply entrenched because they are emphasized in recruitment and selection processes, and are further developed during early socialization processes (Chao et al., 1994; Ostroff & Kozlowski, 1992).

Proposition 13: Organizations that enact a contextual system supportive of change, innovation, and opportunities to use new skills will exhibit more effective aggregate transfer across all training programs and situations.

Proposition 14: Organizations that integrate human resource planning and human resource systems with their long- and short-term strategic plans are more likely to enact congruent contextual systems that support training and facilitate transfer.

The previous discussion raises a final issue that is addressed here. The notion that the context should be congruent with trained skills is all very well, but contexts cannot be enacted or modified overnight. The embedding characteristics that comprise an organizational system unfold as the organization moves through its life cycle. Dramatic change is not easily accomplished. Certainly, piecemeal attempts to modify the contextual system will be doomed. This suggests that efforts to enact supportive contexts must be aligned with well-articulated strategic objectives, both short and long term (Chao & Kozlowski, 1986; Kozlowski, 1987). These objectives must serve to drive alignments throughout the organizational system (Beer & Walton, 1990), but must especially link to the personnel and training subsystem (Jackson & Schuler, 1990; Schuler, 1987; Schuler & Jackson, 1987). Over the long haul, an organizational culture that values innovative change, personnel development, and continuous training can be developed if it is consistent with strategic objectives and organizational characteristics (Jackson, Schuler, & Rivero, 1989). This can help create a general receptivity to training and the use of trained skills. Thus, top leaders who champion change, reward systems that encourage personal development, and training systems that provide useful and applicable skills provide the concrete symbols necessary to create contexts that support training and skill utilization (Beer & Walton, 1990; Jackson & Schuler, 1990; Kozlowski & Hults, 1987). As specific programs are operationalized, more targeted efforts to align the context can be implemented. This approach can help address the uncertainty associated with long-term forecasting and the necessity of ensuring congruent contexts (Kozlowski, 1987). The idea is to consider transfer processes as an integral part of the training and organizational system. However, this will only be possible when the organization's personnel and human resource system is a fully integrated aspect of its strategic orientation.

CONCLUSION

The purpose of this chapter was to develop a theoretical framework, based on organizational theory, that would characterize the factors and processes comprising the context within which training interventions are implemented and transferred. In doing so, this chapter has expanded the conceptualization of transfer processes beyond the narrow, horizontal training to performance environment relationship characteristic of traditional approaches. The framework described herein identifies more complex horizontal links, and, more important, emphasizes vertical relationships across levels that are implicated in transfer. Downward congruence processes focus on the alignment of embedding context features that support the expression of trained skills, thereby enhancing transfer. Upward composition processes focus on the aggregation of training-induced changes to affect higher level targets, thus enhancing the impact of training interventions on organizational objectives.

The issues delineated here make explicit some of the more salient research issues inherent in the framework. Many of the issues raised, although grounded in organizational theory and research, have never been addressed in training research. Many other issues are derived from the integration of the organizational literature and training, and have not been addressed in either domain. In this sense, the model presents a theoretical foundation for new research questions.

In addition to its theoretical and research value, the model serves to identify issues of practical concern during the design, development, and delivery of training. The propositions make salient key issues that, on the basis of available evidence, are expected to influence training effectiveness. Although specific research for the propositions is required, there is considerable support for the underlying theoretical processes. The propositions can provide practical guidance for facilitating transfer during the planning, implementation, and follow-up of training interventions.

Although the model emphasizes an organizational systems perspective for training research, it is not a repudiation of existing research at the individual or intraindividual (cognitive) level. In many ways, the model reemphasizes a focus on the individual, but from a different perspective. It emphasizes a concern with the organizational context and the way the context supports or contradicts trained individual skills. It is concerned with the individual differences of people across a context and the way those differences affect critical behaviors. It is focused on the nature of individual contributions across people comprising higher level entities (teams) and the form of their combination. The individual is still very much in evidence, but must be considered as part of a more extensive configuration of contextual elements.

It is also important to recognize the broader research implications of the model. Transfer is a process that unfolds over time, and often involves a sequence of multiple training interventions (Kozlowski, Ford, & Smith, 1993; Kozlowski et al., 1996). It necessitates longitudinal and process-oriented research. To the extent that research endeavors to address contextual influences from the organizational level, multi-organizational samples exhibiting variance across relevant contextual characteristics will be required (Kozlowski & Hults, 1987). Even at lower levels, greater attention to variance on relevant contextual characteristics will be necessary. Issues of composition, content, and congruence implicate far more precision in criterion measurement than is typically available from supervisory ratings. Research directions suggested by the model necessitate the development of new forms of behavioral performance measurement (Coovert, Cannon-Bowers, & Salas, 1990), with corresponding advances in evaluation theory, methodology, and measurement (Kraiger, Ford, & Salas, 1993).

For many years, leading training researchers have called for theoretical development, expanded perspectives, and new approaches to training research. It appears that researchers have heard the message and are heeding the call. These diverse new efforts are harbingers of a renaissance in training theory, research, and practice.

ACKNOWLEDGMENTS

We acknowledge the helpful comments provided by Irwin L. Goldstein and Susan E. Jackson on earlier drafts of this chapter. The views expressed in this chapter are those of the authors, and do not necessarily reflect the official positions of their organizations.

REFERENCES

Ackerman, P. L., Sternberg, R. J., & Glaser, R. (1989). *Learning and individual differences: Advances in theory and research*. New York: Freeman.

Alliger, G. M., & Janak, E. A. (1989). Kirkpatrick's levels of training criteria: Thirty years later. *Personnel Psychology, 42*, 331–342.

Baldwin, T. T., & Ford, J. K. (1988). Transfer in training: A review and directions for future research. *Personnel Psychology, 41*, 63–105.

Baumgartel, H. J., & Jeanpierre F. (1972). Applying new knowledge in the back-home setting: A study of Indian managers' adoptive efforts. *Journal of Applied Behavioral Science, 8*, 674–694.

Baumgartel, H. J., Reynolds, M., & Pathan, R. (1984). How personality and organizational-climate variables moderate the effectiveness of management development programs: A review and some recent research findings. *Management and Labour Studies, 9*, 1–16.

Baumgartel, H. J., Sullivan, G. J., & Dunn, L. E. (1978). How organizational climate and personality affect the pay-off from advanced management training sessions. *Kansas Business Review, 5*, 1–10.

Beer, M., & Walton, R. E. (1990). Developing the competitive organization: Interventions and strategies. *American Psychologist, 45*, 154–161.

Brass, D. J. (1981). Structural relationships, job characteristics, and worker satisfaction and performance. *Administrative Science Quarterly, 26*, 331–348.

Briggs, G. E., & Naylor, J. C. (1962). The relative efficiency of several training methods as a function of transfer task complexity. *Journal of Experimental Psychology, 64*, 505–512.

Brooks, H. (1982). Social and technological innovation. In S. Lundstedt & E. Colglazier (Eds.), *Managing innovation* (pp. 1–30). New York: Pergamon.

Brown, G. F., & Read, A. R. (1984). Personnel and training policies—some lessons for western companies. *Long Range Planning, 17*(2), 48–57.

Burns, T., & Stalker, G. M. (1961). *The management of innovation*. London: Tavistock.

Campbell, J. P. (1971). Personnel training and development. *Annual Review of Psychology, 22*, 565–602.

Cannon-Bowers, J. A., & Salas, E. (1990, October). *Trainability factors in training effectiveness*. Paper presented at the annual meeting of the Navy's Interdependent Research Symposium, Baltimore, MD.

Cannon-Bowers, J. A., Salas, E., & Converse, S. A. (1990). Cognitive psychology and team training: Training shared mental models of complex systems. *Human Factors Society Bulletin, 33*(12), 1–4.

Cannon-Bowers, J. A., Tannenbaum, S. I., Salas, E., & Converse, S. A. (1991). Toward an integration of training theory and technique. *Human Factors, 33*, 281–292.

Chao, G. T., & Kozlowski, S. W. J. (1986). Employee perceptions on the implementation of robotic manufacturing technology. *Journal of Applied Psychology, 71*, 70–76.

Chao, G. T., O'Leary-Kelly, A. M., Wolf, S., Klein, H. J., & Gardner, P. D. (1994). Organizational socialization: Its content and consequences. *Journal of Applied Psychology, 79*, 730–743.

Comstock, D., & Scott, W. R. (1977). Technology and the structure of subunits: Distinguishing individual and work-group effects. *Administrative Science Quarterly, 20*, 177–202.

Coovert, M., Cannon-Bowers, J. A., & Salas, E. (1990, November). *Applying mathematical modeling technology to the study of team training and performance*. Paper presented at the 12th annual Interservice/Industry Training Systems Conference, Orlando, FL.

Dansereau, F., Alutto, J. A., & Yammarino, F. J. (1984). *Theory testing in organizational behavior: The variant approach*. Englewood Cliffs, NJ: Prentice-Hall.

Denson, R. W. (1981). *Team training: Literature review and annotated bibliography* (A9-A099994). Wright-Patterson AFB, OH: Air Force Human Resources Laboratory.

Dyer, J. L. (1984). Team research and team training: A state-of-the-art review. In F. A. Muckler (Ed.), *Human factors review* (pp. 285–323). Santa Monica, CA: Human Factors Society.

Eden, D., & Ravid, G. (1982). Pygmalion versus self-expectancy: Effects of instructor and self-expectancy on trainee performance. *Organizational Behavior and Human Performance, 30,* 351–364.

Edwards, J. R. (1994). The study of congruence in organizational behavior research: Critique and proposed alternative. *Organizational Behavior and Human Decision Processes, 58,* 51–100.

Ellis, H. C. (1965). *The transfer of learning.* New York: Macmillan.

Fleishman, E. A. (1953). Leadership climate, human relations training, and supervisory behavior. *Personnel Psychology, 6,* 205–222.

Fleishman, E. A., & Zaccaro, S. J. (1992). Toward a taxonomy of team performance functions. In R. W. Swezey & E. Salas (Eds.), *Teams: Their training and performance* (pp. 31–56). Norwood, NJ: Ablex.

Forehand, G. A., & Gilmer, B. H. (1964). Environmental variation in studies of organizational behavior. *Psychological Bulletin, 62,* 361–382.

Friedlander, F., & Brown, L. D. (1974). Organization development. *Annual Review of Psychology, 25,* 313–341.

Galbraith, J. (1973). *Designing complex organizations.* Reading, MA: Addison-Wesley.

Goldstein, I. L. (1980). Training in work organizations. *Annual Review of Psychology, 31,* 229–272.

Goldstein, I. L. (1991). Training in work organizations. In M. D. Dunnette & L. M. Hough (Eds.), *Handbook of industrial and organizational psychology* (Vol. 2, pp. 507–620). Palo Alto, CA: Consulting Psychologists Press.

Goldstein, I. L. (1992). *Training in organizations.* Pacific Grove, CA: Brooks/Cole.

Hackman, J. R., & Morris, C. G. (1975). Group tasks, group interaction process, and group performance effectiveness: A review and proposed integration. In L. Berkowitz (Ed.), *Advances in experimental social psychology* (Vol. 8, pp. 45–99). New York: Academic Press.

Hagman, J. D., & Rose, A. M. (1983). Retention of military tasks: A review. *Human Factors, 25,* 199–213.

Hand, H. H., Richards, M. D., & Slocum, J. M. (1973). Organization climate and the effectiveness of a human relations program. *Academy of Management Journal, 16,* 185–195.

Hattrup, K., & Kozlowski, S. W. J. (1993). An across-organization analysis of the implementation of advanced manufacturing technologies. *Journal of High Technology Management Research, 4,* 175–196.

Herman, J. B., & Hulin, C. L. (1972). Studying organization attributes from the individual and organizational frame of reference. *Organizational Behavior and Human Performance, 8,* 84–108.

Hicks, W. D., & Klimoski, R. J. (1987). Entry into training programs and its effects on training outcomes: A field experiment. *Academy of Management Journal, 30,* 542–552.

Homans, G. C. (1950). *The human group.* New York: Harcourt Brace.

Howell, W. C., & Cooke, N. J. (1989). Training the human information processor: A review of cognitive models. In I. L. Goldstein (Ed.), *Training and career development* (pp. 121–182). San Francisco: Jossey-Bass.

Huczynski, A. A., & Lewis, J. W. (1980). An empirical study into the learning transfer process in management training. *Journal of Management Studies, 17,* 227–240.

Hussey, D. E. (1985). Implementing corporate strategy: Using management education and training. *Long Range Planning, 18*(5), 28–37.

Jackson, S. E., & Schuler, R. S. (1990). Human resource planning: Challenges for industrial/organizational psychologists. *American Psychologist, 45,* 223–239.

Jackson, S. E., Schuler, R. S., & Rivero, J. C. (1989). Organizational characteristics as predictors of personnel practices. *Personnel Psychology, 42,* 727–736.

James, L. R., Demaree, R. G., & Wolf, G. (1984). Estimating within-group interrater reliability with and without response bias. *Journal of Applied Psychology, 69,* 85–98.

James, L. R., & Jones, A. P. (1974). Organizational climate: A review of theory and research. *Psychological Bulletin, 81,* 1096–1112.

James, L. R., & Jones, A. P. (1976). Organizational structure: A review of structural dimensions and their conceptual relationship with individual attitudes and behavior. *Organizational Behavior and Human Performance*, 16, 74–113.

Johnston, W. A. (1966). Transfer of team skills as a function of type of training. *Journal of Applied Psychology*, 52, 89–94.

Jones, A. P., & James, L. R. (1979). Psychological climate: Dimensions and relationships of individual and aggregated work environment perceptions. *Organizational Behavior and Human Performance*, 23, 201–250.

Judd, C. H. (1908). The relation of special training and general intelligence. *Educational Review*, 36, 42–48.

Kanfer, R., & Ackerman, P. L. (1989). Motivation and cognitive abilities: An integrative/aptitude-treatment interaction approach to skill acquisition. *Journal of Applied Psychology*, 74, 657–690.

Katz, D., & Kahn, R. L. (1978). *The social psychology of organizations*. New York: Wiley.

Kirkpatrick, D. L. (1967). Evaluation of training. In R. L. Craig & L. R. Bittel (Eds.), *Training and development handbook* (pp. 87–112). New York: McGraw-Hill.

Klaus, D. J., & Glaser, R. (1970). Reinforcement determinants of team proficiency. *Organizational Behavior and Human Performance*, 5, 33–67.

Kozlowski, S. W. J. (1987). Technological innovation and strategic HRM: Facing the challenge of change. *Human Resource Planning*, 10, 69–79.

Kozlowski, S. W. J., & Doherty, M. L. (1989). Integration of climate and leadership: Examination of a neglected issue. *Journal of Applied Psychology*, 74, 546–553.

Kozlowski, S. W. J., & Farr, J. L. (1988). An integrative model of updating and performance. *Human Performance*, 1, 5–29.

Kozlowski, S. W. J., Ford, J. K., & Smith, E. M. (1993). *Training concepts, principles, and guidelines for the acquisition, transfer, and enhancement of team tactical decision making skills: I. A conceptual framework and literature review*. Orlando, FL: Naval Training Systems Center.

Kozlowski, S. W. J., Gully, S. M., McHugh, P. P., Salas, E., & Cannon-Bowers, J. A. (1996). A dynamic theory of leadership and team effectiveness: Developmental and task contingent leader roles. In G. R. Ferris (Ed.), *Research in personnel and human resource management* (Vol. 14, pp. 253–305). Greenwich, CT: JAI.

Kozlowski, S. W. J., Gully, S. M., Nason, E. R., Ford, J. K., Smith, E. M., Smith, M. R., & Futch, C. J. (1994, April). *A composition theory of team development: Levels, content, process, and learning outcomes*. Paper presented at the 9th annual conference of the Society for Industrial and Organizational Psychology, Nashville, TN.

Kozlowski, S. W. J., & Hattrup, K. (1992). A disagreement about within-group agreement: Disentangling issues of consistency versus consensus. *Journal of Applied Psychology*, 77, 161–167.

Kozlowski, S. W. J., & Hults, B. M. (1987). An exploration of climates for technical updating and performance. *Personnel Psychology*, 40, 539–563.

Kraiger, K., Ford, J. K., & Salas, E. (1993). Integration of cognitive, skill-based, and affective theories of learning outcomes to new methods of training evaluation. *Journal of Applied Psychology*, 78, 311–328.

Kraut, A. I., Pedigo, P. R., McKenna, D. D., & Dunnette, M. D. (1989). The role of the manager: What's really important in different managerial jobs. *Academy of Management Executive*, 3, 286–293.

Latham, G. P. (1988). Human resource training and development. *Annual Review of Psychology*, 39, 545–582.

Lawrence, P. R., & Lorsch, J. W. (1967). Differentiation and integration in complex organizations. *Administrative Science Quarterly*, 12, 1–47.

Lewin, K. (1951). *Field theory in the social sciences*. New York: Harper & Row.

Likert, R. (1967). *The human organization: Its management and value*. New York: McGraw-Hill.

London, M. (1989). *Managing the training enterprise*. San Francisco: Jossey-Bass.

Majchrzak, A. (1988). *The human side of factory automation*. San Francisco: Jossey-Bass.

Marx, R. D. (1982). Relapse prevention for managerial training: A model for maintenance of behavioral change. *Academy of Management Review, 7,* 433–441.

Mathieu, J. E., Tannenbaum, S. I., & Salas, E. (1992). Influences of individual and situational characteristics on measures of training effectiveness. *Academy of Management Journal, 35,* 828–847.

McGehee, W., & Thayer, P. W. (1961). *Training in business and industry.* New York: Wiley.

Mealiea, L. W., & Lee, D. (1979). An alternative to macro-micro contingency theories: An integrative model. *Academy of Management Review, 4,* 333–345.

Miles, R. E., Snow, C. C., Meyer, A. D., & Coleman, H. J. (1978). Organizational strategy, structure and process. *Academy of Management Review, 3,* 546–562.

Morgan, B. B., Glickman, A. S., Woodard, E. A., Blaiwes, A. S., & Salas, E. (1986). *Measurement of team behaviors in a Navy environment* (Rep. No. NTSC TR-86-014). Orlando, FL: Naval Training Systems Center.

Naylor, J. C., & Briggs, G. E. (1963). The effect of task complexity and task organization on the relative efficiency of part and whole training methods. *Journal of Experimental Psychology, 65,* 217–224.

Noe, R. A. (1986). Trainees' attributes and attitudes: Neglected influences on training effectiveness. *Academy of Management Review, 11,* 736–749.

Noe, R. A., & Schmitt, N. (1986). The influence of trainee attitudes on training effectiveness: Test of a model. *Personnel Psychology, 39,* 497–523.

Oldham, G. R., & Hackman, J. R. (1981). Relationships between organizational structure and employee reactions: Comparing alternative frameworks. *Administrative Science Quarterly, 26,* 66–83.

Orasanu, J., & Salas, E. (1993). Team decision making in complex environments. In G. Klein, J. Orasanu, & R. Calderwood (Eds.), *Decision making in action: Models and methods* (pp. 327–345). Norwood, NJ: Ablex.

Ostroff, C., & Ford, J. K. (1989). Introducing a levels perspective to training needs assessment. In I. L. Goldstein (Ed.), *Training and career development* (pp. 25–62). San Francisco: Jossey-Bass.

Ostroff, C., & Kozlowski, S. W. J. (1992). Organizational socialization as a learning process: The role of information acquisition. *Personnel Psychology, 45,* 849–874.

Perrow, C. (1967). A framework for comparative organization analysis. *American Sociological Review, 32,* 194–208.

Peters, L. H., & O'Connor, E. J. (1980). Situational constraints and work outcomes: The influences of a frequently overlooked construct. *Academy of Management Review, 5,* 391–397.

Peters, L. H., O'Connor, E. J., & Rudolf, C. J. (1980). The behavioral and affective consequences of situational variables relevant to performance settings. *Organizational Behavior and Human Performance, 25,* 79–96.

Prince, C., Chidester, T. R., Cannon-Bowers, J. A., & Bowers, C. A. (1992). Aircrew coordination: Achieving teamwork in the cockpit. In R. W. Swezey & E. Salas (Eds.), *Teams: Their training and performance* (pp. 329–354). Norwood, NJ: Ablex.

Randolph, W. A., & Dess, G. G. (1984). The congruence perspective of organization design: A conceptual model and multivariate research approach. *Academy of Management Review, 9,* 114–127.

Reichers, A. E., & Schneider, B. (1990). Climate and culture: An evolution of constructs. In B. Schneider (Ed.), *Organizational climate and culture* (pp. 5–39). San Francisco: Jossey-Bass.

Roberts, K. H., Hulin, C. L., & Rousseau, D. M. (1978). *Developing an interdisciplinary science of organizations.* San Francisco: Jossey-Bass.

Roethlisberger, F. J., & Dickson, W. J. (1939). *Management and the worker.* Cambridge, MA: Harvard University Press.

Rouiller, J. Z., & Goldstein, I. L. (1993). The relationship between organizational transfer climate and positive transfer of training. *Human Resource Development Quarterly, 4,* 377–390.

Rousseau, D. M. (1978a). Characteristics of departments, positions and individuals: Contexts for attitudes and behavior. *Administrative Science Quarterly, 23,* 521–540.

Rousseau, D. M. (1978b). Measures of technology as predictors of employee attitude. *Journal of Applied Psychology*, 63, 213–218.

Rousseau, D. M. (1985). Issues of level in organizational research: Multilevel and cross-level perspectives. In L. L. Cummings & B. M. Staw (Eds.), *Research in organizational behavior* (Vol. 7, pp. 1–38). Greenwich, CT: JAI.

Russell, J. S., Terborg, J. R., & Powers, M. L. (1985). Organizational performance and organizational level training and support. *Personnel Psychology*, 38, 849–863.

Ryman, D. H., & Biersner, R. J. (1975). Attitudes predictive of diving training success. *Personnel Psychology*, 28, 181–188.

Salas, E., Dickinson, T., Converse, S. A., & Tannenbaum, S. I. (1992). Toward an understanding of team performance and training. In R. W. Swezey & E. Salas (Eds.), *Teams: Their training and performance* (pp. 3–29). Norwood, NJ: Ablex.

Schein, E. H. (1968). Organizational socialization and the profession of management. *Industrial Management Review*, 9, 1–16.

Schneider, B. (1981). Work climates: An interactionist perspective. In N. W. Feimer & E. S. Geller (Eds.), *Environmental psychology: Directions and perspectives* (pp. 106–128). New York: Praeger.

Schneider, B., & Bowen, D. E. (1985). Employee and customer perceptions of service in banks: Replication and extension. *Journal of Applied Psychology*, 70, 423–433.

Schneider, B., & Konz, A. (1989). Strategic job analysis. *Human Resource Management*, 28, 51–63.

Schuler, R. S. (1987). Personnel and human resources management practice choices and organizational strategy. *Journal of Human Resource Planning*, 10, 1–21.

Schuler, R. S., & Jackson, S. E. (1987). Linking human resource practices with competitive strategies. *Academy of Management Executive*, 1, 207–219.

Schuler, R. S., & Walker, J. W. (1990). Human resources strategy: Focusing on issues and actions. *Organizational Dynamics*, 19(1), 5–19.

Shortell, S. M., & Zajac, E. J. (1990). Perceptual and archival measures of miles and snow's strategic types: A comprehensive assessment of reliability and validity. *Academy of Management Journal*, 33, 817–812.

Simon, H. A. (1973). The organization of complex systems. In H. H. Pattee (Ed.), *Hierarchy theory: The challenge of complex systems* (pp. 1–28). New York: Braziller.

Slocum, J. W., Jr., & Sims, H. P., Jr. (1980). A typology for integrating technology, organization and job design. *Human Relations*, 33, 193–212.

Sundstrom, E., DeMeuse, K. P., & Futrell, D. (1990). Work teams: Applications and effectiveness. *American Psychologist*, 45, 120–133.

Tannenbaum, S. I., Mathieu, J. E., Salas, E., & Cannon-Bowers, J. A. (1991). Meeting trainees' expectations: The influence of training fulfillment on the development of commitment, self-efficacy, and motivation. *Journal of Applied Psychology*, 76, 759–769.

Tannenbaum, S. I., & Yukl, G. (1992). Training and development in work organizations. *Annual Review of Psychology*, 43, 474–483.

Thompson, J. D. (1967). *Organizations in action*. New York: McGraw-Hill.

Thorndike, E. L., & Woodworth, R. S. (1901). The influence of improvement in one mental function upon the efficiency of other functions. *Psychological Review*, 8, 247–261.

Van de Ven, A., & Drazin, R. (1985). Alternative forms of fit in contingency theory. *Administrative Science Quarterly*, 30, 514–539.

Von Bertalanffy, L. (1975). *Perspectives on general systems theory*. New York: Braziller.

Von Bertalanffy, L. (1980). *General systems theory*. New York: Braziller.

Walton, R. E. (1977). Work innovation at Topeka: After six years. *Journal of Applied Behavioral Science*, 13, 422–433.

Wexley, K. N. (1984). Personnel training. *Annual Review of Psychology*, 35, 519–551.

Wexley, K. N., & Thornton, C. L. (1972). Effect of verbal feedback of test results upon learning. *Journal of Educational Research*, 66, 119–121.

Zohar, D. (1980). Safety climate in industrial organizations: Theoretical and applied implications. *Journal of Applied Psychology*, 65, 96–102.

IV

*Applied Psychology and Training:
Methods for Improving the Linkage
Between Training Research
and Practice*

11

Enhancing Reciprocity Between
Training Theory and Practice:
Principles, Guidelines,
and Specifications

Eduardo Salas
Janis A. Cannon-Bowers
Elizabeth L. Blickensderfer
Naval Air Warfare Center Training
Systems Division

Each year, researchers devote considerable resources to the scientific study of training, learning, and skill acquisition. At the same time, U.S. industry and government pour upward of $200 billion per year into training the workforce (Carnevale, Gainer, & Villet, 1990). Despite the magnitude of these efforts and expenditures, training is not always effective in imparting crucial knowledge and skills. Manufacturers struggle to help workers develop new skills, only later to see these newly acquired skills not retained. Managers grapple with abstract concepts such as "empowerment" or achieving "full potential" in workers, only later to see productivity remain constant. Why does such a situation exist? What is preventing the large body of knowledge on training, learning, and skill acquisition from translating into effective training practice? Why do training research findings seldom affect actual organizational practices?

Although the answers to these questions are not simple, they all involve one central problem: a lack of integration between training theory and training practice. In 1988, Latham pointed out that training practitioners seldom apply results from research literature to their programs. A few years later, Tannenbaum and Yukl (1992) noted that some headway in integration and conceptual development had occurred but also emphasized that considerably more synthesis was needed. Despite further progress in this area, there still exists a variety of reasons why training research and practice are not yet integrated.

The purpose of this chapter is to explore some of the reasons why this is the case, and to offer a framework that extends what others have written on the topic. The notion of a "translation mechanism" is presented as a means to further reciprocity between training theory and practice. To do this, the chapter first defines the notion of "reciprocity" between theory and practice, and reviews a framework offered by Cannon-Bowers, Tannenbaum, Salas, and Converse (1991). Next, it defines additional concepts that can serve as translation mechanisms for applying training research results into actual training practice. Finally, it provides two detailed examples of areas where training theory and practice have employed specific translation mechanisms and have been successful in achieving reciprocity.

WHY IS RECIPROCITY NECESSARY?

Cannon-Bowers et al. (1991) contended that training researchers will achieve more meaningful results when practical relevancies are considered, and training practitioners will have the highest probability of success when training design is based on a solid theoretical and empirical foundation. Training effectiveness in organizations will improve to the extent that training problems, theory, findings, and practices are better integrated, and further, to the extent that training theory and training practice reciprocate to each other.

Reciprocity is defined as a mutual dependence, action, or influence. Reciprocity implies a mutual or equivalent exchange. For researchers, this may include delineating specifics as to how particular research findings should be applied. In addition, researchers should be willing to conduct research that is focused on the problems and concerns of practitioners. On the practitioner's side, reciprocity means providing ideas or hypotheses uncovered while implementing their own training programs; reciprocity implies that practitioners provide feedback—from knowledge acquired during their training implementation experiences—back to researchers. Currently, breakdowns exist in both theory-to-practice and practice-to-theory linkages. This lack of mutual exchange between training theory and practice is one indication of limited integration and reciprocity between training theory and training practice.

So, how does one foster reciprocity? There is not an easy answer or a single path, but a "translation mechanism" may help. Training research needs a set of tools to help make the research and practice links. Before defining translation mechanisms that may help foster reciprocity among training research and practice, it is necessary to provide a context for this discussion. The following sections present and describe a framework borrowed from Cannon-Bowers et al. (1991), which lays out how training theory and practice can be linked.

THE FRAMEWORK:
POTENTIAL RECIPROCITY LINKS

Recent efforts have focused on linking training theory and training practice (Kraiger, Ford, & Salas, 1993). Cannon-Bowers et al. (1991) took a step in this direction by developing a framework including both training-related research and technique. The framework is based on three questions: (a) What should be trained (i.e., what is the nature of the knowledge, skills, and abilities [KSAs] that must be trained)? (b) How should training be designed? and (c) Is training effective and, if so, why? The framework groups numerous conceptual developments and applied techniques within these three questions.

The Cannon-Bowers et al. (1991) framework delineates examples of reciprocity that could introduce new vitality into both theory- and technique-oriented research, and that could also play a critical role in the advancement of the training field. Specifically, theoretical findings can be translated into particular training techniques, whereas the study of techniques can help confirm, refine, and expand related theory. Within the framework, potential linkages/reciprocity include horizontal, vertical, and multiple links (see Fig. 11.1).

Research on the nature of KSAs helps identify appropriate methods for establishing specific task requirements and training needs (Cell 1–Cell 2). In turn, the specific task-analysis techniques can help verify and refine theories about the KSAs and expertise used in a particular task (Cell 2–Cell 1).

Looking at Cells 1 and 3, knowledge about the KSAs used in a task helps propagate hypotheses regarding the most effective training type (Cell 1–Cell 3). Further, research examining the structure of learning and skill acquisition on a particular task can confirm and refine theories about the nature of KSAs and expertise for that task (Cell 3–Cell 1).

The Cell 3–Cell 4 linkage indicates that understanding the learning and skill acquisition for a task helps identify appropriate training techniques and methods (Cell 3–Cell 4). In addition, research examining individual training methods can confirm and refine learning and skill-acquisition theories for a particular task (Cell 4–Cell 3).

Examining the Cell 3–Cell 5 link shows that understanding the structures of learning and skill acquisition for a task can expand hypotheses concerning why training is effective or ineffective and to develop parameters of effectiveness (Cell 3–Cell 5). Conversely, research examining training's effectiveness can confirm and refine learning and skill-acquisition theories (Cell 5–Cell 3).

The Cell 5–Cell 6 link points out that understanding training effectiveness (i.e., the parameters and causes of) can generate methods to assess training effectiveness (Cell 5–Cell 6). In turn, research identifying training effectiveness assessment techniques can confirm and refine theories on why training is effective and under what conditions training is effective (Cell–Cell 5).

RESEARCH QUESTIONS	TRAINING-RELATED THEORY	TRAINING-RELATED TECHNIQUE
WHAT SHOULD BE TRAINED?	**CELL 1** Nature of Expertise (Rasmussen, 1979) Mental Models & Knowledge Structures (Rouse & Morris, 1986) Teamwork Skills (Prince, Chidester, Cannon-Bowers, & Bowers 1992) Expert-Novice Differences (Chase & Simon. 1973; Glaser, 1989) Taxonomies of Task Requirements (Fleishman & Quaintance, 1984) Metacognition (Bereiter & Scardamalia, 1985) Information-Processing Theory (Schneider & Shiffrin, 1977)	**CELL 2** Cognitive Task Analysis (Redding, 1989) Team Task Analysis (Levine & Baker, 1991) Job Analysis Methods (Levine, 1983) Needs Analysis Methods (Goldstein, Braverman, & Goldstein, 1991) Protocol Analysis (Ericsson & Simon, 1984) Critical Incidents (Flanagan, 1954) Future-Oriented Task Analysis (Schneider & Konz, 1989)
HOW SHOULD TRAINING BE DESIGNED?	**CELL 3** Information-Processing Theory (Schneider & Shiffrin, 1977; Fisk & Eggemeier, 1988) Skill Acquisition (Anderson, 1985; Ackerman, 1987) Social Learning Theory (Bandura, 1986) Team Performance (Salas et al., 1992) Learning Principles (Gagne, 1970; Kyllonen & Alluisi, 1987) Taxonomy of Learning Skills (Kyllonen & Shute, 1989) Fidelity (Hays & Singer, 1989) Metacognition (Bereiter & Scardamalia, 1985) Expectancy Theory (Vroom, 1964) Action Control (Kuhl, 1985) Mental Models (Kieras, 1988)	**CELL 4** Behavior Modeling (Goldstein & Sorcher, 1974) Simulators/Training Devices (Cream, Eggemeier, & Klein, 1978) Networked Training (Alluisi, 1991) Part-Task Training (Wightman & Lintern, 1985) Feedback (Ilgen, Fisher, & Taylor, 1979) Relapse Prevention (Marx, 1982) Self-Management (Manz & Sims, 1989) Computer-based Instruction (Crawford & Crawford, 1978) Games & Simulations (Thornton & Cleveland, 1990) Action Learning (Revans, 1982)
IS TRAINING EFFECTIVE and WHY?	**CELL 5** Individual Difference (Noe & Schmitt, 1986; Cronbach & Snow, 1977) Hierarchy of Evaluation (Kirkpatrick, 1976; Tannenbaum, Mathieu, Salas, & Cannon-Bowers, 1991) Transfer of Training (Baldwin & Ford, 1988) Multicomponent Approach (Cannon-Bowers et al., 1989) Attitude/Behavior Relations (Ajzen & Fishbein, 1980) Training Climate (Rouillier & Goldstein, 1993) Self-Fulfilling Prophecy (Eden, 1990) Evaluability Assessment (Rutman, 1980) Content Validity (Ebel, 1977; Guion, 1978) Attribution Theory (Kelley, 1972)	**CELL 6** Scale Development (Anastasi, 1988) Utility Analysis (Cascio, 1991) Quasi-Experimental Methods (Cook, Campbell, & Peracchio, 1991) Work Sample Tests (Asher & Sciarrino, 1974) Team Performance Measures (Coovert & McNelis, 1992) Critical Incidents (Morgan et al., 1986) Content Validation Strategies (Lawshe, 1975) Mental Model Measurement (Moore & Gordon, 1988; Schvaneveldt, 1990) Program Evaluation (Rossi & Freeman, 1982) Walk Through Performance Testing (Hedge & Lipscomb, 1987)

FIG. 11.1. Framework for linking training-related theory and technique (Cannon-Bowers, Tannenbaum, Salas, & Converse, 1991).

Other links include Cell 1–Cell 5, in that an understanding of the nature of KSAs and task expertise aids in developing training effectiveness hypotheses (Cell 1–Cell 5). Research exploring the causes and parameters of training effectiveness helps confirm and refine theories on the nature of KSAs (Cell 5–Cell 1).

Multiple linkages are also possible. Cannon-Bowers et al. (1991) pointed out that tracing through Cells 2, 4, and 6 parallels I. Goldstein's (1980) systems approach to training design. The process would determine training needs, technique choice and design and, finally, evaluation.

In summary, this framework offers a point of departure by which reciprocity can be achieved. This framework sets the stage, such that specifics between research and practice can occur with regards to what to train, how to design training, and how to evaluate it. The next two sections explore why reciprocity is still so elusive and what can be done to achieve it.

WHY RECIPROCITY HAS NOT BEEN ACHIEVED: SOME OBSERVATIONS

Although the Cannon-Bowers et al. (1991) framework is an illustration of the potential that exists for reciprocity, integration of theory and practice in the training field has been relatively rare. Before contemplating what to do to improve this situation, it may be helpful to consider why reciprocity between training theory and technique so seldom appears. Identifying specific reasons is difficult, but the following propositions are offered:

Proposition 1: Training-related theory lacks specificity and concreteness regarding implications for practice.

An important factor in a theory's potential for integration into practice may be the researcher's ability to clearly illustrate its practical implications. Flanagan and Dipboye (1981) performed a meta-analysis of approximately 500 industrial/organizational psychology journal articles written from the mid-1960s to the mid-1970s. One aspect examined was the extent of applicability of the research. The authors concluded that theoretical applicability depended on the researcher's ability to state implications stemming from the results. If a theorist does not state the implications, the theory's applicability will likely decrease (Swezey & Salas, 1992).

In the present context, this conclusion suggests that theories, ideas, and hypotheses be presented in "real-life" contexts, including examples of how the theory may apply. Doing so may encourage practitioners to incorporate the theory into training practice. Practitioners seem more willing to adopt straightforward, concrete theories as opposed to more abstract theories. For example, the proposition from social learning theory—that "people learn by watching others" (Bandura, 1986)—is straightforward and relatively easy to incorporate into training programs (i.e., by providing trainees with appropriate models). It is not surprising that practitioners were quick to adopt behavioral modeling techniques.

The degree of face validity inherent in a theory also appears to encourage integration of theory into practice. To use social learning theory (Bandura, 1986) as an example once again, it appeared valid enough that training practitioners thought it worthy of applying. In addition, the simple, intuitive, and appealing nature of goal setting theory (Locke & Latham, 1990) may have convinced trainers to integrate its tenets into training practice.

> Proposition 2: There is little motivation among researchers and practitioners to incorporate each others' ideas.

The central issue here is how to increase researchers' concern for application, and, similarly, how to increase practitioners' concern for the advancement of knowledge and science. Anything that stimulates a mutual concern would help bridge this gap.

An emphasis on the real-world problem or opportunity driving the training need could help stimulate concern on both fronts. Theories developed in areas that practitioners understand and consider important will meet with the least resistance from practitioners. For example, practitioners can understand the consequences of teams that fail to coordinate and see the importance of teamwork training. This appears to be the case as numerous private airlines, the military, and the Federal Aviation Administration (FAA) have all adopted aircrew coordination training programs (i.e., training practice based on theory; Wiener, Kanki, & Helmreich, 1993).

This is not to suggest that research should follow the fads of training practice. Rather, it is to suggest that when theoretical concepts are not inherently or obviously applicable to training practitioners, theorists must emphasize the real-world application. Emphasizing the real-world applications should help convince and motivate practitioners to utilize the theory. With an increased focus on real-world contexts, theorists might also better realize the value of practitioner input.

> Proposition 3: There are few advocates that help foster reciprocity.

When a new theoretical framework is introduced, someone needs to "take the ball and run," as A. Goldstein and Sorcher (1974) and Latham and Saari (1979) accomplished with the beginnings of applied learning theory. Briefly, Bandura (1969) presented a series of principles that he considered important to observational learning (overt rehearsal, cues shown in modeling scenes). A. Goldstein and Sorcher incorporated these principles into a training approach, which generated considerable interest among practitioners who adopted the same techniques (I. Goldstein, 1993). More important, Latham and Saari provided solid empirical evidence supporting the techniques described by A. Goldstein and Sorcher.

Most likely, without A. Goldstein and Sorcher (1974) advocating the use of the theory by translating this theory into usable techniques, Bandura's (1969) ideas would have spent more time in research journals and less time in actual use. At the same time, Latham and Saari's (1979) solid empirical evidence supporting the ideas helped to convince researchers (who may otherwise have dismissed the flurry of activity as unimportant) of the significance of the techniques. Both A. Goldstein and Sorcher and Latham and Saari played the role of advocate. Their work led to both the development of the applied learning theory and the practitioner acceptance of the applied learning-based techniques. Advocates of this nature are vital to integration of training theory and practice.

> Proposition 4: There is little cross-fertilization among training-related disciplines.

Both researchers and training practitioners have a tendency to limit themselves to a set of similar concepts, theoretical underpinnings, and methods while ignoring others. One example is the division among business/management, educational psychology, instructional technology, cognitive science, human resource development, and industrial/organizational psychology. These fields seldom interact. They have their own organizations, conferences, and trade publications, which make cross-fertilization difficult.

Another factor limiting cross-fertilization and reciprocity may be the physical and geographical separation of practitioners and researchers. Practitioners and researchers usually work in different settings. They are divided by purpose (science) or function (human resources). Military organizations have been one type of setting where research and practice have linked together. In such cases, researchers, training practitioners, and training users work literally side by side. This type of interaction fosters exchange and, ultimately, the derivation of theoretically based and practice-relevant products.

> Proposition 5: Current training practice and research are not always driven by real-world problems and/or opportunities. Therefore, they often remain faddish.

This observation was made by I. Goldstein (1980) over 10 years ago, and today it is still true. Although some progress has been made, training is still a faddish field both in practice and research. Practitioners continue to implement particular training programs simply because they are "in vogue" and not because they are based on need, relevance, or program efficiency; training researchers also conduct one-time studies on the latest construct—all of which generates fragmentation.

Furthermore, the training field has literally exploded in recent years. This brings both good news and bad. The good news is that more solid, theoretically based research is being conducted than ever before (Tannenbaum & Yukl, 1992). Creative practitioners are applying new and innovative training programs using the latest technology (multimedia presentation of training). The bad news is that their programs are often applied without a theoretical basis or with little empirical guidance. Both sides are also having difficulty keeping each other informed and benefiting from the latest findings.

In summary, a number of difficulties in achieving reciprocity exist in the training field: (a) training theory often lacks specific and concrete implications for practice, (b) little motivation exists for researchers and practitioners to incorporate each other's ideas, and (c) few advocates for reciprocity exist. These obstacles are, at best, hindering the integration between theory and practice and, at worst, stalling the training field from achieving its greatest potentials. The obstacles were noted, as was the notion, that current organizational performance problems and/or opportunities should drive *both* training practice and theory. Despite the different directions training research and practice may take, both arenas should begin at the same point: the operational problem.

At this point, a number of questions can be generated regarding the reciprocity of theory and practice. What efforts can be made to keep the two arenas more closely linked to the same path? How can one foster reciprocity and, ultimately, improve the science and practice of training? After a careful review of the observations offered earlier, a common thread appears—that is, how can one better communicate and exchange knowledge and experience? The following sections describe translation mechanisms that can be used to foster communication and exchange between training theory and practice.

TRANSLATION MECHANISM

One potential way to foster the linkages among problems, theories, and techniques that has not received full attention to date is the use of a specific translation mechanism. The term *translation mechanism* refers to a set of tools, including concepts such as principles, guidelines, specifications, and lessons learned. These concepts are not mutually exclusive. The underlying reason for employing these concepts is that they are a means to help communicate information between scientists and practitioners. Packaging training-related information into clear, concise statements is a significant requirement for achieving reciprocity. Before discussing how this translation mechanism may help, definitions of the component concepts must first be presented.

Principle

For the purposes of this chapter, *principle* is defined as an underlying truth or fact about a human phenomenon. In research, the purpose of principles is to extract the fundamental points from empirical research and present them clearly and distinctly to other interested individuals (Chapanis, 1991). In other words, training research must elicit principles, and these principles must be communicated to both the research community and practitioners. Examples of principles, generated from a number of domains in the training field, are delineated in Table 11.1. As is obvious, they are principles about skill acquisition, learning, teamwork, and self-efficacy.

Guideline

Swezey and Salas (1992) defined a *guideline* as, "A brief statement that describes or suggests action(s) or conditions(s) that, if correctly and appropriately applied, could be used to improve or facilitate either instructional or training device

Table 11.1
Example Principles: Information Processing, Learning, and Teams

Subject	Principle and Citation
Information processing	Performance is limited by the number of inconsistent cognitive operations. However, performance may also be limited by the type of task structure (e.g., memory vs. visual vs. hybrid memory/visual search; Fisk, Lee, & Rogers, 1991).
	Part-task training can result in efficient associative learning, at least for semantic-based processing. Target strengthening (priority learning) benefits most from part-task training (Fisk, Lee, & Rogers, 1991).
	Performance improvements will occur only for consistent elements of a task, and the degree of improvement is directly related to the degree of consistency (Fisk, Lee, & Rogers, 1991). Avoid changing requirements midstream (Kyllonen & Alluisi, 1987).
Learning	Train under mild speed stress (Kyllonen & Alluisi, 1987).
	Encourage the use of general problem-solving procedures (Kyllonen & Alluisi, 1987).
	Transfer depends on stimulus and response similarity, and the similarity of performance strategies between two tasks. When the required responses are the same, further task similarities give increasing positive transfer (Holding, 1987).
	Training must be designed to increase the self-efficacy of trainees. Training that includes self-efficacy treatment will help increase performance attainments (Gist, 1989).
	Trainees can learn through observing others (vicarious learning; Bandura, 1982).
Teams	Teamwork judges and measures must be reliable on two levels (interrater agreement, internal consistency and temporal stability; Baker & Salas, 1992).
	There is no escaping observation (in measuring teamwork; Baker & Salas, 1992).

design and development activity" (p. 223). Therefore, guidelines are prescriptive statements that translate principles into statements of "what to do" and, in a general sense, "how to do it." Guidelines aid in the design and development of training programs or systems. Examples of guidelines are listed in Table 11.2.

Specification

A *specification* is a detailed, precise statement of how training should be designed. As viewed here, the purpose of specifications is to operationalize

TABLE 11.2
Example Guidelines: Knowledge and Skill Development and Teams

Subject	Guideline and Citation
Knowledge and skill development	Organize instructional goals around behavioral objectives (Kyllonen & Alluisi, 1987).
	Show positive and negative instances of concept (Kyllonen & Alluisi, 1987).
	The trainer should regulate the supply of information to the learner. Depending on the tack involved, a choice must be made among the methods of telling, showing, or doing (Holding, 1987).
	Verbal instructions are most effective when spaced throughout the execution of a task, unless used for general orientation and for imparting general principles (Holding, 1987).
	Films can present otherwise unavailable lecture or visual material. However, there are disadvantages inherent in the lack of flexibility and audience participation (Holding, 1987).
	Increased precision of knowledge of results is advantageous up to a point, although there maybe an optimum level of precision (Holding, 1987).
	Verbal methods can sometimes be employed to convey useful rules, although a knowledge of theory may be ineffective (Holding, 1987).
Team training	Before team members can focus on developing effective teamwork skills, they must reach some threshold level of competence in their individual knowledge and skills (Guerette, Miller, Glickman, Morgan, & Salas, 1987).
	Individual skills are important components of team performance, and training should be designed to develop both individual and team skills (Davis, Gaddy, & Turney, 1985; Dyer, 1984; Hall & Rizzo, 1975).
	Untrained team members tend to acquire individual performance skills at the same rate, independent of the team training load (Morgan, Coates, Kirby, & Alluisi, 1984).
	The development of norms, and the identification of specific changes in behavior from these norms, may be used as benchmarks of the stages of development of teamwork skills (Glickman et al., 1987).

training guidelines (from any domain: cognitive, team, or managerial skills) for direct application in the development of training programs (Baker & Swezey, 1993). Specifications prescribe precisely what to do and how to do it (Kessler, Macpherson, & Mirabella, 1988), along with when to do it and why to do it.

Specifications can be derived from a number of sources, including task analysis, research findings, and training guidelines. Once they are extracted, they provide a set of specific statements that guide the development and conduct of training for a given task (Baker and Swezey, 1993). Examples of specifications for training are shown in Table 11.3.

Lessons Learned

Lesson's *learned* are new understandings and/or realizations born from experience with a particular situation, problem, or event. The purpose of lessons learned is to exchange among interested parties knowledge drawn from individual experiences. The lessons are not necessarily empirical, but they convey an important piece of information that may be usable by other scientists or practitioners facing the same situation. As such, lessons learned are a crucial source of feedback for practitioners and researchers. In this way, practical experience and knowledge can be passed between researchers and practitioners, and can facilitate reciprocity.

In summary, principles, guidelines, specifications, and lessons learned are translation mechanisms that appear useful in fostering connections between theory and practice. However, the success of such mechanisms hinges on the utility and benefit to both theorists and practitioners that these mechanisms offer. The next section describes how these translation mechanisms may help.

TABLE 11.3
Example Specifications

Specifications
1. The contractor shall ensure that all seven critical skill categories and the aircrew coordination behaviors are addressed in the integrated effort.
2. The contractor shall review existing mission, collective, individual, and occupational task listings to identify collective tasks.
3. The contractor shall list tasks that demand interaction between two or more individuals for successful performance.
4. The training objectives for integrated ACT shall define what training is intended to accomplish by delineating, in behavioral terms, the competencies the trainee will possess at the completion of the integrated ACT.
5. The training objectives shall be written in collaboration with and reviewed by the fleet subject matter experts.

Note. Adapted from the *Draft Statement of Work for Integrated Aircrew Coordination Training and Recurrence Aircrew Coordination Training*, Human Factors Division, Naval Training Systems Center; also appeared in Baker and Swezey (1993).

302   SALAS ET AL.

Using Translation Mechanisms

A model of the roles that translation mechanisms can play in training research and practice is depicted in Fig. 11.2. The purpose of this model is simply to illustrate the concepts surrounding the notion of translation mechanisms. It does not, of course, imply an invariant series of steps or activities that must occur in developing principles, guidelines, specifications, or lessons learned. Instead, the model depicts possible developments in the evolution of a specific training solution.

To illustrate, the evolution of training development begins when a problem or opportunity arises. A *problem* is any training issue that needs to be addressed. Frequently, the presence of a problem also brings opportunity. For example, advanced technology has created a training problem: how to train nonskilled workers the high-tech skills they need for the 21st century.

Once a problem/opportunity is identified, two basic paths may be followed. The most common path is a direct leap from the problem to application of a "solution." The desire to solve a problem as quickly as possible, in addition to the excitement of building a new piece of equipment, often cause designers to skip over the fundamental issues inherent to the problem and proceed directly to the design phase (i.e., the application, Paths 1–2 in the model; or specifica-

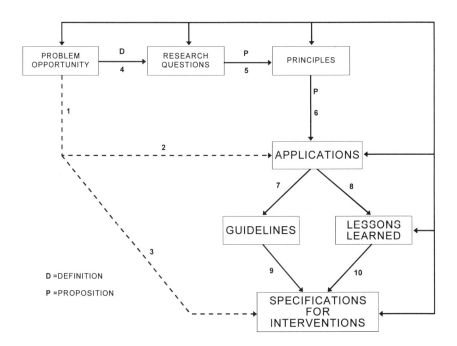

FIG. 11.2. Model of principles, guidelines, and specifications in training design.

tion, Paths 1–3 in the model). An example of this path is a training program that is developed to address a current fad in business operations. Currently, practitioners have jumped at total quality management (TQM) training programs without considering whether these programs solve the fundamental problems faced by the organization. Unfortunately, TQM programs may not necessarily solve the organization's underlying problem.

An even more dramatic example of the problems inherent in these paths lies in developing a simulation for training purposes. Considering that the development of a training simulation can reach into the several hundred thousand (or even million) dollar range, costly mistakes can be made if the training needs have not been examined thoroughly.

An improved path would focus on understanding the fundamental issues involved in a particular problem. The goal is to ensure the design of a training intervention appropriate to the need (I. Goldstein, 1993). Success in this path requires effort and input from both researchers and practitioners. The specific mechanisms (as described previously) will help smooth this path.

Going back to the model, it is suggested here that the problem must be defined properly such that appropriate research questions can be generated (Path 4). Once research questions are generated, appropriate research can begin, or previous theory can be examined so that principles and guidelines from that theory can be applied to the new problem.

At this stage, the link between research and practice is weak at best. The research may be done. The practitioners may be ready to design, and yet training theory is rarely incorporated into training practice. The use of principles (Path 5) is advocated to strengthen the link. Unless researchers synthesize the results of the research into straightforward principles, the likelihood of practitioners incorporating theoretical research into their training design remains small.

Once principles are established, hypotheses regarding training intervention design can be generated. In that way, the particular application (Path 6) is derived directly from research theory. The application stage is the time for training designers to begin testing particular training interventions/applications that were derived from theory; the application stage is the stage where validation of principles generated by research can occur.

When a particular technique is an effective application of the theoretical principle, results can be formulated into guidelines (Path 7). Guidelines can then be used to help formulate specifications (Path 9). In this way, theory is incorporated directly into specifications. If a particular technique is ineffective, the mistake and problems with the method are also important material. Such comments should be summarized in the form of lessons learned (Path 8). Using a particular format (lessons learned) gives researchers and practitioners a common language with which to exchange this type of information. Availability of this genre of information should help prevent others from repeating mistakes and help drive progress forward.

The final product of this evolution of training development is a set of specifications. Specifications give practitioners specific details regarding what to include in the training session or device. Detailed specifications should eliminate the need for practitioners to guess at requirements for training content and delivery. Following specifications derived directly from theoretical guidelines ensures that training theory is incorporated into training practice and, most important, ensures that the fundamental training problem is addressed.

ILLUSTRATIONS OF THEORY
AND PRACTICE LINKAGES

The most natural demonstration of theory and practice reciprocity and the benefits it yields is to discuss previously established and successful links. Unfortunately, integration has been infrequent, and it is relatively rare that training theory feeds directly into development of training technique. One area that has achieved some reciprocity is the team performance field. Team performance research has begun to produce specific training interventions, and has also led to the emergence of new conceptual as well as practical interventions in the team performance field.

This chapter focuses on the team training field because the authors are familiar with the literature, not because the field offers the only model of reciprocity. Even the team training area is not illustrative of true reciprocity—a two-way flow of information from theory to practice. As noted, the theory–practice link appears, but the practice–theory link (where the practice of training leads to new, advanced, or expanded theoretical propositions) is not as strong. The following sections describe how team performance theory is driving the development of team training interventions.

TEAM PERFORMANCE: THE PROBLEM

With teams responsible for increasingly complex operations in both military and civilian life, one current focus of training research is understanding team training and performance. This has been particularly true in light of catastrophic incidents involving teams: the USS Vincennes downing of a civilian airliner, the accidental shooting of two Army helicopters by Air Force personnel, and others. These incidents highlight the need to train decision-making teams, particularly as they operate under stress.

A first step in developing theoretically based training for such teams is to consider the basic definitions of the construct of interest—in this case, the team. Simply defining a *team* can be difficult due to confusion in the literature.

For the purposes of this chapter, a *team* is considered a group of two or more individuals who must interact cooperatively and adaptively in pursuit of shared, valued objectives. Team members have clearly defined, differentiated roles and responsibilities; hold task-relevant knowledge; and are interdependent. They must rely on one another to accomplish goals (Dyer, 1984; Morgan, Glickman, Woodard, Blaiwes, & Salas, 1986; Orasanu & Salas, 1993).

The next step in understanding team training is to develop an appreciation of team performance and the factors that affect it. In the past 50 years, team research has produced a number of team performance models (Hackman, 1983; Nieva, Fleishman, & Reick, 1978; Steiner, 1972). Recently, Salas, Dickinson, Converse, and Tannenbaum (1992) developed an integrative model, based on previous team research and theory, that demonstrates the multiple forces affecting team performance. The Salas et al. (1992) framework is an input, throughput, output model. It demonstrates the links among the organizational and situational context, task characteristics, work structure, individual characteristics, team characteristics, and team processes. Driving the model is the contention that teams do not function in isolation. Numerous factors, both internal and external to the team, feed into each other, interact, and affect a team's performance. A detailed description of the model is beyond the scope of this chapter. Suffice it to say that the model suggests that team performance is a complex phenomenon and is affected by a host of internal and external factors (see Salas et al., 1992 for a full description). To understand and train teams, researchers and practitioners alike must be aware of these factors and the manner in which they affect team performance.

Besides understanding the factors that influence teamwork, one must also understand more directly how teams interact, coordinate, communicate, adapt, and exchange information with one another. These skills have proved highly difficult to identify and explain. Indeed, studies have investigated teams in the past few decades (Cannon-Bowers, Salas, & Converse, 1990), but little concrete knowledge exists regarding the nature of teamwork skills or the most effective methods of team training (Hackman, 1987; Salas et al., 1992).

There are exceptions to this trend, two of which are presented here: (a) decision-making teams under stress, and (b) cockpit aircrew coordination. After reviewing the initial problem that drove the subsequent research and the theoretical developments (principles) from the research, this chapter discusses the influence that this research has had on team training guidelines and interventions.

Illustration 1: Team Decision Making Under Stress

With advances in technology and changes in the world order, demands on the human decision maker are becoming more complicated. Cannon-Bowers, Salas, and Grossman (1991) described modern team scenarios as being characterized by rapidly evolving and changing conditions, severe time compression, and high degrees of ambiguity and uncertainty. These environments can present the decision maker with a barrage of data and require the coordinated performance of a team of operators who must gather, process, integrate, communicate, and act on these data in support of a decision. Numerous other stressors (both environmental and psychological) also exist in the operational setting, not the least of which is the potentially catastrophic cost of making an error. In keeping with the model in Fig. 11.2, a research question can now be generated to guide training development: How can we train team decision making so that the teams are resilient to the impact of stress? One path that team researchers have followed in answering this question involves the "mental model" concept.

Mental Models

Over the past several decades, a number of different research disciplines have adopted some variation of the mental model construct to use as an explanatory mechanism of how humans understand complex systems. With the broad range of topics that the construct has been associated with, different definitions of *mental model* have appeared (see Rouse & Morris, 1986, for review). Team researchers often utilize the definition proposed by Rouse and Morris—that a *mental model* is a "mechanism whereby humans generate descriptions of system purpose and form, explanations of system functioning and observed system states, and predictions of future system states" (p. 351).

Mental models help people describe, explain, and predict system behavior (Rouse & Morris, 1986). Researchers have proposed a number of characteristics that allow mental models to fulfill this role. For example, theorists advocate that mental models are dynamic. This changing nature of mental models allows people to create causal event links and predict ramifications of inputs (or decisions) on particular parts of the model (de Kleer & Brown, 1981, 1983; Klein, 1989; Wilson & Rutherford, 1989). Others have also noted that mental models are manipulable and enable people to predict system states via mental manipulation of model parameters (Johnson-Laird, 1983).

Mental models offer a powerful explanatory mechanism for understanding complex performance. In light of this, an offshoot of mental model theory has developed—a theory of *shared* mental models. Shared mental model theory is currently being used to explain the nature of coordinated team performance and team decision making.

Shared Mental Models

Teamwork behaviors, such as coordinating action, adapting to changing task conditions, and anticipating the needs of the task and team, have proved difficult to delineate in terms of KSAs. Cannon-Bowers, Salas, and Converse (1993) explained that the difficulty inherent in team tasks stems from the characteristics of the team activities, which require team members to predict future events with respect to both task or team requirements. Prediction of future events must occur if team members are to sequence, time, and adjust their behavior appropriately. Because the process by which a team member arrives at the prediction (anticipates a need) cannot be observed, it has been theorized that team members utilize an internal knowledge base that helps them decide which behaviors are necessary and when and how to perform them. The internal knowledge base can be considered the individual's mental model; the overlap among the mental models of several team members allows them to coordinate without the need for overt communication.

In summary, team theorists have taken the concept of a mental model and, instead of using it as an explanation of how humans understand mechanical-type systems, have incorporated it into an explanation of team task performance. This includes explaining how team members can predict needs and actions of other members. Hence, the term shared mental model refers to the extent to which individual team members' mental models overlap, (i.e., the extent to which team members share the same understanding of the task and team).

Principles of Team Performance:
What Must Be Shared?

Although questions about mental models remain, a number of principles have been extracted from the theory and reviewed through empirical work. To date, sufficient progress has been made to allow for the generation of several initial principles. These principles have subsequently driven the design of training interventions.

> *Principle:* "Mature" teams have members who anticipate each others' needs (Glickman et al., 1987).

When team members become familiar with each others' knowledge, skills, abilities, attitudes, motivations, preferences, and style, they are able to better anticipate teammates' task, informational, and interpersonal needs. According to Cannon-Bowers et al. (1993), this is the basis of shared team mental models.

> *Principle:* "Mature" teams can coordinate without the need to communicate overtly (Orasanu, 1990; Rouse, Cannon-Bowers, & Salas, 1992).

Teams with shared mental models do not need to communicate as much under high work load. Communication will decrease when teams have a higher amount of shared information; they have shared expectations and intentions, and can anticipate each other's behavior. This has been referred to as "implicit" coordination (see Kleinman & Serfaty, 1989).

> *Principle:* Effective teams can adjust their strategy under stress
> (Kleinman & Serfaty, 1989).

According to Kleinman and Serfaty, effective teams employ "implicit" coordination strategies under high-work load conditions. This is an example of how teams might change their behavior in response to task demands. Other strategies include: load balancing, performance monitoring, and feedback (Cannon-Bowers, Tannenbaum, Salas, & Volpe, 1995).

Guidelines for Team Training: Cross-Training

The shared mental model idea suggests that training strategies designed to foster development of shared mental models have the potential to improve team performance (Cannon-Bowers, Salas, & Grossman, 1991). Therefore, guidelines for team training design can be delineated. Several techniques to help foster shared mental models have been proposed.

One potential training strategy is through cross-training. In particular, positional rotation has been suggested as a technique to nurture shared knowledge among team members (Cannon-Bowers et al., 1991; Travillian, Volpe, Cannon-Bowers, & Salas, 1993). Positional rotation can be conceptualized as a type of job rotation among team members. This method of cross-training provides team members with an understanding of the basic knowledge necessary to successfully perform the tasks, duties, and/or positions of the other team members, as well as an overall framework within which one's own function is an integral part (Travillian et al., 1993).

Cross-trained teams have achieved team process ratings and team outcome scores higher than those teams without such training (Travillian et al., 1993). More important, cross-training corresponds with a number of the shared mental model principles listed previously. For instance, members who have been cross-trained should have a higher amount of shared information and should be better equipped to anticipate others' needs. Cross-trained teams should be better able to coordinate without depending on overt communication.

By way of specific guidelines for cross-training, several research studies are beginning to offer needed data. In particular, Volpe, Cannon-Bowers, Salas, and Spector (in press) recently found that providing only 10 to 15 minutes of familiarity training on teammates' jobs was sufficient to improve team performance. High-fidelity simulations are also an effective means to provide interpositional knowledge to team members.

So what guidelines can be offered? A number have begun to emerge. Specifically, cross-training should:

1. Provide team members with exposure to the roles, responsibilities, tasks, information needs, and contingencies of their teammates' tasks.

2. Provide team members with limited practice on the roles and tasks of teammates, highlighting the interdependencies of positions as required.
3. Provide team members with an understanding of how other team members operate, why they operate as they do, and the manner in which they are dependent on teammates for information and input.
4. Provide high-fidelity simulations that allow team members to "practice" their teammates' jobs under controlled conditions when job rotation is not feasible (due to safety or other practical considerations).
5. Provide feedback during cross-training exercises that allows team members to formulate accurate explanations for their teammates' behavior and reasonable expectations for their teammates' resource needs.

Specifications

According to the framework offered earlier, the next step in achieving reciprocity in this area is to use these (and other) guidelines to generate specifications for cross-training. This phase of effort is beginning in the cross-training area with the input of various Navy training commands. In particular, the details of implementing cross-training into training for combat information center personnel are being investigated. These specifications will address issues such as:

1. When in the training pipeline should cross-training be implemented?
2. What format should cross-training take (job rotation, simulator practice, knowledge presentation, etc.)?
3. To what extent should team members be cross-trained (how much overlap in job knowledge is required by the task)?
4. Which positions should team members be cross-trained on?
5. What is the criterion measure that indicates that enough interpositional knowledge has been acquired?

Lessons Learned

A final link in the reciprocity chain is to ensure that lessons learned in the course of implementing cross-training are fed back into the research cycle. For example, if it is found that cross-training is only effective (in improving team performance) under certain conditions, it will be of interest to determine how those conditions affect the theoretical assertions about shared knowledge requirements in the task. This finding might suggest that task characteristics moderate the degree of shared knowledge that team members must hold. Alternatively, situational or environmental factors may be most potent in determining the shared knowledge requirements of the task. The important point is that insights gained in the process of applying the training program will affect the original theory that generated it.

Illustration 2: Training Teamwork in the Cockpit

The problem of team coordination in the cockpit did not emerge until technology had pushed pilots to the edge of disaster. Although many early aircraft required only one pilot, the introduction of complex equipment into the cockpit increased work load beyond one individual's capabilities (Prince, Chidester, Cannon-Bowers, & Bowers, 1992). The increase in work load demanded that flight crews be composed of more than one individual. Today, thousands of cockpit crews work daily in an environment with little room for mistakes. Despite the intense environment, it was only recently that aircrews began to receive training in skills necessary for team interaction in the cockpit. Instead, flight training generally emphasized the acquisition of individual technical skills; it taught pilots to focus on their own performance, but did not teach pilots how to perform together effectively as aircrew members (Prince et al., 1992). With little, if any, training on teamwork, numerous problems arose, including incidents of inadequate leadership and monitoring, preoccupation with minor mechanical irregularities, and failures in the delegation of tasks, assignment of responsibilities, and setting of priorities (Prince et al., 1992). The identification of such problems led to research on team coordination skills.

Training Teamwork Skills

Team skill research has revealed some significant findings, which have included evidence that "teamwork" differs from "taskwork" (McIntyre & Salas, 1995). Teamwork skills have been defined as those skills related to functioning effectively as a team member (Cannon-Bowers et al., 1993). In contrast, taskwork skills have been defined as those skills that relate to the execution of the task or the mission (e.g., operating equipment and following procedures; Cannon-Bowers et al., 1993).

Considerable evidence supports the teamwork–taskwork division. First, work has shown that behaviors that are related specifically to team functioning and that are independent of the task at hand are highly important to team outcomes (Oser, McCallum, Salas, & Morgan, 1989; Stout, Cannon-Bowers, Salas, & Morgan, 1990). For example, Oser et al. found that several team behaviors significantly correlated with more effective team performance. These include (a) members offering praise to one another for doing well on a task, (b) members suggesting to one another to recheck work for errors, and (c) members providing suggestions on the best way to locate an error.

Second, team process variables (communication, coordination, compensatory behavior) have been shown to influence team effectiveness (Stout et al., 1990). In other words, the process (communication patterns, coordination) that a team goes through in achieving a particular outcome influences that particular outcome.

Third, effective teamwork behavior has appeared as fairly consistent across tasks (McIntyre & Salas, 1995). McIntyre and Salas examined three teams that operated in similar military environments, but whose tasks were distinctly different. One team faced the task of providing gunfire support to ground troops (naval gunfire support team); another team was responsible for detecting, tracking, and defending against enemy submarines (antisubmarine warfare team); the third team was responsible for detecting, tracking, and defending against enemy surface and subsurface vessels (guided missile teams). McIntyre and Salas identified common teamwork behaviors that all teams exhibited. Thus, crucial teamwork behaviors can be isolated from other task-related behaviors.

After empirical evidence established that teamwork does differ from task-work, the next step was to identify specific team skills. A number of researchers have developed general teamwork skill classifications. For example, one approach to team skill training is a behavioral approach. This was the approach adopted by researchers at the Naval Air Warfare Center Training Systems Division (see Prince & Salas, 1993). The Navy's approach sought to identify the skill dimensions that result in effective flight crew performance and, thus, require training (Prince & Salas, 1993).

A full description of the approach used to determine which teamwork behaviors were related to aircrew coordination appears in Franz, Prince, Cannon-Bowers, and Salas (1990). Briefly, approximately 60 behavioral statements were gathered from reviews of past aircrew coordination literature and team training literature, observations of team development, interviews of job experts, and surveys of the aviation communication. Based on independent classification by job experts, these behaviors were then arranged under seven dimensions: Mission Analysis, Assertiveness, Adaptability/Flexibility, Situational Awareness, Decision Making, Leadership, and Communication. These aircrew coordination dimensions were then decomposed into knowledge skills and attitudes, and a training program was developed.

Validation efforts followed the identification of behaviors. These included a comparison of the perceptions of the importance of aircrew coordination behaviors of aviators from diverse wing communities (Stout, Prince, Baker, Bergondy, & Salas, 1992). In other words, the seven behavioral skill dimensions were the skills that subject matter experts considered vital to effective flight performance. Further, Prince, Brannick, Prince, and Salas (1992) found evidence of discriminant validity between the dimensions, which indicated the multidimensionality of team processes. Helmreich and Foushee (1993) also contributed similar validation efforts. Along with the work by Prince, Salas, and their colleagues, a number of other researchers—focused on a variety of environments—have also approached the team issue from a skill-based perspective. This work has generated a variety of team skill listings. In an effort to synthesize these listings, Cannon-Bowers et al. (1995) consolidated a number of the different teamwork skill labels and definitions found in the literature into the following dimensions: (a) adaptability, (b) shared situational awareness, (c) performance monitoring and feedback, (d) leadership/team management, (e) interpersonal, (f) coordination, (g) communication, and (h) decision making. Associated subskills were also generated for each skill dimension. For example, adaptability is defined as, "The process by which a team is able to use information gathered from the task environment to adjust task strategies through the use of compensatory behavior and reallocation of intrateam resources" (p. 42). The list of alternate labels for adaptability were flexibility, compensatory behavior, and dynamic reallocation of function. In this definition alone, Cannon-Bowers et al. (1995) drew from the work of a number of authors (Johnston & Briggs, 1968; McCallum, Oser, Morgan, & Salas, 1989; McIntyre & Salas, 1995; Oser, Prince, & Morgan, 1990; Streufert & Nogami, 1992). The lengthy list of cited works indicates the large number of teamwork classification/categorization schemata present in current team literature. By sorting through the multitude of definitions and synthesizing them into one succinct list, Cannon-Bowers et al. (1995) demonstrated the links between the different approaches to team skill classification and helped clarify the definition of teamwork.

Principles of Teamwork Skills

Based on the work cited previously, a number of principles pertaining to teamwork skills can be generated.

Principle: Team members need to be trained in teamwork skills.

Because team performance consists of individual and team skills, enhancing team performance involves more than simply training team members individual skills (Denson, 1981; Nieva et al., 1978). Early authors noted that team training usually emphasized instructions of individual skills within a team setting, regardless of the nature of the team task (Briggs & Johnston, 1967; Converse, Dickinson, Tannenbaum, & Salas, 1988; Meister, 1976). Recent writings also noted that team training frequently ignores teamwork skills demanded by interaction requirements of the team task (Salas et al., 1992).

For instance, skills such as situational awareness or decision making require training of team members. It cannot be assumed that these vital skills are automatically possessed by team members (Prince et al., 1992).

Principle: Effective teamwork behavior appears to be consistent across tasks.

Examining a number of different tasks reveals the same basic teamwork behaviors being performed (McIntyre & Salas, 1995). This consistency suggests that team tasks can be conceptualized as requiring separate teamwork skills. It also suggests that some team skills may be generic with respect to the task. That is, it may be possible to train some teamwork skills apart from the task, because they apply to several tasks or task types.

> *Principle:* Process measures are a necessary adjunct to task out-come measures for assessing team performance.

Outcome measures (i.e., the number of targets correctly prosecuted) do not contain information regarding the cause of poor performance, whereas identifying and communicating the behavioral cause of poor performance give team members insight into how to improve performance (Cannon-Bowers, Salas, & Grossman, 1991). This is especially true when the purpose of measurement is to provide feedback that will improve performance (Coovert, Cannon-Bowers, & Salas, 1990).

> *Principle:* Team training must emphasize interaction: mutual dependency.

Some aspects of team training must occur with the actual team. According to Cannon-Bowers et al. (1995), the extent to which actual team members must be present in training depends on the degree of interaction required by the task. In particular, tasks that require extensive coordination will benefit from training in intact teams.

Guidelines for Team Skill Training

Portions of team performance theory have been incorporated into guidelines for training both civilian and military aircraft cockpit crews. Aircrew Coordination Training (ACT) and Cockpit Resource Management (CRM) are training programs built from theory and designed to emphasize the need to integrate and utilize all resources available to the cockpit—human resources as well as hardware and software (Lauber, 1987).

As mentioned earlier, researchers from the U.S. Navy adopted a specific behavioral approach (see Prince & Salas, 1993). Franz et al. (1990) categorized 37 aircrew behaviors under seven skill dimensions: (a) situational awareness, (b) mission analysis, (c) decision making, (d) leadership, (e) communication, (f) adaptability or flexibility, and (g) assertiveness. These aircrew coordination skills were then broken into KSAs, and a training program was developed to parallel the FAA recommendation of aircrew training.

The training program begins by introducing the concepts to the students via lecture and videotaped "action" scenarios. Once introduced to the skills, trainees must have the opportunity to practice the newly learned skills. Simulators have offered this opportunity. Researchers and practitioners work together to create scenarios for simulators. The scenarios depict incidents, situations, and environments that demand the use of team coordination skills. Pilots are given the opportunity to practice the skills in conditions highly similar to the conditions they will encounter in the air.

In light of this, specific guidelines for team training have emerged. Teamwork skills training should:

1. Focus on the behavioral and cognitive requirements of the task to include the following teamwork skills: (a) communication, (b) compensatory behavior, (c) team leadership, (d) assertiveness, (e) decision making, (f) planning, and (g) situation awareness.
2. Provide for presentation of requisite knowledge, demonstration of teamwork behaviors, practice (via role plays and simulation) on teamwork skills, and feedback regarding the quality of teamwork behavior.
3. Provide for specific measurement and diagnosis of teamwork skills via tracking and assessment of moment-to-moment team interactions.
4. Allow team members to gain experience and confidence in exercising teamwork behaviors when required by the task.
5. Provide training in "generic" teamwork skills (communication, leadership, interpersonal) when team members must accomplish a variety of team tasks.

Specifications for Team Training

Based on these and other guidelines, a series of specifications for implementing teamwork skills training for cockpit crews has been generated. Although an exhaustive list of these is too detailed to present here, the following examples are offered (adapted from the Naval Air Warfare Center Training Systems Division, 1993):

1. *Draft List of Tasks; Training Objectives.* The contractor shall develop draft list of collective procedures and tasks for routine flight, emergencies, and each mission type. The draft list should not be a complete task analysis listing, but shall consist of all of the collective tasks and those individual tasks which directly impact the execution of collective tasks...The contractor shall write no fewer than one training objective for each instructional approach (i.e., practice/feedback, demonstration, information) for each collective task. For each collective task, all aircrew coordination behaviors important to the performance of that task shall be addressed in the training objectives. (p. 8)

2. *Produce Training Objectives for Practice/Feedback.* The contractor shall produce training objectives for using the instructional approach of practice and feedback for the tasks selected in accordance with aircrew coordination behaviors. These objectives shall be written such that trainees, in order to fulfill the

objectives, shall be required in simulated or actual conditions to perform the specific aircrew coordination behaviors required for successful performance of the tasks and behaviors selected for Integrated ACT. (p. 12)

3. *Instructor Rating Forms.* The contractor shall modify and adapt one or more of the sample instructor rating forms in Appendix N for instructors and trainees to use during administration of the exercise. The rating form shall contain a list of the aircrew coordination behaviors defined in the training objectives produced for the exercise. The rating form shall permit observers to record whether or not an aircrew coordination behavior has been displayed. (p. 17)

4. *Produce Scenario.* The contractor shall choose a scenario that depicts the aircrew coordination behaviors targeted in the training objectives. The contractor shall draw upon existing sources (e.g., aircraft mishap summaries, transcripts, and subject-matter experts) during the production of mission related scenarios. The contractor shall produce a story board that describes the sequence of events, the visual components, and the audio components of the scenario. (p. 21)

As can be seen from the previous examples, specifications give detailed descriptions of what to do, along with when, how, and why to do it. In these and other specifications, aircrew coordination theory was operationalized for direct application in the development of training programs.

Lessons Learned

Finally, in the process of initial implementation of teamwork skills training, several important lessons learned are beginning to become evident. This feedback has required that particular theoretical assertions be revisited. Briefly, these include (excerpts from Naval Air Warfare Center, Training Systems Division, 1991):

1. Three of the planned eight Aircrew Coordination Training modules (i.e., Mission Analysis, Leadership, Situational Awareness, Decision Making, Communication, Adaptability/Flexibility, Assertiveness, and Introduction) were successfully taught as separate, stand-alone instructional modules. The modularized focus of the training is intended to provide flexibility so that modules can be utilized individually, or together in any combination, as dictated by the Navy/Marine Corps' instructional requirements in a specific situation. (p. 2)

Implications for theory: The finding that teamwork skills can be trained relatively independently has implications for our conceptualization of the notion of teamwork and its training. Specifically, we have begun to hypothesize that the particular configuration of team skills (and related training strategies) depend on task and contextual factors (Cannon-Bowers et al., 1995).

2. It was noted that the introduction module should be tailored for trainee experience level. For example, the full introduction, as presented in the demonstration, may be most suitable for Undergraduate Pilot Training (UPT), and an abbreviated introduction, to review concepts, may be most relevant for Fleet Replacement Squadron (FRS) and squadron level training. (p 26)

Implications for theory: This finding caused us to consider more carefully the potential novice–expert differences in crew coordination behaviors. In particular, we are investigating the manner in which teamwork behaviors are acquired, maintained, and expanded over the course of a crew member's career (Prince & Salas, 1993; Salas, Bowers, Braun, & Jentsch, 1994).

3. While the standardization of the experiences of crews during the scenario was enhanced by the script utilized by the simulator facilitator, it was evident that more detailed "scripting" of contingencies during the introduction of emergencies, when crew reactions are most variable, would improve the sensitivity of the TARGET methodology (i.e., targeted acceptable responses to generated events or tasks). (p. 27)

Implications for research methods: As our ability to define and measure crucial team work behaviors evolves, we are able to specify more detailed event-to-action sequences that define effective performance. The TARGETS framework has been continually enhanced based on lessons from field research and implementation (Fowlkes, Lane, Salas, Franz, & Oser, 1994). As implementation efforts mature, additional feedback will be generated and can serve to validate, refute, expand, and/or enrich the theories of team performance and training.

CONCLUSION

This chapter attempted to highlight a limitation in the training field—that research and practice are not closely coupled. This was done at the risk of sounding overly critical and pretentious. It is hoped that the important message delivered was not lost for this reason. After all, training is one of the most dynamic and exciting fields in which applied psychologists and other professionals can be involved. It is one of the few areas where researchers can actually watch their theories and findings be applied to the solution of important organizational problems. By the same token, practitioners in training are fortunate to have a large body of knowledge on which to draw in addressing training challenges. Where else can the two communities come together and exchange ideas, information, and feedback so that the end user benefits directly from a better product?

The concepts and ideas presented here should give training researchers and practitioners a common language for fostering reciprocity. In particular, the notion of translation mechanisms—if enthusiastically applied—can provide an excellent means to enable and encourage communication among constituents. The outcome will benefit both the science and practice of training.

ACKNOWLEDGMENTS

The views expressed herein are those of the authors and do not reflect the official position of the organization with which they are affiliated.

REFERENCES

Ackerman, P. L. (1987). Individual differences in skill learning: An integration of psychometric and information processing perspectives. *Psychological Bulletin, 102,* 3–37.

Ajzen, I., & Fishbein, M. (1980). *Understanding attitudes and prediction social behavior.* Englewood Cliffs, NJ: Prentice-Hall.

Alluisi, E. A. (1991). The development of technology for collective training: SIMNET, a case history. *Human Factors, 33,* 343–362.

Anastasi, A. (1988). *Psychological testing* (6th ed.). New York: Macmillan.

Anderson, J. R. (1985). *Cognitive psychology and its implications.* New York: Freeman.

Asher, J. J., & Sciarrino, J. A. (1974). Realistic work sample tests: A review. *Personnel Psychology, 27,* 519–534.

Baker, D. P., & Swezey, R. W. (1993). *Transitioning guidelines to specifications: Mixing team training theory and practice.* Unpublished manuscript.

Baker, D. P., & Salas, E. (1992). Principles for measuring teamwork skills. *Human Factors, 34,* 469–475.

Baldwin, T. T., & Ford, J. K. (1988). Transfer training: A review and directions for future research. *Personnel Psychology, 41,* 63–101.

Bandura, A. (1969). *Principles of behavior modification.* New York: Holt, Rinehart & Winston.

Bandura, A. (1982). Self efficacy mechanism in human agency. *American Psychologist, 37,* 122–147.

Bandura, A. (1986). *Social foundations of thought and action.* Englewood Cliffs, NJ: Prentice-Hall.

Bereiter, C., & Scardamalia, M. (1985). Cognitive coping strategies and the problem of "inert" knowledge. In S. Chipman, J. W. Segal, & R. Glaser (Eds.), *Thinking and learning skills: Current research and open questions* (Vol. 2, pp. 65–80). Hillsdale, NJ: Lawrence Erlbaum Associates.

Briggs, G. E., & Johnston, W. A, (1967). *Team training* (NTDC Tech. Rep. No. 1327-4). Orlando, FL: Naval Training Device Center.

Cannon-Bowers, J. A., Prince, C., Salas, E., Owens, J. M., Morgan, B. B., Jr., & Gonos, G. H. (1989). Determinng aircrew coordination effectiveness. In *Proceedings of the Interservice/Industry Training Systems Conference* (Vol. 1, pp. 128–135). Washington, DC: American Defense Preparedness Association.

Cannon-Bowers, J. A., Salas, E., & Converse, S. A. (1990). Cognitive psychology and team training: Training shared mental models and complex systems. *Human Factors Society Bulletin, 33,* 1–4.

Cannon-Bowers, J. A., Salas, E., & Converse, S. A. (1993). Shared mental models in expert team decision making. In J. Castellan, Jr. (Ed.), *Current issues in individual and group decision making* (pp. 221–246). Hillsdale, NJ: Lawrence Erlbaum Associates.

Cannon-Bowers, J. A., Salas, E., & Grossman, J. D. (1991, June). *Improving tactical decision making under stress: Research directions and applied implications.* Paper presented at the International Applied Military Psychology Symposium, Stockholm, Sweden.

Cannon-Bowers, J. A., Tannenbaum, S. I., Salas, E., & Converse, S. A. (1991). Toward an integration of training theory and technique. *Human Factors, 33*, 281–292.

Cannon-Bowers, J. A., Tannenbaum, S. I., Salas, E., & Volpe, C. E. (1995). Defining competencies and establishing team training requirements. In R. Guzzo & E. Salas (Eds.), *Team effectiveness and decision making in organizations* (pp. 330–380). San Francisco: Jossey-Bass.

Carnevale, A., Gainer, L., & Villet, J. (1990). *Training and development in work organizations*. San Francisco: Jossey-Bass.

Cascio, W. F. (1991). *Costing human resources: The financial impact of behavior in organizations* (3rd ed.). Boston: Kent.

Chapanis, A. (1991). To communicate the human factors message, you have to know what the message is and how to communicate it. *Human Factors Society Bulletin, 34*(11), 1–4.

Chase, W. G., & Simon, H. A. (1973). The mind's eye in chess. In W. G. Chase (Ed.), *Visual information processing* (pp. 215–281). New York: Academic Press.

Converse, S. A., Dickinson, T. L., Tannenbaum, S. I., & Salas, E. (1988, April). *Team training and performance: A meta-analysis*. Paper presented at the annual meeting of the Southeastern Psychological Association, New Orleans, LA.

Cook, T. D., Campbell, D. T., & Peracchio, L. (1991). Quasi-experiments. In M. D. Dunnette & L. M. Hough (Eds.), *Handbook of industrial/organizational psychology* (2nd ed., Vol. 2, pp. 4991–5076). Palo Alto, CA: Consulting Psychologists Press.

Coovert, M. D., Cannon-Bowers, J. A., & Salas, E. (1990). Applying mathematical modeling technology to the study of team training and performance. In *Proceedings of the 12th Annual Interservice/Industry Training Systems Conference* (pp. 326–333). Washington, DC: National Security Industrial Association.

Coovert, M. D., & McNelis, K. (1992). Team decision making and performance: A review and proposed approach employing Petri nets. In R. W. Swezey & E. Salas (Eds.), *Teams: Their training and performance* (pp. 247–282). Norwood, NJ: Ablex.

Crawford, A. M., & Crawford, K. S. (1978). Simulation of operational equipment with a computer-based instructional system: A low cost training technology. *Human Factors, 20*, 215–224.

Cream, B. W., Eggemeier, F. T., & Klein, G. A. (1978). A strategy for the development of training devices. *Human Factors, 20*, 145–158.

Cronbach, L. J., & Snow, R. E. (1977). *Aptitudes and instructional methods: A handbook for research on interactions*. New York: Irvington.

Davis, L. T., Gaddy, C. D., & Turney, J. R. (1985). *An approach to team skills training of nuclear power plant control room crews* (NUREG/CR=4255GP-R-123022). Columbia, MD: General Physics Corporation.

de Kleer, J., & Brown, J. S. (1981). Mental models of physical mechanisms and their acquisition. In J. Anderson (Ed.), *Cognitive skills and their acquisition* (pp. 285–309). Hillsdale, NJ: Lawrence Erlbaum Associates.

de Kleer, J., & Brown, J. S. (1983). Assumptions and ambiguities in mechanistic mental models. In D. Gentner & A. L. Stevens (Eds.), *Mental models* (pp. 155–190). Hillsdale, NJ: Lawrence Erlbaum Associates.

Denson, R. W. (1981). *Team training: Literature review and annotated bibliography* (AFHRL-TR-80-40, A9-A099994). Wright-Patterson AFB, OH: Logistics and Technical Training Division, Air Force Human Resources Laboratory.

Dyer, J. L. (1984). Team research and team training: A state of the art review. In F. A. Muckler (Ed.), *Human factors review: 1984* (pp. 285–323). Santa Monica, CA: Human Factors Society.

Ebel, R. L. (1977). Prediction? Validation? Construct validity? *Personnel Psychology, 30*, 55–63.

Eden, D. (1990). *Pygmalion in management*. Lexington, MA: Lexington.

Ericsson, K. A., & Simon, H. A. (1984). *Protocol analysis: Verbal reports as data*. Cambridge, MA: MIT Press.

Fisk, A. D., & Eggemeier, F. T. (1988). Application of automatic/controlled processing theory to training tactical command and control skills: I. Background and analytic methodology. In

Proceedings of the Human Factors Society 32nd annual meeting (pp. 1227–1231). Santa Monica, CA: The Human Factors Society.

Fisk, A. D., Lee, M. D., & Rogers, W. A. (1991). Recombination of automatic processing components: The effects of transfer, reversal, and conflict situations. *Human Factors, 33*(3), 267–280.

Flanagan, J. C. (1954). The critical incident technique. *Psychological Bulletin, 51*, 327–358.

Flanagan, M. F., & Dipboye, R. L. (1981). Research settings in industrial and organizational psychology: Facts, fallacies, and the future. *Personnel Psychology, 34*(1), 37–47.

Fleishman, E. A., & Quaintance, M. K. (1984). *Taxonomies of human performance*. Orlando, FL: Academic Press.

Fowlkes, J. E., Lane, N. E., Salas, E., Franz, T., & Oser, R. (1994). Improving the measurement of team performance: The TARGETs methodology. *Military Psychology, 6*(1), 47–61.

Franz, T. M., Prince, C., Cannon-Bowers, J. A., & Salas, E. (1990). The identification of aircrew coordination skills. In *Proceedings of the 12th Symposium Psychology in the Department of Defense* (pp. 92–96). Springfield, VA: National Technical Information Services.

Gagne, R. M. (1970). *The conditions for learning*. New York: Holt, Rinehart & Winston.

Gist, M. E. (1989). The influence of training method on self-efficacy and idea generation among managers. *Personnel Psychology, 42*, 787–805.

Glaser, R. (1989). Expertise and learning: How do we think about instructional processes now that we have discovered knowledge structures? In D. Klahr & K. Kotovsky (Eds.), *Complex information processing* (pp. 269–282). Hillsdale, NJ: Lawrence Erlbaum Associates.

Glickman, A. S., Zimmer, S., Montero, R. C., Guerette, P. J., Campbell, W. J., Morgan, B. B., Jr., & Salas, E. (1987). *The evolution of teamwork skills: An empirical assessment with implications for training* (Tech. Rep. NTSC 87-016). Arlington, VA: Office of Naval Research.

Goldstein, A. P., & Sorcher, M. (1974). *Changing supervisory behavior*. New York: Pergamon.

Goldstein, I. L. (1980). Training in work organizations. *Annual Review of Psychology, 31*, 229–272.

Goldstein, I. L. (1993). *Training in organizations*. Pacific Grove, CA: Brooks/Cole.

Goldstein, I. L., Braverman, E. P., & Goldstein, H. W. (1991). The use of needs assessment in training systems design. In K. Wexley (Ed.), *Developing human resources* (Vol. 5, pp. 35–75). Washington, DC: BNA Books.

Guerette, P. J., Miller, D. L., Glickman, A. S., Morgan, B. B., Jr., & Salas, E. (1987). *Instructional processes and strategies in team training* (NTSC Tech. Rep. No. 87-016). Orlando, FL: Naval Training Systems Center.

Guion, R. M. (1978). Content validity in moderation. *Personnel Psychology, 31*, 205–214.

Hackman, J. R. (1983). *A normative model of work team effectiveness* (Tech. Rep. No. 2). New Haven, CT: Yale University Press.

Hackman, J. R. (1987). The design of workteams. In J. Lorsch (Ed.), *Handbook of organizational behavior* (pp. 315–342). Eglewood Cliffs, NJ: Prentice-Hall.

Hall, E., & Rizzo, W. (1975). *An assessment of U.S. Navy tactical team training* (TAEG Report No. 18). Orlando, FL: Training Analysis and Evaluation Group.

Hays, R. T., & Singer, M. J. (1989). *Simulation fidelity in training system design*. New York: Springer-Verlag.

Hedge, J. W., & Lipscomb, M. S. (1987). *Walk through performance testing: An innovative approach to work sample testing* (Tech. Rep. AFHRL-TP-87-8). Brooks AFB, TX: Training Systems Division, Air Force Human Resources Laboratory.

Helmreich, R. L., & Foushee, H. C. (1993). Why crew resource management? Empirical and theoretical bases of human factors training in aviation. In E. L. Wiener, R. L. Helmreich, & B. G. Kanki (Eds.), *Cockpit resource management* (pp. 3–46). San Diego, CA: Academic Press.

Holding, D. H. (1987). Concepts of training. In G. Salvendy (Ed.), *Handbook of human factors* (pp. 939–962). Canada: Wiley.

Ilgen, D. R., Fisher, C. D., & Taylor, M. S. (1979). Consequences of individual feedback on behavior in organizations. *Journal of Applied Psychology, 64*, 349–371.

Johnson-Laird, P. (1983). *Mental models*. Cambridge, MA: Harvard University Press.

Johnston, W. A., & Briggs, G. E. (1968). Team performance as a function of team arrangement and workload. *Journal of Applied Psychology, 52*(2), 89–94.

Kelley, H. H. (1972). Attribution in social interaction. In W. W. Jones, D. E. Kanhouse, H. H. Kelly, S. Valins, & B. Weiner (Eds.), *Attribution: Perceiving the causes of behavior*. Morristown, NJ: General Learning Press.

Kessler, J., Macpherson, L., & Mirabella, A. (1988). *Army maintenance training and evaluation simulation systems (AMTESS): Lessons learned* (Research Rep. No. 1471). Alexandria, VA: U.S. Army Research Institute.

Kieras, D. E. (1988). What mental model should be taught: Choosing instructional content for complex engineering systems. In J. Psotka, L. D. Massey, & S. A. Mutter (Eds.), *Intelligent tutoring systems: Lessons learned* (pp. 85–111). Hillsdale, NJ: Lawrence Erlbaum Associates.

Kirkpatrick, D. L. (1976). Evaluation of training. In R. L. Craig (Ed.), *Training and development handbook: A guide to human resources development* (pp. 18-1–18-27). New York: McGraw-Hill.

Klein, G. A. (1989). Recognition-primed decisions. In W. B. Rouse (Ed.), *Advances in man-machine systems research* (Vol. 5, pp. 47–92). Greenwich, CT: JAI.

Kleinman, D. L., & Serfaty, D. (1989). In R. Gilson, J. P. Kincaid, & B. Goldiez (Eds.), *Proceedings of the Interservice Networked Simulation for Training Conference* (pp. 22-27). Orlando, FL.

Kraiger, K., Ford, J. K., & Salas, E. (1993). Application of cognitive, skill-based and affective theories of learning outcomes to new methods of training evaluation [Monograph]. *Journal of Applied Psychology, 78*(2), 311–328.

Kuhl, J. (1985). Volitional mediators of cognition-behavior consistency: Self-regulatory processes and action versus state orientation. In J. Kuhl & J. Beckman (Eds.), *Action control: From cognition to behavior* (pp. 11–39). Berlin: Springer-Verlag.

Kyllonen, P. C., & Alluisi, E. A. (1987). Learning and forgetting facts and skills. In G. Salvendy (Ed.), *Handbook of human factors* (pp. 124–153). New York: Wiley.

Kyllonen, P. C., & Shute, V. J. (1989). A taxonomy of learning skills. In P. L. Ackerman, R. J. Sternberg, & R. Glaser (Eds.), *Learning and individual differences: Advances in theory and research* (pp. 117–163). New York: Freeman.

Latham, G. P. (1988). Human resource training and development. *Annual Review of Psychology, 39*, 545–582.

Latham, G. P., & Saari, L. (1979). The application of social learning theory to training supervisors through behavior modeling. *Journal of Applied Psychology, 64*, 239–246.

Lauber, J. K. (1987). Cockpit resource management: Background studies and rationale. In H. W. Orlady & H. C. Foushee (Eds.), *Cockpit resource management training* (Tech. Rep. No. NASA CP2455). Moffett Field, CA: NASA Ames Research Center.

Lawshe, C. H. (1975). A quantitative approach to content validity. *Personnel Psychology, 28*, 563–575.

Levine, E. L. (1983). *Everything you ever wanted to know about job analysis*. Tampa, FL: Mariner.

Levine, E. L., & Baker, C. V. (1991, April). *Team task analysis: A procedural guide and test of the methodology*. Paper presented at the annual meeting of the Society of Industrial and Organizational Psychology, St. Louis, MO.

Locke, E. A, & Latham, G. P. (1990). *A theory of goal setting and task performance*. Englewood Cliffs, NJ: Prentice-Hall.

Manz, C., & Sims, H. P., Jr. (1989). *Superleadership: Leading others to lead themselves*. New York: Simon & Schuster.

Marx, R. D. (1982). Relapse prevention for managerial training: A model for maintenance of behavior change. *Academy of Management Review, 7*, 433–441.

McCallum, G. A., Oser, R., Morgan, B. B., Jr., & Salas, E. (1989, August). *An investigation of the behavioral components of teamwork*. Paper presented at the annual meeting of the American Psychological Association, New Orleans, LA.

McIntyre, R. M., & Salas, E. (1995). Measuring and managing for team performance: Emerging principles from complex environments. In R. Guzzo & E. Salas (Eds.), *Team effectiveness and decision making in organizations* (pp. 9–45). San Francisco: Jossey-Bass.

Meister, D. (1976). Team functions. In D. Meister (Ed.), *Behavioral foundations of system development* (pp.231-296). New York: Wiley.

Moore, J. L., & Gordon, S. C. (1988). Conceptual graphs as instructional tools. *Proceedings of the Human Factors Society 32nd annual meeting* (pp. 1289–1293). Santa Monica, CA: The Human Factors Society.

Morgan, B. B., Jr., Coates, G. D., Kirby, H., & Alluisi, E. A. (1984). Individual and group performances as functions of the team-training load. *Human Factors, 26* (2), 127–142.

Morgan, B. B., Jr., Glickman, A. S., Woodard, E. A., Blaiwes, A. S., & Salas, E. (1986). *Measurement of team behaviors in a navy environment* (Tech. Rep. No. TR-86-014). Orlando, FL: Naval Training Systems Center.

Naval Air Warfare Center Training Systems Division. (1991). *Draft lessons learned from the demonstration of aircrew coordination training methodology in the CH-53 community.* Orlando, FL: Author.

Naval Air Warfare Center Training Systems Division. (1993). *Draft lessons learned from the demonstration of aircrew coordination training methodology in the CH-53 community.* Orlando, FL: Author.

Nieva, V. F., Fleishman, E. A., & Reick, A. (1978). *Team dimensions: Their identity, their measurement and their relationships* (Final Tech. Rep. Contract No. DAH19-78-C-001). Washington, DC: Advanced Research Resources Organization.

Noe, R. A., & Schmitt, N. (1986). The influence of trainee attitudes on training effectiveness: Test of a model. *Personnel Psychology, 39,* 497–524.

Orasanu, J. M. (1990). Diagnostic approaches to learning: Measuring what, how and how much. In N. Frederiksen, R. Glaser, A. Lesgold, & M. Shafto (Eds.), *Diagnostic monitoring of skill and knowledge acquisition* (pp. 393–405). Hillsdale, NJ: Lawrence Erlbaum Associates.

Orasanu, J. M., & Salas, E. (1993). Team decision making in complex environments. In G. Klein, J. M. Orasanu, & R. Calderwood (Eds.), *Decision making in action: Models and methods* (pp. 327–345). Norwood, NJ: Ablex.

Oser, R. L., McCallum, G. A., Salas, E., & Morgan, B. B., Jr. (1989). *Toward a definition of teamwork: An analysis of critical team behavior* (NTSC Tech. Rep. No. 89-004). Orlando, FL: Naval Training Systems Center.

Oser, R. L., Prince, C., & Morgan, B. B., Jr. (1990, October). *Differences in aircrew communication content as a function of flight requirement: Implications for operational aircrew training.* Poster presented at the 34th annual meeting of the Human Factors Society, Orlando, FL.

Prince, A., Brannick, M. T., Prince, C., & Salas, E. (1992). Team process measurement and implications for training. In *Proceedings of the 36th annual meeting of the Human Factors Society* (pp. 1351–1355). Atlanta, GA: The Human Factors Society.

Prince, C., Chidester, T. R., Cannon-Bowers, J. A., & Bowers, C. A. (1992). Aircrew coordination: Achieving teamwork in the cockpit. In R. W. Swezey & E. Salas (Eds.), *Teams: Their training and performance* (pp. 329–353). Norwood, NJ: Ablex.

Prince, C., & Salas, E. (1993). Training and research for teamwork in the military aircrew. In E. L. Wiener, B. G. Kanki, & R. L. Helmreich (Eds.), *Cockpit resource management* (pp. 337–366). San Diego, CA: Academic Press.

Rasmussen, J. (1979). *On the structure of knowledge—a morphology of mental models in a man-machine system context* (Tech. Rep. Riso-M-2192). Roskilde, Denmark: Riso National Laboratory.

Redding, R. E. (1989). Perspectives on cognitive task-analysis: The state of the state of the art. In *Proceedings of the Human Factors Society 33rd annual meeting* (pp. 1348–1352). Santa Monica, CA: The Human Factors Society.

Revans, R. W. (1982). *The origin and growth of action learning.* Hunt, England: Chatwell-Bratt, Bickley.

Rossi, P. H., & Freeman, H. E. (1982). *Evaluation: A systematic approach* (2nd ed.). Beverly Hills, CA: Sage.

Rouiller, J. Z., & Goldstein, I. L. (1993). The relationship between organizational transfer climate and positive transfer of training. *Human Resource Development Quarterly, 4,* 377–390.

Rouse, W. B., Cannon-Bowers, J. A., & Salas, E. (1992). The role of mental models in team performance in complex systems. *IEEE Transactions on Systems, Man, and Cybernetics, 22*(6), 1296–1308.

Rouse, W. B., & Morris, N. M. (1986). On looking into the black box: Prospects and limits in the search for mental models. *Psychological Bulletin, 100,* 349–363.

Rutman, L. (1980). *Planning useful evaluations.* Beverly Hills, CA: Sage.

Salas, E., Bowers, C. A., Braun, C. C., & Jentsch, F. G. (1994, April). *The development of team process: An empirical investigation.* Paper presented at the 9th annual conference of the Society for Industrial and Organizational Psychology, Nashville, TN.

Salas, E., Dickinson, T. L., Converse, S. A., & Tannenbaum, S. I. (1992). Toward an understanding of team performance and training. In R. W. Swezey & E. Salas (Eds.), *Teams: Their training and performance* (pp. 3–29). Norwood, NJ: Ablex.

Schneider, B., & Konz, A. (1989). Strategic job analysis. *Human Resource Management, 28,* 51–63.

Schneider, W., & Shiffrin, R. M. (1977). Controlled and automatic human information processing: I. Detection, search, attention. *Psychological Review, 84,* 1–66.

Schvaneveldt, R. W. (1990). *Pathfinder associative networks: Studies in knowledge organization.* Norwood, NJ: Ablex.

Steiner, I. D. (1972). *Group process and productivity.* Orlando, FL: Academic Press.

Stout, R. J., Cannon-Bowers, J. A., Morgan, B. B., Jr., & Salas, E. (1990). Does crew coordination behavior impact performance? *Proceedings fothe Human Factors Society 34th annual meeting* (pp. 1382–1386). Santa Monica, CA: The Human Factors Society.

Stout, R. J., Prince, C., Baker, D. P., Bergondy,, M. L., & Salas, E. (1992). Aircrew coordination: What does it take? In *Proceedings of the 13th Biennial Psychology in the Department of Defense Symposium* (pp. 133–137). Colorado Springs, CO: U.S. Air Force Academy Government Printing.

Streufert, S., & Nogami, G. (1992). Cognitive complexity and team decision making. In R. W. Swezey & E. Salas (Eds.), *Teams: Their training and performance* (pp. 127–152). Norwood, NJ: Ablex.

Swezey, R. W., & Salas, E. (1992). Guidelines for use in team-training development. In R. W. Swezey & E. Salas (Eds.), *Teams: Their training and performance* (pp. 219–245). Norwood, NJ: Ablex.

Tannenbaum, S. I., Mathieu, J. E., Salas, E., & Cannon-Bowers, J. A. (1991, April). *An examination of the factors that influence training effectiveness: A model and research agenda.* Paper presented at the annual meeting of the Society for Industrial and Organizational Psychology, St. Louis, MO.

Tannenbaum, S. I., & Yukl, G. (1992). Training and development in work organizations. *Annual Review of Psychology, 43,* 399–441.

Thornton, G. C. III., & Cleveland, J. N. (1990). Developing managerial talent through simulation. *American Psychologist, 45,* 190–199.

Travillian, K. K., Volpe, C. E., Cannon-Bowers, J. A., & Salas, E. (1993). Cross-training highly interdependent teams: Effects on team process and team performance. In *Proceedings of the 37th annual Human Factors and Ergonomics Society Conference* (pp. 1243–1247), Santa Monica, CA: The Human Factors Society.

Volpe, C. E., Cannon-Bowers, J. A., Salas, E., & Spector, A. (in press). The impact of cross-training on team functioning. *Human Factors.*

Vroom, V. H. (1964). *Work and motivation.* New York: Wiley.

Wiener, E. L., Kanki, B. G., & Helmreich, R. L. (1993). *Cockpit resource management.* San Diego, CA: Academic Press.

Wightman, D. C., & Lintern, G. (1985). Part-task training for tracking and manual control. *Human Factors, 27,* 267–283.

Wilson, J. R., & Rutherford, A. (1989). Mental models: Theory and application in human factors. *Human Factors, 31,* 617–634.

12

The Unintended Organizational Consequences of Technology Training: Implications for Training Theory, Research, and Practice

Katherine J. Klein
University of Maryland at College Park

R. Scott Ralls
North Carolina Department of Commerce

Traditional models of training evaluation and effectiveness are rational and micro, designed to assess the extent to which individual trainees meet the intended and predetermined goals of training (Arvey & Cole, 1989; Cascio, 1989; Wexley & Latham, 1991). Yet training in organizations is often haphazard, its goals poorly defined and uncertain, and its effects both unexpected and diffuse (cf. March & Olsen, 1976; Weick, 1976). In this chapter, we offer a novel approach to training evaluation and effectiveness. Focusing on technology training, we eschew the rational and micro, exploring instead the potential unanticipated and unintended consequences of training on workplace processes and characteristics.

In outlining this perspective, we draw on our in-depth, qualitative research on the implementation of computerized manufacturing technologies. The qualitative findings are not used as evidence or proof, but as a starting point for the development of novel research propositions regarding the unintended consequences of technology training on: (a) employee sense-making regarding the new technology; (b) the distribution of expertise and power in supervisor–supervisee relationships, and in organizations in general; and (c) job design, organizational structure, and culture. The findings of this qualitative research suggest that technology training may have unintended and unanticipated effects—some positive, some negative—on each of these three domains. The three domains represent differing levels of organizational analysis: individuals, dyads, and organizations. Further, the certainty and immediacy of training effects on each domain vary substantially. Training's effects on employee sense–making appear most certain and immediate. Training's effects on job design, organizational structure, and culture appear most uncertain and most distal in time. The three domains represent the likely range of the unintended consequences of technology training.

We begin with a brief overview of the nature and effects of new computerized technologies in the workplace. We then describe our qualitative research methods. Next, we explore, and present research propositions regarding the unintended effects of technology training on each of the three domains listed earlier. In the final sections of the chapter, we discuss the generalizability of our propositions and highlight the distinctive elements of out perspective for the conceptualization and study of organizational training.

COMPUTERIZED TECHNOLOGIES AT WORK: A BRIEF DESCRIPTION

In the past decade, computerized technologies have changed the face of the workplace. Between the years 1984 and 1989 (the latest year census figures were available), the number of workers who reported using a computer at work increased by over 50%, from 24.6% to 37.4% of the workforce (Krueger, 1993). Over 35% of business establishments reported that they had personal computers in 1989, compared with fewer than 10% in 1984. This trend reflects, in large part, the 28% annual decline in the adjusted real price of microcomputers between 1982 and 1988 (Berndt & Griliches, 1990; Krueger, 1993). Experts predict that, by the year 2010, new information technologies will affect the jobs of approximately 90% of the workforce (Hines, 1994).

Sophisticated computerized technologies are now common in both factories and offices. On the factory floor, traditional blue-collar work has been revolutionized by such new technologies as computerized numerical control, flexible manufacturing systems, robotics, computer-assisted manufacturing, and computer-assisted process planning (Majchrzak & Klein, 1987; Office of Technology Assessment, 1984). In offices, white collar work has been forever changed by such technologies as the microcomputer, computer-aided design (CAD), intelligent systems, and other forms of office automation, such as facsimile (FAX) technology and electronic mail (e-mail) systems (Office of Technology Assessment, 1985). Training plays a crucial role in the implementation of computerized technologies in the workplace. In our review of research on the implementation of computerized technologies (Klein & Ralls, 1995), we found that training was mentioned as a key determinant of implementation success in 67% of the 18 qualitative technology implementation studies identified.

McKersie and Walton (1991) reported that, in their six case studies of technology implementation, "everyone we interviewed underscored the importance of training for facilitating organizational change and the introduction of new technology" (p. 258). Quantitative studies of technology implementation, although more limited in number than qualitative studies of the topic, have also underscored the importance of training for effective computerized technology implementation. Fleischer, Liker, and Arnsdorf (1988) found that the number of hours of CAD training that users received was significantly and positively related to users' self-rated CAD proficiency, and that user proficiency was in turn positively correlated with the impact of CAD on core functions of the design task.

Despite the importance of training for successful computerized technology implementation, industry observers and academic researchers alike are typically quite critical of the quantity (too little) and quality (poor) of much of the computerized technology training that organizations provide (Anderson Soft-Teach, 1993; Klein & Ralls, 1995; Stamps, 1993). A 1987 survey of 1,368 U.S. establishments in 21 different manufacturing industries found that, although 56% of workers in companies with programmable automation had some responsibility for programming machinery, only 16% of these work sites offered classes in parts programming (Kelley, 1989). The establishments most likely to provide training in programming—very large plants of multiplant corporations—were the least likely to allow front-line machinists to program the machines. Smaller, less hierarchical, plants in which front-line employees were more likely to have programming responsibilities, were least likely to offer training. Not only do too few employers offer training, this study concluded, but training is often least available to those most in need.

THE IMPACT OF COMPUTERIZED TECHNOLOGIES ON ORGANIZATIONAL PROCESSES AND CHARACTERISTICS

With the growth of computerization, research on the consequences of computerization on performance, productivity, structure, job characteristics, employee satisfaction, and related outcomes has burgeoned (e.g., Attewell, 1992; Chao & Kozlowski, 1986; Ettlie & Reza, 1992; Finholt & Sproull, 1990; Klein, Hall, & Laliberte, 1990; March & Sproull, 1990; Osterman, 1991; Snell & Dean, 1992; Wall, Jackson & Davids, 1992). The studies paint an inconsistent picture of the effects of computerization. Some studies conclude that computerization increases productivity; others conclude that it does not. Some studies conclude that computerization increases centralization and deskills jobs; others conclude that it has the opposite effects. Some studies show that it enhances job satisfaction; some conclude that it does not.

The results of these studies defy technological determinism—the view that specific technologies have direct and uniform effects across organizational settings. Abandoning technological determinism, analysts now suggest that the impact of identical computerized systems may vary significantly from organization to organization as a function of managerial choice regarding how the technology is implemented and used.

For example, Zuboff (1988) suggested that new computerized technologies have the capacity to either "automate" or "informate" work. Computers can be used to either routinize tasks or to enrich them:

As long as the technology is treated narrowly in its automating function, it perpetuates the logic of the industrial machine that, over the course of this century, has made it possible to rationalize work while decreasing the dependence on human skills. However, when the technology also informates the processes to which it is applied, it increases the explicit information content of tasks and sets into motion a series of dynamics that will ultimately reconfigure the nature of work and the social relationships that organize productive activity. (pp. 10–11)

Similarly, Zammuto and O'Connor (1992) argued that benefits gained from advanced manufacturing technologies are "not solely attributable to these new technologies" (p. 703), but depend instead on the culture of the manufacturing organization. Recent research (Barley, 1986; Wall et al., 1992) lends empirical support to the assertion that the same technology may have differing consequences in different settings (or even the same setting, over time), depending on the nature of managerial choices during implementation.

In this chapter, we build on existing research and theory describing the variable effects of computerized technology implementation across settings. Our contribution to the discussion is to argue that the impact of the technology on the organization is shaped in part by the training process; the nature and content of the training, who is trained, and equally importantly, who is not trained (Klein et al., 1990). We argue, as suggested above, that technology training may influence not only the outcomes of traditional training research (employee knowledge and skills), but also employee attitudes, supervisor–subordinate relations, organizational power, job design, organizational structure, and organizational culture.

AN OVERVIEW OF OUR QUALITATIVE RESEARCH ON COMPUTERIZED TECHNOLOGY IMPLEMENTATION

During the late 1980s and early 1990s, we conducted several qualitative case studies of the implementation of computerized technologies in office and manufacturing settings. We rely on the results of qualitative case studies of: (a) a construction and engineering firm in the process of implementing computer–aided design and drafting (CADD), (b) a wire manufacturer in the process of implementing computerized manufacturing resource planning (MRP II), and (c) a food products manufacturer also implementing MRP II.

In the construction and engineering firm, we interviewed 26 managers, engineers, designers, and drafters following the initial purchase and implementation of CADD. In the wire company, we interviewed 37 managers, supervisors, and production and production–support personnel following the initial purchase and implementation of MRP II. Finally, in the food products company, we first interviewed 31 division managers and professional, staff personnel prior to the MRP II implementation, and later conducted interviews in two of the division's plants following the MRP II implementation in these plants. In these two plants, we interviewed, respectively, 20 and 27 managers, supervisors, and production and production–support personnel. Thus, the results highlighted here were drawn from interviews with 141 individuals.

Following the recommendations of Yin (1981, 1984) and Eisenhardt (1989), our qualitative studies were intentionally exploratory, designed to develop rather than test hypotheses regarding the dynamics of computerized technology implementation. Using structured interviews, employees were questioned about numerous aspects of the implementation process, including: adequacy of training, user friendliness of software, level of top management support for the technology, extent of user support, nature of rewards for technology use, and so on. Technology training was not the focus of this research, but, given the fundamental role of training in technology implementation, training was a central topic in the interviews.

At each site, employees were interviewed either singly or in small groups of two to four employees. Employees ranged from top management to production operators. Except at the highest levels of management, employees were randomly sampled to participate in the interviews. Employees interviewed in groups held approximately the same status level within the organization, and at no time were both a supervisor and his or her subordinate interviewed simultaneously. The interviews followed a structured format to ensure that all employees holding similar jobs at similar ranks in the organization received the same questions.

Two researchers were present at each interview and made detailed notes of all responses. Some interviews were also taped and transcribed. Members of the research team read over the transcripts of the interviews from each setting, generating setting-specific themes articulated in multiple interviews within the setting. These themes inform our understanding of technology implementation and offer a starting point for our exploration of the possible unintended consequences of technology training.

THE UNINTENDED CONSEQUENCES
OF TECHNOLOGY TRAINING:
EMPLOYEE SENSE-MAKING REGARDING
THE NEW TECHNOLOGY

Organizational changes arouse uncertainty and anxiety (Isabella, 1990; Kotter & Schlesinger, 1979). Having learned that changes are forthcoming, employees struggle to make sense of the news, so as to anticipate how the changes will affect them. Computerized technologies are no exception. With the news that a new computerized system is coming, employees endeavor to make sense of the impending event: Why are we getting a new computer system? Will the new system make my job easier or harder, more boring or more interesting? Does the computer purchase mean that management finds employees expendable or worthy of investment?

Weick (1990) captured this view in his discussion of "technology as equivoque":

> An *equivoque* is something that admits of several possible or plausible interpretations and therefore can be esoteric, subject to misunderstandings, uncertain, complex, and recondite. . . . [New technologies] make limited sense because so little is visible and so much is transient, and they make many different kinds of sense because the dense interactions that occur within them can be modeled in so many different ways. Because new technologies are equivocal, they require ongoing structuring and sense–making if they are to be managed. (p. 2)

As employees attempt to make sense of new computerized equipment, they develop—alone and in concert—interpretations of the new technology. Their interpretations are unlikely to be the result of a careful and knowledgeable evaluation of the computer system. Employees lack the technical ability for such an analysis. Computerized systems are too complex, and their potential applications are too numerous. The answers to employees' questions are often the product of employee discussion and speculation, tempered by employees' experience of their organization and of the new technology. Over time, employees' interpretations, fears, hopes, and rumors are confirmed or rebutted, and the sense employees have made of the computer system takes on the aura of truth. Thus, Goodman, Griffith, and Fenner (1990) argued that the sense-making or social construction process may influence employees' views of a new computer system:

> This social construction of the meaning of the technology partly determines how people use and react to the technology. ... For example, if the employees attribute favorable, human-like qualities to the robot, their acceptance of and behavior toward the robot will be more positive than if they attribute negative, machinelike qualities. ... The process of introducing technological change is independent of

the technology, and yet the process is the major way people learn and, hence, construct an image of the technology. (pp. 52–53)

On the basis of our case study research, we suggest that technology training may profoundly influence the sense employees make of their new technology, and thus employees' ultimate acceptance or rejection of the technology. Training may have unintended, but positive, effects on employee sense-making. An organization's failure to anticipate these potential benefits, and to use technology training accordingly, represents a lost opportunity to facilitate employee acceptance of the new technology.

Case Study Highlights

In every company in which we have studied the implementation of computerized technologies, we have heard employees wonder aloud about the meaning and consequences of increasing computerization. Employee questions and concerns were most acute and insistent, however, at the wire company—a company that offered its employees minimal training regarding the new computerized inventory control and barcoding system. The following comments from two production employees were typical:

I feel lost. The day it arrived, they said, "Well, here it is. It's a computer. You better grow up and use it." I was explained nothing, not what it will do for the company, not what it'll do for me.

I don't totally understand the system. They didn't really tell people much about it. What is the end goal for the system? What will it do for me? I don't know the answers to these questions.

Supervisors, too, were uncertain of the meaning and benefits of the new system:

I remember the day we picked the system like it was yesterday. About the time to sign the check, Jones (a pseudonym for the president of the company) called a meeting and asked, "Why are we doing this?" But no real answer ever came out. To this day, I still don't know if they know. I'm sure upper management must have a goal, but it has never been communicated to me, and if it hasn't been communicated to me and other supervisors, I can't believe that it has been communicated to the operators.

Most employees, we have observed, will not tolerate such ambiguity for long. Through a process of interactive social construction, many employees will come to a conclusion about the meaning—the sense—of the new technology. Many employees at the wire company no longer pondered what sense to make of the new technology. Their sense of the technology was clear: They came to see the new computer system as an insult—an indicator of management's disdain for and distrust of production employees. Some saw the new system as beneath them, requiring demeaning paperwork:

> When you're a machine operator, you shouldn't have to deal with paperwork. They should ask someone else to do it. It feels like you're a secretary having to handle all that paperwork.

Others saw the technology as proof that management would rather invest in machines than people:

> They're investing all this money in this system, but they won't give a decent increase in wages. If they gave more money, people would work better at it. Money is talk.

Finally, some saw the computer system as both a burden and a "Big Brother":

> The system records who screwed up and who didn't. If you mess up any bars, they know it. Maybe if they paid us for that, we wouldn't mind. It doesn't make the job any easier. It's just something else you've gotta do.

Such conclusions are by no means inevitable. Under some circumstances, employees may make more positive sense of new computerized systems. They may come to see new technologies as benign and even helpful to themselves and their organizations. Technology training may play a powerful role in this regard.

The food products company that we studied implemented a computerized system similar to the one used by the wire company. Employees in that company's plants readily described the benefits of their new system. Employees had not directly experienced these benefits; the computer system was too new for that. The employees expressed positive views and interpretations of the systems—views that they first heard during training:

> In the future, if everything works the way it is supposed to work, I would see a smoother running operation with less cycle counting and less variances that we have to track down because we don't know where it is at. That sounds like kind of a utopia, but it was presented in this utopia kind of fashion.

> The way I understand it, the new system was installed so that the plant could more accurately pinpoint a problem in a product. Now, we could pinpoint the problem and instead of destroying $20,000 worth of material, we would destroy only $4,000 to $5,000.

The company wanted a better way to trace the vendors' lots for reasons of a recall or a problem somewhere out in the field. With the new system, they'll be able to look back and trace, "Well, this vendor lot number went in this, so we know this is the one."

This company appeared to manage the sense–making process and influence the social construction of the new computer system's meaning, at least in part, through their training program, in which all of the employees quoted earlier participated. Based on these qualitative findings, we suggest that computer training may not only teach employees how to use the new technology, but it may also have the often unintended, yet typically, positive effect of teaching employees what to think of the new technology.

Research Propositions

The discussion above rests upon two fundamental propositions:

> Proposition 1: Employees perceive workplace computerization to be an ambiguous, uncertainty-arousing event. To employees, the consequences of computerization are not obvious.
>
> Proposition 2: Employees engage in sense-making regarding workplace phenomena when those phenomena are perceived to have significant, but uncertain, consequences.

These propositions are fairly well established in the organizational behavior and technology literatures (Barley, 1986; Goodman et al., 1990; Weick, 1990), although, to our knowledge, neither proposition has been formally tested.

Based on these propositions and our case study findings, we suggest a third proposition:

> Proposition 3: Technology training may influence the sense that employees make of new workplace computerization.

The results of our case studies suggest that technology training is not simply a medium through which employees acquire new technical skills. It is a conduit of intended and unintended messages that employees use to make sense of the new technology.

The messages of greatest significance to employees may be those describing the purposes of the new technology: Why was the technology purchased? What are the benefits to the company? If technology training teaches employees *how* to use the new system, but not *why* to use it, employees will reach their own conclusions; they will make their own sense of the technology. Thus:

Proposition 4:   Technology training is most likely to influence em-
                 ployee sense-making regarding the new technology if
                 the training provides employees with an explanation
                 of the intended benefits of the new technology for the
                 organization (rather than simply teaching employees to
                 operate the new technology).

The sense of the new technology that employees develop in response to
explanations of the benefits of the new technology to the organization
depends, in part, on employees' perceptions of the link between employees'
fate and their organization's fate. In employee eyes, what good is a new
technology that benefits the organization and yet has no positive impact
upon employees? Thus:

Proposition 5:   Technology training that provides employees with an
                 explanation of the intended benefits of the new technol-
                 ogy for the organization will have a positive influence on
                 employee sense-making if employees perceive that they
                 benefit personally from improvements in organizational
                 performance.

The power of technology training to influence employee sense-making may
vary from employee to employee and from organization to organization. The
previously stated propositions suggest that employees are most likely to engage
in sense-making and are most open to the influence of technology training (on
sense-making) when they are uncertain about the likely consequences of
computerization. If, for whatever reason, employees are certain that they can
correctly anticipate the consequences of computerization, their sense of the
new computer system is relatively unlikely to change as a result of participation
in technology training; their minds may already be made up.

We speculate that four factors may influence how certain employees are in
their views of a new computer system, and how susceptible they are to the
sense-making impact of technology training. First, an employee's prior
experience with computerization may influence the certainty of his or her sense
of a new computer system:

Proposition 6:   The less experience an employee has had with com-
                 puter systems (both prior computer systems and the
                 specific computer system in question), the less certain
                 the employee's sense of the new computer will be,
                 and the more technology training will influence the
                 employee's sense of the new technology.

If an employee has had a great deal of experience with computers in general, and/or with the specific computer system in question, his or her assessment of the new computer system is likely to be quite fixed. Thus, the influence of training on employee sense-making regarding computerization is likely to be greatest for those employees who are least experienced with and knowledgeable about computers.

Several organizational characteristics may also influence the certainty of an employee's sense of a new computer system. First, the consequences of past organizational interventions may influence the certainty of employees' views of the new computer system. If past interventions have been uniformly beneficial to employees, employees are likely to be relatively certain that the new computer system will also yield benefits. Conversely, if past interventions have been uniformly detrimental to employees, employees are likely to be relatively certain that the new computer system will, like past interventions, prove damaging to employees' interests. Thus:

> Proposition 7: If organizational interventions in the past have proved neither uniformly beneficial nor uniformly detrimental to employees, employees' sense of the new computer is likely to be relatively uncertain, and employees are likely to be relatively susceptible to the influence of technology training on sense-making.

Employees' trust in management may have a comparable effect. If employees have a great deal of trust in their managers, employees are likely to approach the new computer system with positive and relatively certain expectations. However, if employees distrust management, convinced of their deviousness and ill will, employees are likely to approach the new computer system with negative and relatively certain expectations. Employees who view management with a mixture of respect and suspicion, enthusiasm and cynicism, are likely to be more uncertain of the likely consequences of computerization. "One can't be sure what our management will do," they may think. Thus:

> Proposition 8: If organizational managers are viewed by employees as neither exceptionally good nor exceptionally bad, employees' sense of the new computer system is likely to be relatively uncertain, and employees are likely to be relatively susceptible to the influence of technology training on sense-making.

The certainty of employees' views of computerization may be influenced by the organization's recent financial performance. If the organization's recent financial performance has been very poor, employees are likely to view the new technology as an attempt to cut labor costs. If the organization's recent financial performance has been very good, employees are likely to view the new technology as the fruits of financial success and little or no threat to their job security. Thus:

> Proposition 9:   If the organization's recent financial performance has been neither exceptionally good nor exceptionally bad, employees' sense of the new computer is likely to be relatively uncertain, and employees are likely to be relatively susceptible to the influence of technology training on sense-making.

Practical Implications

The previous discussion suggests five implications for managers of organizations implementing new computerized technologies. First, it alerts managers to employees' thirst for information during the technological change process. Uncertainty is uncomfortable; employees want answers, shared interpretations.

Second, it invites managers to broaden their training goals. Employees acquire new skills in training, as well as new attitudes and interpretations. Accordingly, managers should take charge of this process, noting with care what messages or cues they want trainers to communicate to trainees during training. To do less is to miss a prime opportunity to influence employees' perceptions of the new technology.

Third, it suggests that training should begin early in the technology implementation process at which time employees are most uncertain about the impending change, most eager for information, and most open to the influence of training on sense-making. Training may well continue, periodically, over a period of weeks, months, or years, but an early start seems appropriate.

Fourth, it suggests that training is likely to be most influential on employee sense-making when the organization is in the middle ground—in terms of the effectiveness of its past organizational interventions, its managerial relations, and its financial performance. If employees have a great deal of trust and confidence in management (because of effective past changes, positive managerial relations, and good financial performance), employees are relatively likely to develop a positive sense of the new technology, with or without the influence of technology training. If employees neither trust nor have confidence in management, training is likely to be relatively inconsequential in shaping employee attitudes.

Technology training is but one influence on employee sense-making. Because technology training typically occurs relatively early during the implementation of a new technology, it may be very consequential. If, in the absence of effective technology training, employees develop a negative sense of the new technology, they may never accept the new technology, never learn the skills to use it, and never even try to use it. Once employees have constructed a negative interpretation of a new technology, that construction—that sense—may be extremely difficult to overcome.

THE UNINTENDED CONSEQUENCES OF TECHNOLOGY TRAINING: SUPERVISOR–SUBORDINATE RELATIONS AND ORGANIZATIONAL POWER

Supervisors are as skilled, or more skilled, than their subordinates. Supervisors understand their subordinates' work procedures and performance requirements. These are the assumptions by which organizations live. These assumptions are embedded in many organizational theories of leadership, yet these assumptions may be shattered by technology training.

Consider path-goal leadership theory (House & Mitchell, 1983). The theory suggests that leaders may enhance subordinate motivation and performance by:

> (1) recognizing and/or arousing subordinates' needs for outcomes over which the leader has some control, (2) increasing personal payoffs to subordinates for work–goal attainment, (3) making the path to those payoffs easier to travel by coaching and direction, (4) helping subordinates clarify expectancies, (5) reducing frustrating barriers, and (6) increasing the opportunities for personal satisfaction contingent on effective performance. (House & Mitchell, 1983, p. 495)

Surely, supervisors cannot perform the vast majority of these functions if they do not understand their subordinates' tasks and do not recognize appropriate performance standards. When supervisors lack such knowledge, they cannot coach and direct their subordinates. Moreover, they can not assess their subordinates' "work-goal attainment" and cannot offer performance-contingent rewards.

Not all theories of leadership assume that supervisors' technical expertise exceeds their subordinates'. Kerr's (1983) substitutes for leadership theory expressly addresses the nature of the leadership role when subordinates' technical expertise surpasses their supervisors' technical expertise. Kerr suggested that professionals, by virtue of their specialized knowledge, do not look to their hierarchical leaders for coaching, direction, or even performance feedback. As Filley, House, and Kerr (1976) noted: "First, professionals may deny that their hierarchical superiors have the skills to determine whether performance standards are being met. From the professional's viewpoint, only fellow professionals know enough about their work to evaluate it competently. Second, professionals may deny that their superior's performance standards are even relevant" (p. 385).

This section suggests that technology training may alter the relative distribution of technical expertise between supervisors and subordinates. When subordinates receive technology training and supervisors do not (Kelley & Brooks, 1988), as is commonly the case, subordinates may acquire specialized skills that their supervisors lack. This shift in the relative distribution of expertise may fundamentally transform the supervisor–subordinate relationship. Supervisors may be unable to perform the expected leadership functions outlined in pathgoal theory, yet supervisors may hesitate to regard and treat their subordinates as the professionals described in substitutes for leadership theory.

The consequences of a shift in the distribution of specialized expertise, and hence expert power (French & Raven, 1959), may surpass the supervisory relationship to affect the distribution of power throughout an organization. Strategic contingencies theory (Hickson, Hinings, Lee, Schneck, & Pennings, 1971; Pfeffer & Salancik, 1978) suggests that power accrues to organizational actors who: (a) are skilled in coping with important problems, (b) perform central functions within an organization's or unit's work flow, and (c) have a unique expertise. Through technology training, employees may acquire relatively unsubstitutable skills in coping with important problems, and thus new, more central roles within their organizations.

We use data from a qualitative case study of the implementation of CADD to illustrate the potential unintended consequences of technology training on the distribution of expertise and power within supervisor–subordinate dyads and, more broadly, within organizations. We build on our qualitative results, and the theoretical works described earlier, to suggest several new research propositions, and conclude with a discussion of the practical implications of the propositions.

Case Study Highlights

The likely users of a new technology often receive training in how to use the new system while their supervisors and managers do not (Kelley & Brooks, 1988). In the engineering and construction company implementing three–dimensional CADD, we saw the substantial, and unintended, consequences of this choice for the distribution of expertise and power within the supervisor–subordinate relationship. (See Klein et al., 1990 for a longer discussion of this case.)

Within the company, drafters—trained to use the new CADD system—complained about their managers' and supervisors' relative ignorance of the system:

Because supervisors don't know CADD, if you go up to them with a problem, they don't understand. They start yelling at you for no reason. How can you supervise someone if you can't answer their questions?

Supervisors, too, complained of their inability to guide their subordinates:

I don't feel as if I have as good a handle on things. The new CADD system is a black box with a lot of stuff in it. To see a whole building on screen, you have to pull up five or six computer files. You can't visualize where everything is. Those of us who grew up on drawing boards can just scan a drawing and pick up a problem. As a result of CADD, we've lost the personal touch.

I'm less confident of the product because I'm not as involved, because I don't review as much. The more contact you have with each step of the way, the more familiar you are with it and the more confidence you have in knowing whether you can make potential changes. Now, because drafters are using CADD, I don't have as much information stored in my mind. I don't know the ramifications of design changes.

In summary, the decision to train drafters, but not their supervisors and managers, to use CADD undermined supervisors' and managers' confidence and credibility. In two sets of propositions, we explore the implications of technology training for the distribution of power within the supervisor–subordinate dyad and within the organization as a whole.

Research Propositions: Supervisor–Subordinate Relations

The qualitative results and theoretical works described suggest the following fundamental proposition:

Proposition 10: When subordinates receive technology training and their supervisors do not, the resulting shift in the relative distribution of expertise may decrease both subordinates' and supervisors' confidence in supervisors' ability to provide meaningful guidance and feedback to subordinates.

The remaining propositions in this section suggest conditions that may moderate this dynamic: When is a training–induced shift in the relative distribution of supervisors' and subordinates' expertise likely to be most and least dysfunctional for their relationship?

If supervisors are to effectively coach and monitor their subordinates, supervisors must understand subordinates' basic work procedures and must provide reasonable performance standards. But supervisors need not know every detail of their subordinates' work. If technology training modifies trainees' work tasks in a fairly limited way, the redistribution of technical expertise between nontrained supervisors and trained subordinates appears unlikely to be sufficient to damage the supervisor–subordinate relationship. Thus:

> Proposition 11: Training-induced shifts in the relative technical expertise of supervisors and subordinates are most likely to disrupt the supervisor–subordinate relationship when trainees' new skills are fundamental, rather than peripheral, to their work.

Under the circumstances described in the preceding proposition, supervisors would seem likely to take steps to restore the former distribution of technical expertise unless supervisors question their own ability to acquire their subordinates' new found expertise. Accordingly:

> Proposition 12: Training-induced shifts in the relative technical expertise of supervisors and subordinates are most likely to disrupt the supervisor–subordinate relationship when supervisors' perceive trainees' new skills to be difficult and time-consuming to learn and maintain.

It is not surprising that a shift in power was observed as a result of training for CADD—an extremely difficult and time-consuming computer system to master.

Building on Kerr's (1983) substitutes for leadership theory, we posit that subordinates who, following training, perceive that their specialized skills now exceed their supervisors' specialized skills may desire to be treated like professionals. Thus:

> Proposition 13: If supervisors respond to subordinates' acquisition of substantial specialized skills by giving subordinates new authority to self-direct and self-monitor, subordinates are likely to be satisfied with their relationships with their supervisors.

Such a recalibration in the supervisor–subordinate relationship is likely to be foreign to and resisted by supervisors under many circumstances. However, the larger organizational context may influence supervisors' willingness to alter their supervisory style and procedures in this way:

Proposition 14:   The less hierarchical and bureaucratic the organization, the more likely supervisors are to respond to a shift in the relative distribution of specialized expertise by increasing subordinates' ability to self-direct and self-monitor.

Research Propositions: Organizational Power

An individual's acquisition of computer expertise may result in the individual's acquisition of new power not only vis-à-vis his or her supervisor, but also more broadly within the organization. However, expertise only begets power within an organization if others in the organization value that expertise (Pfeffer, 1981). The propositions in this section describe the factors that make computer expertise more valuable within an organization, and thus likely to engender increases—typically unanticipated—in individual power.

Power stems from relative, not absolute, expertise. If everyone in an organization acquires the same computer expertise through technology training, the training program is likely to have little impact on the distribution of power. Accordingly:

Proposition 15:   The acquisition of computer expertise in training is most likely to engender an increase in a trainee's power if, other things being equal, computer expertise is a relatively rare commodity within the organization.

An employee's expertise is of greater value if others in the organization believe that it would be difficult to acquire comparable expertise. Expertise regarding relatively simple word-processing packages is likely to be less valued than expertise regarding relatively complex computer packages (CAD, expert systems). Thus:

Proposition 16:   The acquisition of computer expertise in training is most likely to engender an increase in a trainee's power if, other things being equal, the computer system is perceived as relatively difficult to learn.

Power accrues to those whose expertise is central to the fundamental mission of the organization (or subunit). The acquisition of expertise regarding tangential matters (e.g. technologies peripheral to the organization's or subunit's central tasks) is unlikely to engender a shift in power. Thus:

Proposition 17:   The acquisition of computer expertise in training is most likely to engender an increase in a trainee's power if, other things being equal, the computer system is central to the organization's (or subunit's) fundamental mission.

Computer expertise is likely to be a valuable source of organizational power in organizations that regard computer expertise as a key to credibility and advancement. As a form of technical expertise among drafters, designers, and engineers, computer expertise was held in high regard in the case study company. Within universities, computer expertise is positively regarded, but it is not as intimately linked to advancement, credibility, and power as is, for example, research productivity. Thus:

> Proposition 18:   The acquisition of computer expertise in training is most likely to engender an increase in a trainee's power if, other things being equal, computer expertise is considered a key to advancement and credibility within the organization.

Finally, there may be ceiling effects on the acquisition of power during technology training (cf. Burkhardt & Brass, 1990). If an employee is already powerful, the acquisition of new computer expertise is unlikely to engender a significant increase in organizational power. Hence:

> Proposition 19:   The acquisition of computer expertise in training is not likely to engender an increase in a trainee's power if the trainee is already powerful.

Practical Implications

The prior discussion suggests four training guidelines for managers of organizations that are implementing or plan to implement new computerized systems. First, it suggests that the decision to exclude certain employees from technology training may be just as important and consequential as the decision to include other employees. Obviously the two decisions go hand in hand, yet managers appear far more likely to contemplate the repercussions of training an employee than of not training an employee. Clearly, being trained has real consequences—both intended and unintended—for an employee, as does not being trained.

Second, it suggests that managers should consider the implications of technology training for supervisor–subordinate relations. If subordinates receive training that their supervisors lack, both supervisors and subordinates may question the right and ability of supervisors to monitor and evaluate subordinate performance. In such a case, it may be appropriate and effective for the employing organization to establish new mechanisms, commensurate with trainees' new expertise, to carry out supervisory functions. For example, train-ees, as professionals within the organization, may assume new responsibility for self-monitoring and self-management.

Third, it suggests that managers may also wish to evaluate the consequences of technology training for the distribution of power within the organizations. As specialized professionals within the organization, trainees may acquire new power. Will any existing power-holder be threatened and, thus, inclined to denigrate the value of both the new technology and technological knowledge? Managers may eschew such political battles—perhaps by providing widespread computer technology training—if they can anticipate them.

A final implication is that the organizational costs of providing technology training for select members of an organization may ultimately exceed the costs of offering technology training to everyone in the organization. The consequences of training only a select few may, depending on the nature of supervisor–subordinate relations and distribution of power in the organization, prove very disruptive.

THE UNINTENDED CONSEQUENCES OF TECHNOLOGY TRAINING: JOB DESIGN, ORGANIZATIONAL STRUCTURE, AND CULTURE

Traditional training models (Goldstein, 1993) urge training designers to conduct job and organizational analyses prior to designing the training program. The goal is to design training to fit the needs, requirements, and style of existing jobs and the organization as a whole. This assumes that the job and the organization's structure and culture precede training and are impervious to training effects. The design of existing jobs, structure, and culture are expected to shape the design and content of the training program. This sequence may be reversed in the case of computerized technology training. Technology training may precede and shape the job, the structure of the organization, and its culture. Organizations typically purchase computerized systems with the goal of chang-ing the status quo. Yet, given the variety of uses and applications of given computerized technologies, managers often have only a general, amorphous knowledge of how they intend to use technology (Dean, 1987). Accordingly, there may well be no computerized job or task to analyze before designing training; that job and those tasks may not exist, and no one may be certain just what the job or the tasks will be. Similarly, organizational analysis may be moot because the technology may well change the organization.

In such cases, managerial choices, embodied in the technology training, may determine the impact of the technology on trainees' jobs. The nature and breadth of the tasks that employees learn during training may determine whether, for example, employees' jobs grow or shrink in autonomy, variety, task identity, task significance, and feedback (Hackman & Lawler, 1971; Hackman & Oldham, 1980) following training.

In a similar fashion, managerial choices, embodied in technology training, may shape the impact of the technology on the structure of the organization. Who is trained to use the new system? What skills do they learn? The answers to these questions may determine whether the new technology enhances or diminishes centralization, communication, and intraorganizational integration (cf. Barley, 1986).

The nature and design of technology training also sends employees a message about the organization's values and priorities. As such, training appears to be an organizational practice or procedure that may influence the organizational climate(s) that employees perceive and the cultural interpretations and attributions that they make (O'Reilly, 1991; Schein, 1991; Schneider, 1990; Schneider & Gunnarson, 1991).

In drawing attention to the potential unintended effects of technology training on job characteristics, organizational structure, and culture, we rearrange the causal chains that dominate existing training models (Goldstein, 1993; Holding, 1965). Here, job and organizational characteristics are treated not as predictors of training design or moderators of training effectiveness, but as dependent variables influenced, in part, by technology training.

This perspective also defies much of the existing literature on job and organizational design. Normative in character, job and organizational design models (Galbraith, 1973; Griffin, 1982; Hackman & Oldham, 1980; Lawler, 1986; Perrow, 1967; Peters, 1987) commonly advise managers to redesign employees' jobs and the organization's structure to achieve a variety of organizational objectives (e.g., job satisfaction, organizational flexibility, organizational productivity, etc.). In describing the potential effects of technology training on job and organizational characteristics, we highlight the ways in which job and organizational characteristics may evolve, in the absence of intentional redesign, in response to technology training. The next section draws on our case study findings to suggest possible effects of technology training on jobs, structure, and culture.

Case Study Highlights

Interview data from three separate settings illustrate the potential influence of training on jobs, structure, and culture, respectively. In implementing CAD, the construction and engineering firm chose to train all of its designers to perform comparable tasks, compressing the company's traditional career progression ladder. Employees found that the distinctive features of their jobs were diminished. This case suggests the potential influence of training on jobs.

Before CADD, there was a structure where you progressed from junior drafter to designer and up. With CAD, you have different grades sitting next to each other, doing the same work.

There's so much overlap. The Grade 5 does the same CAD work as the Grade 9. Even if I got a promotion, I'd be doing the same thing. The company is getting a good deal because I'm a 5 and doing 9 work.

Depending on the character and status of their pretraining jobs, some employees felt that their jobs were upgraded following CAD training while others felt that their jobs were downgraded:

I'm one of the lower people in my discipline. I don't know as much technically, but I may know the machine better than others do. So, I don't feel like an idiot. It's increased my satisfaction.

I don't know how long I can do this. It's like being a professional TV watcher. You don't have to think anymore. The machine does it all.

At the food products company, we saw the potential effects of technology training on organizational structure, particularly the relationship among the plants. With the purchase of an MRP II system designed to put all the plants on a common software system for the first time, managers feared that the traditional autonomy of the plants would be compromised:

The underlying assumption of the new MRP II system is that there is a strong commonality of plant missions and processes. That assumption is false. In reality, we have quite different plants that have no business being linked together.

The new MRP II system will shift us toward facilitative management. Our business is not organized as a football team sending in plays. It's more like a volleyball game with no superstars and no plays, just skilled reactions.

The effects of the new MRP II system on the plants depend, to a considerable extent, on how technology training is structured: Will all of the plants be trained to use the system in an identical fashion, or will technology training be customized such that plants may use the software as they choose?

Within one of the company's plants, a manager intentionally used MRP II training to send a message to employees and to the company as a whole about the plant's culture. Bucking the norms of the larger company, the plant put two nonsupervisory employees in charge of technology training and implementation. The message: "We're different here. Nonsupervisory employees are capable of assuming the responsibility of implementing the system." Two managers explained:

We made a decision that we were going to let Peggy and Bruce (pseudonyms) carry the ball on this one. Even though we pride ourselves in the company as being very TQM–ish, to really relinquish control and give it to those people was difficult to handle—not for us, but for those at headquarters. Still, the proof was in the pudding as we started up with very few glitches.

We used hourly people to drive the implementation of PRISM. That's a difference between us and the rest of the company. We are in more of an empowerment mode. There was some nervousness about that from headquarters. They'd ask, "Why isn't management more involved? Why isn't management driving it?" I think that the people from headquarters learned from this whole thing that maybe it can happen in different ways. There are several different ways to skin a cat.

Drawing on these findings, we explore the possible effects of technology training on job design, structure, and culture.

Research Propositions and Strategies

The available theoretical and empirical literature on the effects of computerization (Attewell, 1992; Dean & Snell, 1991; Walton, 1989; Zuboff, 1988) suggests that computerized technologies—even the same computerized technology—may upgrade (informate) or downgrade (automate) jobs. Our case study results suggest that the content of technology training may, in large part, determine the job consequences of computerization. Thus:

> Proposition 20: If technology training teaches employees how to perform new tasks that are more varied or cognitively complex than their existing tasks, employees' jobs will be enriched and enlarged as a result of technology training.

This proposition rests on the assumption that employees actually use the new skills that they have learned in training on the job. In some cases, such skills may not transfer to the job (Baldwin & Ford, 1988; Rouiller & Goldstein, 1993). In our experience, this occurs most often because computer terminals and other equipment are not readily accessible for employee use. Under these circumstances, the content of training may have no discernable impact on job characteristics, but may influence employee attitudes:

> Proposition 21: If employees acquire new and relatively varied or cognitively complex skills during technology training, but are not able to transfer these skills to their jobs following training, they may feel dissatisfied, frustrated, and resentful.

Employees may resent having had to learn new skills that they cannot use. In some cases, they feel disappointed that the promise of more interesting and challenging work has not materialized.

The composition of the trainee group may also influence the consequences of technology implementation. First, the vertical or hierarchical composition of the trainee group may influence the outcomes of computerization. That is:

Proposition 22:   If employees from differing hierarchical levels are taught the same computer skills, the organization's chain of command or hierarchical ladder will be compressed.

This, again, assumes that employees do use their newly acquired skills on the job, and that technology skills are central to the required job tasks. If so, training employees from diverse hierarchical groups in the same computer skills will reduce the distinctions among the groups. This may have the effect of increasing the status, job variety, job complexity, and resulting job satisfaction for employees within the lower hierarchical levels. It may have some of the opposite consequences for employees within the higher hierarchical levels.

The composition of the trainee group may also influence who may communicate with whom about the computer system following computerization. The smaller the number or percentage of employees trained to use a new computer system, the more technology implementation fosters or reinforces the division of labor (i.e., some employees possess new skills that others lack). Conversely:

Proposition 23:   The greater the number or percentage of employees who receive technology training, the more technology implementation fosters or reinforces decentralization, flexibility, a team orientation, and perhaps conformity.

The greater the percentage of employees trained to use a new computer system, the more the technology acts as an equalizing force, reducing divisions of labor, expertise, information access, and status. In this way, training a broad spectrum of organizational members to use a new computer system increases the flexibility of the organization; employees can substitute for each other when the need arises. Training a broad spectrum of employees lays the groundwork for the use of teams within an organization; employees have a common base of skills and knowledge. However, training a large number of people to operate a new computerized system in the same way may foster conformity among trainees, forcing employees to do their work in a common fashion. This is what the plants in the food products company feared and resisted.

Technology training may not only influence job characteristics and organizational structure, but also organizational culture. The content of technology training not only sends employees a message about the meaning of the new technology, but also may send employees a message about organizational values. For example, training content conducive to "information," not automation (i.e., training content that serves to enrich, rather than routinize, employee tasks), sends employees a message that management believes in employees' ability and seeks a relatively empowered and expert workforce. Equally important are the messages implicit in management's choices regarding who should offer and who should receive training. If nonmanagerial, nonprofessional employees take on the task of providing technology training, managers send employees a message—through the training—that the technology is for everyone; it is not the province of the managerial or technical elite. If managers and supervisors receive no technology training, management sends employees a message that the technology is beneath managers and supervisors, that managers and supervisors are above technology uses. However, if only managers and professionals receive training, the organization risks sending the message that technology, and the information available through it, are off limits to nonmanagerial employees. In summary:

Proposition 24: The content of training as well as the choice of who provides training and who receives it all send a message to employees about the culture of the organization and the content of management values.

Technology training is but one manifestation of organizational culture. Nevertheless, during times of organizational change, it seems likely to be a powerful and often unintended carrier of cultural information.

Practical Implications

The previous discussion again underscores the importance of technology training. In numerous ways, technology training has the power to influence the consequences of technology implementation. Too often technology training is an afterthought during the technology implementation process, overshadowed in the rush to get the hardware and software up and running. The earlier propositions invite managers to give serious attention to the design of technology training, recognizing the potential implications of the training program for job design, organizational structure, and culture.

First, the discussion above highlights the potential limitations of basing the design of technology training on employees' current job requirements and characteristics. Managers and trainers who base training on existing job characteristics may, by default, not only recreate the characteristics of existing work, but also limit the potential uses and benefits of the new technology. Technology implementation yields its greatest benefits not when the technology is used merely to regulate or speed up the performance of existing skills and procedures, but when it fosters the development of new abilities and strengths.

Caveats are sprinkled throughout the discussion: "assuming that employees actually use the new skills that they have learned in training on the job" we cautioned repeatedly. A second, although not original, practical implication of the discussion is: transfer of training is essential (Baldwin & Ford, 1988; Rouiller & Goldstein, 1993). Transfer of training does not occur in and of itself; it must be fostered. Managers and trainers must devote attention not only to the design of training, but to its application on the job. The availability of the computerized equipment—on which employees may use their skills—is only the most obvious determinant of training transfer. Training transfer, not training per se, ultimately determines the influence of training on job characteristics, structure, and culture. When skills learned in training do not transfer, training fosters not improvements in employee jobs, organizational structure, and culture, but cynicism.

A third practical implication relates to senior employees' fears that career ladders may be compressed by the provision of widespread computer training. On the one hand, such fears may be unrealistic. Learning CAD may enable someone to produce a blueprint or draft, but will not provide one with the analytical or creative skills of an experienced engineer, architect, or drafter. Learning statistical software may enable someone to generate a statistical analysis, but will not provide the quantitative skills of a skilled statistician. On the other hand, the upgrading of lower level employees' skills almost inevitably threatens and encroaches on supervisors' perceived skills and prerogatives. The organizational challenge is to determine how technology implementation and training may be used to enhance all employees' skills and contributions to the organization. When training has this effect, it truly is an organizational intervention with far-ranging effects on job characteristics, organizational structure, and culture.

Given that the provision of technology training to a broad spectrum of employees may prove beneficial for organizational flexibility and employee teamwork, managers and trainers should evaluate strategies for increasing the availability of technology training. The provision of training to a broad spectrum of employees may be difficult in an era of simultaneous budget cutbacks and increasing technology training requirements due to the increasing number of software applications. A final practical implication of the earlier discussion is: Training departments must be creative in developing new and effective methods for meeting technology training demand. The Federal National Mortgage Association (Fannie Mae) provides one example. The organization is making greater use of CD–ROM and online training programs for individual, self-paced training, and has developed a "train-the-trainer" program through which designated technology representatives teach their peers about technology information and applications that they learn through the program. Financial realities may temper, but need not quash, ambitious hopes for technology training.

BEYOND TECHNOLOGY TRAINING: GENERALIZING TO OTHER TYPES OF TRAINING

In exploring training's potential unintended organizational consequences, we have focused exclusively on technology training. Yet much of our discussion appears generalizable to other forms of organizational training. We have argued that the prospect of computerization generates employee uncertainty and employee sense–making efforts. Surely the prospect of other kinds of organizational change may also generate uncertainty and sense-making. If these forms of organizational change are accompanied by training, training for the change may influence employee sense-making regarding the change. For example, TQM training, may influence employees' interpretations of the meaning of their organization's TQM efforts.

Similarly, training regarding a variety of subjects—not just new technologies—may influence the distribution of expertise and power within an organization. If a training program concerns a skill that is central to the organization, known by relatively few organizational members and perceived to be difficult to learn, that training program may confer new expertise and power on trainees. If a training program teaches employees skills and knowledge that were formerly the province of supervisors alone, the training program may alter the organization's balance of power, thus threatening supervisors.

Training programs regarding nontechnological interventions may also influence job design, organizational structure, and culture. Skills learned in training may, if used on the job, alter the characteristics of trainees' jobs. Training programs regarding almost any topic will unite trainees and divide them from nontrainees, potentially reinforcing or changing the division of labor within an organization, centralization of information, and/or patterns of communication. Training programs of all kinds send employees messages regarding the organization's cultural values: "managers care about this topic," a training program says to employees. Who teaches the training course and who takes it? The answers to these questions send employees a message about the standing of the various groups in management's eyes: Who is competent to train coworkers and even supervisors? Who is above or below training?

In summary, technology training and other forms of training are likely to have far-reaching and often unintended organizational consequences. These consequences are ripe for research, and they merit managers' attention.

CONCLUSION

Five distinctive features underlie the research propositions discussed earlier:

1. *Training as a subsystem of the open organizational system.* Within the organizational literature, open systems theorists (e.g., Katz & Kahn, 1978) have suggested that:

> Systems are like Chinese boxes in that they always contain wholes within wholes. Thus, organizations contain individuals (who are systems of their own account) who belong to groups or departments, which belong to larger organizational divisions. And so on. If we define the whole organization as a system, then the other levels can be understood as subsystems . . . [that] are complex open systems on their own account. (Morgan, 1986, p. 45)

In this chapter, we have described *organizational training* as an open system in its own right, buffeted by and buffeting other organizational subsystems. With some exceptions (e.g., Baldwin & Ford, 1988; Ford, Quiñones, Sego, & Sorra, 1992; Rouiller & Goldstein, 1993), training researchers have drawn relatively little attention to the interplay between training and other organizational "subsystems" (leadership, culture, and structure). Our training perspective brings the interplay of training and other organizational subsystems to the forefront for further empirical and theoretical analyses.

2. *The unintended consequences of training.* Traditional training research is rational and experimental, examining issues such as: (a) the effects of trainee characteristics on skill acquisition and training performance (Gist, Stevens, & Bavetta, 1991; Martocchio & Webster, 1992; Stevens, Bavetta, & Gist, 1993), (b) the effectiveness of different types of training methods (Bretz & Thompsett, 1992; Eden & Aviram, 1993; Stamoulis & Hauenstein, 1993), and (c) the relative merits of different methods of training evaluation (Kraiger, Ford, & Salas, 1993; Ostroff, 1991; Sackett & Mullen, 1993). The benefits of such research are obvious. However, the effects of training, may transcend the intended. Our perspective invites training theorists and researchers to consider not only the intended consequences of training, but also the unintended consequences of training.

3. *Organizational characteristics and processes as potential training outcomes.* Training theorists and researchers have typically conceptualized the organizational environment as either (a) a precursor to training, or independent variable, that should, ideally, shape the content, format, and outcomes of organizational training (Goldstein, 1993) or (b) a moderating variable that determines the extent to which skills learned during training transfer to the work environment (Baldwin & Ford, 1988; Rouiller & Goldstein, 1993). Within our training propositions presented above, we present a third conceptualization: organizational characteristics and dynamics as unintended training outcomes, or dependent variables. This training perspective encourages examination of

the extent to which training may affect a range of organizational processes and characteristics that have often been overlooked by training researchers.

4. *Training's multilevel effects.* Training researchers typically conduct individual-level research, assessing the consequences of training on individual skills or behaviors within a single organization (Bretz & Thompsett, 1992; Ganster, Williams, & Poppler, 1991; Harrison, 1992) or university-based laboratory setting (Gist et al., 1991; Stamoulis & Hauenstein, 1993; Stevens et al., 1993). Ostroff and Ford (1989)encouraged training researchers to take a multilevel approach to training. In the previous propositions, we have illustrated such an approach. Many of the propositions describe between-organization differences in the consequences of training (e.g., Propositions 9, 14, 17, and 23). To test organization-level hypotheses, researchers must move beyond single-organization samples to multiorganizational samples. Organizational processes and dynamics are inherently multilevel (Klein, Dansereau, & Hall, 1994). The propositions herein begin to describe the range of training's multilevel consequences.

5. *Qualitative and quantitative research methods.* In developing the research propositions, we built on our qualitative studies of technology implementation. Qualitative studies of training are relatively rare within industrial and organizational psychology and related disciplines, yet they may provide training researchers with stimulating new insights for future theory and qualitative or quantitative research.

In opting to use qualitative research methods, training researchers expand their research arsenal, but need not reject familiar quantitative methods. Quantitative research is most effective in testing theory. When the goal is to build, rather than test, theory, however, qualitative case study research may be most apt:

> Theory developed from case study research is likely to have important strengths like novelty, testability, and empirical validity, which arise from the intimate linkage with empirical evidence. . . . [G]iven the strengths of this theory-building approach and its independence from prior literature or past empirical observation, it is particularly well-suited to new research. (Eisenhardt, 1989, pp. 548–549)

Eisenhardt's (1989) prescriptions for theory-building qualitative research provide a valuable primer for training researchers more familiar with experimental than qualitative research.

In summary, our perspective differs in several respects from the mainstream of training research and theory. We advocate our perspective not as a substitute to mainstream training research and theory, but as a complement that may extend and enrich current training theory and research. The 24 propositions described in this chapter offer a starting point for new research and theory regarding the unintended organizational consequences of technology training and other forms of training as well.

ACKNOWLEDGMENTS

Many of our colleagues assisted in conducting these qualitative studies. We are particularly indebted to Lori Berman, Sylvia Bittle, Greg Bodzioch, Pamela Carter, Elizabeth Clemmer, and Rosalie Hall.

REFERENCES

Anderson Soft–Teach. (1993). *Survey of personal computing in corporate America: Survey results and analysis.* Los Gatos, CA: Author.

Arvey, R. D., & Cole, D. A. (1989). Evaluating change due to training. In I. L. Goldstein (Ed.), *Training and development in organizations* (pp. 89–117). San Francisco: Jossey–Bass.

Attewell, P. (1992). Skill and occupational changes in U.S. manufacturing. In P. S. Adler (Ed.), *Technology and the future of work* (pp. 46–88). New York: Oxford University Press.

Baldwin, T. T., & Ford, J. K. (1988). Transfer of training: A review and directions for future research. *Personnel Psychology, 41,* 63–105.

Barley, S. R. (1986). Technology as an occasion for structuring: Evidence from observations of CT scanners and the social order of radiology departments. *Administrative Science Quarterly, 31,* 78–108.

Berndt, E., & Griliches, Z. (1990, June). Price indexes for microcomputers: An exploratory study. *NBER Working Paper No. 3378.*

Bretz, R. D., Jr., & Thompsett, R. E. (1992). Comparing traditional and integrative learning methods in organizational training programs. *Journal of Applied Psychology, 77,* 941–951.

Burkhardt, M. E., & Brass, D. J. (1990). Changing patterns or patterns of change: The effects of a change in technology on social nextwork structure and power. *Administrative Science Quarterly, 35,* 104–127.

Cascio, W. F. (1989). Using utility analysis to assess training outcomes. In I. L. Goldstein (Ed.), *Training and development in organizations* (pp. 63–88). San Francisco: Jossey–Bass.

Chao, G. T., & Kozlowski, S. W. J. (1986). Employee perceptions on the implementation of robotic manufacturing technology. *Journal of Applied Psychology, 71,* 70–76.

Dean, J. W., Jr. (1987). Building the future: The justification process for new technology. In J. M. Pennings & A. Buitendam (Eds.), *New technology as organizational innovation* (pp. 35–88). Cambridge, MA: Ballinger.

Dean, J. W., Jr., & Snell, S. A. (1991). Integrated manufacturing and job design: Moderating effects of organizational inertia. *Academy of Management Journal, 34,* 776–804.

Eden, D., & Aviram, A. (1993). Self–efficacy training to speed reemployment: Helping people to help themselves. *Journal of Applied Psychology, 78,* 352–360.

Eisenhardt, K. M. (1989). Building theories from case study research. *Academy of Management Review, 14,* 532–550.

Ettlie, J. E., & Reza, E. M. (1992). Organizational integration and process innovation. *Academy of Management Journal, 35,* 795–827.

Filley, A. C., House, R. J., & Kerr, S. (1976). *Managerial process and organizational behavior* (2nd ed.). Glenview, IL: Scott, Foresman.

Finholt, T., & Sproull, L. S. (1990). Electronic groups at work. *Organizational Science, 1,* 41–64.

Fleischer, M., Liker, J., & Arnsdorf, D. (1988). *Effective use of computer–aided design and computer–aided engineering in manufacturing.* Ann Arbor, MI: Industrial Technology Institute.

Ford, J. K., Quiñones, M. A., Sego, D. J., & Sorra, J. S. (1992). Factors affecting the opportunity to perform trained tasks on the job. *Personnel Psychology, 45,* 511–527.

French, J., & Raven, B. H. (1959). The bases of social power. In D. Cartwright (Ed.), *Studies of social power* (pp. 150–167). Ann Arbor, MI: Institute for Social Research.

Galbraith, J. (1973). *Designing complex organizations.* Reading, MA: Addison–Wesley.

Ganster, D. C., Williams, S., & Poppler, P. (1991). Does training in problem solving improve the quality of group decisions? *Journal of Applied Psychology, 76,* 479–483.

Gist, M. E., Stevens, C. K., & Bavetta, A. G. (1991). Effects of self–efficacy and post–training intervention on the acquisition and maintenance of complex interpersonal skills. *Personnel Psychology, 44,* 837–861.

Goldstein, I. L. (1993). *Training in organizations* (3rd ed.). Pacific Grove, CA: Brooks/Cole.

Goodman, P. S., Griffith, T. L., & Fenner, D. B. (1990). Understanding technology and the individual in an organizational context. In P. S. Goodman & L. S. Sproull (Eds.), *Technology and organizations* (pp. 45–86). San Francisco: Jossey–Bass.

Griffin, R. W. (1982). *Task design: An integrative approach.* Glenview, IL: Scott, Foresman.

Hackman, J. R., & Lawler, E. (1971). Employee reactions to job characteristics. *Journal of Applied Psychology, 55,* 259–286.

Hackman, J. R., & Oldham, G. R. (1980). *Work redesign.* Reading, MA: Addison–Wesley.

Harrison, J. K. (1992). Individual and combined effects of behavior modeling and the cultural assimilator in cross-cultural management training. *Journal of Applied Psychology, 77,* 952–962.

Hickson, D. J., Hinings, C. R., Lee, C. A., Schneck, R. E., & Pennings, J. M. (1971). A strategic contingencies' theory of intraorganizational power. *Administrative Science Quarterly, 16,* 216–229.

Hines, A. (1994, January–February). Jobs and infotech: Work in the information society. *The Futurist,* pp. 9–13.

Holding, D. H. (1965). *Principles of training.* London: Pergamon.

House, R. J., & Mitchell, T. R. (1983). Path-goal theory of leadership. In J. R. Hackman, E. E. Lawler III., & L. W. Porter (Eds.), *Perspectives on behavior in organizations* (pp. 493–501). New York: McGraw-Hill.

Isabella, L. A. (1990). Evolving interpretations as a change unfolds: How managers construe key organizational events. *Academy of Management Journal, 33,* 7–41.

Katz, D., & Kahn, R. L. (1978). *The social psychology of organizations.* New York: Wiley.

Kelley, M. R. (1989). *An assessment of the skill upgrading and training opportunities for blue–collar workers under programmable automation* (Working Paper No. 89–5). Pittsburgh, PA: Carnegie Mellon University, School of Urban and Public Affairs.

Kelley, M. R., & Brooks, H., (1988). *The state of computerized automation in U.S. manufacturing.* Cambridge, MA: John F. Kennedy School of Government.

Kerr, S. (1983). Substitutes for leadership: Some implications for organizational design. In J. R. Hackman, E. E. Lawler III., & L. W. Porter (Eds.), *Perspectives on behavior in organizations* (pp. 515–522). New York: McGraw–Hill.

Klein, K. J., Dansereau, F., & Hall, R. J. (1994). Levels issues in theory development, data collection, and analysis. *Academy of Management Review, 19,* 195–229.

Klein, K. J., Hall, R. J., & Laliberte, M. (1990). Training and the organizational consequences of technological change: A case study of computer–aided design and drafting. In U. E. Gattiker & L. Larwood (Eds.), *Technological and end–user training* (pp. 7–35). New York: Walter de Gruyter.

Klein, K. J., & Ralls, R. S. (1995). The organizational dynamics of computerized technology implementation: A review of the empirical literature. In L. R. Gomez-Mejia & M. W. Lawless (Eds.), *Advances in global high- technology management* (Vol. 5, pp. 31–79). Greenwich, CT: JAI.

Kotter, J. P., & Schlesinger, L. (1979). Choosing strategies for change. *Harvard Business Review, 57,* 106–114.

Kraiger, K., Ford, J. K., & Salas, E. (1993). Application of cognitive, skill–based, and affective theories of learning outcomes to new methods of training evaluation. *Journal of Applied Psychology, 78,* 311–328.

Krueger, A. B. (1993, February). How computers have changed the wage structure: Evidence from microdata, 1984–1989. *The Quarterly Journal of Economics,* pp. 33–60.

Lawler, E. E. III. (1986). *High–involvement management.* San Francisco: Jossey–Bass.

Majchrzak, A., & Klein, K. J. (1987). Things are always more complicated than you think: An open systems approach to the organizational effects of computer–automated technology. *Journal of Business and Psychology, 2,* 27–49.

March, J. G., & Olsen, J. P. (1976). *Ambiguity and choice in organizations.* Bergen: Universitetsforlaget.

March, J. G., & Sproull, L. S. (1990). Technology, management, and competitive advantage. In P. S. Goodman & L. S. Sproull (Eds.), *Technology and organizations* (pp. 144–173). San Francisco: Jossey–Bass.

Martocchio, J. J., & Webster, J. (1992). Effects of feedback and cognitive playfulness on performance in microcomputer software training. *Personnel Psychology, 45,* 553–578.

McKersie, R. B., & Walton, R. E. (1991). Organizational change. In M. S. Morton (Ed.), *The corporation of the 1990s: Information technology and organizational transformation* (pp. 244–277). New York: Oxford University Press.

Morgan, G. (1986). *Images of organization.* Beverly Hills, CA: Sage.

O'Reilly, C. (1991). Corporations, culture, and commitment: Motivation and social control in organizations. In B. M. Staw (Ed.), *Psychological dimensions of organizational behavior* (pp. 293–305). New York: Macmillan.

Office of Technology assessment. (1984). *Computerized manufacturing automation: Employment, educaiton, and the workplace.* Washington, DC: U.S. Congress (OTA-CIT-235).

Office of Technology Assessment. (1985). *Automation of American's offices.* Washington, DC: U.S. Congress (OTA-CIT-287).

Osterman, P. (1991). Impact of IT on jobs and skills. In M. S. Morton (Ed.), *The corporation of the 1990s: Information technology and organizational transformation* (pp. 220–243). New York: Oxford University Press.

Ostroff, C. (1991). Training effectiveness measures and scoring schemes: A comparison. *Personnel Psychology, 44,* 353–374.

Ostroff, C., & Ford, J. K. (1989). Assessing training needs: Critical levels of analysis. In I. L. Goldstein (Ed.), *Training and development in organizations* (pp. 25–62). San Francisco: Jossey–Bass.

Perrow, C. A. (1967). A framework for the comparative analysis of organization. *American Sociological Review, 32,* 194–208.

Peters, T. (1987). *Thriving on chaos: Handbook for a management.* New York: Knopf.

Pfeffer, J. (1981). *Power in organizations.* Marshfield, MA: Pitman.

Pfeffer, J., & Salancik, G. R. (1978). *The external control of organizations.* New York: Harper & Row.

Rouiller, J. Z., & Goldstein, I. L. (1993). The relationship between organizational transfer climate and positive transfer of training. *Human Resource Development Quarterly, 4,* 377–390.

Sackett, P. R., & Mullen, E. J. (1993). Beyond formal experimental design: Towards an expanded view of the training evaluation process. *Personnel Psychology, 46,* 613–627.

Schein, E. H. (1991). The role of the founder in creating organizational culture. In B. M. Staw (Ed.), *Psychological dimensions of organizational behavior* (pp. 312–326). New York: Macmillan.

Schneider, B. (1990). The climate for service: An application of the climate construct. In B. Schneider (Ed.), *Organizational climate and culture* (pp. 383–412). San Francisco: Jossey–Bass.

Schneider, B., & Gunnarson, S. (1991). Organizational climate and culture: The psychology of the workplace. In J. W. Jones, B. Steffy, & D. W. Bray (Eds.), *Applying psychology in business: The manager's handbook* (pp. 542–551). Lexington, MA: Lexington Books.

Snell, S. A., & Dean, J. W., Jr. (1992). Integrated manufacturing and human resource management: A human capital perspective. *Academy of Management Journal, 35,* 467–504.

Stamoulis, D. T., & Hauenstein, N. M. A. (1993). Rater training and rating accuracy: Training for dimensional accuracy versus training for ratee differentiation. *Journal of Applied Psychology, 78,* 994–1003.

Stamps, D. (1993, November). Stalking the elusive technology payoff. *Training,* pp. 47–53.

Stevens, C. K., Bavetta, A. G., & Gist, M. E. (1993). Gender differences in the acquisition of salary negotiation skills: The role of goals, self–efficacy, and perceived control. *Journal of Applied Psychology, 78*, 723–735.

Wall, T. D., Jackson, P. R., & Davids, K. (1992). Operator work design and robotics system performance: A serendipitous field study. *Journal of Applied Psychology, 77*, 353–362.

Walton, R. E. (1989). *Up and running: Integrating information technology and the organization.* Boston, MA: Harvard Business School Press.

Weick, K. E. (1976). Educational organizations as loosely coupled systems. *Administrative Science Quarterly, 21*, 1–19.

Weick, K. E. (1990). Technology as equivoque: Sensemaking in new technologies. In P. S. Goodman & L. S. Sproull (Eds.), *Technology and organizations* (pp. 1–44). San Francisco: Jossey–Bass.

Wexley, K. N., & Latham, G. P. (1991). *Developing and training human resources in organizations* (2nd ed.). New York: Harper Collins.

Yin, R. (1981). The case study crisis: Some answers. *Administrative Science Quarterly, 26*, 58–65.

Yin, R. (1984). *Case study research.* Beverly Hills, CA: Sage.

Zammuto, R. F., & O'Connor, E. J. (1992). Gaining advanced manufacturing technologies' benefits: The roles of organization design and culture. *Academy of Management Review, 17*, 701–728.

Zuboff, S. (1988). *In the age of the smart machine: The future of work and power.* New York: Basic Books.

V

Final Observations

13

The Science and Practice of Training—Current Trends and Emerging Themes

Eduardo Salas
Janis A. Cannon-Bowers
Naval Air Warfare Center Training Systems Divison

Steve W. J. Kozlowski
Michigan State University

Organizations invest considerable resources and effort into training their workforce. In fact, some estimate that organizations spend over $30 billion a year on formal training and about $180 billion a year for on-the-job training (Carnevale, Gainer, & Villet, 1990).To justify an investment of this magnitude, it is reasonable to pose questions such as: What is the value of training to the "bottom line"? How can organizations know that training is effective? How can organizations optimize the design and delivery of training? How can organizations create opportunities for employees to practice acquired skills? How can learning environments best be designed by organizations? What factors motivate training effectiveness in organizations? The answers to these questions are neither simple nor straightforward. They demand careful consideration of *what* needs to be trained, for what *purpose*, with what *value*, and with what assurance that learning *goals* are accomplished.

Fortunately, training research has begun to answer these questions, at least to some extent. As illustrated in this volume, there has been an explosion of training research. In the last few years, the training field has seen new theories and constructs (Cannon-Bowers, Salas, Tannenbaum, & Mathieu, 1995), fresh tools (Haccoun & Hamitaux, 1994; Kraiger, Ford, & Salas, 1993), emerging instructional strategies (Salas, Cannon-Bowers, & Johnston, in press; Schmidt & Bjork, 1992), and exciting, practical findings (Baldwin, Magjuka, & Loher, 1991; Leedom & Simon, 1995).

In fact, progress is being made so quickly in some areas that periodic reflection regarding where we are in the training field and, perhaps more important, where we would like to be is advisable. Therefore, the purpose of this postscript is twofold. First, it briefly outlines a number of trends that are indicative of recent progress in the science and practice of training. These serve as a representative, but not exhaustive, list; other forums are available for that purpose (see Ford & Kraiger, 1995; Goldstein, 1993; Tannenbaum & Yukl, 1992). These trends are used to accomplish the second purpose of this post-script—to discuss emerging themes and key research questions that need attention as we move into the 21st century.

CURRENT TRENDS IN THE SCIENCE
AND PRACTICE OF TRAINING

Taken together, the chapters in this volume show that there is coherence and order to the apparent "piecemeal" approach that was evident in training research, and to the faddish nature that typified training practice. Although the early criticisms by Campbell (1971) and Goldstein (1980) are not completely answered, progress has been made. The science and practice of training in the late 20th century are dynamic, exciting, and rich, with new insights about the design, delivery, and evaluation of training interventions. The field is now positioned to make significant contributions to organizations. The future looks promising.

In reviewing and integrating the literature in this volume, a number of trends have emerged that are worth highlighting. In compiling these trends, we looked for similarities, interconnections, and common threads in how authors approached and described the science and/or practice of training in a particular area. The following sections delineate the current trends that were uncovered.

Theme 1: Theories Abound

The training field has been criticized on numerous occasions for being atheoretical. This criticism has been addressed of late by the emergence of many theoretical constructs, frameworks, and models. In fact, it is safe to say that the training field is now theoretically rich. Inspection of the chapters in this volume reveals that a number of new constructs have emerged to guide research (knowledge structures), and that other constructs have gained more acceptance (self-efficacy, opportunity to preform). For example, Rogers, Maurer, Salas, and Fisk (chap. 2) use controlled and automatic processing theory to guide the development of their task-analytic methodology. This is a well-accepted theoretical framework making significant contributions to instructional practice (see Fisk, Lee, & Rogers, 1991). Similarly, Baldwin and Magjuka (chap. 5) base their notion of training as an organizational episode on social cognitive theory. The same theory is employed by Mathieu and Martineau (chap. 8) to outline a series of properties associated with training motivation. Salas, Cannon-Bowers, and Blickensderfer (chap. 11) develop their teamwork training intervention from a syntheses of team performance models. These models have been applied to military training for a number of years (Salas, Bowers, & Cannon-Bowers, 1995). Noe and his colleagues (chap. 7) illustrate how a number of theories (e.g., goal setting and expectancy theory) can help explain employee developmental activities. On the macro side, organizational system theory and levels of analysis are the point of departure for Kozlowski and Salas' (chap. 10) propositions about how to implement training (design and delivery issues) and how to create an appropriate organizational context to enhance transfer and training effectiveness.

Training theories now range across a spectrum, from individual-level cognitive processes to organizational-level systems. In summary, the field has profited from researchers drawing from a broader and deeper set of conceptual developments to better understand training effectiveness.

Theme 2: Show Us, Don't Tell Us

The search for answers to the questions posed at the onset of this chapter—whether training works, how it works, why it does or does not work, and under what conditions it is effective—has led to more empirical investigations. Fortunately, the unrelenting call to show why training works has begun to be answered in recent years. In fact, the body of knowledge used by the authors of this volume to discuss their views on training is largely based on recent empirical studies aimed at understanding the underlying mechanisms of skill acquisition (Rogers et al., chap. 2), training motivation (Baldwin & Magjuka, chap. 5; Noe et al., chap. 7; and Mathieu & Martineau, chap. 8), knowledge structures (Goldsmith & Kraiger, chap. 4), transfer of training (Kozlowski & Salas, chap. 10), training evaluation (Alliger & Katzman, chap. 9), and organizational developmental events (Chao, chap. 6; Klein & Ralls, chap. 12). Basing recent training theories on well-established empirical findings provides a strong foundation for progress in training research and practice.

This trend has emerged as organizations demand more data, accountability, and results regarding their return on training investment, and as scientists derive new constructs in need of testing and validation. The need for empirical analysis on a variety of topics (mental models and on line diagnosis) will continue in the coming years.

Theme 3: Making a Difference
in Practice and Searching for Reciprocity

Recently, training researchers have emphasized relevancy (to practice and application) in their research. That is, there is a trend toward providing organizations with clear, specific, and concise answers to the question, "So what?" Historically, scientifically rigorous training research that generates practically relevant, usable products for practitioners has not been forthcoming. Some have argued (Campbell, 1988; Cannon-Bowers, Tannenbaum, Salas, & Converse, 1991; Goldstein, 1993) that one of the problems in this regard has been the lack of state-of-the-art training principles that generate precise guidelines for the design, delivery, and evaluation of training. Others have argued that, although information is available, it is not organized enough for practitioners to use (Swezey & Salas, 1992). Therefore, it is important to generate a dialogue between science and practice.

For example, Salas et al. (chap.11) present a heuristic model of how reciprocity between science and practice may occur. They offer a "translation" mechanism and a way to define and clarify terms that scientists use to communicate information to practitioners. They draw on other people's own experiences to illustrate how this might work. Significantly, Chao (chap. 6) as well as Klein and Ralls (chap. 12) remind us of how we can structure work experiences into learning events, and how these learning events have beneficial organizational consequences. Other work has developed targeted, theoretical propositions (Kozlowski, Gully, McHugh, Salas, & Cannon-Bowers, 1996), and has translated the propositions into application-oriented guidelines designed for work settings (Kozlowski, Gully, Salas, & Cannon-Bowers, 1996).

In summary, there is a higher demand of late for drawing implications of training research for practice. Scientists (and practitioners alike) have answered this call by emphasizing the need to articulate principles, derive precise guidelines, and transform routine organizational practices into learning events.

Theme 4: Toward a Broader View of Training

The notion of sending a trainee to a training program and expecting a skilled worker in return, simply as a consequence of the training, is no longer valid. Recent models and modern views of training suggest that training effectiveness is influenced by a number of factors. Researchers have expanded the conception of training by studying a wider range of variables than in the past. Clearly, the collection of chapters in this volume illustrates that quite convincingly. They represent topics ranging from organizational characteristics (Chao, chap. 6; Kozlowski & Salas, chap. 10), to situational influences (Mathieu & Martineau, chap. 8), to pretaining motivation (Baldwin & Magjuka, chap. 5), to task demands (Rogers et al., chap. 2), to individual characteristics (Noe et al., chap. 7), to posttraining activities (Kozlowski & Salas, chap. 10).

The influence of cognitive science in training research has also broadened the view of training and, more specifically, learning (Kraiger et al., 1993). Discussions about mental models, knowledge organization, knowledge structures, controlled processes, cognitive demands, and knowledge assessment reflect the current thinking and research about learning. This highlights the importance of balancing behavioral, affective, and cognitive aspects of learning as one designs, delivers, and evaluates training.

This broader view of training also creates a multidisiplinary "push." That is, researchers rely more and more on cross-disciplinary constructs, tools, and methods. Understanding learning and training today demands that industrial/organizational (I/O), educational, cognitive, and military psychologists, as well as instructional designers, computer scientists, and human factors specialists, combine their talents to collaborate, coordinate, and communicate.

In summary, training can no longer be considered solely a behavioral event. Instead, training is best conceptualized as a series of behavioral, affective, and cognitive events embedded in a dynamic work setting. Training, as demonstrated in this volume, embodies a complex set of individual and organizational variables that interact dynamically, independent of training quality, to produce learning outcomes of benefit to individuals, groups, and organizations.

Theme 5: Renewed Focus on Tools

A number of researchers have enriched the notion of training tools, such as measurement and evaluation. It has been argued that measurement is paramount to training (Salas & Cannon-Bowers, in press). That is, without performance measurement, there is no opportunity to assess learning, nor is there an opportunity to guide remediation or improve performance. More important, without sound assessment procedures, one cannot understand the many factors that may contribute to, or detract from, training effectiveness. Although progress has been made in this area, until recently, we were relying on old tools that did not provide a deep understanding of what had been learned (and why) by the trainee. Fortunately, the training field has finally gone beyond Kirkpatrick's (1976) typology as demonstrated in this volume. The tools are broader; they are aimed at assessing cognitive states and providing added information about the trainee. For example, Kraiger et al. (1993) expanded the notion of learning assessment by providing specific recommendations for measuring behavioral, cognitive, and affective learning outcomes. The same approach and expansion is also reflected in this volume by several authors. Coovert and Craiger (chap. 3) discuss a number of emerging tools (Petri Nets) for modeling human behavior in training. Similarly, Goldsmith and Kraiger (chap. 4) offer tools (e.g., Pathfinder) for the assessment of cognitive structures. Rogers and colleagues (chap. 2) describe in detail methodological tools for determining the performance demands of complex, cognitive-oriented tasks. A note of caution is needed, however. These emerging tools are in need of further development, refinement, and validation.

In summary, the five trends briefly discussed here constitute a snapshot of what is going on in the science and practice of training. We now turn to the future. To begin this discussion, this section focuses on the factors that have the most significant impact on the development of training; it then transitions to a number of themes in training research and practice that should shape the field in the future.

THE FUTURE: NEW WINE IN OLD BOTTLES

People sometimes employ the phrase "old wine in new bottles" to refer to situations where seemingly new ideas are proposed that are actually a restate-ment of existing ones, but "dressed-up" to appear new or innovative. Exactly the opposite situation describes the future of training. That is, the phrase "new wine in old bottles" is employed to characterize the future as we see it. The following paragraphs help to explain.

The chapters in this volume give a number of messages—"new wine"—about the future of training research and practice. These messages are influenced by a number of factors, some of which have been described already by several of the authors in this volume. At the same time, a number of training delivery methods have existed for a number of years—the "old bottles." The nature of both of these topics is described next.

First, there are organizational influences that dictate how training research should be conducted and applied in practice. These factors include issues such as constrained budgets and, as stated earlier, the growing demand in organiza-tions for accountability. Essentially, we need to do more with less as budgets shrink, and to prove that training investments have a demonstrable and long-lasting payoff. Organizations are pushing to cut costs by investing in things like distance learning and just-in-time training. Furthermore, organizations are demanding transportable training systems—in industry and the military—as a means to optimize their investment. These organizational influence suggest that training must be researched and practiced differently in the next century.

A second influence on the future of training has to do with the nature of training. In its most basic form, training involves the instigation of a stable change in cognition and/or behavior relative to a particular task and setting. The "vessels" or mechanisms (shaped by learning principles) available to accomplish this—lectures, role plays, modeling, simulations, computer-based training, on-the-job training (OJT), active practice, feedback, and others—have all been around for a number of years, and are not likely to disappear in the future. Instead, it seems more likely that progress will be made by revisiting these techniques and principles ("old bottles"), armed with the advances recently made, illustrated in this volume, and captured by the five trends discussed earlier.

As stated earlier, looking at the future in this way leads us to assert that training interventions (or delivery) might best be served by focusing on "new wine in old bottles." That is, we may have the most to gain by applying newfound advances (embedded in the trends) to what is already known, instead of trying to invent brand new methods of training. These include things already discussed from the chapters: enhanced theoretical notions, data-driven conclusions, improved tools, reciprocity as a goal, and broader perspectives. Of course, it is clear that factors such as advanced technology will affect the nature of training delivery systems and access, at least on the surface. Overall, however, there is more to be gained by investing in and improving techniques (computer-based training) and principles (active practice) that already exist. With these influences in mind, this postscript turns to a discussion of the future. In particular, it delineates three themes that should drive the field.

The Nature of Practice

Everyone has heard at least once in life, from coaches, instructors, or tutors, "practice, practice, practice" or "practice makes perfect." This belief is an "old bottle" principle. Although the importance of practice in training cannot be refuted, there is evidence that suggests that all practice is not equivalent (Schmidt & Bjork, 1992). Therefore, the term *practice* does not describe a simple concept. Rather, some types of practice may not improve performances as well as others.

The chapters by Noe et al. (chap. 4), Rogers et al. (chap. 2), Baldwin and Magjuka (chap. 5), as well as recent work by Ford and Kraiger (1995) and Noe and Ford (1992), all suggest that some "new wine" may enhance the mechanisms of practice. For example, Ford and Kraiger suggested that cognitive apprenticeships may provide a richer, more systematic approach to practice, particularly as a means to develop expertise on the job. Advances in technology may also help. Cannon-Bowers and Salas (in press) suggested that, as computers facilitate intelligent diagnosis of performance, it may be possible to improve practice sessions by providing on line feedback. The key tool to this development is the capability of modeling expert performance, as illustrated by Coovert and Craiger (chap. 3).

The thinking described here will help to provide mechanisms and principles for guided practice. However, these new perspectives notwithstanding, a number of research questions emerge. First, what are the boundaries of practice? How much practice is enough? What kind of practice is required for complex jobs? Second, what theoretical framework(s) can guide this research? Constructs such as socialization (Chao, chap. 6), guided practice (Cannon-Bowers & Salas, in press), on-the-job training, and continuous learning environments require richer theoretical foundations. Third, what tools (and of what kind) are needed to guide practice? For example, new tools are needed for structuring learning events on the job and in real time (Kozlowski, Gully, McHugh, et al., 1996). Fourth, as implied by Chao (chap. 6), Kozlowski and Salas (chap. 10), and Klein and Ralls (chap. 12), how can opportunities be created for practice in the organization?

Computer-Based Training: Engineering and Restructuring Knowledge

Computer-based training—another "old bottle"—has been around for decades. There are known computer-based training contributions to training practice, such as self-paced instruction tutoring and interactive courseware (Crawford & Crawford, 1978; Shute & Regian, 1993; Towne & Munro, 1991). However, this technology has had a limited impact on the science and practice of training, primarily due to its simplistic assumptions about knowledge and its emphasis on content rather than presentation formats and medium characteristics.

Today, the advent of multimedia technology, coupled with new insights about cognition (Rogers et al., chap. 2, Goldsmith & Kraiger, chap. 4) and learning (Ford, chap. 1; Mathieu & Martineau, chap. 8)—"new wine"—offer an opportunity to improve the quality of computer-based training systems. In fact, a promising line of research lies ahead. To begin, it is necessary to further investigate the nature of expertise and, more particularly, as suggested by Goldsmith and Kraiger, how the organization of knowledge supports expert performance. That is, how do experts learn in a particular domain, and how do they employ knowledge in support of higher order skills (decision making)? From here, it is of interest to determine how various knowledge presentation formats (text, graphics, animation, simulation, video) affect the acquisition and organization of knowledge. In this manner, it may be possible to build and even accelerate expertise by presenting knowledge in a way that fosters its utility in performance situations.

A related opportunity involves the enhanced use of high-fidelity training systems. Modern theories of decision making (e.g., Klein, 1989) suggest that experts rely on a store of well-organized memories that are triggered by situational cues. This type of thinking suggests that at least some types of training should focus on helping trainees make associations between situational cues and appropriate responses. Computer-based simulations, which are becoming more widely available, have the potential to present a variety of cue/strategy associations in relatively low-cost, safe environments. Training imparted by such systems also has a high probability of transfer due to the high degree of similarity between the training and operational environments.

Overall, the area of computer-based training holds vast potential as a means to improve the effectiveness of training. The chapters in this volume offer rich and broader constructs, a number of potential tools, and opportunities to impact the practice of computer-based training. If this area is to progress, research needs to: (a) investigate the relationship between knowledge organization and expertise, (b) determine the characteristics of the various knowledge presentation formats, and (c) establish the relationship between presentation formats and knowledge acquisition.

Training Effectiveness

A final theme for the future involves a topic already given some attention—namely, training effectiveness. As highlighted in the chapters of this book, the concept of training effectiveness has been expanded in recent years to incorporate notions about individual (trainee) and organizational characteristics. It is now time for the field of training to expand further. Specifically, training needs to be viewed as more central to the functioning of organizations by being granted a place of importance alongside financial, strategic, and operational concerns. Training researchers have the potential to contribute to issues such as worker motivation and productivity, diversity, career development, retraining, obsolescence, and profit margins. In military terms, training can be a "force multiplier" (i.e., a factor that improves mission effectiveness with fewer resources).

Therefore, the challenge for training researchers is to infuse the "old bottles"—current training effectiveness paradigms—with "new wine"—expanded and enhanced thinking about the potential offered through sound training design. Two major obstacles to be confronted in this regard include: (a) the manner in which training researchers communicate what they have to offer, and (b) creating mechanisms to demonstrate the potential of training. In both cases, the solution may lie in conducting more action research—empirical studies that are perceived to be relevant to organizational functioning.

CONCLUDING REMARKS

This postscript has summarized recent contributions in the training field, and has offered some suggestions for the future. In doing so, a few things have become apparent. First, the field of training has witnessed exciting and dramatic advances in the past 10 years. There are more varied and rich theories underlying training design; better, more useful tools to support training; wider perspectives on training; more empirical studies; and more relevant and practically applicable research findings. Moreover, the themes outlined for the future—to investigate more completely the nature and uses of practice, expand understanding of expertise and the relationship between presentation formats and its development, and push the envelope regarding the impact of training effectiveness issues on organizational functioning—are all stimulating as well.

In conclusion, the chapter authors hope they have provided the training community with some reasonable points of departure, they hope that the theories represented herein help to dispel the oft-cited criticisms that training is atheoretical and faddish. Above all, it is hoped that the field continues to thrive as the broader challenges of society are faces—fiscal austerity, exploding technology, and an aging workforce. Clearly, if the last 10 years are indicative of the progress we can expect in training science and practice, the future looks bright.

ACKNOWLEDGMENTS

The views expressed herein are those of the authors and do not reflect the official position of the organization with which they are affiliated.

REFERENCES

Baldwin, T., Magjuka, R. J., & Loher, B. T. (1991). The perils of participation: Effects of trainee choice on motivation and learning. *Personnel Psychology, 44*, 51–66.
Campbell, J. P. (1971). Personnel training and development. *Annual Review of Psychology, 22*, 565–595.
Campbell, J. P. (1988). Training design for performance investment. In J. P. Campbell & R. J. Campbell (Eds.), *Productivity in organizations* (pp.177–216). San Francisco: Jossey-Bass.
Cannon-Bowers, J. A., & Salas, E. (in press). A framework for developing team performance measures in training. In M. T. Brannick, E. Salas, & C. Prince (Eds.), *Team performance measurement: Theory, methods, and applications.* Mahwah, NJ: Lawrence Erlbaum Associates.
Cannon-Bowers, J. A., Salas, E., Tannenbaum, S. I., & Mathieu, J. E. (1995). Toward theoretically based principles of training effectiveness: A model and initial empirical investigation. *Military Psychology, 7*, 141–164.
Cannon-Bowers, J. A., Tannenbaum, S. I., Salas, E., & Converse, S. A. (1991). Toward an integration of training theory and practice. *Human Factors, 33*, 281–292.
Carnevale, A., Gainer, L., & Villet, J. (1990). *Training and development in work organizations.* San Francisco: Jossey-Bass.
Crawford, A. M., & Crawford, K. S. (1978). Simulation of operational equipment with a computer-based instructional system: A low cost training technology. *Human Factors, 20*, 215–224.
Fisk, A. D., Lee, M. D., & Rogers, W. A. (1991). Recombination of automatic processing components: The effects of transfer, reversal, and conflict situations. *Human Factors, 33*, 267–280.
Ford, J. K., & Kraiger, K. (1995). The application of cognitive constructs and principles to the instructional systems model of training: Implications for needs assessment, design, and transfer. In C. I. Cooper & I. T. Robertson (Eds.), *International review of industrial and organizational psychology* (Vol. 10, pp. 1–48). New York: Wiley.
Goldstein, I. L. (1980). Training in work organizations. *Annual Review of Psychology, 31*, 229–272.
Goldstein, I. L. (Ed.). (1989). *Training and development in organizations.* San Francisco: Jossey-Bass.
Goldstein, I. L. (1993). *Training in organizations* (3rd ed.). Belmont, CA: Wadsworth.
Haccoun, R. R., & Hamtiaux, T. (1994). Optimizing knowledge tests for inferring learning acquisition levels in single group training evaluation designs: The internal referencing strategy. *Personnel Psychology, 47*, 593–604.
Kirkpatrick, D. L. (1976). Evaluation of training. In R. L. Craig (Ed.), *Training and development handbook* (2nd ed.; pp. 18-1–18-27). New York: McGraw-Hill.

Klein, G. A. (1989). Recognition-primed decisions. In W. B. Rouse (Ed.), *Advances in man-machine system research* (Vol. 5, pp. 47–92). Greenwich, CT: JAI.

Kozlowski, S. W. J., Gully, S. M., McHugh, P. P., Salas, E., & Cannon-Bowers, J. A. (1996). A dynamic theory of leadership and team effectiveness: Developmental and task contingent leader roles. In G. R. Ferris (Ed.), *Research in personnel and human resource management* (Vol. 14, pp. 253–305). Greenwich, CT: JAI.

Kozlowski, S. W. J., Gully, S. M., Salas, E., & Cannon-Bowers, J. A. (in press). Team leadership and development: Theory, principles, and guidelines for training leaders and teams. In M. Beyerlein, S. Beyerlein, & D. Johnson (Eds.), *Advances in interdisciplinary studies of work teams: Team leadership* (Vol. 3, pp. 251–289). Greenwich, CT: JAI.

Kraiger, K., Ford, J. K., & Salas, E. (1993). Application of cognitive, skill-based, and affective theories of learning outcomes to new methods of training evaluation [monograph]. *Journal of Applied Psychology, 78*, 311–328.

Leedom, D. K., & Simon, R. (1995). Improving team coordination: A case for behavior-based training. *Military Psychology, 7*, 109–122.

Noe, R. A., & Ford, J. K. (1992). Emerging issues and new directions for training research. *Research in Personnel and Human Resources Management, 10*, 345–384.

Salas, E., Bowers, C. A., & Cannon-Bowers, J. A.. (1995). Military team research: Ten years of progress. *Military Psychology, 7*, 55–75.

Salas, E., & Cannon-Bowers, J. A. (in press). Methods, tools, and strategies for team training. In M. A. Quiñones & A. Dutta (Eds.), *Training for 21st century technology: Applications of psychological research*. Washington, DC: American Psychological Association.

Salas, E., Cannon-Bowers, J. A., & Johnston, J. H. (in press). How can you turn a team of experts into an expert team?: Emerging training strategies. In C. Zsambok & G. Klein (Eds.), *Naturalistic decision making*. Mahwah, NJ: Lawrence Erlbaum Associates.

Schmidt, R. A., & Bjork, R. A. (1992). New conceptualizations of practice: Common principles in three paradigms suggest new concepts for training. *Psychological Science, 3*, 207–217.

Shute, V. J., & Regian, W. (1993). Principles for evaluating intelligent tutoring systems. *Journal for Artificial Intelligence in Education, 4*, 245–271.

Swezey, R. W., & Salas, E. (1992). Guidelines for use in team-training development. In R. W. Swezey & E. Salas (Eds.), *Teams: Their training and performance* (pp. 219–245). Norwood, NJ: Ablex.

Tannenbaum, S. I., & Yukl, G. (1992). Training and development in work organizations. *Annual Review of Psychology, 43*, 399–441.

Towne, D. M., & Munro, A. (1991). Simulation-based instruction of technical skills. *Human Factors, 33*, 325–342.

About the Authors

George M. Alliger is an associate professor of Psychology and Organizational Studies at the University of New York at Albany, State University of New York. He received his BA in 1973 from the College of Wooster, Ohio, an MA in 1980 from Xavier University, Ohio, and his PhD in 1985 from the University of Akron. He publishes in the areas of job analysis, selection tests, training, and meta-analysis. He consults in the areas of training efficiency and effectiveness.

Timothy T. Baldwin is Dow Teaching Fellow and associate professor of management at the Indiana University Graduate School of Business. Professor Baldwin holds a BA, M.BA, and PhD in management from Michigan State University. His research has focused on effective human resource management, particularly within the area of training and development. He is a prolific writer and has published his research work in leading academic and professional outlets such as: *Journal of Applied Psychology, Personnel Psychology, Academy of Management Journal, Training and Development Journal,* and *Human Resource Development Quarterly.* He has won several national research awards, including three from the National Academy of Management. He was also the 1995 recipient of the Richard A. Swanson Excellence in Research Award presented by the American Society for Training & Development (ASTD).

Elizabeth L. Blickensderfer is a research psychologist with the Training Technology Development branch at the Naval Air Warfare Center Training Systems Division. She received her BS degree (1991) in psychology from the University of Nebraska at Kearney and is enrolled in the Human Factors doctoral program at the University of Central Florida. Her research interests include team decision making, team self-correction training development, and cognitive perspectives of training evaluation.

369

Janis A. Cannon-Bowers is a senior research psychologist in the Training Technology Development Branch of the Naval Air Warfare Center Training Systems Division. She holds an MA and PhD in industrial/organizational psychology from the University of South Florida, Tampa. Her research interests include team training and performance, shared mental models in team performance, training effectiveness, and tactical decision making. Currently, Cannon-Bowers is a team leader for advance surface training research, which includes projects associated with development of advanced embedded training, shipboard instructor training and support, and automated performance measurement.

Georgia T. Chao is an associate professor in the Department of Management at Michigan State University. She received her MS and PhD in industrial/organizational psychology from the Pennsylvania State University. Prior to joining Michigan State University in 1985, she was Section Head of the Department of Management at the GMI Engineering and Management Institute. Dr. Chao's research interests are in the areas of career development, organizational socialization, international human resource management, and organizational downsizing. She has published her research in journals such as the *Journal of Applied Psychology* and *Personnel Psychology*. Dr. Chao was recently elected to the HRM and Careers Divisions' Executive Committees in the Academy of Management, and currently chairs the Committee for International HRM Research. She has served as a consultant to the United Nation's Association for Training Institutions for Foreign Trade in Asia and the Pacific, AT&T, and Ford Motor, and has also served as a personnel specialist for HRB-Singer and General Motors. Currently she is the Director of the Asia Pacific Economic Cooperation Study Center at MSU. She is a member of the Academy of Management and the Society for Industrial and Organizational Psychology, Inc.

Michael D. Coovert is an associate professor of psychology at the University of South Florida, where he is also the founding director of the Institute for Human Performance, Decision Making, and Cybernetics. He received his BA (1979) from Chaminade University of Honolulu in computer science and psychology, his MS (1981) from Illinois State University in psychology, and his PhD (1985) from The Ohio State University in industrial/organizational psychology with a minor in computer science. Dr. Coovert's research interests include human–computer interaction, the impact of technologies on organizations, quantitative methods, and statistical models of human performance.

J. Philip Craiger is an assistant professor at the University of Nebraska at Omaha. He received his PhD in 1992 in industrial/organizational psychology with a minor in artificial intelligence. His research interests include computer simulation and modeling, fuzzy logic, neural networks, expert systems, computer-based training, and the use of technology in organizations.

Arthur D. Fisk is a professor of psychology at the Georgia Institute of Technology. He is Coordinator of the Engineering Psychology program within the School of Psychology and Director of the Human Attention and Performance Laboratory at Georgia Tech. He holds a PhD from the University of Illinois, and is a Certificant from the Board of Certification in Professional Ergonomics. His laboratory is currently addressing issues aimed at understanding age-related influences on learning mechanisms responsible for skill development, retention of skilled performance, as well as development of training for improving dynamic decision making. Prior to his academic position, he was a Manager, Human Factors Engineering, at AT&T. Dr. Fisk is a Fellow of the Human Factors and Ergonomics Society as well as the American Psychological Association's Divisions 20 and 21. He has served as editor of *Human Factors* and as a member of Executive Council of the Human Factors and Ergonomics Society. He is President-Elect of the Human Factors and Ergonomics Society and President of the American Psychological Association's Division of Applied Experimental and Engineering Psychologists.

J. Kevin Ford is a professor of psychology at Michigan State University. His major research interests involve improving training effectiveness through efforts to advance our understanding of training needs assessment, design, evaluation, and transfer. Dr. Ford also concentrates on increasing our understanding of training as a system and the building of continuous learning orientations within organizations. He has published over 30 articles and chapters, serves on the editorial board of *Personnel Psychology*, *Academy of Management Journal*, and *The Training Research Journal*, and is an active consultant with private industry and the public sector on training and organizational development issues. He is a Fellow of the American Psychological Association and the Society of Industrial and Organizational Psychology. He received his BS in psychology from the University of Maryland and his MA and PhD in psychology from The Ohio State University.

Timothy E. Goldsmith is an assistant professor of psychology at the University of New Mexico. He received his BS (1976) in mathematics and psychology from Northern Arizona University, and his MA (1980) and PhD (1984) from New Mexico State University in experimental psychology with a minor in artificial intelligence. Dr. Goldsmith's research interests include methods for eliciting and representing domain knowledge, computer models of human performance, and quantitative methods.

Steven Katzman is an assistant professor of psychology at Baruch College, City University of New York. Prior to his appointment at Baruch, he was a faculty member in the psychology department at the Illinois Institute of Technology. He has also taught at the University at Albany, SUNY, and at Rennselaer Polytechnic Institute. Steven received his BA from Binghamton University, and is in the process of completing PhD requirements at Albany. His recent interests have focused on organizational training, research methods, and statistics.

Katherine J. Klein is an associate professor of psychology at the University of Maryland at College Park. She received her BA (1978) in psychology from Yale University and her PhD (1984) from the University of Texas at Austin. Her research interests include technology implementation and organizational change, levels of analysis issues, part-time work, and employee ownership. She is on the editorial board of the *Academy of Management Journal,* and in 1988 won the Organizational Behavior Division of the Academy of Management's award for the Outstanding Publication in Organizational Psychology.

Steve W. J. Kozlowski is a professor of organizational psychology at Michigan State University. His major research interests focus on organizational innovation and change, and on the processes by which people adapt to novel or changing situations. His work addresses: effects of organizational downsizing; implementation of advanced manufacturing technologies; skill obsolescence, updating, and development; training interventions to enhance adaptive expertise; team training; and informal learning during organizational socialization. In his applied work on innovation and adaptation, Dr. Kozlowski serves as a consultant to federal research laboratories and private industry. He has published over 30 articles and chapters, is a consulting editor for the *Journal of Applied Psychology,* and serves on the Editorial Board for the *Academy of Management Journal.* He also regularly reviews for the *Academy of Management Review, Organizational Behavior and Human Decision Processes,* and *Personnel Psychology.* He is a Fellow of the American Psychological Association and of the Society for Industrial and Organizational Psychology. He received his BA (1976) in psychology from the University of Rhode Island, and his MS (1979) and PhD (1982) from The Pennsylvania State University.

Kurt Kraiger is an associate professor of psychology at the University of Colorado at Denver. He is an active researcher and consultant in the areas of training and training evaluation. He has published or presented over 50 papers on various topics in industrial/organizational psychology, including raining theory, training evaluation, and performance measurement. Along with Kevin Ford and Eduardo Salas, he was awarded the Scholarly Achievement Award in 1993 by the Human Resources Division of the Academy of Management. He has consulted in these areas with a number of organizations, including McDonalds, Miller Brewing, Warner Lambert, US WEST, the National Institute of Occupational Safety and Health, and the U.S. Air Force. Dr. Kraiger is a member of the American Psychological Association, the Academy of Management, and the National Society for Performance and Instruction. He is also the current editor of the *Training Research Journal.* Dr. Kraiger received his BA (1979) in psychology from the University of Cincinnati and his PhD (1983) in industrial/organizational psychology from The Ohio State University.

Richard J. Magjuka is an associate professor in the Department of Management at the Indiana University School of Business. He received his PhD in sociology from the University of Chicago and an MBA from Notre Dame. His research interests are in the areas of employee involvement, team-based organizational structures, and training and development. His work has been published widely in a number of leading professional journals, and he is a former co-editor of the *Journal of Research in Sociology*. Prior to joining the faculty of IU, he held positions at Arthur Andersen & Co. and Northern Illinois University.

Jennifer W. Martineau is a research associate at the Center for Creative Leadership. Her research interests center around the system of training effectiveness, examining both individual and situational influences on training effectiveness, the impact of training on individual and organizational outcomes, and the removal of barriers to transfer of training. She has been with the Center since 1993 and received her PhD (1995) in industrial/organizational psychology from The Pennsylvania State University.

John E. Mathieu is an associate professor of psychology at The Pennsylvania State University. He received his PhD (1985) in industrial/organizational psychology from Old Dominion University. His research, teaching, and practice interests center on multilevel and cross-level theories of organizational behavior. In particular, his recent efforts have concentrated on individual–organizational attachment processes, and training and team effectiveness applications.

Todd J. Maurer is an assistant professor of psychology at Georgia Institute of Technology. He received his BS (1984) at the University of Pittsburgh, and his MS (1988) and PhD (1990) degrees in industrial/organizational psychology at The University of Akron. Dr. Maurer's research interests include employee development, performance appraisal, employment testing, and job analysis.

Ellen J. Mullen is currently an assistant professor in the Education and Technology Department at Iowa State University. Professor Mullen received her PhD (1994) in industrial relations from the University of Minnesota. Her research focuses on training and development issues, including mentoring relationships, outcomes associated with serving as a mentor, information sharing among mentors and proteges, and the effects of trainee attitudes and perceptions on learning, particularly in the context of workplace, literacy training. Professor Mullen's articles have been published in the *Journal of Organizational Behavior*, *Human Resource Management*, *Personnel Psychology*, and *Journal of Vocational Behavior*.

Raymond A. Noe is an associate professor in the Department of Management at Michigan State University. A former professor in the Industrial Relations Center of the Carlson School of Management, University of Minnesota, he received his B.S. in psychology from The Ohio State University and his MA and PhD (1985) in psychology from Michigan State University. Professor Noe conducts research and teaches undergraduate, MBA and PhD students in human resource management, managerial skills, quantitative methods, human resource information systems, training, employee development, and organizational behavior. He has published articles in the leading management and psychology journals and is co-author of two textbooks. Professor Noe is currently on the Editorial Board of *Personnel Psychology, Journal of Training Research,* and *Journal of Business and Psychology*. Professor Noe has received awards for his teaching and research excellence, including the Herbert G. Heneman Distinguished Teaching Award in 1991 and the Ernest J. McCormick Award for Distinguished Early Career Contribution from the Society for Industrial and Organizational Psychology in 1993.

R. Scott Ralls is director of the Division of Employment and Training for the North Carolina Department of Commerce. A doctoral candidate in the Industrial and Organizational Psychology Program at the University of Maryland at College Park, Scott received his BA (1986) in psychology from the University of North Carolina and his MA (1990) from the University of Maryland. He wrote the 1994 U.S. Department of Labor report, *Integrating Technology with Workers in the New American Workplace*. He was formerly manager of Workforce Programs for the Manufacturing Extension Partnership at the National Institute of Standards and Technology.

Wendy A. Rogers is an assistant professor of psychology at The University of Georgia. She received her BA in psychology from Southeastern Massachusetts University and her MS (1989) and PhD (1991) in experimental psychology from Georgia Institute of Technology. Her research interests include skill acquisition and training, ability determinants of performance, human factors, and general issues in attention. In addition, she is interested in the changes in cognition that occur as a function of age.

Eduardo Salas is a senior research psychologist and head of the Training Technology Development Branch of the Naval Air Warfare Center Training Systems Division. He received his PhD (1984) in industrial/organizational psychology from Old Dominion University. He is a Fellow of the American Psychological Association. He also has courtesy appointments at the University of South Florida and the University of Central Florida. He has co-authored over 50 journal articles and book chapters and has co-edited four books. He is on the Editorial Board of *Human Factors, Personnel Psychology,* and *Training Research*

Journal. His research interests include team training and performance, training effectiveness, tactical decision making under stress, team decision making, performance measurement, and learning strategies for teams.

Mark S. Teachout is a performance technology specialist at USAA. He was formally a senior research psychologist at the USAF Armstrong Laboratory where he worked for more than 10 years. He holds a PhD in industrial/organizational psychology from Old Dominion University. His research interests include criterion development, the measurement of work performance and work experience, and issues of training efficiency, effectiveness, and improvement. He is currently developing a systems approach to training effectiveness and is working on practical applications of training to the workplace.

James E. Wanek is currently a lecturer in the Industrial Relations Center, Carlson School of Management, University of Minnesota. Professor Wanek received his B.S. in business administration from Winona State University and his MA and PhD (1995) in Industrial Relations from the University of Minnesota. His research interests include instruments and methods of employee selection, including personality measures of integrity and conscientiousness, and issues of fairness, justice, and diversity in human resource management.

Steffanie L. Wilk is an assistant professor of management at the Wharton School of the University of Pennsylvania. She received her BA from Rockhurst College in Industrial and Labor Relations and her PhD (1994) from the Industrial Relations Center at the University of Minnesota. In her graduate work, she specialized in selection, training and development, and organizational behavior. Her research has been published in *Journal of Applied Psychology* and *American Psychologist.* Her research interests include the relationship of occupational mobility patterns of individuals in the labor to changes in person-job fit, organizational selection and subgroup norming, and the relationship between selection and training initiatives and organizational strategy.

Author Index

A

Abelson, R. P., 49, *71*
Ackerman, P. L., 24, 28, *41*, 109, *125*,
    225, 239, 241, *243*, 247, 268,
    283, 285, 294, *317*
Acton, W. H., 77, 80, 83, 87, 88, 93, *95*
Ajzen, I., 180, *185*, 294, *317*
Alexander, R. A., 241, *243*
Allen, N. J., 131, *149*, 173, *187*
Alliger, G. M., 74, *93*, 229, 241, 242,
    243, 248, 283
Alluisi, E. A., 294, 299, 300, *317*, 320,
    321
Alutto, J. A., 259, *283*
Ambler, R. K., 201, *217*
Ames, C., 204, *217*
Anastasi, A., 224, *243*, 294, *317*
Anderson, J. H., 77, *94*
Anderson, J. R., 21, 32, *41*, 136, *149*,
    225, *243*, 294, *317*
Anderson, M., 23, 29, *42*
Anderson, R. C., 107, *124*
Annett, J., 240, *243*
Archer, J., 204, *217*
Argyris, C., 143, *149*

B

Arnold, J., 131, *150*
Arnsdorf, D., 325, *351*
Arvey, R. D., 226, 227, 233, 234, 235,
    236, *243*, 244, 323, *350*
Ash, R. A., 143, 145, *149*, 163, *185*
Asher, J. J., 294, *317*
Ashford, S. J., 167, *184*, *189*
Attewell, P., 325, 344, *350*
Atwater, L., 167, *184*
Ault, C., 82, *95*
Ausubel, D. P., 90, *94*
Aviram, A., 349, *351*

B

Bainbridge, L., 67, 68, 69
Baker, C. V., 294, *320*
Baker, D. P., 299, 301, 311, *317*, *322*
Baldwin, T. T., 47, 69, 74, *94*, 102, 106,
    107, 108, 109, 117, 118, 120,
    124, 135, *149*, 163, 170, 172,
    174, 182, *185*, *189*, 195, 209,
    211, 213, *217*, 221, 248, 255,
    256, 257, *283*, 294, *317*, 344,
    346, 349, *351*, 358, 366
Bale, R. M., 201, *217*

377

Subject Index

A

Ability, 201
Assessment centers, 160
Advanced organizers, 90
Adventure learning, 163
Age, 170
Applied learning theory, 296–297
Attentional resources, 20–21, 29
Automatic and controlled processing,
    20–22
  benefits of, 22
  identification of consistencies, 27,
    32–33
  interview regarding, 34
  principles of automatic development,
    27–30
  Task analytic methodology, 30–31
Automaticity, see automatic and control-
    led processing

B

Benchmarks, 159
Business strategy, 174–175

C

Career planning, 206
Change scores
  effect size calculations, 233–234
  individual-level models of, 248
  measurement of, 226
  power, 234–236
  score reliabilities, 232–233
Climate, see transfer climate
Cognitive ability, 171
Cognitive control
  skill-based, rule-based, and knowl-
    edge-based, 49–50
Cognitive structure, 76, see also struc-
    tural assessment
Compensation system, 176
  group incentives, 178
  skill-based pay, 212–213
  pay level, 177
  pay mix, 177
Competitive advantage, 2
Compressed time procedure, 23–24
Computational psychology, 65–66
  effective calculability, 66
Computer-aided design and drafting, 327